Longmen's Stone Buddhas
and Cultural Heritage

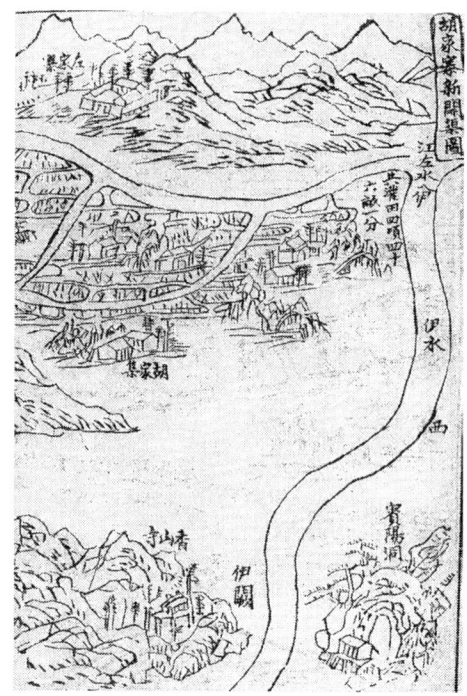

Longmen in a local gazetteer, 1745, vol. 1, Tukao.
Source: Gong, Songlin, and Wang Jian, comp. *Luoyang xianzhi* (Luoyang gazetteer). u.p.: 1924, reprint of 1745 ed., 24 vols.

Longmen's Stone Buddhas and Cultural Heritage

When Antiquity Met Modernity in China

Dong Wang

ROWMAN & LITTLEFIELD
Lanham • Boulder • New York • London

Published by Rowman & Littlefield
An imprint of The Rowman & Littlefield Publishing Group, Inc.
4501 Forbes Boulevard, Suite 200, Lanham, Maryland 20706
www.rowman.com

6 Tinworth Street, London SE11 5AL, United Kingdom

British Library Cataloguing in Publication Information Available

Library of Congress Cataloging-in-Publication Data Available

Names: Wang, Dong, 1967– author.
Title: Longmen's stone buddhas and cultural heritage : when antiquity met modernity in
    China / Dong Wang.
Description: Lanham : Rowman & Littlefield, [2020] | Series: Asia/Pacific/perspectives |
    Includes bibliographical references and index.
Identifiers: LCCN 2020007284 (print) | LCCN 2020007285 (ebook) |
    ISBN 9781538141106 (cloth) | ISBN 9781538141113 (paperback) |
    ISBN 9781538141120 (epub)
Subjects: LCSH: Longmen Caves (China) | Cultural property—Protection—China—
    Longmen Caves. | Cultural property—Protection—Social aspects. | Culture and
    globalization. | China—Relations. | Civilization—Chinese influences.
Classification: LCC DS797.44.L84 W36 2020 (print) | LCC DS797.44.L84 (ebook) |
    DDC 951/.18—dc23
LC record available at https://lccn.loc.gov/2020007284
LC ebook record available at https://lccn.loc.gov/2020007285

♾ ™ The paper used in this publication meets the minimum requirements of American
National Standard for Information Sciences—Permanence of Paper for Printed Library
Materials, ANSI/NISO Z39.48-1992.

This book is dedicated to the memory of Daniel H. Bays (1942–2019),
my mentor and friend who was an inspiration for me.

Contents

List of Figures

Acknowledgments

This book was written during the last fifteen years on the North Shore of Boston, Massachusetts, in Pikisaari at the Finnish-Swedish archipelago, in Xanten—the Roman city on the Lower Rhine of Germany—in Shanghai, and between airports, railway stations, and sea ports around the globe. Longmen's story and its home city Luoyang carry personal and professional significance to me.

I was born in Luoyang, and lived there until 1983 when I left to study history at Shandong University. As part of the local heritage, Longmen was the most favored spring outing site in my memory. But if it were not for this book, I would not have gotten to know of all those extraordinary human beings, Chinese and foreign, who were closely tied to Longmen.

In mid-August 2005, an excursion to Longmen's caves together with my parents titillated my intellectual curiosity about the ancient cultural site. On that cloudy summer day after a good rain, I was struck by the face-lift that Longmen had experienced due to its new UNESCO World Heritage status. From that point on, I began to collect sources in Chinese, English, French, German, Italian, Japanese, and Swedish languages on Longmen and Luoyang. Longmen opened a brand new world for me, which, among many meaningful things, motivated me to learn French and German at a late age.

Studying Longmen and its modern rebirth has been a humble yet privileged journey for me. The nearly first two decades of my life were spent in the same compound in Luoyang as Wen Yucheng and his family. Mr. Wen is a pioneering and leading scholar in the study of Longmen. In Mr. Wen's own words, he inherited his knowledge and skills from two teachers: one was Yan Wenru (1912–1994), who focused on the Jinshi epigraphic system; the other was Su Bai (1922–2018), a founder of Chinese Buddhist archaeology.[1] A trained archaeologist, Wen graduated from Peking University in 1964, and was assigned to work at what was then the Longmen Grottoes Institute for the Protection of Cultural Relics, which had only eight full-time employees at the time. In June 2008, I had the fortune to visit the Wens at their home in Beijing. Gratitude is expressed herewith for Mr. Wen's generosity with his time and in sharing with me about Longmen.

My first article on Longmen and cultural heritage was prompted by a UNESCO history conference held at King's College, Cambridge University in early April 2009 organized by the International Scientific Committee for the UNESCO History Project. Since then, various invited talks on the subject were given at the University of Helsinki, the University of Cologne, the University of Hamburg, the Hudson Institute, the M at the Bund Shanghai, Shanghai University, Westmont College and other places.

Over the years, I have also received support, in various forms, from the UNESCO History Project, the UNESCO Archives, the UNESCO World Heritage Centre, the East-West Institute at Gordon College, the German Ministry of Education and Research, the U.S. National Endowment for Humanities, Shanghai University, the Freer Gallery of Art and Arthur M. Sackler Gallery, the Smithsonian Institution Libraries, the Longfellow House-Washington's Headquarters NHS, the Longfellow National Historic Site, the Isabella Stewart Gardner Museum Archives, the Office of Gazetteers and Local History of Luoyang, the Luoyang Municipal Library, the Administration of Longmen Cultural Tourism Zone, the Royal Ontario Museum Library & Archives, the Center for Archaeological Excavations and Research in Asia at the Istituto Italiano Per L'Africa E L'Oriente, Sapienza University of Rome, the Harvard University Archives, Pusey Library, Houghton Library, and Östasiatiska Museets (Museum of Far Eastern Antiquities) in Stockholm, Sweden, the Institute of Modern History Library at the Chinese Academy of Social Sciences, the Metropolitan Museum of Art Archives and the Nelson-Atkins Museum of Art in Kansas City, Missouri. A modified version of chapter 4 appeared in *The Journal of The Royal Asiatic Society China* 79, no. 1, 2019 (January 2020): 44–70. Permission to reuse the image of Laurence Sickman in Luoyang, China 1932 (Laurence Sickman Papers, MSS 001) by the Nelson-Atkins Museum of Art is acknowledged here as well.

Tim Wright, Mark Selden, Flemming Christiansen, and anonymous reviewers have read the book manuscript in its entirety with overall and chapter-by-chapter comments and suggestions, which reshaped my thinking and writing. With decades of experience in publishing China books, Susan McEachern at Rowman & Littlefield, alongside her editorial team including Katelyn Turner, Jehanne Schweizer, and Jayanthi Chander, has provided me sustained support and speedy assistance. My own long-time editor, Paul Sorrell, never failed to lend his superb skills and send the edits even when he had a short turnaround time.

I also wish to express sincere appreciation of countless other individuals who played a helpful role in the preparation of my Longmen book. Omissions are predictably certain owing to the length of time of this book project and extensive contacts in Asia, Africa, Europe, North America, and the Oceania. They include Stanley Abe, Christopher I. Beckwith, Kerstin Bergström, Jens Boel, Melissa Bowling, Charlotte Chaffey, Paul A. Cohen, David R. Daly, Francesco D'Arelli, Prasenjit Duara, Paul Dunscomb, Fan Jinshi, Rainer Feldbacher, Feng Jing, Michael Friedrich, Gao Shihua, Jessica Gienow-Hecht, Vincent Goossaert, David Hogge, Joshua Howard, Ian Johnson, Shin Kawashima, Martin Kern, Klaus Koschorke, Lai Xuezhai, Michel Lee, Li Hong, Li Yong, Liang Shan, Liu Xian, Lu Wei, Amy McNair, Richard Madsen, Mao Yangguang, Shana McKenna, Caroline Michotte, Tak-Wing Ngo, Paul Nietupski, Lauri Paltimaa, Edward Rhoads, Lucy Rhymer, James Robson, Helena Rundkranz, Shang Renjie, Stacey Sherman, Si Han, K. Ian Shin, Richard J. Smith, Daniel Stevenson, Youli Sun, Anna Maria Thunman, Bill Tsutsui, Franciscus Verellen, Matt Wacke, Richard Weitz, Ellen Widmer, Chris Wirth, Dorothy C. Wong, Wang Jianlang, Wang Xianming, Wang Yunhong, Tom Wells, Xiaoqun Xu, Xu Jinxing, Xue Ruize, Zhang Junyi, and Suisheng Zhao.

Colleagues and my own twenty graduate students in Shanghai shared ideas and sources, and supported me in many ways. Among them are Cai Yaming, Kai Yin Chan, Chen Juxia, Galen Ford, Guo Hong, Guo Luxia, Tugrul Keskin, Li Shengling, Liang Shuang, Roland Livins, Rajiv Ranjan, Bunlay Suy, Tao Feiya, Wu Jing, Xu Youwei, Yang Weijian, Antonio Zapata, and Zhang Yong'an. Rupert Arrowsmith, Michael Falser, and other participants in my conference, "Historical Monuments and Modern Society," held at Shanghai University in early December 2018, critiqued my paper, which formed a large part of chapter 4 of the present study. I am indebted to the vibrant Shanghai expat community and the Royal Asiatic Society China colleagues, Tracey Willard, Julie Chun, John Van Fleet, Parul Rewal, Frank Tsai, and Gábor Holch for their resourceful help.

My parents, brother Peng, and sister Jing alongside her Italian family in Rome, Italy, helped me gather historical sources, and even accompanied me on some of my field trips to Longmen and Rome, Italy. I am grateful to my daughter Rose at the Massachusetts Institute of Technology for all the joy and realization that the meaning of living can be enriched not only with luck but also in adversity.

Finally, this book is dedicated to the memory of Daniel H. Bays (1942–2019) for his mentorship, friendship as well as inspiration. Parkinson's disease sadly took him away, but Dan's spirit and legacy live on.

Dong WANG, Xanten, Northwest Germany, January 20, 2020

NOTE

1. Wen Yucheng, "Dangnian manfu lingyunzhi, erjin wuren bu baitou," *Shijie zongjiao yanjiu* 3 (2001): 6–7.

Introduction

In July 2018, *The Guardian* published an editorial which read in part: "UNESCO has been attacked as a bloated bureaucracy, but it is also itself the expression of a noble dream: that there could be places and buildings so beautiful that they transcend nationality and even culture and speak in some way to the whole human race."[1] The subject of this book, a UNESCO World Heritage site—Longmen's Buddhist rock caves, stone carvings, epigraphic inscriptions, and other objects of faith, devotion, and efficacy—testifies not only to the recasting of tradition in the age of modernity, but more importantly to a historical aspiration that encompasses the whole of humanity, as *The Guardian* piece noted so eloquently. While Eric Hobsbawm and other scholars have traced the invention of tradition by nation-states, elements that simultaneously embraced all of humanity during the same historical process are rarely examined in relation to the pursuit of nationalism.[2] The dynamic interplay between national tradition and a one-world universalism—two ways of thinking about culture, heritage, geopolitics, and international relations in history—takes us closer to the historical realities at stake.[3]

This book refracts modern and contemporary China through the lens of the stone Buddhas at Longmen, an ancient landmark laden with political and cultural symbolism. It highlights the manifold traffic and expanded contact between China and other countries, at the same time as these nations were reorienting themselves in order to adapt their own cultural traditions to the newly industrialized and industrializing societies of the modern age. I trace the changing attitudes, both in China and across the globe, toward ancient monuments and antiquities as exemplified by the Longmen caves of Luoyang. Luoyang was a key geopolitical, administrative, and cultural center throughout the first millennium BCE and CE. It later deteriorated into what was called a "Chinese Babylon"[4] (Figure 0.1).

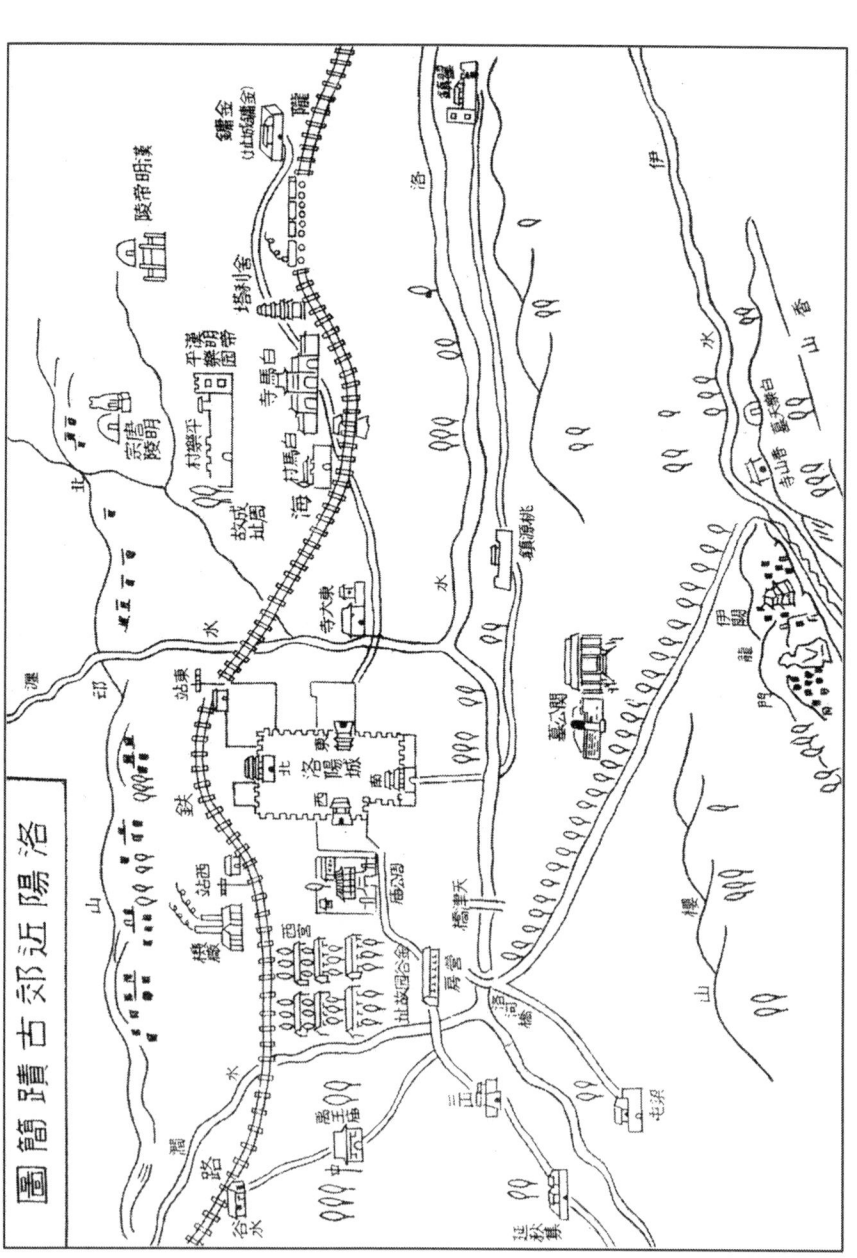

Figure 0.1 Map of Luoyang's Ancient Sites Including the Image of Vairocana at the Center Bottom.
Source: Ni Xiying, Luoyang youji (Travel accounts of Luoyang) (Shanghai: Zhonghua shuju, 1935), frontispiece.

Rediscovered by American, British, Chinese, French, German, Japanese, and Swedish scholars, collectors, and connoisseurs around the turn of the twentieth century, in modern history Longmen came to embody the values of universalism, modernity, and the modern impulse for both China and the world. The treasures at Longmen—preeminently stone sculptures dating from the fifth to the tenth centuries CE—were the object of a global quest that can be compared with the exploits of Indiana Jones.

Based on extensive investigation of original and secondary sources in multiple languages, as well as fieldwork by the author, this book unravels the interconnections between ideas and historical practices from which the contemporary advocacy for the preservation of the world's cultural patrimony, held in trust by the whole of humanity, has sprung. Moreover, Longmen's story invites us to look beyond the familiar narrative detailing how modern China was transformed through its engagement with the outside world: the other side of the coin—how the outside world was likewise changed through its interactions with China—should be given equal scrutiny. Here the focus is on the juncture—not just the oft-repeated story of how China joined the modern world, but also how the world reached out to and learned from China, albeit for different ends.[5]

The global resurgence of populist nationalism and the return to great power rivalry[6] since 2016 prompt us to take a fresh look at the all-but-forgotten mutual empowering of China and the world in modern times through the prism of Longmen. Exploring the Longmen story may explain why a Buddhist votive site created 1,500 years ago in Luoyang proved to be more representative of China at the turn of the twentieth century (or even today) than in first- and second-tier cities—extensively studied in current scholarship—and, more importantly, how it became a potent source of inspiration on the world stage. Industrialization and the advent of modernity propelled nations of both East and West to reposition themselves and ultimately see each other in a new light, while each attempted to revitalize their own cultural heritage through the unifying power of art and the scientific study of other cultures and national traditions. This book opens a window onto a cultural and geopolitical history unfolding in China's hinterland, one with international ramifications—a subject that has not been adequately addressed hitherto.

LONGMEN AND THE CITY OF LUOYANG

Meaning "dragon gate," the name Longmen refers to the scenic mountain ravine between the East (303.5 meters altitude) and West Hills (Longmenshan, 263.9 meters altitude) through which the Yi River flows, a place also known as Yique, about 13 kilometers (around 8 miles, or 25 *li*) south of Luoyang in Henan Province, the central province of the North China Plain, the heartland and imperial capital of thirteen Chinese dynasties, mostly south of the Yellow River (Figure 0.2). Dating from 493 CE during the Northern Wei dynasty (386–534),[7] the Longmen Grottoes as we see today comprise an assemblage of more than 2,000 stone niches and caves, over 100,000 fine-grained limestone sculptures and reliefs, and around 2,800 memorial steles (stone tablets) containing more than 300,000 words of inscribed text.[8] The caves are carved into a 1-kilometer stretch of limestone cliffs on either side of the Yi River. While many of Longmen's sculptures are low relief carvings on the walls and ceilings of the caves, some are spectacularly hewn out of the limestone in situ. The inscriptions are also mostly chiseled into walls and ceilings, alongside the images to which they refer.[9] The production of stone images at Longmen continued in the Eastern Wei (534–550), Western Wei (535–556), Northern Qi (550–577), Northern Zhou (557–581), and Sui (581–618) dynasties, tailing off after the Tang dynasty (618–907) as Luoyang was repeatedly subject to war and communal violence and gradually waned in status, although new carving projects were likely undertaken until the early seventeenth century during the Ming dynasty (1368–1644). Irregular efforts at maintenance and repair were made, probably the most significant on the occasion of the Qianlong emperor's visit in 1750.[10] Over time, to counter the damaging effects of vibration and erosion, roofs, covers, gutters, and a drainage system were installed on the West Hill.

The beginnings of Longmen's caves and icons are attributed to the Tuoba clan of the Tabgatch (Tabgach, Xianbei) tribe from southern Manchuria, who established the Northern Wei dynasty in 386 CE, with its capital in Shengle (near Hohhot, Inner Mongolia); the capital was moved to Pingcheng (Datong, north Shanxi Province) in 398. Led by the Xiaowen emperor (r. 471–499), some of the Tuoba leaders sought to consolidate their dominance in North China by moving the capital from Pingcheng to Luoyang on the Yellow River in 493—home to the first Buddhist temple in China, the Temple of the White Horse (Baima Si), built in 68 AD during the Eastern Han.[11]

Despite the fluctuating patronage of Buddhism by various emperors, the Northern Wei's Tuoba ancestors had practiced a half century or more of devotion to Buddhism, which was transmitted to China via Central and West Asia from India.[12] The Tuoba people had also mastered the art of casting statues and carving rocks into memorial images in honor of revered parents, relatives, and significant clan figures. In 454, the Wencheng emperor ordered that five standing Sakyamuni Buddha statues be cast in copper and gold to commemorate the five emperors who had preceded him. The significant presence of Buddhism in the Northern Wei can also be inferred from the fact that in 476 the capital, Datong, was home to hundreds of Buddhist temples and

Figure 0.2   Longmen's Location in the City of Luoyang.
Source: Courtesy of the UNESCO Archives and the World Heritage Centre. WHC Nomination Documentation, file no. 1003, December 2, 2000, Longmen Grottoes (34°28′N, 112°28′ E), p. 107, https://whc.unesco.org/uploads/nominations/1003.pdf (accessed on January 11, 2020).

monasteries housing over 2,000 monks and nuns; in the area around Datong there were 6,478 temples served by 77,250 monks and nuns.[13] The Yungang Grottoes, carved and painted out of the rock cliffs on Wuzhou Hill, 16 kilometers west of Datong, were an earlier court project of the Northern Wei before their relocation to the hub of Han Chinese economic activity, politics, and civilization.[14]

Like Yungang, Longmen's caves not only were augustly imperial but also served the religious needs of ordinary Chinese—shown not only in the colossal images dedicated to and sponsored by emperors, empresses, empress dowagers, imperial court families, eunuchs, aristocrats, and prominent monks, but also in the small niches donated by lay commoners, especially women, during the Tang dynasty.[15] Tens of thousands of small niches or shrines dedicated by known and unknown donors were dug side by side like beehives along the cliffs and pathways.[16]

In the new capital Luoyang, Xiaowen carried on the Xianbei custom of excavation and stone carving which resulted in the completion of the Guyang Cave, the oldest grotto at Longmen, consisting of eight large shrines carved between 493 and around 528.[17] While the Northern Wei produced around 30 percent of the surviving cave sculptures, the craftsmen of the Tang dynasty (618–907) were responsible for approximately 60 percent of the total. Among the Tang caves, the Fengxian Temple, also known as *Jiujianfang*, housing the 17.14-meter-high statue of the Huayan (Avataṃsaka) and esoteric Buddha Vairocana, is the most photographed, iconic monument of Longmen. Completed in 675/676 (and most probably started in 666), the Fengxian Temple was constructed by a team of workmen including Li Junzan, Cheng Renwei, and Yao Shiji, led by Wei Ji, Fan Xuanze, and two prominent master monks under the auspices of the Tang emperor Gaozong (r. 650–680).[18]

The fate of Longmen's cave temples, stupas, icons, and stone inscriptions is inseparable from the rise and fall of Luoyang. The splendor of the early city, described by Charles Lang Freer (1854–1919) as "the nursery of Chinese culture and civilization,"[19] can only be imagined today. According to historian Victor Cunrui Xiong, "Luoyang [before the tenth century] was not merely a Weberian 'princely residence,' but a world-class urban center of political power, social interaction, business transactions, and cultural enrichment."[20] As a consequence of the cycles of violence that befell Luoyang, the city was reduced to ruins at the hands of regional warlords during the tenth century and later. By the early twentieth century, Luoyang was "deserted by modern civilization, left alone on the Central China Plain with nobody caring for it." Modern Luoyang became a center of rampant banditry, activity in which almost the entire population of West and South Henan were alleged to be involved.[21]

Prominently featured in Chinese mythology and early records, Luoyang and Longmen were both sacred and imperial centers, in striking contrast to their post-thirteenth century decline. Located in a narrow, mountain-rimmed basin formed by the Rivers Yi and Luo, Luoyang was the capital of thirteen dynasties, the first of which was founded over 1,500 years before the Common Era. During the seventh century, Luoyang's status reached its zenith as a *shendu* (divine capital).[22]

The corridor linking the Guanzhong Wei River valley to west Luoyang and the Yi–Luo River valley, where Luoyang was set, holds the key to understanding the emergence of historical China, its politics, society, culture, and religion. Luoyang was the eastern capital of the Western Zhou state, which built the twin cities of Luoyi, the first being Wangcheng, located between the Jian and Chan Rivers (both tributaries of the Luo River) and the other, Chengzhou, to the east of the Chan River; although the exact location of Chengzhou is still in dispute.[23] During the Han and Wei, the walled city of inner Luoyang, a rectangle with a 14-kilometer perimeter and encompassing an area of 6×9 *li* (about 15 square kilometers), was home to over 109,000 households. Greater Luoyang covered 85 square kilometers.[24] The Sui dynasty dug a canal (disused after 1855 due to the Yellow River having changed its course) of 2,000 kilometers that reached both south and north to link Luoyang, the region's political and economic hub, with today's Hangzhou and Beijing. In 622, during the Tang dynasty, Luoyang had a population of 400,000, and the largest inland harbor in China. After the thirteenth century, it gradually lost its geopolitical and cultural centrality becoming the seat of Henan Prefecture during the Ming (1368–1644) and Qing (1644–1911) dynasties, a political, economic, and cultural backwater, anticipating the undeveloped, agricultural character of Henan Province in the early modern and modern periods.[25] By the early twentieth century, among the nineteen Chinese provinces, only Henan, Shanxi, Shaanxi, Gansu, and Guizhou had no treaty ports.[26] In the modern Chinese experience, Henan carried limited weight culturally and internationally—or that is the perception. Describing its architecture in 1913, Murdoch MacKenzie (1858–1938), who arrived in North Henan as a Canadian Presbyterian missionary in 1889 and lived there almost continuously until 1936, wrote:

> To a foreigner it does not seem as if they [houses] were erected with a view to comfort, health or cheerfulness, yet contact with those who dwell in them convinces one that they find their houses suited to all the purposes of their lives. The day of glass windows, wooden floors, good doors, grates and chimneys, convenient cellars, pictures on some walls at least, as well as a certain measure of regard for air and light, will yet come in Honan.[27]

The railway line between Kaifeng and Luoyang was completed in 1908, facilitating both the appreciation and pillage of Longmen as a treasure trove.[28] In 1920, warlord Wu Peifu set up his headquarters in Luoyang, and in 1923, for a short time, the city functioned as the capital of Henan Province. Most of Luoyang's streets were renamed when another warlord, Feng Yuxiang, took charge there in 1927. In 1932, the city became a provisional capital for almost a year under Chiang Kai-shek in Republican China. In October 1936, together with Madame Song Meiling, Chiang celebrated his fiftieth birthday in the two-story villa built for him by the local authorities on Longmen's East Hill.[29] Three years later, Luoyang became the capital of Henan Province for the second time. In April 1948, the People's Liberation Army took over the city, which by then had only 70,000 inhabitants living in a much diminished area of 4.5 square kilometers.[30]

The establishment of the People's Republic of China (PRC) in 1949 awarded new strategic, economic, and cultural importance to Luoyang in the First Five-Year Plan. Seven of the 156 priority national projects were allotted to Luoyang. The city had a population of around 30,000 households and 140,000 residents according to a first census in 1953, exclusive of suburban and county residents.[31] The first thirty years of the People's Republic witnessed a substantial expansion of the urban area with the construction of large *danwei* (work unit) compounds. During the 1950s and 1960s, Luoyang became a key city for national defense, aviation, and missile research as well as industrial development in the mid-South region (Zhongnan qu).[32] In 1954, the State Planning Commission's proposals for a ball-bearing plant, a mining machinery factory—both began operations in 1958—a nonferrous metals processing factory, a copper processing factory, and a tractor plant were approved for construction in Luoyang by Chairman Mao Zedong. As part of a mass campaign to achieve rapid industrialization,[33] the Great Leap Forward of 1958–1960 introduced heavy industry to Luoyang for the first time in history.

In 1958, 76,000 residents—equivalent to the entire population of Luoyang when the People's Liberation Army took over the city in 1948—were transferred into industrial production, over a third of whom were skilled migrants. This was followed by the relocation of 17 factories and 88 shops and around 2,800 workers from Shanghai and Guangzhou in 1955–1956, the transfer of the No. 10 Architecture and Design Institute (dishi shejiyuan) from Beijing in 1958, and the establishment of a refractory factory, a cement plant and other heavy industries in Luoyang.[34] In 1958–1960, 7,000 workers were recruited for these newly founded factories, most of them poor peasants from eastern Henan. On the other hand, the rural areas of the peri-urban zone around Luoyang underwent only limited industrialization. At the same time, the push for immediate industrialization and a decline in grain production were compounded by a three-year period of natural disasters involving floods, droughts, and pest infestations. To alleviate its salary burden, the city government decided to slash the number of urban workers in Luoyang by almost 35,000, most of who were sent back to the countryside.[35]

During the Mao years (1949–1976), preliminary survey, maintenance, repair, and reorganization work were conducted at Longmen, affording the site "relatively good protection."[36] In 1951, the Forest and Ancient Relics Committee of Longmen (Longmen Senlin Guji Baohu Weiyuanhui) was established. In April 1953, the Longmen wenwu baoguansuo (the Longmen Institute for the Protection of Relics) was formed with four staff members, and maintenance and repair work was conducted simultaneously.[37] One can get a sense of the rising significance of Longmen from the short list of visiting dignitaries in 1960. They included Chairman Liu Shaoqi, Premier Zhou Enlai, Vice Premier Tan Zhenlin, Vice Chairman Dong Biwu, Vice Premier Chen Yun, the American journalist Edgar Snow, and the British general Bernard Law Montgomery.[38] In October 1961, accompanying King Mahendra and Queen Ratna of Nepal on a tour of the site, Premier Chen Yi handwrote the two Chinese words spelling "Longmen," which were later inscribed and can be seen on the Longmen Bridge at the north entrance. In March 1961, the site was designated as China's first protected *danwei* (unit) of national significance (*quanguo diyipi wenwu baohu danwei*). In September 1963, the Longmen Protection Area was demarcated. Weekly inspections were carried out by the Longmen Institute for the Protection of Relics until 1990.

Miraculously, Longmen's caves and relics remained mostly unscathed during the Cultural Revolution of 1966–1976, although events could easily have turned out differently. In summer 1966, instigated by Mao Zedong, Luoyang's Red Guards, mostly middle, high school and college students, mobilized to attack the establishment and destroy the "four olds" (*sijiu*)—old ideas, habits, customs, and culture. Amid the resulting chaos, the nation's antiquities and cultural treasures were deliberately targeted and vandalized. One afternoon in August 1966, the Red Guards[39] stormed the White Horse Temple in Luoyang, burning more than 55,000 tomes of Buddhist scriptures and smashing 91 religious statues. In response, the city's party secretary Lü Ying asked faculty and students—an opposing Red Guards faction, according to some accounts—at the Luoyang Agriculture and Machinery College (today's Henan Science and Technology University) to guard Longmen day and night for an entire week.[40] Thus did Longmen escape a major catastrophe during the Mao years.

Throughout the 1970s–1980s, supported by the CCP Central Committee, measures were taken to strengthen the collapsing caves and preserve the sculptures. In 1982, Longmen was designated a site of national scenic importance. In 1983–1989, the local government banned the use of groundwater and the construction of unnecessary buildings and facilities at Longmen, while installing protective barriers, walls, plank roads, weatherproofing, and epoxy and waterproof concrete sealer.[41]

On a personal note, as a Luoyang native, I remember my typical spring excursion, before 1993 when I left for the United States, was a trip to the Longmen caves (Figure 0.3). My older brother recalled that in the 1970s he would ride with my father on a motor tricycle to the caves. He had fond memories of holding onto the legs of the *Jingangs* (warrior attendants) before the tourism boom when protective metal bars and fences were erected to stop visitors from touching the major statues.

Figure 0.3   Dong Wang (*Right*) and Her Classmate in 1982 at Longmen on a School-Organized Spring Excursion.
Source: Photo from the author's collection.

By the late 1980s, the city of Luoyang covered an area of 546.5 square kilometers containing over one million people.[42] Since 1983, the city has hosted a popular Peony Festival (Mudan Huahui) each April. The post-Mao decades of the mid-1980s–1990s saw a flourishing of tourism at Longmen, which was visited by a million people a year, surpassing visitor numbers of the famous Dunhuang and Yungang caves.[43] In 1990, the Longmen Institute briefly merged with the Longmen Institute for Landscape Management (Longmen Yuanlin Guanlisuo, Fengjingqu Guanbaochu) which shared the same office facilities under two separate names—Longmen Shiku Yanjiusuo (The Longmen Institute for Research) and Longmen Guanliju (the Longmen Scenery Management Bureau). However, in October 1992 the Longmen Institute for Research began operating as an independent unit once more, with seventy-two employees.[44]

In 2001, more than 1,500 years after the initial stone carving activities had ceased on the site, Longmen became a UNESCO World Heritage site under the protection of the UNESCO World Heritage Convention and Chinese law, prompting further urbanization and development in Luoyang. The following year, the Research Academy of the Longmen Grottoes (Longmen Yanjiuyuan, Longmen Research Academy for short) was founded to replace the Longmen Institute for Research, and has undergone large-scale expansion since that time. In 2007, Longmen became China's first national 5A-level scenic site, and the Longmen Research Academy fell under the newly formed Longmen Culture and Tourism Management Committee (Longmen Wenhua Lüyou Yuanqu Guanli Weiyuanhui), under whose auspices it continues to function. During the 2010s, the Longmen Research Academy began operating from a new office complex in the eastern corner of the main northeast entrance to the caves.[45] In October 2017, Harvard University welcomed members from the Longmen Grottoes Research Academy to inaugurate an international joint initiative focusing on digital conservation and restoration. In 2018 and 2019, research interest in Longmen apparently peaked in China, with the author getting forty-five and fifty-four hits, respectively, in a keyword search for "Longmen Shiku" on China National Knowledge Infrastructure (CNKI), the most widely used Chinese academic search database.[46]

As for Longmen's host city, in 2016, the prefecture-level city of Luoyang, including seven city districts, one county-level city, and eight counties, had grown to cover 803 square kilometers with a population of over 6.5 million residents, of whom 2 million lived in its urban centers.[47] In the same year, Luoyang was classified as a central regional city and a second-tier, sub-core city of the Central Plain City Cluster in North China centered on Zhengzhou, the capital of Henan Province.[48]

CULTURAL HERITAGE AND MODERNITY

Interrogating the linkages between cultural heritage and modernity, this book explores a variety of historical and contemporary viewpoints on cultural relics through the lens of modern and contemporary China's Longmen in a local, national, and global context. Current scholarship mostly holds that cultural heritage—as an idea, a legal category, and as something in need of protection—emerged out of armed conflict and is embedded within nation-states.[49] Heritage—entities, both tangible and intangible, passed down from preceding generations—commonly refers to "features belonging to the culture of a particular society, such as traditions, languages, or buildings, that were created in the past and still have historical importance."[50] As for modernity, Marshall Berman defines it as "a mode of vital experience—experience of space and time, of the self and others, of life's possibilities and perils—that is shared by men and women all over the world today." Modernity unites all mankind.[51] Rooted in European and American thought, modernity introduced new perspectives and theories about art, philosophy, and aesthetics. While this movement questioned and rejected realism in the arts, the very essence of Western fine art, it ended up by reconstituting the concepts of heritage and tradition. The mass experience of malaise, stress, and loss of certainty were characteristics of life in industrial societies. Where there was initially a strong reaction against the formalism of classical heritage in such societies, heritage was soon refashioned as a source of national identity. Cultural heritage and modernity thus became mutually corrective mechanisms.

On the Chinese side, the terms antiquities, artifacts, ancient sites, cultural property, cultural relics, cultural objects, and cultural heritage are interchangeable, all expressed as *wenwu* in contemporary China, alongside *guwu* and *guji*, appellations widely used in the late nineteenth and first half of the twentieth century. These phrases denote objects or sites of artistic, archaeological, ethnological, ecological, and historical interest. The concept of culture or civilization refers to an amorphous complex of knowledge, beliefs, ideas, art, morals, law, customs, and "any other capacities and habits acquired by man as a member of society."[52] It implies the notion of heritage as fixed and permanent, tangible and intangible property, or simply things handed down from the past. One commentator has enumerated over 160 definitions of culture and cultural property,[53] and many more could no doubt be found.

The 1972 UNESCO Convention Concerning the Protection of the World Cultural and Natural Heritage (the World Heritage Convention, WHL) defines "cultural heritage" (*wenhua yichan*) to include monuments (architectural works, examples of monumental sculpture and painting, archaeological structures and materials, inscriptions, cave dwellings and combinations of features, which are of outstanding universal value), groups of buildings (which, because of their architecture, their homogeneity or their place in the landscape, are of outstanding universal value), and sites (works of man or the combined works of nature and man, and areas including archaeological sites which are of outstanding universal value).[54] As of July 2019, there are 1,121 properties on the World Heritage List (WHL)—869 are designated as cultural, 213 as natural, and 39 as mixed (both cultural and natural).[55] Acknowledging the internationally recognized concept of cultural heritage, China joined the World Heritage Convention (Shiyi) in 1985. China increased its listed sites dramatically from 37 in 2009 to 55 in August 2019, climbing within a single decade from third place in 2009 to first, equaling Italy (41 in 2009 and 55 in 2019) among the 167 state parties which owned WHL properties.[56]

Notions of cultural heritage mediate the past in the present and are intimately associated with global affairs. Through the case of Longmen, this study examines the modern history of cultural heritage in China as an evolving concept, and the ways in which it is claimed, constructed, perceived, and, more importantly, impacts modern society around the world.[57] Closely linked to the concepts of protection, preservation, and conservation, "cultural heritage" has also been defined in terms of a special relationship with a particular culture or nation-state, or the wider community of mankind. Historically, this general concept has been embodied in statements on cultural property such as those pronounced by Theoderic the Great (454–526 CE) in the sixth century CE; the 1462 Bull of Pius II during the Italian Renaissance; the 1819 order of the French Ministry of the Interior; the 1830 Guizot France "Rapport au Roi sur la creation d'une inspection générale des monumens historiques"; the 1877 English "Manifesto" of the Society for the Protection of Ancient Buildings founded by William Morris; and the resolution adopted by the Sixth International Congress of Architects in Madrid, Spain, in 1904. The 1904 Madrid resolution divided monuments into two classes: "dead monuments, i.e., those belonging to a past civilization or serving obsolete purposes, and living monuments, i.e., those which continue to serve the purpose for which they were originally intended."[58]

Controversies over cultural property most commonly arise over questions of ownership: whether the things in question should be viewed as components of a common human culture independent of property rights and national jurisdiction, or whether they should belong exclusively to a specific nation-state, or to an indigenous group, or should be regarded as the inviolable property of individuals. On the one hand, the paradox of cultural property can be attributed to the inconsistencies in international law and domestic law, with their differing emphases on cultural internationalism and cultural nationalism. On the other hand, disputes over cultural property bring to the fore the logic of ownership and the relationship between market nations (countries engaging in the antiquity trade) and source nations (countries supplying antiquities for sale), which place a special value on both tangible and intangible cultural objects possessed by one group of people.[59] To some legal scholars, the May 1954 Hague Convention for the Protection of Cultural Property in the Event of Armed Conflict (hereinafter The 1954 Hague Convention) places the legal emphasis on a shared, international culture. In comparison, the UNESCO 1970 Convention on the Means of Prohibiting and Preventing the Illicit Import, Export and Transfer of Ownership of Cultural Property gives individual nations a special interest and legitimizes national export controls over cultural property. Legal scholar John Henry Merryman plumps for the 1954 Hague Convention: "where choices have to be made between the two ways of thinking, then the values of cultural internationalism—preservation, integrity and distribution/access—seem to carry greater weight."[60]

Similarly, Michael Brown and Naomi Menzy oppose the view of cultural heritage as a form of property which has the effect of commodifying culture and shrinking the public domain.[61] However, approaching cultural property as marketable goods, Eric Posner argues against international treaties and

UNESCO conventions relating to cultural property on the grounds that they have been a "failure" and that "[t]he distinct features of cultural property do not justify the existing treaty regimes or proposals to strengthen them. . . . The treatment of cultural property would improve, even during wartime, if the current regime of international regulations were abolished."[62] Defending cultural property as a form of non-fungible property linked to a common humanity and under collective stewardship, Kristen Carpenter and her coauthors see "great potential—in both cultural property law and practice—for a more nuanced approach to ownership that reflects both broad values of fairness and equality and indigenous legal traditions of relatedness to the land."[63]

Closely linked to the concept of cultural heritage is the question of modernity in cultural relations between East and West, an issue which has largely been framed in terms of imperial projects carried out under the auspices of nations, empires, colonialism, imperialism, postcolonialism, and post-imperialism. In her introduction to a special volume of the *Journal of American-East Asian Relations*, historian Jane Hunter questions the validity of master narratives based on nation-states and imperialism as a conceptual frame for East-West cultural relations in the context of Christian overseas missions.[64] Do we privilege race over questions of faith and spirituality in academic research? Is there a universal love that permeates human activities and interactions beyond the restrictions of time, place, and culture?

Mounting empirical evidence supports Hunter's doubts about current academic framing of East-West cultural relations, suggesting that compassion has been a motivating force in history. From the modern era, ancient sites around the world have been reevaluated as a source of inspiration, both intellectual and spiritual, that embody transcultural aspects of modernity within a complex milieu of local, regional, national, and international forces. At the turn of the twentieth century, Eastern monuments such as the Buddhist rock temples of Longmen were promoted by a diverse and influential group of intellectuals including art historians, collectors, connoisseurs, and Orientalists in Europe, the United States, and Asia as "fully equal, if not superior, to Western products of corresponding kind."[65] In 1956, Osvald Sirén (1879–1966), a Swedish art historian and an important figure in the modern history of Longmen, confirmed the conviction that had been pronounced in 1907 by Ernest Francisco Fenollosa (1853–1908) and others that "the artistic creations of the Far East were not inferior to those of the Western world, and that consequently the figurative arts of the Far East should be placed on the same level as the corresponding products from various European countries."[66] Modernity brought multidirectional change to the ways in which East and West viewed each other.

As mentioned above, modernity has strong roots in the Protestant Reformation, the scientific revolution, the Enlightenment, romanticism, and other influential social and intellectual movements. In economic terms, modernity refers to the industrialized division of labor, the primacy of the market economy, and ever-expanding technologies and modes of communication.[67] Politically, some have defined modernity as the replacement of personal forms of rule with impersonal bureaucracies.[68] Others see modernity from a social viewpoint as the liberation of individuals from the restrictions imposed by family and local communities and their transformation into a "lonely crowd of consumers." Still others characterize modernity from the perspective of secularization and the decline of religion, destabilizing and transforming the fabric of premodern, preindustrial society.

Although fluid in its meaning, modernity—when applied to Chinese history—here refers both to the modern period, which conventionally includes the nineteenth and twentieth centuries, and the state of being modern—an aggregation of norms, institutions, ways of thinking, and existential conditions that are often associated with industrialization and urbanization. In premodern China, Longmen was frequently denounced as a blatant example of the squandering of resources on gaudy frippery by elites and commoners alike. Modernity gave birth to a new Longmen, and Longmen in its turn enriched modernity. As a cultural consequence of modernity, the modern appreciation of Longmen by Chinese and foreigners—mostly opposed to radical social upheaval—took the form of a social and cultural shift that was, however, held fast in an iron cage—reflecting the painful contradiction between scientific standards and sentimental fantasy, between the individual's aspiration for goods and personal fulfillment, and the reality of their limited choices, "firmly channeled into paths laid down by the modern market economy and bureaucratic states."[69]

CHAPTER OVERVIEW

The modern and contemporary story of the Longmen Grottoes helps us answer three major research questions: How did the appreciation of historical sites and ancient stone sculptures as a valuable form of tangible heritage emerge, persist and change in public discourse in twentieth-century China? What lessons can be learned from the historical development of both domestic and international legal frameworks in China for the protection of historical monuments and the return of missing artifacts? Third, how have ancient sites been managed and sustained in face of the issues thrown up by modernity and urbanization?

As sociologist Richard Madsen has observed, the Chinese government has been pushing to "sinicize" all aspects of Chinese life. In the case of religion, sinicization might mean "the imposition of a particular version of a putative

'traditional' culture" constructed and propagated for the agenda of a powerful modern state.[70] For different reasons, many mainland Chinese scholars
consider the development of Buddhist culture with Chinese characteristics
(*Zhongguo tese*)—as expressed in President Xi Jinping's 2014 UNESCO
speech—as an issue of paramount importance in guiding national studies of
the Chinese influence on Buddhism.[71] For a long time, sinicization (*Zhongguohua*) has remained a fault line that has determined the direction of much
research in English on Chinese Buddhism.[72]

With the question of sinicization in mind, chapter 1 explores how Buddhism—historically known as *Xiangjiao* (arguably understood as the teaching of images)[73]—particularly as manifest in the massive groups of stone
images in Luoyang, was remembered, not remembered, and misremembered
in Chinese historical accounts, literary poetry, prose, inscribed epitaphs
(some newly discovered from archaeological excavation), gazetteers, and
other documents dating from the fifth to the eighteenth centuries.[74] Within
their *original* contexts, did the historical witnesses to Buddhist images in Chinese tradition, whether believers or nonbelievers, think and comment about
the artifacts they saw in ethnographically polarized terms of Chinese versus
non-Chinese? Was "sinicization" a major concern of these observers, as it is
today? How were the Buddhist stone images of Longmen characterized in
local literary sources?

Turning next to the manifestation of modernity in the rebirth of Longmen,
chapter 2 traces the developing discussion in China about antiquities and
historical sites that took place from the late nineteenth to the early twentieth
centuries. Previous scholarship has failed to fully explain the apparent contradiction exemplified by an influential group of cultural figures including Kang
Youwei (1858–1927) and Luo Zhenyu (1866–1940) between their historic,
innovative role in renewing Chinese civilization and their political conserva-
tism that was concerned to preserve the existing social order under China's
monarchical polity in the age of republicanism and revolution.[75] Illustrative
of the modern reshaping of Chinese culture and identity, the Longmen story
helps clarify the dynamic processes whereby both the nature and scope of
antiquities were consciously redefined and promoted from the realm of private property to become priceless treasures, potent symbols of nation and
culture, and objects of scientific study. Through public debate and action
surrounding the protection of antiquities (*guwu baocun*), the sovereignty of
antiquities (*guwu zhuquan*) and their public ownership, concepts of tradition
and modernity were refashioned and ultimately fused—a historical movement and a typology that defy the prevailing wisdom "that held (and continue
to hold) categories of tradition and modernity in uneasy separation."[76] In her
book on Tianjin and *weisheng*, Ruth Rogaski argues compellingly that the

Chinese elites steered a parallel course to their Western and Japanese counterparts by systematically reflecting on and critiquing their own traditions and cultural habits—a hallmark of modernity.

Nevertheless, much contemporary scholarship devotes considerable attention to the conflict and incompatibility between tradition and modernity in modern Chinese intellectual and cultural history. Chapter 2 suggests that modern Chinese discourse around heritage did not present a clear cut picture—it was not a simple question of reviling tradition and lauding modernity. Historian Xiaoqun Xu has revealed the complexities of the cultural mood in early twentieth-century China:

> A cosmopolitan outlook would not exclude Chinese culture but regard it as a contributing part to a world culture, and thus it is perfectly legitimate for a Chinese cosmopolitan to be engaged in researching, interpreting, and preserving national heritage, which at the same time was a nationalistic endeavor, at least in the sense of reaffirming the value of Chinese culture. Furthermore, the kind of research, writing, and publishing was an individual calling, freely chosen based on the person's intellectual sensibilities and aesthetic tastes. On all these counts, it was intellectually and morally satisfying to practice reorganizing national heritage[.] Chinese intellectuals from Liang Qichao to Hu Shi, and many others, came to rest on this modest level of self-fulfillment in the trying time of the 1920s.[77]

In chapter 3, the focus shifts to the European—and particularly French—discovery of China's historical ruins, offering an analytical account of the foreign fascination with Longmen. This section locates the origins of Longmen's French connection within a broader context of European historical interest in the East. The establishment of engineering, industrial production, and scientific norms and practices in France, Britain, Germany, the United States, and Japan by the late nineteenth century aided North Atlantic elites and their Japanese colleagues to garner new knowledge of humanity from all parts of the globe in a rational, secular, empirical, and dispassionate manner—although motives based on nationalism, imperialism, colonialism, and geopolitical expediency loomed large in the background. I first examine the historical context of Longmen's French ties before investigating the key figures and ideas of Philippe Berthelot (1866–1934), Édouard Chavannes (1865–1918, a leading sinologist of the early twentieth century), Victor Segalen (1878–1919) and André Malraux (1901–1976).

This investigation shows how the East helped inspire modernity in the West—refuting the conventional trope of Chinese backwardness in the modern era repeated by both camps. In many discussions of culture and modernity in modern world history, this trope takes the form: "During the peak of

European colonialism, appealing to modernity was a method for asserting the 'civilizational' superiority of the West, as European powers claimed their own cultures as the source of modernity."[78] A refreshing take on Orientalism, however, is found in the work of historian Marie-Paule Ha; she examines colonial literature and finds in it a surprising awareness of the complex and ambiguous relationship between colonizers and colonized, and the existential problems that the relationship entailed.[79] I take a different direction, noting that by the first half of the twentieth century French scholars and connoisseurs had invested the ancient Chinese stone images and inscriptions at Longmen with an epiphanic power, by subjecting them and their history to meticulous scrutiny in an effort to reveal that these Buddhist cave temples represented a universal spirituality and aesthetic quality and that they demonstrated the transmission of culture and religion between India, Greece, and China.

Complementing the developments in Europe, chapter 4 turns to the United States and Japan, two new world powers in both collaboration and competition, and their interest in ancient Chinese sites in their respective pursuit of modernity and global cultural status.[80] In both Chinese and Western historiography, Chinese influence, whether considered benign or threatening, on the advanced nations of Europe, Asia and North America conventionally "disappeared" during the late eighteenth century and reemerged in 1949, with a yawning gap in between. To some degree at least, this chapter seeks to fill this gap, indicating how ideas about China made a significant impact on both the United States and Japan—"[a]n influence from the souls of these stone saints,"[81] as Charles Lang Freer put it in 1910 during a visit to Longmen.

More than a century ago, the stone Buddhas of North China became an object of fascination for many influential and wealthy Americans and Japanese. As newly precious commodities, they not only found their way onto world markets but also awakened imaginings of cultural bonds spanning the continents. In a collective imagination driven by a host of individual, national, imperial, and cosmopolitan factors, these sculpted Buddhas came to symbolize the urge to resume human connections long lost and to recover a cultural unity that had once stretched across Asia and formed a bridge between America's European and Asiatic heritage. Together with some European and Chinese elites, a circle of privileged Americans and Japanese, including Ernest Fenollosa (1853–1908), Okakura Kakuzō (1862–1913), Charles Lang Freer (1854–1919), and Langdon Warner (1881–1955), passionately promoted Chinese cultural artifacts as an authentic form of art, albeit reflecting disparate political messages. The dissonant, fin-de-siècle discourses centered on Longmen intersected and ultimately strengthened each other.

Chapter 5 further explores foreign recognition of China's ancient landmarks as a source of ideas of common humanity and modernity through the eyes of Osvald Sirén (1879–1966), the first recipient of the coveted Charles

Lang Freer Medal. I argue that the modern cultural reevaluation of Asia involved the reappropriation of stone statues as works of art and cultural innovations—although, in the case of Longmen and other sites, most Chinese had long been disenchanted with them as symbols of waste and ill-placed faith in their original environment until the advent of modernity. Sirén's eminence as a historiographer can be glimpsed in a eulogy published on his death in 1966: "Sirén's bent was throughout academic: if in him the scholar's coolness wins over the aesthete's advocacy, that is inseparable from his great gifts for synthesis, thoroughness, and lucid exposition. The study of Chinese sculpture and painting in the West still owes more to him than to any other man."[82]

The Chinese verdict on Sirén[83] and his role in the modern recovery of the Longmen Grottoes also highlights the special contribution made by him, alongside a small circle of Euro-American, Japanese, and Chinese connoisseurs and scholars in the East Asia field. According to Wen Yucheng, an archaeologist specializing in Longmen studies, Sirén and Édouard Chavannes had "minds that were as open as a valley and eyes exceptionally perceptive to be able to see what others cannot see. Using cultural comparison, they paid serious attention to Chinese sculpture" at a time when China was "stagnantly confined by feudalism, under siege from the West."[84] Sirén was an important figure in transforming Longmen's stone Buddhas into symbols of timeless beauty—trans-human, trans-religious, and trans-racial—on a par with corresponding Western forms of art.

Cleaving to traditional illusionistic representation with the intention of reviving Chinese heritage so as to "bring forth the new" (*fugu er gengxin*), Sirén's Chinese contemporary Kang Youwei, a world traveler and cultural reform theorist and practitioner, promoted a form of realism in the fine arts which approached the "optical accuracy of shape, color, texture, space and volume."[85] In contrast, with an art-historical background in Renaissance primitivism, Sirén rejected the mundane realism of his own tradition as overbearingly constraining, while identifying the "primitive" and "abstraction" as emerging aesthetics.

Although a historical empiricist, Sirén emphasized the detached imagination which had the power to break the bonds of mundane constraints. For him, the emotionally detached flâneur figure of modernity had no interest, yet his career and demeanor were discretely stage-managed and he regularly feigned modesty when presenting his findings. Using photography in documenting historical ruins, the technical reproducibility of photographs was not something that disturbed him. Sirén juxtaposed art works in innovative ways, a practice André Malraux later developed into the notion of an imaginary museum,[86] a virtual museum in today's terms, yet each man sought different ends in taking the comparative path. Sirén's interest in the stone Buddhas of Longmen suggests that he yearned for both a spiritual epiphany and also to trace their complete history as human artistic creations rather than as vessels of the devotion they once had attracted. Tracing Sirén's role in such a complex process helps clarify the idiosyncrasies, contingencies as well as the predicament of modernity in the East-West cultural world of the first half of the twentieth century.

The legal ramifications of a Janus-faced modernity antagonistic to ancient landmarks is featured in chapter 6, which discusses the institutional measures taken in modern and contemporary China and globally for heritage protection. As Chinese antiquities, especially stone sculptures and stupas, were assigned economic value in art markets in China and across the world, their destruction and removal from their original sites escalated dramatically. Today, as in the past, growing appreciation and commercially motivated vandalism—forms of attention both wanted and unwanted—continue to pit scientific interests, moral scruples, monetary gain, legal judgment, and aesthetic spectacle against each other in a turbulent, never-ending contest.

The global hunt for Chinese antiquities in the nineteenth and early twentieth centuries has been richly documented.[87] However, few have considered the plundering of these treasures in the context of evolving legal frameworks, both domestic and foreign—a subject referred to by one commentator as a "still insufficiently known domain."[88] Nonetheless, as "a most injurious calamity in the modern history of Chinese antiquities"—as the Shanghai daily *Shenbao* called the fate of Longmen's artifacts in 1937—in the modern period Longmen[89] not only prompted a strong emotional reaction, but also constituted a milestone on the way to establishing a legal framework and cultural institutions tasked with protecting China's cultural heritage.

Three legal issues are discussed in detail in chapter 6. I first outline Chinese law on cultural property in the first half of the twentieth century relevant to Longmen and its stone sculptures, which brought to the fore issues of "antiquities sovereignty" and public ownership. The second section explores parallel trends in global legal frameworks and their role in the modern Chinese discourse on the protection of antiquities. In the third section, I discuss various accounts in Chinese and English of the detachment of two important bas-reliefs from Longmen. From the legal and historical perspective, the passions and interests aroused over Longmen reveal that the protection of antiquities in both domestic and international law has proceeded through a winding and contrary procession of alignments, clashes, compromises, and balancing acts.[90]

The final chapter turns the spotlight on Longmen during the People's Republic from 1949 to the present through urbanization and cultural heritage. Longmen is poised at the intersection of national rejuvenation and urbanization, core to PRC's reforms since 1979, on the one hand, and the UNESCO's WHL which has sought to promote universal values and the sense of a shared global culture since 1972, on the other.

From a local perspective, Longmen's new status illustrates how contemporary China has actively participated in and utilized the world order since its admission to the United Nations in 1971 to promote its domestic agendas through top-down political mobilization and mass campaigns.[91] As a new but influential multinational as well as a local institution, UNESCO's WHL is becoming an important sector of urban governance in China, one which has yet to be acknowledged by many scholars researching urbanization in China and the nation's ambitions for increased cultural clout and soft power on the world stage.[92] Since the 1980s, urbanization has been the major driver of China's unceasing push for modernization and national rejuvenation, although an official urbanization policy was not announced until 2014. Longmen became a UNESCO World Heritage site in 2001 in the newly created Luolong District of the city of Luoyang. Within this context, chapter 7 focuses on the local workings of the WHL and heritage governance as it is implemented in China, a synergistic mode of interaction aimed at incorporating local rules, norms, procedures, and technology with the demands made of players at international, national, regional, city, district, township, and village level.

Three aspects are discussed in detail. The first is the clean-up campaign carried out in preparation for the nomination of Longmen for the WHL. A complex array of local, national, and international agencies and actors at governmental, intergovernmental, and nongovernmental levels formed a variety of hybrid coalitions aimed at conserving and refurbishing the site. The biggest challenge to Longmen's nomination was its poor infrastructure and dilapidated environment—the "most difficult, burdensome, demanding, yet essential task," as one document described it.[93] During the environmental makeover, the Chinese state was the driving force—a role designated by the World Heritage Convention, which emphasizes the primary importance of nation-states in nominating and maintaining properties of cultural and natural significance.[94] At Longmen, this centralized process gave more power to the state, enabling it to override the disparate decision-making processes at regional, district, and village levels and thus to overcome the dialectic between the universal and the local.

Second, World Heritage listing has brought about a simultaneous interaction and interdependence of the many actors involved, which has in turn borne fruit in a growing social pluralism including the dissemination of international concepts and institutions, economic benefits, international collaboration, and the development of internationalizing coalitions at the civic level. The UNESCO listing has encouraged ordinary citizens to form networks to protect heritage properties and take part in the burgeoning social pluralism that is developing in inland China. Today's environmental movement is not only a top-down process, but also a spontaneous grassroots phenomenon exhibiting a profound social transformation unfolding at Longmen that is in striking contrast to conditions a century ago.

Third, heritage governance is increasingly being inserted into debates about urbanization and the individual in China. Throughout history Longmen has bound many human lives together, and its elevation to the WHL has involved the rehousing of over 700 households near their former homes in eight peri-urban villages clustered around Longmen's northern entrance. The residents of these villages have experienced in situ urbanization in two major waves—in 1999–2000 and again from 2012, primarily driven by the changed status of the Longmen Grottoes, in concert with China's ongoing urban spread and the New Style Urbanization Plan. Will these developments make for a "Better City, Better Life," to quote the official motto of Expo 2010 Shanghai?

The story of Longmen and its admirers goes some way to providing an answer: "The great mask of the Shang Dynasty is a masterpiece, but Longmen is a world."[95]

NOTES

1. https://www.theguardian.com/commentisfree/2018/jul/04/the-guardian-view-on-world-heritage-in-the-beginning-was-the-dream (accessed on July 12, 2018). The United Nations Educational, Scientific and Cultural Organization is abbreviated as UNESCO hereafter. All translations of Chinese, French, German, and Japanese are mine unless otherwise indicated.

2. Eric J. Hobsbawm, ed., *The Invention of Tradition* (Cambridge: Cambridge University Press, 1992). Works that flesh out the historical interface between national tradition and global commonalities include Xiaoqun Xu, *Cosmopolitanism, Nationalism, and Individualism in Modern China: The Chenbao Fukan and the New Culture Era, 1918–1928* (Lanham, Md.: Lexington Books, 2014); John Fitzgerald and Hon-ming Yip, eds., *Chinese Diaspora Charity and the Cantonese Pacific, 1850–1949* (Hong Kong: University of Hong Kong Press, 2020).

3. Jo-Anne Pemberton, *Global Metaphors: Modernity and the Quest for One World* (Sydney: Pluto, 2001). In arguing for more comprehensive histories of the Cold War era, Laura Elizabeth Wong documents the persistent transnational efforts to disarm fears stemming from war, empire, racism, and ignorance in the period 1957–1966. Laura Elizabeth Wong, "Relocating East and West: UNESCO's Major Project on the Mutual Appreciation of Eastern and Western Cultural Values," *Journal of World History* 19, no. 3 (2008): 349–74.

4. Ni Xiying (1911–42), *Luoyang youji* (Shanghai: Zhonghua shuju, 1935), p. 1.

5. Shellen Xiao Wu, *Empires of Coal: Fueling China's Entry into the Modern World Order, 1860–1920* (Stanford, Calif.: Stanford University Press, 2015), pp. 2–3.

6. BBC Radio4, "Land Power v Sea Power," August 13, 2019, http://www.bbc.co.uk/programmes/m0007kk3 (accessed on August 15, 2019).

7. Stone carving activities took place much earlier than the fifth century, as evidenced by Lu Ji (261–303 CE) of the Western Jin dynasty. See Li Daoyuan (?–527), annotated and transl. by Chen Qiaoyi and supplemented by Wang Dong, *Shuijing zhu* (Beijing: Zhonghua shuju, 2017), 1st ed. 2016, vol. 15, pp. 119–21. Li served in the Northern Wei court. Stanley Abe puts the date at 495 in his *Ordinary Images* (Chicago, Ill.: University of Chicago Press, 2002), ch. 4. Some Chinese scholars have argued for 483 rather than 493 as the beginning of the massive undertakings. Liu Jinglong, ed., *Longmen shiku zaoxiang quanji*, Beijing, 2002, vol. 1, preface, p. 1. For a Chinese bibliography of pre-1995 research in Chinese on Longmen, see Luoyang difang shizhi bianzuan weiyuanhui, comp., *Luoyang shizhi* (Zhengzhou: Zhongzhou guji chubanshe, 1996), vol. 15, pp. 368–86.

8. The State Administration of Cultural Heritage of the PRC, World Heritage Convention, Nomination of Cultural Properties for Inscription on the WHL: China, Longmen Grottoes, 2001. UNESCO World Heritage Centre, archives, CLT/WHC/ NOM 542. Like the exact year construction began, the number of these various categories of artifacts also lacks consensus. The number of stone inscriptions was put at 2,840 individual pieces in Longmen shiku yanjiusuo, Liu Jinglong, and Li Yukun, comp., *Longmen Shiku beike tiji huilu* (Beijing: Zhongguo dabaike quanshu chubanshe, 1998), vol. 1, p. 11.

9. The Longmen of the Northern Wei can be seen in a popular computer game, "Tomb Raider," featuring heroine Lara Croft, https://tombraiderhorizons.com/2017 /01/18/tomb-raider-china-publishes-3-part-article-on-the-wei-mirror/. For a photographic survey of Longmen's caves, see Robert D. Fiala's website on Asian historical architecture, https://www.orientalarchitecture.com/sid/98/china/luoyang/longmen -grottoes (accessed on October 29, 2019). A solid art-historical study of Longmen in English is Amy McNair's *Donors of Longmen: Faith, Politics, and Patronage in Medieval Chinese Buddhist Sculpture* (Honolulu, Hawaii: University of Hawaii, 2007). The book focuses on the relationship between faith, politics, donors to monasteries, lay groups and individual lay men and women (including daughters of aristocrats and widows), and other benefactors of Longmen's Buddhist rock sculptures. Contemporary publications in Chinese mainly discuss the site from the fifth to the tenth centuries and its artistic, religious, visual, and archaeological values, but not its modern history and significance in the formation of modern Chinese and world culture.

10. Lu Jilu and Wei Xiang, comp., *Luoyang xianzhi* (u.p.: 1813, 60 vols.), devoted vol. 2 to Qianlong's visit. For a chronology of Longmen's caves and stone images, see Liu Jinglong, Chang Qing, and Wang Zhenguo, *Longmen shiku diaoke cuibian* (Beijing: Wenwu chubanshe, 1995), pp. 295–310; Li Wensheng, "Longmen Shiku dashiji," in Longmen wenwu baoguansuo and Beijing daxue kaoguxi, comp., *Zhongguo shiku: Longmen Shiku* (Tokyo/Beijing: Heibonsha/Wenwu chubanshe, 1992), vol. 2, pp. 284–95.

11. The collapse of the Han dynasty (206BCE–220) ushered in 369 years of political fragmentation and religious and cultural cross-fertilization when nomads including those from the north Asian steppe came south, vying for control of northern China. During this time, Buddhism—imported first to Luoyang, capital of the Eastern

Han (25–220), from India through Serindia (Xinjiang, Chinese Turkistan) during the Han dynasty—took firm root in China. It appealed to the upper classes including the Tuoba people, and tens of thousands of Buddhist temples and monasteries were constructed throughout both northern and southern China.

12. The ancestors of the Northern Wei were probably exposed to Buddhism during visits to Luoyang, then the capital of the ethnic Chinese regimes of Wei (220–280) and Jin (265–317). For an extensive chronology of Buddhism and Daoism in the Han and Northern Wei dynasties, see Wei Shou (b. 505–572), *Weishu* (Beijing: Zhonghua shuju, 1999), vol. 2, pp. 2011–31.

13. Wei Shou, *Weishu*, vol. 2, p. 2020. Xue Ruize, *Qinhan Weijin Nanbeichao Huanghe wenhua yu caoyuan wenhua de jiaorong* (Beijing: Kexue chubanshe, 2010), pp. 334–39.

14. Also a World Heritage site since 2001, the Yungang Grottoes contain five huge caves, known as the *Tanyao wuku*, probably excavated during the years 460–493, and named after the monk Tanyao. The Northern Wei fell into chaos in 528 when Empress Dowager Hu murdered her eighteen-year-old son, the Xiaoming emperor. Eager to gain the imperial throne himself, General Erzhu Rong stormed Luoyang and tricked and then slaughtered more than 2,000 Xianbei and Chinese court nobles and officials in Heyin (Xingyang), an event known as the Heyin Massacre. Shortly afterward, General Gao Huan turned against the Erzhu family, leading to the split of the Northern Wei into Eastern and Western Wei. In 534, Gao established the Eastern Wei dynasty, moving the capital, more than 400,000 residents, and palace construction material from Luoyang to Yecheng in Hebei. In 535, General Yu Wentai in Xi'an created the Western Wei. In 550 and 557, respectively, General Gao and Yu's sons themselves founded new dynasties, the Northern Qi and Northern Zhou, in place of the Eastern and Western Wei. Wei Shou, *Weishu*, pp. 225–27, pp. 1111–22, pp. 1935–78.

15. These included laywoman Song Jingfei; see McNair, *Donors of Longmen*, pp. 57–8. The empresses of the Northern Wei were mostly Buddhist believers. Koreans and Central Asians also contributed to some of the Longmen caves. During the Tang, more than thirty high-ranking monks including some from Chinese Turkistan were buried on the West Hill at Longmen. Wen Yucheng, "Longmen Tangku painian," in Longmen wenwu baoguansuo and Beijing daxue kaoguxi, comp., *Zhongguo shiku: Longmen shiku*, vol. 2, pp. 172–216.

16. The smallest niche at Longmen is 1.9 cm high, and the smallest sitting Buddha is 1.3 cm, both located in the Guyang Cave. The head of the largest image, Buddha Vairocana, is 4 meters long (with 1.9-meter-long ears), and its shoulders are 6 meters broad.

17. Long Hui, "Xiao Wendi yu Longmen shiku de kaizao," in Longmen shiku yanjiusuo, ed., *Longmen shiku yiqian wubai zhounian guoji xueshu taolunhui lunwenji* (Beijing: Wenwu chubanshe, 1996), pp. 1–8.

18. Zhang Kaisheng, "Luoyang Longmen Fengxiansi daxiangkan kaizao niandai qianshuo," in Longmen shiku yanjiusuo, ed., *Longmen shiku yiqian wubai zhounian guoji xueshu taolunhui lunwenji*, pp. 151–56.

19. Charles Lang Freer, handwritten travel journal from Honanfu (Luoyang), dated October 19 and October 28, 1910, Charles Lang Freer Papers (CLF Papers thereafter),

Freer and Sackler Gallery of Art Archive, Smithsonian Institution in Washington, DC; Freer's lecture on Longmen given in Japan during his homeward trip was probably delivered in 1911, CLF Papers, provided by David Hogge.

20. Victor Cunrui Xiong, *Capital Cities and Urban Form in Premodern China: Luoyang, 1038 BEC to 938 CE* (London: Routledge, 2017), p. 53.

21. Ni, *Luoyang youji*, p. 1. F. H. Hedges, "Bandits: A Growing Menace in China," *Current History* 18 (1923): 606–10; Phil Billingsley, "Bandits, Bosses, and Bare Sticks: Beneath the Surface of Local Control in Early Republican China," *Modern China* 7, no. 3 (July 1981): 235–87, p. 236.

22. This refers to the Wuzhou period of the Tang dynasty, the reign of China's only female emperor (*nühuang*), Wu Zetian (624–705), wife of the Tang emperor Gaozong, who ruled in her own name unlike other empresses in Chinese history. Dangdai Luoyang chengshi jianshe bianwenhui, *Dangdai Luoyang chengshi jianshe* (Anhui: Nongcun duwu chubanshe, 1990), pp. 9–10. Dynastic information was compiled from national and local histories in English and Chinese, including Endymion Wilkinson, *Chinese History: A New Manual* (Cambridge, Mass.: Harvard University Asia Center, 2012), introduction; Angela Falco Howard, Li Song, Wu Hung, and Yang Hong, *Chinese Sculpture* (New Haven, Conn.: Yale University Press and Foreign Languages Press, 2006), chronology; Wan Guoding, comp., Wan Sinian and Chen Mengjia, supplemented, *Zhongguo lishi jinianbiao* (Beijing: Zhonghua shuju, 2005), 1st ed. 1978, and Luoyang difang shizhi bianzuan weiyuanhui, comp., *Luoyang shizhi* (Zhengzhou: Zhongzhou guji chubanshe, 2002), 18 vols., vol. 1. Discrepancies between these sources, especially in the dates of the historical dynasties, should be noted. For instance, there is no consensus on the exact dates of the Xia dynasty and the various sites of its capital. The Erlitou archaeological excavation underway near Luoyang promises to illuminate the earliest state formations of China. Feng Li, *Landscape and Power in Early China: The Crisis and Fall of the Western Zhou 1045–771 BC* (Cambridge: University of Cambridge Press, 2006).

23. Li, *Landscape and Power in Early China*, pp. 62–6, pp. 211–17, fn. 111 on p. 243. The construction of Luoyi (Luoyang) is documented in two chapters, Shaogao and Luogao, of the *Shangshu* (p. 15) and other records and bronze inscriptions. According to the *Zhushu jinian* (Bamboo annals), the construction of Luoyi began in the fifth year of the Duke of Zhou's regency when King Cheng of the Zhou was a boy.

24. These figures differ from those published in Xiong, *Capital Cities and Urban Form in Premodern China*, p. 95. W. J. F. Jenner, *Memories of Loyang: Yang Hsuan-chih and the Lost Capital (439–534)* (Oxford: Clarendon Press, 1981), p. 271. Duan Pengqi, *Hanwei Luoyang gucheng* (Beijing: Wenwu chubanshe, 2009); Xu Song, proofed and supplemented by Zhang Mu, *Tang liangjing chengfang kao* (Beijing: Zhonghua shuju, 2013), 1st ed. 1985; Xin Deyong, *Suitang liangjing congkao* (Xi'an: Sanqin chubanshe, 2006).

25. Roger V. Des Forges argues that Henan, the central province of the central plain, serves as a microcosm of China; *Cultural Centrality and Political Change in Chinese History: Northeast Henan in the Fall of the Ming* (Stanford, Calif.: Stanford University, 2003).

26. In English-language historiography, modern Henan has received most attention for subjects such as violent revolution, military figures, famine, banditry, and

the Christian missions of the 1920–1940s. For a theory-rich study of Southwest (Nanyang) and North Henan (Anyang and Xinxiang), see Xin Zhang, *Social Transformation in Modern China: The State and Local Elites in Henan, 1900–1937* (Cambridge: Cambridge University Press, 2000). See also Micah S. Muscolino, *The Ecology of War in China: Henan Province, the Yellow River, and Beyond, 1938–1950* (Cambridge: Cambridge University Press, 2014); Anthony Garnaut, "A Quantitative Description of the Henan Famine of 1942," *Modern Asian Studies* 47, no. 6 (November 2013): 2007–45; Sonya Grypma, *Healing Henan: Canadian Nurses at the North China Mission, 1888–1947* (Vancouver: UBC Press, 2008); Erleen J. Christensen, *War and Famine: Missionaries in China's Henan Province in the 1940s* (Montreal: McGill-Queen's University Press, 2005); Odoric Y. K. Wou, *Mobilizing the Masses: Building Revolution in Henan* (Stanford, Calif.: Stanford University Press, 1994).

27. Murdoch Mackenzie, *Twenty-Five Years in Honan* (Toronto: Board of Foreign Missions Presbyterian Church in Canada, 1913), p. 5.

28. Odoric Y. K. Wou assesses the uneven economic impact of the introduction of railways to Henan in "Development, Underdevelopment and Degeneration: The Introduction of Rail Transport into Honan," *Asia Profile* (Hong Kong) 12, no. 3 (June 1984): 215–30.

29. The Chiangs stayed in and around Longmen for over a month before departing for Xi'an in December 1936 when Chiang was taken hostage by Zhang Xueliang, an event known as the Xi'an Incident. The Incident forced Chiang to forge the Second United Front with the Chinese Communist Party to jointly resist Japanese aggression. Today, the renovated Chiang-Soong Villa is open to the public.

30. Dangdai Luoyang, *Dangdai Luoyang chengshi jianshe*, preface, pp. 8–29. Wu Shaomin, *Huihuang de Luoyang* (Kaifeng: Henan daxue chubanshe, rev. ed. 2003), 1st ed. 1995. Another source indicates during an April 1948 census conducted by the Public Security Bureau (Gong'an'ju), the city of Luoyang had more than 100,000 people and near 20,000 households, in *Luoyang dashiji* (BCE 50,000–CE 1990), ed. by Luoyang difangshizhi bianzuan weiyuanhui, unknown place and publication date, p. 334.

31. Luoyang difangshizhi bianzuan weiyuanhui, comp., *Luoyang dashiji*, p. 354.

32. Luoshu wang, "Luoyang gailan," http://www.luoshuw.com/lygl.php (accessed on May 15, 2014).

33. The Great Leap Forward aimed to increase in steel, coal, and electricity production by almost 20 percent over three years, and for China to overtake Britain in industrial output within fifteen years; see Michael Dillon, ed. *China: A Cultural and Historical Dictionary* (Surrey: Curzon Press, 1998), pp. 120–1.

34. Luoyang difangshizhi bianzuan weiyuanhui, comp., *Luoyang dashi*, pp. 357–75.

35. Luoyang difangshizhi bianzuan weiyuanhui, comp., *Luoyang dashi*, p. 384. Luoyang's story reflected the national situation. See R. Keith Schoppa, *Twentieth Century China: A History in Documents* (Oxford: Oxford University Press, 2004), ch. 9.

36. Wang Zhenguo, "Longmen Shiku pohuai canji diaocha," in Shanghai remin chubanshe, and Longmen shiku yanjiuyuan, comp., *Longmen liusan diaoxiang ji*, p. 107.

37. Luoyang difangshizhi bianzuan weiyuanhui, comp., *Luoyang dashiji*, p. 349.

38. Luoyang difangshizhi bianzuan weiyuanhui, ed., *Luoyang shizhi* (Zhengzhou: Zhongzhou guji chubanshe, 1996), vol. 15, p. 363.

39. Some accounts indicate that the villagers of Baimasi Village were responsible, carrying out the raid on August 26, 1966. Luoyang difangshizhi bianzuan weiyuanhui, ed., *Luoyang shizhi*, vol. 15, p. 19.

40. Wang, "Longmen Shiku pohuai canji diaocha," p. 107. Luoyang difangshizhi bianzuan weiyuanhui, comp., *Luoyang dashiji*, p. 394. Concurring with Wang, *Luoyang shizhi*, vol. 15, ed. by Luoyang difangshizhi bianzuan weiyuanhui (p. 351), also noted that the destruction of the White Horse Temple took place in June 1966.

41. For thematic and chronological details, see Luoyang difangshizhi bianzuan weiyuanhui, ed., *Luoyang shizhi*, vol. 15, ch. 6.

42. Henansheng Minzhengting, *Henansheng zhengqu biaozhun diming tuji* (Xi'an: Xi'an ditu chubanshe, 1997), pp. 21–3. The different statistical sources show huge discrepancies. For instance, according to the fourth census recorded in *Luoyangshi dashiji* (p. 581), in 1990 the urban population of Luoyang stood at over 5.6 million, a 13.56 percent increase from the 1982 census, which might have included suburban areas and subordinate counties (*jiaoxian*).

43. Liu Jinglong, "Longmen baohu sishinian," *Zhongyuan wenwu* 4 (1993): 1–4. Liu Jinglong, "Longmen Shiku de weixiu gongcheng," *Henan wenbo tongxun* 7 (1978): 48–9.

44. Liu, "Longmen baohu sishinian," p. 2.

45. On the author's field visits of June 2017 and April 2018, the main northwest entrance to Longmen was still closed, the area being under construction for a bio park.

46. Prior to 2018, searches for "Longmen Shiku" on CNKI had never surpassed 30 hits; http://cnki.net (accessed on November 12, 2019).

47. Henansheng minzhengting, *Henansheng zhengqu biaozhun diming tuji*, pp. 21–3.

48. Guowuyuan, "Cujin Zhongbu diqu queqi 'Shisanwu' guihua"; Guojia fazhan gaige weiyuanhui, "Guojia Fazhan Gaige Weiyuanhui guanyu yinfa Zhongyuan chengshiqun guihua de tongzhi," announced on December 29, 2016, http://www.ndrc .gov.cn/zcfb/zcfbtz/201701/t20170105_834444.html (accessed on August 20, 2018). For the full plan (51 pages), see http://www.ndrc.gov.cn/zcfb/zcfbtz/201701/W02 0170105517946834722.pdf (accessed on August 20, 2018).

49. Jane Anderson and Haidy Geismars, eds., *The Routledge Companion to Cultural Property* (London: Routledge, 2017), introduction.

50. https://www.thefreedictionary.com/heritage and https://dictionary.cambridge. org/dictionary/english/heritage (accessed on November 3, 2017 and June 25, 2019).

51. Marshall Berman, *All That is Solid Melts into Air: The Experience of Modernity* (London: Verso, 2010), 1st ed. 1982 by Simon and Schuster. For a different take on modernity, see Christopher A. Hall, "Back to the Fathers," an interview with Thomas Oden, *Christianity Today*, September 24, 1990. http://www.christianityto day.com/ct/2011/octoberweb-only/back-fathers.html (accessed on August 19, 2017).

52. Edward B. Tylor, *Primitive Culture: Researches into the Development of Mythology, Philosophy, Religion, Language, Art, and Custom* (London: John Murray, 1920), 1st ed. pub. 1871, 2 vols., vol. 1, p. 1. J. Jokilehto, "Definition of Cultural

Heritage: References to Documents in History," ed. by ICCROM Working Group "Heritage and Society," 2005, http://cif.icomos.org/pdf_docs/Documents%20on%20 line/Heritage%20definitions.pdf (accessed on January 31, 2019).

53. Jokilehto, "Definition of Cultural Heritage."

54. http://whc.unesco.org/en/conventiontext/ (accessed on February 11, 2019).

55. https://whc.unesco.org/en/list/ (accessed on July 8, 2019).

56. Spain ranks as the second country with the most WHL sites—39 in 2009 and 48 in 2019—and Germany ranks third, with 46 sites as of August 2019. UNESCO, World Heritage Convention, et al., "World Heritage, 2008-09." For August 2019 statistics, https://whc.unesco.org/en/list/stat#s2 (accessed on August 13, 2019).

57. Janet Blake, "On Defining the Cultural Heritage," *International and Comparative Law Quarterly* 49 (January 2000): 61–85.

58. Jokilehto, "Definition of Cultural Heritage," p. 13. Further examples are the 1666 Swedish antiquities ordinance; the 1794 decisions and instructions during the French Revolution to protect cultural relics from iconoclasm and plunder made by the Commission temporaire des arts appointed by the Comité d'instruction publique de la convention nationale; the 1802 Papal State edict by Cardinal Doria Pamphilj, Pro-Camerlengo of the Papal States on behalf of Pope Pius VII; the 1815 book *Le Jupiter olympien ou l'art de la sculpture antique* published in France by Quatremère de Quincy.

59. Today many countries including China are both market nations and source nations.

60. John Henry Merryman, "Two Ways of Thinking about Cultural Property," *The American Journal of International Law* 80, no. 4 (October 1986): 831–53. The 1954 Hague, May 14, 1954, http://portal.unesco.org/en/ev.php-URL_ID=13637&UR L_DO=DO_TOPIC&URL_SECTION=201.html (accessed on February 13, 2019). Patrick J. O'Keefe, *Commentary on the UNESCO 1970 Convention on the Means of Prohibiting and Preventing the Illicit Import, Export and Transfer of Ownership of Cultural Property* (Leicester: Institute of Art and Law, 2007).

61. Michael F. Brown, *Who Owns Native Culture?* (Cambridge, Mass.: Harvard University Press, 2004); Naomi Mezey, "The Paradoxes of Cultural Property," *Columbia Law Review* 107 (2007): 2004–46.

62. Eric A. Posner, "The International Protection of Cultural Property: Some Skeptical Observations," *Chicago Journal of International Law* 8, no. 1 (summer 2007), Article 12, pp. 213–31, https://chicagounbound.uchicago.edu/cjil/vol8/iss1/12 (accessed on February 5, 2019), p. 215. Posner's point is a strong one. One study of seven major museums and individual antiquities collections revealed that around 75 percent of the 1,396 items surveyed were of unknown origin, with many surfacing for the first time long after the passage of national antiquities regulations. See Baker, "Selling the Past," under "The Numbers." Regarding China, one commentator has alleged that "100,000 looters are active in China, with more than 400,000 ancient graves robbed in the last 20 years alone," in Lauren Hilgers in 2013, http://savingan tiquities.org/a-global-concern/china (accessed on January 31, 2019).

63. Kristen A. Carpenter, Sonia K. Katyal, and Angela R. Riley, "In Defense of Property," *The Yale Law Journal* 118, no. 6 (April 2009): 1022–125, p. 1125.

64. Jane Hunter, "Introduction: "Christianity, Gender, and the Language of the World," *Journal of American-East Asian Relations* 24:3–4 (2017): 305–20.

65. Osvald Sirén, "Professor Sirén's Address," in Freer Gallery of Art, *First Presentation of the Charles Lang Freer Medal* (Washington, DC: Freer Gallery of Art, Smithsonian Institution, 1956), p. 18 and p. 10. Ernest Francisco Fenollosa, "The Collection of Mr. Charles L. Freer," *Pacific Era* 1, no. 2 (November 1907), p. 58.

66. Fenollosa, "The Collection of Mr. Charles L. Freer," p. 58. Fenollosa's formulation was at variance with the conventional wisdom of the time and has been subject to contemporary criticism as well. He was a pioneer in treating Japanese and Chinese art objects as equal to their Western counterparts and in developing the history of art as a scientific field of study. Critical of the philistinism of art education in the United States, Fenollosa wrote: "Our art books seem written rather to merit the appearance of scholars than to inform the public about the treasures of appreciation hidden in their own souls."

67. Richard Madsen, William M. Sullivan, Ann Swidler, and Steven M. Tipton, eds., *Meaning and Modernity: Religion, Polity, and Self* (Berkeley, Calif.: University of California Press, 2002), introduction; David L. McMahan, *The Making of Buddhist Modernism* (Oxford: Oxford University Press, 2018), introduction.

68. Although some may argue that China has a long tradition of bureaucracy, premodern China does not fit the multidimensional prescription for modernity. For example, Max Weber has in *Die Wirtschaftsethik der Weltreligionen: Konfzianismus und Taoismus* (Tübingen: J.C.B. Mohr, 1991) and other writings discussed Chinese bureaucracy throughout history in terms that broadly indicate that it never fulfilled the hallmarks of the modern bureaucracy which Weber has famously helped conceptualize.

69. Madsen, et al., *Meaning and Modernity*, ix.

70. Richard Madsen, "'Sinicization' of Religion in China: From Above and Below," description of a workshop held at the University of California at San Diego, March 21, 2018. In Chinese scholarship, sinicization is referred to as *hanhua* and *Zhongguohua*.

71. Cited from an internal document relating to a Chinese national research project in the humanities and social sciences distributed in March 2017. Xi Jinping, "Xi Jinping zai Lianheguo Jiaokewen Zuzhi zongbu de yanjiang," March 28, 2014, http://www.xinhuanet.com/world/2014-03/28/c_119982831_2.htm (accessed on November 17, 2019).

72. Sinicization as a prevailing paradigm in Qing studies has been questioned by Pamela Kyle Crossley, "Thinking about Ethnicity in Early Modern China," *Late Imperial China* 11, no. 2 (June 1990): 1–35.

73. Eric Greene explains, along the line of Chinese vs. foreign, that how image worship was discussed in Chinese literary sources. He suggests that worship of sacred images became distinctly Buddhist in the late fifth century in his "The "Religion of Images"? Buddhist Image Worship in the Early Medieval Chinese Imagination," *Journal of the American Oriental Society* 138, no. 3 (July–September 2018): 455–84. Paul Pelliot argued that the *Xiangjiao* did not mean the doctrine of images in the meaning of "worshipping statues" and in the issue of aniconism versus iconism, but

that Buddhism had three phases, the first of which is the "correct law" (*Zhengfa*), the second, the period we live in, a thousand years where the law is *Xiangjiao*, an image or counterfeit impression, to be followed by the third, final *Mofa* period of ten thousand years. Pelliot claimed that this reading should have precedence over whatever Chinese dictionaries said. Paul Pelliot, "Le terme de 象教 siang-kiao comme designation du bouddhisme," *T'oung Pao* 25 (1928): 92–94. According to Pelliot, the real meaning of the *Xiangjiao* is the teaching of the medium law stage of Buddhism. He followed Sylvain Levi and Édouard Chavannes, "Les seize Arhat proteteurs de la loi," ii, *Journal Asiatique*, September–October 1916, pp. 189–304 (footnote page 194), which stated that the original Sanskrit word "pratirupaka" had the double meaning of image and counterfeit in between the proven law (*Zhengfa*) and the final law (*Mofa*). It was thus the present stage of Buddhism. In my view, the issue is entirely a matter of translation and philological explanation. I thank James Robson for providing me with information about these references.

74. Longmen also boasts the largest number of rock cave *tiji* in China, carved epigraphs associated with stone images. During the Northern Wei in the fifth century, grottoes and stone chapels were also carved at places such as Gongxian, a site near Luoyang that attracted similar attention from foreigners and Chinese alike at the turn of the twentieth century.

75. Aida Yuen Wong, *The Other Kang Youwei: Calligrapher, Art Activist, and Aesthetic Reformer in Modern China* (Leiden: Brill, 2016); Yang Chia-Ling and Roderick Whitfield, eds., *Lost Generation: Luo Zhenyu, Qing Loyalists and the Formation of Modern Chinese Culture* (London: Saffron Books, 2012); Shana J. Brown, *Pastimes: From Art and Antiquarianism to Modern Chinese Historiography* (Honolulu, Hawaii: University of Hawai'i Press, 2011). Kang Youwei, organized by Lou Yulie, *Kang Nanhai zibian nianpu (wai erzhong)* (Beijing: Zhonghua shuju, reprint 2017, based on the 1992 ed. This autobiographical chronicle (pp. 237–70) also contains in the appendix a biography of Kang Youwei by Liang Qichao, a well-known essayist and publicist. Liang characterized Kang as an educator and *xianshi zhi renwu* (someone ahead of his time).

76. Ruth Rogaski, *Hygienic Modernity: Meanings of Health and Disease in Treaty-Port China* (Berkeley, Calif.: University of California Press, 2004), pp. 20–1. A classic work, along the same lines, is Joseph R. Levenson's *Confucian China and its Modern Fate: A Trilogy* (Berkeley, Calif.: University of California Press, 1965).

77. Xu, *Cosmopolitanism, Nationalism, and Individualism in Modern China*, p. 192.

78. Stephen Pascoe, Virginie Rey, and Paul James, eds., *Making Modernity: From the Mashriq to the Maghreb* (Melbourne: Arena Publications, 2015), p. 10.

79. Marie-Paule Ha, *Figuring the East: Segalen, Malraux, Duras, and Barthes* (Albany, N.Y.: State University of New York, 2000).

80. These developments are relevant to the contemporary debate over Chinese influence in the politics, education, finances, technology, and industries of the United States, Australia, Britain, and other countries. For a representative sample of different opinions over time, see Zhu Qianzhi's classic work, *Zhongguo zhexue duiyu Ouzhou de yingxiang* (Shanghai: Shangwu shuju, 1940), 2nd ed. 1983 by Fujian renmin chubanshe in Fuzhou. Nancy Bernkopf Tucker, *The China Threat: Memories, Myths, and*

Realities in the 1950s (New York: Columbia University Press, 2012). Bill Gates, "I worry about U.S.-China relations," Davos, January 25, 2019, https://www.youtube.com/watch?v=fGYz5SszZ74 (accessed on June 28, 2019). Critical of the zero–sum mentality, Gates notes that actors build on each other and, in the civilian sector, innovation is the key. Larry Diamond and Orville Schell, et al., *Chinese Influence & American Interests: Promoting Constructive Vigilance* (Stanford, Calif.: Hoover Institution Press, 2018); Mike Pence, "Remarks by Vice President Pence on the Administration's Policy toward China," issued on October 4, 2018 https://www.whitehouse.gov/briefings-statements/remarks-vice-pre (accessed on October 5, 2019). Robert Sutter, "Pushback: America's New China Strategy," *The Diplomat*, November 2, 2018, https://thediplomat.com/2018/11/pushback-americas-new-china-strategy (accessed on November 8, 2018).

81. Travel journal, November 14, 1910, CLF Papers. Freer Gallery of Art and Arthur M. Sackler Gallery Archives. Smithsonian Institution, Washington, DC.

82. William Watson (1917–2007), obituary of Osvald Sirén, 1966, "Professor Osvald Sirén," *The Burlington Magazine* 108, no. 762 (September 1966): 484–5. Alexander Coburn Soper, "Review of Chinese Sculpture from the Fifth to the Fourteenth Century," *Artibus Asiae* 32 (1970): 336–8.

83. Sirén is known in China as Xi Longren or Xi Leng. The Chinese pass issued to Sirén to visit Shanxi, Hebei, Qahar, Henan, Anhui, Jiangsu, and Zhejiang, dated April 1929 and valid for one year, is held in the Östasiatiska Museet in Stockholm, Sirénarkiv, A2: 1921–29; letter from Feng Yuxiang to Sirén, Sirénarkiv, A2: 1921–29, November 30, 1921.

84. Wen Yucheng, "Zheren weixiao, qiangu miaodi," in *Longmen liusan diaoxiang ji*, ed. by Longmen shiku yanjiusuo, Shanghai: Shanghai renmin meishu chubanshe, 1993, p. 1.

85. Wong, *The Other Kang Youwei*, p. 7.

86. Malraux (and/or his assistants) borrowed ideas and observations from Sirén for his work on the imaginary museum, in most cases with little or no acknowledgment of his sources. For examples of Malraux's failure to credit Sirén and others' works, see André Malraux, *The Voices of Silence* (London: Secker & Warburg, 1954), transl. by Stuart Gilbert, p. 12. Walter Grasskamp, *The Book on the Floor and the Imaginary Museum* (Los Angeles, Calif.: Getty Publications, 2016), transl. by Fiona Elliott, pp. 56–64.

87. K. Ian Shin, "The Chinese Art 'Arms Race': Cosmopolitanism and Nationalism in Chinese Art Collecting and Scholarship between the United States and Europe, 1900–1920,"*The Journal of American-East Asian Relations* 23 (2016): 229–56; Kin-Yee Ian Shin, "Making 'Chinese Art:' Knowledge and Authority in the Transpacific Progressive Era," doctoral dissertation, Columbia University, 2016. Shin's dissertation deals with the production of American knowledge about Chinese art, and does not engage with the Chinese context, or with Japan, an important shaper of American knowledge. Other sources worth noting include Michael St. Clair, *The Great Chinese Art Transfer: How So Much of China's Art Came to America* (Madison, N.J.: Fairleigh Dickinson University Press, 2016); Karl E. Meyer and Shareen Blair Brysac, *The China Collectors: America's Century-Long Hunt for Asian Art Treasures* (New York: Palgrave Macmillan, 2015); Perry Johansson, *Saluting the Yellow Emperor:*

A Case of Swedish Sinography (Boston, Mass.: Brill, 2012); Constance J. S. Chen, "From Passion to Discipline: East Asian Art and the Culture of Modernity in the United States, 1876–1945," doctoral dissertation, University of California at Los Angeles, 2000.

88. Vincent Kelly Pollard, review of Jocelyne Fresnais' *La protection du patrimoine en Républic Populaire de Chine, 1949-1999* (Paris: 2001), *China Review International* 10, no. 2 (Fall 2003): 385–9. Peng Lei, *Wenwu fanhuan fazhi kao* (Nanjing: Yilin chubanshe, 2012). Focusing on smuggling and the expanded regulatory capacity of the state authorities, Philip Thai explores their symbiotic and dialectic relationship and argues that the fight against illicit trade along the China coast helped empower the modern Chinese state. Philip Thai, *China's War on Smuggling: Law, Economic Life, and the Making of the Modern State, 1842–1965* (New York: Columbia University, 2018).

89. In a discussion of Dunhuang and the oracle bones, Zuozhen Liu touches on Longmen in *The Case for Repatriating China's Cultural Objects* (Singapore: Springer, 2016), p. 13. Popular works in Chinese include: Zhang Zicheng, ed., *Bainian Zhongguo wenwu liushi beiwanglu* (Beijing: Zhongguo lüyou chubanshe, 2001); see pp. 224–30 on the losses suffered by Longmen and the "collusion" between Beijing dealer Yue Bin (1896–1955) and Alan Priest; Zhang Jian, *Guobao jienan beiwanglu* (Beijing: Zhongguo lüyou chubanshe, 2000); Xu Senyu, ed., *Zhongguo jiawu yihou liuru Riben zhi wenwu mulu* (Shanghai: Zhongxi shuju, 2012).

90. Li Yuxue, "Yingdui wenwu weiji de lujing xuanze: Yi guoneifa he guojifa dui wenwu de baohu wei fenxi kuangjia," *Falü kexue (Xibei Zhengfa Daxue xuebao)* no. 3 (2009): 106–18.

91. Prior to joining the UN in 1971, P.R. China was considered to be a potential "radicalizer" of the world system. Samuel S. Kim, "The People's Republic of China in the United Nations: A Preliminary Analysis," *World Politics* 26, no. 3 (April 1974): 299–330; Samuel S. Kim, *China, the United Nations and World Order* (Princeton, N.J.: Princeton University Press, 1979); Yongjin Zhang, *China in International Society since 1949: Alienation and Beyond* (New York: St. Martin's Press, 1998).

92. For useful annotated bibliographies of urban studies, heritage management, and China, see Kristin Stapleton, "Urban Change and Modernity"; and Tracey L-D Lu, "Heritage Management," both ed. by Tim Wright, *Oxford Bibliographies in Chinese Studies* (New York: Oxford University Press, 2013), online database. For a helpful treatment of heritage management, see Graham Fairclough, Rodney Harrison, John H. Jameson Jr., and John Schofield, eds., *The Heritage Reader* (New York: Routledge, 2008).

93. "Zuohao shenyi gongzuo, tisheng gudu xingxiang," undated (2008, my inference), manuscript provided by Lu Wei.

94. http://whc.unesco.org/en/164/ (accessed January 1, 2009).

95. André Malraux, *Le musée imaginaire de la sculpture mondiale: Des bas-reliefs aux grottes sacrées* (Paris, 1954), p. 55, where Malraux implied that Longmen was an awe-inspiring repository of the past. Contemporary tour guides describe the site as a "huge museum," *baoluo wanxiang* (all encompassing), in agreement with Malraux. "Longmen daoyouci," dated July 25, 2008, http://www.doc88.com/p-30 92266291369.html (accessed on November 6, 2019).

Chapter 1

How Longmen Was Remembered, Not Remembered, and Misremembered as an Ancient Site in Premodern China

The Tathāgata Buddha founded Buddhism, and focused on mercy. Was Buddhism ever meant to disturb people with gaudy superficial adornment?

—Sima Guang (1019–1086)[1]

The breakup of the Northern Wei state was the result of its excessively large number of stone buddhas.

—Peng Gang (Ming dynasty scholar-official)[2]

The hermeneutic paradigm of sinicization (sinification, *Zhongguohua*, *hanhua*) dominates our contemporary reading of the historical links between China and Buddhism. Underlying this approach are assumptions which have previously been questioned, albeit unsystematically, by a handful of scholars working in different disciplines.[3] Two of these assumptions have framed not only the current ideological emphasis on sinicization in China but also academic approaches to Chinese religious history.

The first of these is the clear separation of different cultures—whether Han Chinese, non-Han ethnic minorities, Western, or Eastern—into clear cut vectors of influence which enjoyed unequal relationships and historical impact. The second assumption is that the premodern history of Buddhism in China was largely a matter of ethnic, racial, and cultural allegiance, acculturation, or sinicization.[4]

These assumptions have taken at least three broad directions in historiography. One is the notion of the Buddhist "occupation" of China, or the Indianization of China, as suggested by the title of Hu Shi (Hu Shih)'s 1937 article and Erik Zürcher's 1959 book, or the heavy Buddhist influence on Chinese material culture.[5] This approach has been countered by the viewpoint that Buddhism is a subsidiary cultural form to native Chinese tradition. For instance, in 1973, Kenneth K. S. Ch'en's *The Chinese Transformation of Buddhism* highlighted how the Chinese modified Buddhism to fit into their situation.[6] In the 1980s, Ren Jiyu, an eminent Chinese philosopher, argued that Buddhism was auxiliary to indigenous culture in China.[7] Chan and popular Buddhism are examples of the sinicization of Buddhism.

A third stream of scholarship emphasizes the social dynamics and interdependent elements at work in the spread of Buddhism in China, with complex implications for an active Chinese contribution.[8] In his book *Fojiao de Zhongguohua*, Chinese scholar Xu Kangsheng states that Buddhism is "an integral and important component of Chinese culture that is represented by Confucianism, Buddhism and Daoism."[9]

Two introductions, written by Li Song and Angela Falco Howard, respectively, for a multiauthored book on Chinese sculpture published in 2006, display a subtle divergence, with Li emphasizing the "sinicization of the Indian tradition as it moved east," and Howard highlighting the "Han assimilation" of foreign inspiration and imperial patronage.[10] At the present, paraphrasing President Xi Jinping's 2014 UNESCO speech, many mainland Chinese scholars deem the development of a Buddhist culture with Chinese characteristics (*Fojiao Zhonguohua, Zhonguo tese de Fojiao wenhua*) as an issue of "paramount importance" in guiding national studies of the Chinese influence on Buddhism.[11]

Given the above diverse recognitions of the crucial role that sinicization of Buddhism has played in the study of Buddhism in China, we should consider the startling reaction of French intellectual Victor Segalen, a sinophile, to Longmen's stone Buddhas on his visit to Luoyang in the early twentieth century. Segalen denounced the Buddhist stone artifacts of Luoyang as adulterated, and thus he regarded them as not part of authentic Chinese culture.[12]

With the question of sinicization in mind, in this chapter I explore how Buddhism—historically known as *Xiangjiao* (arguably the teaching of images)—particularly as manifest in the massive groups of stone images in Luoyang, was remembered, not remembered, and misremembered in historical accounts, literary poetry, prose, local gazetteers, and other documents dating from the fifth to the eighteenth century, before the modern rebirth of Longmen as a result of its discovery by Japanese, European, American, and Chinese scholars, art collectors, and adventurers.[13] Within their original contexts, did the historical witnesses to stone Buddhas (*shifo*), whether believers or nonbelievers, think and comment about the artifacts they saw in ethnographically polarized terms, that is, Han versus non-Han? Was "sinicization" a major concern of these observers, as it is today? How were the Buddhist stone images of Longmen characterized in local literary sources?

In lieu of the relatively well-documented record of the city by the standards of ancient and medieval history, there are at least three reasons why Luoyang is a suitable place to seek answers to these questions. First, greater Luoyang, the capital of the Northern Wei (386–534 CE) dynasty from 495 to 534, was traditionally known as the land of Buddhas, with over one thousand Buddhist holy sites.[14] Its 700,000 inhabitants and area of 75 square kilometers (29 square miles) made it the world's largest and most populous city for its time.[15] Second, although Luoyang's Longmen,[16] located in today's Luolong District of south Luoyang, has the largest concentration of historical stone carvings in China, their role as a form of Chinese cultural construct is rarely discussed by scholars.[17]

Third, Luoyang is the putative birthplace of Daoism, a place where Buddhism found its first home in China and a city where large Nestorian, Persian, and other Central Asian communities settled, Confucianism thrived, and Neo-Confucianism arose.[18] As a place where the powerful and rich, aristocrats and luminaries, as well as ordinary people preferred to live and to be buried, the *Shiji* and other historical records labeled Luoyang the center of the universe. It was characterized by Sima Guang (1019–1086), historian and statesman of the Song dynasty, as the barometer of all worldly affairs.[19] Like Rome, Luoyang was ransacked in wars and suffered violence and cruel destruction but, unlike Rome, it declined over the course of two millennia so that, by the early twentieth century, this once grand metropolis had become a dilapidated township of 70,000 souls, "China's Babylon deserted by civilization"—only to be transformed into a manufacturing city in Western Henan Province after the founding of the People's Republic.

Thus, given that places such as the Yangzi delta (Jiangnan) and other areas in south China have received much more attention in studies of Chinese religious history, these perspectives from Luoyang, in the heart of the North China Plain, shed new light on the understanding of questions of Buddhism and sinicization in premodern Chinese society.[20]

SHIFO, SHIXIANG, AND LUOYANG: EARLY REFERENCES

As pointed out in the Introduction, Buddhism, the rock cave temples, and the numerous carved sculptures in Luoyang were inseparable from the rise and fall of the city. I shall examine historical references to the Buddhist images, in addition to written records from the Eastern Han,[21] Jin, Cao Wei, and

Northern Wei, as well as the sources of the Northern and Southern dynasties before the seventh century.

Historically and arguably, Buddhism, "the teaching of images," conjures up images of icons, stupas, temples, tonsured, robed clergy, monasteries, bells, and incense. Most commentators agree that Buddhist reverence for images and icons of the Buddha, Bodhisattvas, Ānanda, Arhat, and other cult figures began during the first century of the Common Era, before the religion's entry into China during the Eastern Han dynasty.[22] According to one legend, when the Buddha Tathāgata ascended to the Trāyastriṃśa, the heaven of the thirty-three, to pray for his dead mother, King Udyāna became so despondent that the Buddha's disciple Mu-lien made the first image of the Buddha out of sandalwood to comfort him. King Prasenajit is also said to have made a similar image in gold.[23]

Buddhism spread overland from India to China, probably between 147 and 189 CE, through Serindia (Xinjiang in Chinese Turkistan) during the Eastern Han dynasty.[24] The collapse of the Han dynasty (206 BCE–220 CE) ushered in nearly four centuries of political fragmentation and religious and cultural cross-fertilization when nomads intruding from the north Asian steppe came south, vying for control of North China. During this time, Buddhism took firm root in China. As the capital of the Eastern/Later Han (25–220), Luoyang was a hub for early Buddhist activities and home to what is commonly believed to be the first Buddhist temple in China, the Temple of the White Horse (Baima Si), founded in 68 CE by Emperor Mingdi, which is still functioning on its original site today.[25]

According to Alexander Coburn Soper and Fang Hao, the first Buddhist bronze images in China that can be historically verified were probably made around 190 by Ze Rong (?–195), the preeminent Buddhist propagandist, in the Luoyang, Xuchang (Henan) and Jiangsu (Xuzhou-Yangzhou) areas. "He erected a Buddha shrine, making a human figure of bronze whose body he coated with gold and clad in brocades. He hung up nine tiers of bronze plates [on the spire] over a multi-storeyed pavilion."[26] On the basis of epigraphical evidence preserved in literary sources, Minku Kim argues that the first icons used by Chinese Buddhists appeared only from the mid third century.[27] We should also note here that *Zaoxiang liangdu jing*, a manual for making Buddhist images, was translated into Chinese by Gongbuchabu from a Tibetan translation and published in 1742 during the reign of the Qianlong emperor.[28]

Three types of historical sources suggest how Buddhist images in Luoyang were referenced before the seventh century. The first, a text by a court official, Yang Xuanzhi of the Northern Wei, described the city's major Buddhist temples as a window on the splendor, excess, and ensuing tragedy of Luoyang in the mid sixth century. Second, the final chapter of *Weishu* contains an extensive chronology of Buddhism and Daoism in the Han and Northern

Wei dynasties, recorded by the Northern Qi courtier-scholar Wei Shou in the late sixth century.[29] The third type of source is the dedicatory tomb epitaphs recovered from archaeological excavations.[30]

In 547—more than a decade after the forced relocation of Northern Wei's capital from Luoyang to Yecheng in Hebei—when court official Yang Xuan-zhi returned to Luoyang, he encountered ruined buildings, broken walls, and streets and whole city wards covered in wild grass and wormwood. As Yang recalled, "Luoyang and its vicinity was once filled with over one thousand Buddhist temples, but now all is emptiness and desolation, where one rarely hears the sound of temple bells anymore."[31] Yang wrote *Luoyang qielan ji* in order that later generations should remember the city's lost past.[32]

In this work, Yang told the story, set in Zhaoyi Nisi (nunnery) in the inner city of Luoyang, of miraculously recovered statues inscribed with the name of a historical figure dating from 266. Whether credible or not, this type of story indicates the important role played by icons in Buddhist faith and practice:

> South of the nunnery [Zhaoyi Nisi] is Yishou Li, where stood the mansion of Duan Hui, magistrate of Baoxin County (today's Xixian [Henan]) . . . The ring-ing of a bell was continually heard underground and often a five-colored glow was seen, lighting up the buildings. Hui was so curious that he finally had an excavation made at the place from which the light came, and found a gilded image about three feet high, with two Bodhisattvas. On the pedestal was an inscription saying: "Jin, Taishi second year [266], fifth month and fifteenth day; made by courtier secretary Xun Xu." Hui therefore gave up his mansion and had it turned into the Guangming Temple. People at the time all said that that was where Xun Xu's mansion had stood. Later a thief tried to make off with the statue, upon which it and the two Bodhisattvas all shouted at the thief. The thief was so terrified that he fell in a dead swoon, and so was captured by the monks who came when they heard the statue's cry.[33]

The same chapter also lavishly praised the sculptural skills, which was rarely seen in premodern literary texts from Luoyang: "The nunnery [Zhaoyi Nisi] had one Buddha and two Bodhisattva statues. The sculpting techniques were perfect and unsurpassed in the capital."[34]

Aside from his vivid portrayal of the more ostentatious features of the Buddhist presence in Luoyang, including statuary, Yang Xuanzhi struggled to make sense of the rapid downfall of the Northern Wei that he witnessed in rational, ethical, and class terms—rather than explaining it in terms of Han Chinese versus "barbarian" non-Han, as implied in the sinification approach. In his opening chapter on the extravagant Temple of Yongning founded by Empress Dowager Hu, Yang criticized her lust for power and excess in con-structing ornate Buddhist pagodas, temples, images, and other lavish material expressions of the Buddhist faith.

The Northern Wei fell into disarray in 528 when Empress Dowager Hu allegedly murdered her own eighteen-year-old son, the Xiaoming emperor, who himself had no heir. "Power-hungry to control the court," she placed the three-year-old heir to Prince Lin Tao on the throne.[35] Eager to ascend the imperial throne himself, General Erzhu Rong stormed Luoyang and, together with Prince Changle, duped and then slaughtered more than 2,000 court nobles and officials in the Heyin (Xingyang) Massacre, bringing Luoyang's golden era to a bloody end. Shortly afterward, General Gao Huan turned against the Erzhu family, leading to the split of the Northern Wei into the Eastern and Western Wei. In 534, Gao established the Eastern Wei dynasty, moving the capital, more than 400,000 residents, and palace construction material from Luoyang to Yecheng (in Hebei). In 535, General Yu Wentai in Xi'an created the Western Wei. In 550 and 557, respectively, the sons of Generals Gao and Yu themselves founded new dynasties, the Northern Qi and Northern Zhou, in place of the Eastern and Western Wei.[36]

Yang laid the blame for the excessive scale of the Temple of Yongning squarely on Empress Dowager Hu, who was allegedly influenced by a supernatural tale about the discovery of thirty Buddhist statues beneath the site:

> In the beginning, when the foundations [for the grand nine-story wooden pagoda] were dug, they went deep underground, and thirty gold [bronze] statues were found. The Empress Dowager considered this to be a propitious manifestation of her faith in Dharma, making her even more determined to pursue a lavish construction program . . . The pagoda was nine-story tall, with golden bells hung from every corner—120 in all, from top to bottom. Each door had five rows of golden studs—a total of 5,400—with golden rings mounted in holders. The absolute perfection achieved by this wooden Buddhist building in both design and construction is hard to believe.[37]

In early 534, when the Northern Wei fell, the ornate pagoda which was the centerpiece of the temple caught fire and burned for three months, despite the efforts of a thousand imperial troops who attempted to put out the blaze. "People from all walks of life, clerical and lay, came out to watch, making the capital tremble with their sobs. Three monks went into the fire and killed themselves."[38]

In his final chapter, Yang referred briefly to the stone caves and images at Longmen: "In the passes to the south of Luoyang was Shiku Si."[39] This stone monastery, also known as the Guyang Cave (Guyang Dong), was considered by some to have been built by Empress Dowager Hu in 516, along with another stone cave temple called Lingyan Si, the Binyang Cave (Binyang Dong).[40] In *Weishu*, Wei Shou noted that quarrying the limestone hills at Longmen to build cave temples was an extremely costly and difficult undertaking.[41]

Yang Xuanzhi also devoted considerable space to the figure of Song Yun, a Dunhuang man who had taken up residence in Luoyang, and who had been on a mission to Central Asia via Xinjiang in 517/518, together with the monk Huisheng. Five years later he had returned bringing back 170 Greater Vehicle (Mahayana) classics that became popular Buddhist texts.[42] Yang's account contains a reference to stone images: One *li* (a few hundred meters) north of the city of Foshafu on the Kābul River[43] was the White Elephant Palace, "which was full of stone images—a great number of them—which were grand and majestic, covered in gold leaf. They were a dazzling sight."[44]

Drawing on a wide range of then contemporary sources, this chapter was a "document of the first importance for the history of Central Asia" during the early sixth century. In it, Yang also clearly traced the stone images and cave chapels in Luoyang, especially those at Longmen, to their antecedents, which were said to be found throughout Udyāna and Gandhāra,[45] via Khotan, the Congling Mountains, the Wakhan, the Ephthalites, and Pashai in the Hindu Kush, between Zebak and Chitral.

According to Yang, Song Yun had been well received by the king of Udyāna, who "ate vegetarian food and worshipped the Buddha morning and night, accompanied by drums, mandolins, harps, and pipes." He continued: "On learning that the Empress Dowager honored the Buddha's Law, he [the king] turned east, put his hands together, and prostrated himself as he paid his respects to her from afar." Through an interpreter, the king also responded to the Northern Wei envoy, saying: "If it is as you just said, yours is indeed a land of the Buddha. I hope to be reborn there when this life of mine ends." While in Udyāyana, the two Northern Wei men were also seeking the traces, including the stone footprints, of Tathāgata Buddha—the places where the Buddha was said to have preached, sat, dried his clothes, given his body to feed a hungry tigress while practicing asceticism, taken off his skin to make paper, and broken off his own bones to serve as pens.

In these accounts, Buddhist beliefs, practices, and stone images not only opened up new connections and sacred meanings but also clearly suggested that food, customs, cultural and social differences—not just in terms of Han versus non-Han, but also in terms of recognizing the differences between Northerners and Southerners, among others—were discussed in and around Luoyang's Buddhist temples, although they were mostly treated in light-hearted vein by Yang Xuanzhi.

According to Yang, the founder of the temple Zhengjue Si, Wang Su, a learned and brilliant man, came to Luoyang in 494 to submit to the Northern Wei from the Southern Qi in south China, where Wang was deputy privy secretary. The dietary differences between Luoyang's Northern Wei people and those in south China became the subject of humor, even in a court setting:

When he arrived in Luoyang, he could not eat mutton, yogurt and other local foods, feeding himself instead on carp broth and drinking tea. When the aristocrats of the capital saw that he could down a gallon of it at a sitting, they nicknamed him the Bottomless Drinking Cup. Several years later, at a palace banquet with Kaozu (the Xiaowen emperor, r. 471–499 CE), he consumed large quantities of mutton and yogurt. Surprised, Kaozu asked Wang: "You have tasted the foods of China: how does mutton compare with fish soup and tea with yoghurt, then?" Wang replied: "Mutton is the finest produce of the land, and fish the best of the watery tribe. They are both delicacies in their different ways. As far as flavor goes, there is a great gulf between them. Mutton is like big territories such as the Qi and Lu, and fish are like small states such as the Zhu and Ju. Tea is in a different category altogether and is the very slave of yoghurt."[46] When asked why he still preferred fish and tea, Wang replied: "One cannot help liking the best products of one's hometown."[47]

This story illustrates the self-confidence of the Northern Wei in relation to its southern rivals such as the Nanqi. Thus, in Luoyang, tea-drinking became the object of ridicule and political satire, associated with the politically weak Jiangnan region in south China.

In addition, the low status of the defeated descendants of the Shang dynasty remnants,[48] and the craftsmen and merchants who lived among them, attracted comment from Yang as he described the social life unfolding around the town's Buddhist temples. The former Shang descendants lived in northeast Luoyang in a neighborhood known as Wenyi Li. Shortly after the Northern Wei relocated its capital to Luoyang, many courtiers settled there without being aware of the political and social implications of living in this ward. Subject to constant derision, they all eventually moved away, leaving the area to the city's potters who produced all the capital's tiles. Wenyi Li was perceived as a marginal community, despised and avoided by aristocrats and courtiers during the early sixth century.[49]

This story clearly shows that social discrimination in Luoyang did not simply follow along ethnic lines, as social discrimination was directed toward such groups as craftsmen, manual laborers, merchants, southerners, and the former subjects of the Shang and southern dynasties who settled there. These attitudes also prevailed in the case of foreigners, who were partly responsible for the region's flourishing commercial life and the diverse array of goods imported from all over the world. South of the Luo River, five hostels housed foreign residents, seasonal foreign visitors (*yanchen*), and southern Chinese who had submitted to the powerful Northern Wei.[50] Xiao Baoyin, prince of Jian'an of the rival Nanqi, was one of them. According to Yang, he "felt humiliated at being put in the same class as foreigners, so he made the princess [of Nanyang, Henan, his wife] petition the Shizong emperor to allow him to live in the inner city. His request was granted."[51] The tale of the Prince of Jian'an indicates that while social prejudice was present in Luoyang, like anywhere else, it was not rigidly enforced or unchangeable.[52]

Significantly, sinicization was not a predominant concern, if present at all, in discourses about Buddhism and stone images in Luoyang, and is even less evident in later literary sources on Longmen and its stone images by Buddhist and non-Buddhist literati from the late seventh to the tenth centuries.

POLITICAL AND CULTURAL CONSTRUCTS: THE STONE ICONS OF LONGMEN DURING THE TANG (618–907 CE) AND THE FIVE DYNASTIES (907–960 CE)

This section focuses on Longmen's stone sculptures through surviving eye-witness accounts of scholar-officials dating from the seventh to the tenth centuries. Eschewing political and moral themes, most Tang lay texts about Longmen expressed the writer's subjectivity and covered a wide range of emotional responses. Common topics included friendship and drinking, romantic love, homesickness and parting, history and nostalgia, leisure, and nature. In other words, they went well beyond pure Buddhism in their thematic range. Tang poetry about Longmen was also concerned with the relationship between human emotion and the external environment, and its carved stone niches, if they were mentioned at all, were seen as part of this nexus. This school of poetry sought to identify the self with the object of contemplation in order to establish a form of spiritual connection. Compared with the formal *tiji* (stone inscriptions), in this body of poetry Buddhist doctrines were secularized and popularized, and expressed in a variety of forms.[53] Considering stone images as a manifestation of faith, Tang poetry mostly shied away from an explicit spiritual affinity or aesthetic identification, inflecting the original monuments with new, subjective intent and meaning.[54]

While at least four intertwined thematic strands can be discerned in these early sources, they are rarely and ostensibly concerned with sinicization or the distinctions between Han Chinese and non-Han people. First is the literary treatment of natural features including mountains, valleys, rivers, streams, trees, and the moon, along with visits to the area by scholars, monks, and female entertainers.

Second, there are numerous disparaging references to Buddhist material culture in the monasteries and hostels of Longmen. Unlike visitors to the area from the early twentieth century onward, most educated observers, believers, and nonbelievers alike, did not regard the stone images and carvings at Longmen as a form of art or as aesthetic objects revealing superior artistic taste. Rather, stone Buddhas of Luoyang were condemned as examples of gaudy adornment, waste of government resources, social decadence and, above all, as a betrayal of the true intentions of the Buddha—attitudes which marked Chinese political discourse from the Tang until the late nineteenth century, and are still invoked from time to time in government religious policy.

In autumn 700, Empress Wu expressed a desire to build a large Buddhist image, urging Luoyang's monks and nuns to donate one penny (*qian*) a day to the project. Her chancellor Di Renjie reportedly advised her that: "Until now, Buddhism has been obsessed with building lavish palaces. Manual work does not involve ghosts, but only human beings. Materials do not drop down from heaven, but rather originate from the earth. So who would not believe that this kind of public project does not harm the interests of ordinary people?"[55]

Third, archaeological evidence shows that large communities from Central Asia and southern China were active in the Luoyang area and exerted significant influence on social and economic life.[56] Fourth, rather than being an exclusively Buddhist preserve, Longmen was an imperial and public space where political propaganda, filial piety, belief in merit accumulation, Daoist and folk beliefs, Nestorianism, and a variety of other faiths and practices all coexisted.[57] Although some contemporary scholars note that Buddhism used preexisting Daoist terminology to ensure acceptance in ancient China, in this period Daoism itself had yet to develop an iconological tradition, so that very little, if any, Daoist imagery can be seen at Longmen, and there is even less evidence of Nestorianism, which was only introduced to China during the Tang dynasty.[58] Daoist, Confucian, and Buddhist influences not only competed with one another but also enmeshed and enriched one another, jockeying for recognition in medieval Chinese court politics.

Affiliations with particular sages, gods, and political and cultural heroes and ancestors played a vital role in establishing political legitimation. The skilled Empress Wu of the Tang dynasty "necessarily possessed a keen awareness of, and sensitivity towards, the diverse constituencies of her empire: men and women; Han and non-Han; Buddhist, Daoist, and Confucian; and newly risen families and long-established clans."[59] Consequently, she sought to project herself as the reverent heir and conscientious guardian of the enduring glorious Confucian lineage of ruler-sages, ancient goddesses, dynastic mothers, exemplary mother figures, female Daoist divinities, and Buddhist devils and goddesses alike—a pantheon of political ancestors, constructing the extended self,[60] echoed in rhetoric, texts, and iconography.

To further explain the above four themes on Longmen in historical and literary sources, we shall next look into more records from the Tang dynasty. In Tang times, Longmen was favored by mandarins and scholars as a place to visit for its landscape, Buddhist monasteries, and social gatherings. The three most famous Tang poets—Li Bai (701–762), Du Fu (712–770), and especially Bai Juyi (772–846)—have all left poems and other written records celebrating their time at Longmen.[61] Although Longmen was a popular site for outings for the elite, its thousands of rock caves and images were neither a particular focus of attention nor conceived as art or beautiful objects; rather, in Tang literature they were seen as part of the larger natural environment.

Endowed with a free-roaming imagination bolstered by classical Chinese and Daoist learning, Li Bai possessed a fondness for nature, often retreating into the wilderness to compose poems that reflect a personal consciousness prompted by exposure to the natural world. In 733, at the invitation of his good friend, the recluse Yuan Danqiu, Li Bai spent some time on Mt. Song, and traveled through the Dengfeng and Luoyang areas. Li commemorated his stay at Longmen's Xiangshan Monastery in a poem of five-character lines. Oblivious to the stone images at Longmen, Li regarded the region's Buddhist temples as integral to the Longmen landscape:[62]

Cold currents flow so swift at dusk
Bare trees fill empty hills in fall
Heaven transcends a boundless infinity
Serenity sinks down on earth
The stars catch homes in shiny webs
The galaxy brightens temple walls
My desire drifts to places far away
My joy for Jiangxi friends abides
My ache for absent friends dissolves in the limpid waters of the Yi [River]
How is it that plenty thus fades away?

Presenting Buddhism as a human reflection of the universe, the poem moved from an autumnal scene, through the incorporation of human life and faith into a timeless universality, culminating in the sublimation of individual desire through the use of simple language and imagery.

Similarly friendly to Buddhism, Du Fu—who was ten years Li Bai's junior, a high-born aristocrat from Gongxian, near Luoyang, and author of more than 1,400 poems—produced a poem on his visit to the Fengxian Monastery[63] at Longmen, where he stayed overnight in 736. At the age of twenty-five, he had just failed the imperial examination in Luoyang:

Showed around, I followed
Offered lodging, I rested
Dark ravines whistled empty tunes
Moonlit woods cast crisp shadows
Heaven's watchtower wove me tight
Crouched in the clouds, my clothes were cold
As I woke, the morning bell tolled
and thrust me into deep reflection.[64]

Confronted with his bad examination results, young Du Fu submitted himself
to the atmosphere of the Buddhist temple, the bells, the priests, and the eerie
beauty of Longmen as their "guest," freeing his mind and allowing himself to
be drawn into self-reflection. In 745, during the poet's years of wandering—
and disappointed by his reception at the imperial court in Xi'an—Du revisited
Longmen, where he contemplated the evanescence of life, contrasting it with
the permanence of the river:

> Longmen struck through the wilderness
> The tree-lined post road emerged from the city
> The imperial palace gleamed nearby
> The gilded Buddhist temples sparkled
> On my return all has changed
> Only the waters flow freely
> Life is but a journey in passing
> A calling of few returns.[65]

For Du Fu, constancy lay in the endless flow of the river, not in human life.
The power of nature, gold, silver, the manifold niches (*qiankan*), flowery
alcoves, and detachment from the mundane world are recurrent tropes in the
poetry of Longmen. Of thirty-five Tang poems on Longmen as a group, only
one referred to the naturalization of foreigners during the Tang dynasty, albeit
in an ostentatiously positive light. Written by Song Yu (?–?) who served
as *Zhongshu sheren* (a secretarial official) during the reign of the Tianbao
(the Xuanzong emperor), this poem praised the Xiaowen emperor's ability
to invite luck (*yaofu*) by building temples and carving flying *apsaras* and
auspicious lotuses, as evidence to the naturalization of foreigners, although it
admitted the passing of that ruling generation.[66]

The third and most celebrated of the three poets, Bai Juyi, a devout Buddhist, bequeathed a literary legacy that made him a cultural hero after the
Tang. Bai spent the last seventeen years of his life (829–846) in Luoyang with
his friends, including Buddhist monks, mainly at the Xiangshan Monastery
on the East Hill across the Yi River—accessible by raft or small boat from
the north, allowing access to the most elaborately carved stone monuments
on the West Hill. Together with his good friend, poet and chancellor Yuan
Zhen, Bai pioneered the new vernacular movement, eschewing the rigidity
and exclusivity of Tang literary tradition, and thereby drawing sharp criticism
from some members of the elite.

In 832, as a deed of merit accumulation, Bai used funds gifted by Yuan
Zhen's family to have the Xiangshan Monastery repaired. Bai wrote: "Of all
the scenery in the area around the capital (Luoyang), Longmen has the best.
Of all the scenic spots to visit among Longmen's ten monasteries, Xiangshan

tops the list . . . The Xiangshan [Monastery] was long in need of renovation. Its towers and pavilions were broken and had tumbled down in decay, and the Buddhist temples had no roofs . . . The Buddhist faithful were ashamed of this situation, and so was I."[67]

Bai Juyi resigned from office in the Huichang years (840–846) of the anti-Buddhist Emperor Wuzong and lived at Monk Ruman's residence.[68] In 840, Bai sponsored the construction of the scripture hall at the Xiangshan Monastery; he is said to have donated 5,000 copies of the Buddhist scriptures and over 800 of his own poems, composed in Luoyang, to be kept there.[69] In 844, together with the monk Beizhi, he organized local people to clear the channels of the Yi River, where two major snags, known as *Bajie tan* and *Jiuqiao shi*, often caused accidents to rafts making the crossing to the East Hill.[70]

Bai Juyi's works "have puzzled some critics who find piety and levity an incongruous pair . . . Clearly, over the many years that Pai [Bai] versified on Buddhist subjects, he adopted a wide range of personae, making simple characterizations of his attitudes impossible."[71] As an instance of such humor, Bai referred to the topknots worn by stone Buddhas and Bodhisattvas as an allegory of the seven-jewel hat.[72] While in his over 2,800 poems, prose pieces, dedicatory inscriptions, and other writings, Bai often referred to Buddhist priests and monasteries at Longmen, the site's rock caves and images received limited attention.[73] While Bai certainly saw Buddhist shrines and images while crossing south down the Yi River in order to get to the Xiangshan Monastery, he very rarely, if ever, noted the rock caves on the East and West Hills (Figure 1.1).[74]

On the other hand, many of Bai's poems lack explicit Buddhist content, leading one commentator to conclude that "the entire group of literati shunned the Longmen Grottoes . . . Of all the Longmen icons, not a single one was sponsored by the literati."[75] This response is supported by a good deal of evidence in the works, where Bai seems to go out of his way to avoid mentioning them. For example, Bai Juyi wrote of one spring outing: "I went out of the capital's [Luoyang] city gates and gazed nearby and far into the distance, seeing only water and mountains. Green vegetation covers the grand Yique Pass [Longmen]. Slowly flows the clear Yi River. [I saw] stately ancient houses [temples], with their doors and windows open."[76]

After Bai Juyi's death, some learned Chinese travelers recorded the dilapidated condition of the site, giving free rein to traditional sentiments of emptiness and impermanence, particularly in relation to the passing of dynasties,[77] but showing no concern over the destruction of religious and urban life depicted by Yang Xuanzhi in 547 (see above). The ten Buddhist temples at Longmen gradually fell into disrepair, and disappeared altogether following the end of the Yuan dynasty (1279–1368), with the possible exception of

Figure 1.1   Xiangshan Monastery Original Site.
Source: Photo by the author, April 25, 2018.

Bai's favorite Xiangshan Monastery.[78] The remaining stone Buddhas on the site were valued not for their own sake, but as a catalyst for prompting the expression of subjective feelings about nature, life, faith, and freedom.

Despite his ambiguous attitudes toward Longmen, Bai Juyi was elevated to the status of a cultural ancestor of the place, repeatedly invoked by visitors to Longmen alongside the legendary Yu emperor and the themes of geomantic power, desolation, and the need to draw lessons from the past—all shared markers and sentiments that became increasingly associated with Longmen.

REPROGRAMING ORTHODOXY AND
ESTABLISHING NEW NORMS AT LONGMEN:
A POSTMODERN TURN IN THE SONG (960–1279)
AND THE JIN (1115–1234) DYNASTIES?[79]

Conventionally, the Song dynasty is known for its promotion of Confucian orthodoxy and the revival of classical Confucian texts to the extent that some scholar-officials distanced themselves from Buddhism. But older intellectual traditions were maintained, albeit in unsystematic fashion.[80] Concerning Longmen, three observations can be corroborated by both archaeological and textual evidence.

First, in this period few new stone carving activities were undertaken at Longmen, perhaps because of the lack of suitable rock faces and perhaps because such undertakings were increasingly perceived as a waste of public resources. Second, the stone caves and images were seen as a part of the secularized, multifaith—rather than purely religious and Buddhist—environment at Longmen. Imperial visits to the site also displayed a high degree of ambivalence in this regard. Third, a group of important official records linked Longmen's stone statues to the abuse of state power and waste of labor, while referring to Buddhism as foreign teaching (*waijiao*), compared with native Daoism. The distinction between northern (*beiren*) and southern customs and people is referred to in Sima Guang's orthodox, pre-Song, monumental historical work *Zizhi tongjian*.[81]

During this period, Luoyang was the secondary, western capital (*xijing*) of the Song empire, complementing the eastern capital of Bianliang (Kaifeng).[82] Political, cultural, and religious activities were all recorded from Longmen during the Song dynasty, and surviving records allow us to assess the diverse political functions of Longmen and its stone images and pathways. Taizu (b. 927–976, r. 960–976), the first emperor of the Song dynasty, visited Luoyang in late spring 975 to worship heaven and had his subordinates pray in local temples for an end to the torrential rain that was affecting the region. Taizu also visited Longmen's Guanghua Temple for the opening of the Śubhakarasiṃha Pagoda.[83]

In 1007, during a trip to Luoyang, the pro-Daoist Zhenzong emperor toured eighteen Buddhist temples including Longmen's Guanghua, Xiangshan, and the caves, in addition to paying his respects to the Zhou dynasty temples and imperial tombs in Luoyang. He "saw that many of the stone Buddhas had been destroyed during the Huichang disaster. The officials accompanying the emperor commented: 'If it were not maintained by the government, it could not have become a famous site.' The emperor responded: 'National resources should not be expended on foreign teachings, for fear of the extreme costs involved.'"[84] However, Zhipan, a Buddhist historian of the Southern Song, gives a different account: "Seeing the damage to Longmen's niche images, in 1015 the emperor ordered the monks to hire craftsmen to repair a total of 17,339 statues."[85]

Zhenzong was attracted to Longmen for its great natural beauty, cave temples, and, most importantly, its rich antiquity and profound geomantic significance. In this politically loaded landscape, in 1022, Zhenzong had a lyric—elucidated in a lengthy preface—inscribed on the cliff face at Longmen that laid claim to everything the sacred site contained:[86]

> When Yu of the Xia deepened the rivers, he began by unclosing the sealed pylon; Cheng of the Zhou surveyed the realm, and began building the kingly city. This is where wind and rain unite; this is where the power of the land resides. Miraculous flowers and rare trees spread their fragrance by the side of the road; rugged boulders and spouting wells resound with vehemence in the current of the stream. Precious pagodas rise a thousand feet; dark cliffs tower a myriad spans.[87]

Interestingly, in the lyric, Zhenzong cemented his claim to the past by adding a further reference to the landscape, linking the topknots sported by these stone Buddhas with the spirits of the landscape and of the ancestors. Zhenzong also had Bai Juyi's tomb repaired.[88] Bai Juyi's cultural ancestry was reiterated and reinforced during the Song period. Many scholarly works on Longmen produced during this period display an entangled, ambiguous mix of Buddhism, Daoism, Confucianism, and other beliefs.[89]

In some poems, the stone images in the caves were, as in earlier times, celebrated as part of the natural landscape. On a visit to the Xiangshan Monastery on the East Hill, known in his time as the Stone Building (Shilou), Mei Yaochen wrote: "Halfway up the hill at the old Stone Building, on the stone stairs in the morning sun looking down over the canopies, I saw the statues on the other [river] bank."[90] An exceptionally learned scholar and poet of eleventh-century China, Shao Yong (1011–1077) helped reformulate and revitalize classical Confucian learning. In a poem that displayed his varied talents as a cosmologist, ethicist, historian, and prognosticator, Shao referred to the "tens of thousands of rock niches and the two or three shops and lodgings" in the pretty terrain around Longmen.[91] Such an interest was not unusual in Shao Yong's world, as he grew up influenced by his mother who was a practicing Buddhist.

For many public officials, Longmen was a private, free space for self-enjoyment; whereas in their writings they alluded to the cave monasteries, the stone statues barely featured. For the influential essayist Ouyang Xiu (1007–1072) at the age of twenty-six, the appeal of Longmen's mountains and water lay in "rafting on the torrents of the Yi River, accompanied by the fish and the birds in freedom." Such simple comforts could not be enjoyed by the political power-holders who, if they came out to Longmen, invariably brought a large, noisy entourage with them.[92] Buddhist monasteries, temple bells, and floating clouds figured in Ouyang's fifteen poems on his outings to Longmen, although the stone images and caves were ignored. Another frequenter of Longmen, Sima Guang (1019–1086), again omitted these grandiose stone icons in his poem on the site:

> The Stone Building touches the sunny sky, but I gaze afar into the south.
> People love the scenery of the mountains and the air, but I venerate
>   the beauty of Yu the Great's [circa 2200–2101 BCE] work.
> I visualize how before [Yu] dredged [the riverbed],
>   everything was a waterlogged swamp.[93]

Often regarded as anti-Buddhist, Ouyang Xiu's close association with many monks confounds this view. Moreover, in his ten-volume work *Jigu lu* (1063), the earliest collection of its kind to survive, Ouyang Xiu surveyed stele epigraphs and their calligraphy and included a considerable number of devotional inscriptions taken from Buddhist tombs and temples. He also spent time in Longmen's Buddhist monasteries and refers to the stone images of the Binyang trio caves, the Longmen Sankan, although his main focus was the calligraphy of Cen Wenben of the Tang dynasty: "The calligraphy [of the Longmen Sankan inscription] is especially magnificent, located on Henan's Longmen Hill. The Yi River is flanked by hills, and its east and west sides are scenically lovely. . . . Hundreds of Buddhist images were chiseled out of the rock cliffs during the later Wei and Tang. These three caves of images are the largest, and were created by the Prince of Wei, [Li] Tai, for Empress Zhangsun."[94]

Scholarly representations of Longmen underwent three major changes during the Song–Yuan transition, while still acknowledging the heritage of the past. One was the reinvention of Bai Juyi as a "cultural ancestor" of Longmen and a role model for those seeking independence and detachment from officialdom. "One should follow Letian [Bai] in abandoning the robes of office."[95] Second, Buddhist activity at Longmen was dwindling by the twelfth century, accounting for the disappearance of most of the Buddhist monasteries there. We can sense this decline in Su Guo's line: "There are few monks and one can barely hear them chant the scriptures."[96]

Third, Longmen's imposing stone statues were increasingly identified as symbols of the transience of life, offering moral and sociopolitical lessons linked with the downfall of the Northern Wei. "I deplore the slighting of human labor and the wasting of time."[97] In his often cited historical magnum opus, *Zizhi tongjian*, Sima Guang spared no effort in attacking Empress

Dowager Hu of the Northern Wei and the construction of the Binyang Caves. First, the empress's Buddhist construction projects, especially the Shiku Temple (Binyang Cave) and Yongning Temple, were unprecedentedly profligate, exhausting all the materials the earth could offer. Observers were scandalized by the thousands of rooms built for the monks, decorated with precious stones and luxurious appointments. Sima's second charge was the negative influence that the Empress Dowager had on ordinary people. She was obsessed with Buddhist affairs and the people blindly followed, flocking to join the Sangha. "Impiety trumps the three thousand offenses, and child-lessness trumps impiety." Third, Buddhism was a cult of ghosts, and thus incompatible with traditional beliefs. "Confucius said: 'This life cannot even be known, so how can one claim to know the afterlife?' How can one abandon the decent ways of this life pursued by the scholar-official?"[98]

DENOUNCING THE TUOBA: LONGMEN IN RUINS DURING THE YUAN (1271–1368) AND MING (1368–1644) DYNASTIES

Although evidence from the thirteenth century suggests that Longmen was in poor physical condition, it continued to attract visitors, albeit somewhat on a reduced scale. Some were drawn to its stone images because of their symbolic power, which found expression and reinforcement in their ties with the state. For others, the stone Buddhas portrayed an extravagant religiosity which reflected the corruption of the age that created them; for others again, the sacrifice and industry demanded by such projects was worthy of emulation. Finally, Longmen's Buddhist temples continued to evoke highly personal feelings of impermanence, filial piety, and nostalgia. These varying responses were the result of fundamental changes within the Buddhist and classical traditions in China, resulting at times in the use of the site's stone images as frames of reference for observers to assess politics, history and society, like elsewhere in China.

During this period, conventional attitudes can still be seen in tributes to Longmen's two great political and cultural heroes—Yu the Great and Bai Juyi—especially in sentiments about the transience of life, and in employing wet drops of green to represent Buddhist topknots.[99] By the fifteenth century, Longmen lay in ruins, with broken steles abandoned to the tall, wild grass of the mountain valleys, and countless stone Buddhas of varied sizes, postures and conditions, sitting or standing, several feet or an inch high, damaged or undamaged, strewn across the landscape. On the other hand, hearing and tasting the clear water of the mountain springs, drinking a glass of wine and grilling river fish while singing ancient poems kindled memories of the past—sad, enthralling, poetic, or merry—for a local magistrate and his scholar-official friends.[100]

Criticism of Longmen's stone images became increasingly harsh and didactic during the Yuan and the Ming dynasties. The didactic view of literature coupled a functionalist viewpoint with a concern for tradition. The fundamental purpose of literature was seen as self-cultivation and the betterment of society. In this new atmosphere, ethical considerations were paramount, leading to negative moral judgments on Longmen and the Tuoba.

One of the earliest extant witnesses to the natural and human damage inflicted on Longmen was Sa Tianxi (Sa Dula, Sadula, 1272–1355), a Muslim poet and official of the Yuan dynasty:

> Between the two cliffs, people of former times had carved out large caves and small niches. There must be thousands of them. There are carved stone images of buddhas, dodhisattvas, amitabhas, and warrior attendants. . . . There must be at least tens of thousands of them. These stone figures, however, have cracks caused by natural processes and human damage. Some have broken heads, others broken bodies, and some are missing noses, hands and feet, or parts of them. Decorative gold and green paint is peeling off.[101]

Showing no disquiet over this destruction, Sa Tianxi instead condemned the senseless expenditure of human and financial resources that had gone into creating the grottoes, which, in his view, violated the teachings and practices of Sage Śākyamuni about simple living and opposing idolatry:

> Hewing rocks into sculptures with gaudy embellishments is no more than an act designed to gain attention. . . . Benevolent rulers, according to Buddhism, should show compassion for the sake of the public good; they should neither pursue private gratification at the expense of others, nor should they be concerned with using fantastic images to beguile people. I have written this essay to stress the need to undo the bewilderment felt by lovers of Buddhism and to admonish Buddhist students not to disobey their masters by seeking Buddhahood in external things rather than from within.[102]

This perceived wasteful spending on rock images chiseled into the mountains—sapping their vitality, it was believed—and then coated with gold or other colors for worship, remained a predominant concern during the Ming dynasty. Such practices were in stark contrast to the deeds of the sage, king and sovereign, Yu the Great. Uneasy about the tens of thousands of Buddhist cave-temples at Longmen, Tang Shu (1497–1574) commented: "Stonework is labor-intensive. It exhausts human and financial resources. These must have been the product of an age of decadence. . . . While the cost [of these projects] might be comparable to that of opening up the water channel [at

Longmen] accomplished by Yu, the former harmed the people while the latter benefited them."[103]

Longmen's stone images became a clear target for scathing criticism of the abuse of power: Peng Gang's seven-stanza poem was explicit in attributing the demise of the Northern Wei to the Tuoba and their licentious empresses for their adulation of Buddhism and exploitation of the common people as well as natural resources such as mountains and rocks: "At the time, they extracted flesh and blood from the people in order to make these carvings, and tens of thousands of gold units were lavished on all the miracles of the netherworld . . . No wonder that the Buddhas died without a nimbus, and that their demons were embodied as apes howling in the night."[104]

A similar sense of desolation was shared by Wen Ruzhang of Luoyang, a provincial official and 1556 imperial degree holder, who was sympathetic to Buddhism. Since Longmen's monasteries and hostels no longer existed, he was forced to spend an entire night in a rock cave amid pouring rain: "One looks at the tens of thousands of Buddhas on the cliffs, and cannot stop lamenting the transient, solitary dynasties gone in the miserable wind and rain."[105]

Inheriting negative perceptions of Buddhist activities at Longmen from the past, Gong Ding (1558–1626), a poet and politician, composed fifty-two lines of five-character couplets which rendered a harsh political, moral, and sexist verdict on Longmen's stone figures. "Female rulers [Northern Wei empress dowagers and Empress Wu] were real evildoers, and foreign monks believed in monsters. How could they invoke good luck in the afterlife? It simply promoted mad frenzies. The country collapsed, and the people were so devastatingly poor that even heaven was moved."[106]

Such references to Buddhist monasteries, stone inscriptions, religious practices, and broken rock statues were intended to cast a favorable moral, theological, and economic light on the legendary emperor Yu the Great and, by contrast, condemn the promiscuous Northern Wei and Tang leaders. By the seventeenth century, a complex mix of political, cultural, religious, and social factors led to the seemingly universal neglect of Longmen's Buddhist cave sculptures—images that were equated with vernacular craftsmanship implying low social status in China, although other historical voices cautioned against simplistic conclusions.[107]

CONCLUSION: POLITICS AND ETHICS IN
THE POSTMODERN CONSTRUCT

Concerned to judge the relevance of the sinicization paradigm to the history of Chinese religion and stone sculpture, in this chapter I have surveyed the historical cultural reception of Luoyang's Buddhist stone images from the first surviving records in the fifth century to the premodern era of the seventeenth century. My aim has been to discover whether and how the issue of ethnicity—Han versus non-Han—featured in then contemporary sources commenting on Luoyang's Buddhist stone imagery. The following two conclusions should be considered in the context of Luoyang's central role in Early and Medieval China and the modern reevaluation of Longmen's sculptures and other artifacts in international art markets and museums and as a UNESCO World Heritage site.

First, the sinicization paradigm assumes that influence and acculturation always operate in a particular direction—in the case of Longmen, for example, the progression from a foreign-influenced style to fully sinicized Buddhist images. However, the Han versus non-Han dichotomy was not so visible from historical references to Longmen's stone imagery for quite some time. Therefore, the search for alternative models of interpretation should always be open to other possibilities and constructs that are based in historical reality.

Second, Confucianism, Daoism, Buddhism, Christianity, and other faiths all found a place at Luoyang's Longmen, a site laden with political, cultural, and religious values, but not in an organized, orderly, or externally coordinated manner. Historical witness accounts, whether prose or poetry, subordinated the stone figures to the appreciation of nature, veneration of politico-cultural ancestors, such as Yu the Great and Bai Juyi, and the abiding of political and ethical concerns, especially in travel literature, emanating from what was a an important sphere of elite activity in premodern China. Discussion of ethnic issues was notable by its absence.

In autumn 1750, the Qianlong emperor visited the three Binyang Caves and Xiangshan Monastery, staying overnight in nearby Li Village.[108] Of the many options at his disposal in terms of paying his respects to Longmen, Qianlong chose a "safe" site, the celebrated Xiangshan Monastery on its new location built during his grandfather Kangxi's reign. Avoiding commenting on the controversial stone figures, Qianlong composed two five-stanza poems which struck a middle course by focusing on the area's natural scenery, the autumn season, and its water features, doing a "cut and paste" job on Bai Juyi's famous lines, which had made Longmen a common cultural and social icon in China, irrespective of its historical significance.[109]

As a particular manifestation of Buddhism, Luoyang and the cave sculptures at Longmen were closely knitted into the fabric of Chinese society and culture and have been so since the Northern Wei. Thus, the sinicization debate can be seen to reflect shifting approaches to the site over time, depending on whether scholars and political power-holders sought to embrace and celebrate or, alternatively, eschew and repress a rich and vibrant part of

China's cultural heritage. Sinicization and its opposite—the rejection of part of the self or one's extended self as something foreign or monstrous—have developed over centuries from a set of ambiguous and poorly understood preferences and antagonisms into a history marked by recurrent political and cultural mood swings.

NOTES

1. Sima Guang, comp., *Zizhi tongjian* (Beijing: Zhonghua shuju, 2017, 15th printing), based on 2007 ed., vol. 3, p. 2529. All translations are mine, unless otherwise indicated.

2. Peng Gang (imperial degree holder of 1475), "Ti Longmen shixiang," in Zhengzhou shi tushuguan wenxian bianji weiyuanhui, comp., *Songyue wenxian congkan*, vol. 3, reprint of *Shuosong*, by Jing Rizhen (1658–?), vol. 31, *Fengshi 4* (Zhengzhou: Zhongzhou guji chubanshe, 2003), p. 764. Some limited biographical information on Peng can be found in Zhang Tingyu, et al., *Mingshi* (Beijing: Zhonghua shuju, 1974), vol. 180, pp. 4783–5.

3. Pamela Kyle Crossley, "Thinking about Ethnicity in Early Modern China," *Late Imperial China* 11, no. 2 (June 1990): 1–35. Richard J. Smith, *China's Cultural Heritage: The Qing Dynasty, 1644–1912* (Boulder, Colo.: Westview Press, 2nd ed. 1994), introduction and chs. 2 & 7–8, 1st ed. in 1983, 3rd and expanded ed. in 2015 by Rowman & Littlefield. Stanley K. Abe has challenged the application of the sinicization model to Buddhist sculpture and other artifacts in *Ordinary Images* (Chicago, Ill.: University of Chicago Press, 2002), ch. 4. Also see Katherine R. Tsiang's review of Abe's work, in *Artibus Asiae* 64, no. 1 (2004): 112–21. Similarly, Robert H. Sharf critiques the master trope of sinification with which contemporary scholarship misleadingly frames discussions of Chinese Buddhism. For more see the footnote below and Sharf's works: *Coming to Terms with Chinese Buddhism: A Reading of the Treasure Store Treatise* (Honolulu, Hawaii: University of Hawaii Press, 2002); "The Scripture on the Production of Buddha Images," in *Religions of China in Practice*, ed. by Jr. Donald S. Lopez, Princeton, NJ.: Princeton University Press, 1996, pp. 261–7 and "On the Allure of Buddhist Relics," *Representations* 66 (1999): 75–99.

4. Acute to the tensions between sinology and Buddhology, Robert H. Sharf points out both fields did have one thing in common: they both regarded Chinese Buddhism as the result of a protracted encounter, or conversation, or dialogue between Indian Buddhism and Chinese civilization, "an encounter that led to the sinification of Buddhist teachings and practices." According to Sharf, this narrative trope is "historically and hermeneutically misleading," because the "conversation" had only one side, the Chinese who conversed with themselves on the Chinese soil and in the Chinese language with a severely limited or false understanding of original Buddhist scriptures. Sharf, *Coming to Terms with Chinese Buddhism*, p. 2 and throughout the Introduction.

5. Hu Shih, "The Indianization of China: A Case Study in Cultural Borrowing," in *Independence, Convergence, and Borrowing in Institutions, Thought and*

Art (Cambridge, Mass.: Harvard University Press, 1937), pp. 219–47. Erik Zürcher, *The Buddhist Conquest of China: The Spread and Adaptation of Buddhism in Early Medieval China*, with a foreword by Stephen F. Teiser, 2007, 3rd ed. Leiden: Brill, 1st ed. 1959. John Kieschnick, *The Impact of Buddhism on Chinese Material Culture* (Princeton: Princeton University Press, 2003).

6. Kenneth K. S. Ch'en, *The Chinese Transformation of Buddhism* (Princeton, NJ.: Princeton University Press, 1973).

7. Ren Jiyu, ed., *Zhongguo fojiao shi* (Beijing: Zhongguo shehui kexue chubanshe, 1988), 3 vols. 2018 reprint. The sinicization narrative of Buddhist history in China is widely adopted by many prominent scholars of different stripes. Craig Clunas argues that the gradual "naturalization" of Buddhism at all levels of Chinese society was "neither a single, nor an evenly occurring process." Craig Clunas, *Art in China* (Oxford: Oxford University Press, 1997), p. 89. Victor Cunrui Xiong, *Capital Cities and Urban Form in Premodern China: Luoyang, 1038 BCE to 938 CE* (London: Routledge, 2016); Dorothy Wong, *Chinese Steles: Pre-Buddhist and Buddhist Use of a Symbolic Form* (Honolulu, Hawaii: University of Hawaii Press, 2004); William Theodore de Bary, ed., *The Buddhist Tradition in India, China and Japan* (New York: Vantage Books, 1972, 2nd ed.), p. 241, 1st ed. in 1969.

8. Mark Halperin, *Out of the Cloister: Literati Perspectives on Buddhism in Sung China, 960–1279* (Cambridge, Mass.: Harvard University Asia Center, 2006). Angela Falco Howard, Li Song, Wu Hung, Yang Hong, *Chinese Sculpture* (New Haven, Conn.: Yale University Press and Foreign Languages Press, 2006).

9. Xu Kangsheng, *Fojiao de Zhongguohua* (Beijing: Zongjiao wenhua chubanshe, 2008). Xu's book is regarded in mainland China as one of the most significant conceptual advances in Chinese historiography since the 1980s. A reflection of this trend can be found in Shi Jun, Lou Yulie, Fang Litian, Xu Kangsheng, and Le Shouming, comp., *Zhongguo Fojiao sixiang ziliao xuanbian* (Beijing: Zhonghua shuju, 2014), 10 vols.

10. Howard et al., *Chinese Sculpture*, pp. 1–14.

11. Xi Jinping, "Xi Jinping zai Lianheguo Jiaokewen Zuzhi zongbu de yanjiang," March 28, 2014, http://www.xinhuanet.com/world/2014-03/28/c_119982831_2.htm (accessed on November 17, 2019).

12. Victor Segalen, *Chine. La grande statuaire. Les origines de la statuaire en Chine* (Chicoutimi, Québec: Bibliothèque Paul-Émile-Boulet de l'Université du Québec, 2004), 1st ed. 1972 in Paris, ch. 7, "L'hérésie bouddhique," esp. pp. 77 and 81.

13. Luoyang's Longmen also has the greatest number of rock cave *tiji* in China, inscriptions carved on stone images. Longmen Shiku Yanjiusuo, Liu Jinglong, and Li Yukun, eds., *Longmen Shiku beike tiji huilu* (Beijing: Zhongguo dabaike quanshu chubanshe, 1998), 2 vols.

14. Yang Xuanzhi (?–?), *Luoyang qielan ji*, annotated and trans. by Xiang Rong, Beijing: Zhonghua shuju, 2012. Xiang's preface, p. 9 and Yang's own count on pp. 398–9 list 1,367 temples, a dramatic increase from the 500 or so recorded in 493 shortly after the Northern Wei had relocated its capital to Luoyang. However, in 534 there were only 421 temples standing following the fall of the Northern Wei due to internal conflict and external wars.

15. Xiong, *Capital Cities and Urban Form in Premodern China*, p. 95.

16. There are several places named Longmen in China, for example, the town in Hancheng, Shaanxi Province.

17. Stone icons and sculpture are not addressed in Kieschnick, *The Impact of Buddhism on Chinese Material Culture*, p. 11 and ch. 1; Endymion Wilkinson, *Chinese History: A New Manual* (Cambridge, Mass.: Harvard University Asia Center, 2012), p. 419.

18. See, for example, Don J. Wyatt, *The Recluse of Loyang: Shao Yung and the Moral Evolution of Early Sung Thought* (Honolulu, Hawaii: University of Hawaii Press, 1996). Also, for Luoyang's connection with Lao Zi, founder of Daoism, and Kong Zi (Confucius), founder of Confucianism, see Wu Shaomin, *Huihuang de Luoyang* (Kaifeng: Henan daxue chubanshe, rev. ed. 2003), 1st ed. 1995, pp. 130–55.

19. Sima Qian (ca. 145 BCE–?), annotated Pei Yin (between 420–479 CE), *Shiji: Zhou benji* (Beijing: Zhonghua shuju, 1999), 1st ed. in 1959, vol. 1, pp. 81–123, p. 97. Solomon Katz, *The Decline of Rome and the Rise of Medieval Europe* (Ithaca, N.Y.: Cornell University Press, 1955); C. R. Whittaker, *Frontiers of the Roman Empire: A Social and Economic Study* (Baltimore, Md.: Johns Hopkins University Press, rev. ed. 1997), 1st ed. 1994.

20. Major historical studies of the function of Buddhism in society, its internal organization and beliefs, changing literati attitudes to Buddhism, and the material culture of Buddhism have frequently ignored Buddhist rock sculpture. In noting the dramatic changes in the landscape of Buddhism in the Song, Halperin discusses Jiangnan, Jiangsu, and Zhejiang in south China, but says nothing about changing attitudes toward Buddhist material culture in North China, including the derogation of stone statues and images and the gradual disappearance of many of Longmen and Luoyang's Buddhist temples. Halperin, *Out of the Cloister*, p. 20.

21. Rafe de Crespigny, *Fire over Luoyang: A History of the Later Han Dynasty 23–220 AD* (Leiden: Brill, 2016).

22. Two differing opinions can be found in Alexander Coburn Soper, *Literary Evidence for Early Buddhist Art in China* (Ascona: Artibus Asiae Publishers, 1959), p. 3; Kieschnick, *The Impact of Buddhism on Chinese Material Culture*, p. 53. Yuvraj Krishan, *The Buddha Image: Its Origin and Development* (New Dehli: Munshiram Manoharlal, 1996), argues that the early phase of Buddhist image-making was aniconic, and that the subsequent emergence of the anthropomorphic Buddha image resulted from Hellenistic influence.

23. I am grateful to James Robson for correcting my errors here. For a critical treatment of this legend, see Soper, *Literary Evidence for Early Buddhist Art in China*, pp. 259–65. *Zeng yi ahan jing* (Skt. Ekottarāgama-sūtra), in Takakusu Junjirō (1866–1945) and Watanabe Kaikyoku (1872–1933), eds. et al., *Taishō shinshū daizōkyō* (Tokyo: Taishō Issaikyō Kankōkai, 1924–35), 100 vols., vol. 2, no. 125, pp. 703–08. Halperin, *Out of the Cloister*, p. 270, fn. 74. Sharf, "The Scripture on the Production of Buddha Images." B. Rowland, "A Note on the Invention of the Buddha Image," *Harvard Journal of Asiatic Studies* 11, no. 1–2 (1948): pp. 181 ff.

24. For a critical commentary on the spread of Buddhism to China, see Fang Hao (1910–1980) , *Zhongxi jiaotongshi* (Changsha: Yuelu shushe, 1987), 2 vols., vol. 1, pp. 124–30, 1st. ed. in 5 vols. published in Taipei by Zhonghua wenhua chubanshiye weiyuanhui, 1953–4.

25. Yang, *Luoyang qielan ji*, pp. 276–80. The beginnings of Baima Si were closely linked with the apocryphal tale of Emperor Mingdi's dream, a mission to bring Buddhist scriptures to Luoyang, and the arrival there of two Indian monks, Kāśyapa Mātaṇga and Dharmaratna. Zürcher, *The Buddhist Conquest of China*, pp. 28–32. Emperor Mingdi "dreamed of a golden man, ten feet six inches high, with the light of the sun and moon behind his head. Foreigners called him the Buddha. The Emperor dispatched Cai Yin, Qin Jing and others to the West (Xiyu) to look for the image. Over there, sūtras and statues were acquired. The monastery was given its name after the white horse that came carrying the scriptures." (Yang, p. 277; Wei Shou (505–72), *Weishu* (Beijing: Zhonghua shuju, 1999), p. 2011) According to Yang, the pomegranates and grapes grown at the White Horse Temple were unusually large and delicious. Jenner, *Memories of Loyang*, pp. 232, has a different rendering of this passage.

26. Soper, *Literary Evidence for Early Buddhist Art in China*, p. 4. This interpretation largely conforms with Fang Hao, *Zhongxi jiaotongshi*, vol. 1, p. 130. Fang put the first appearance of Buddhist images and temples—an event attended by more than 5,000 worshippers—between 188 CE and 195 CE. Fang's work summarized the historical evidence including Guan Rong (Ze Rong)'s activities that can be found in Chen Shou (?–297), annotated by Pei Songzhi (372–451), *Sanguo zhi: Wushu*, vol. 4 (Beijing: Zhonghua shuju, 1999), p. 876, based on 1959 ed.; and Fang Ye (398–445), annotated by Li Xian et al., *Houhan Shu* (Beijing: Zhonghua shuju, 1999, based on 1965 ed.), vol. 73, p. 1599, and other historical records.

27. Minku Kim, "Image Worship in Early Chinese Buddhist Art," PhD dissertation, University of California at Los Angeles, 2011.

28. The 1748 published version of this work was reprinted in 2016 by Wenwu chubanshe in Beijing, Gongbuchabu (1690–1750, also known as Shuaibuzhazhen), *Foshuo zaoxiang liangdu jing*. For a note on Gongbuchabu and the different versions of the manual, see the epilogue of the above 2016 reprint by Dong Furong; Liang Sicheng (1901–1972, posthumous), and Lin Zhu, ed., *Foxiang de lishi* (Beijing: Zhongguo qingnian chubanshe, 11th reprinting 2018), 1st ed. 2010; Wang Ti, *Fojiao zaoxiang fa* (Tianjin: Tianjin renmin chubanshe, 1999).

29. Wei Shou, *Weishu*, vol. 2, pp. 2011–31.

30. Examples are Yang Zuolong, Zhao Shuisen, et al., comp., *Luoyang xin chutu muzhi shilu* (Beijing: Beijing tushuguan chubanshe, 2004); Yang Zuolong, ed., *Luoyang guanli shiyue* (Beijing: Zhaohua chubanshe, 2007). Luoyangshi wenwu shiyeju and Luoyangshi wenwu gongzuodui, comp., *Cishi xingshi lu* (Beijing: Beijing tushuguan chubanshe, 2006). Longmen Shiku Yanjiuyuan, Beijing Daxue Kaogu Wenboyuan and Zhongguo shehui kexueyuan shijie zongjiao yanjiusuo, *Longmen Shiku kaogu baogao: Dongshan Leigutai qu* (Beijing: Kexue chubanshe, 2018), 6 vols.

31. Yang Xuanzhi, *Luoyang qielan ji*, pp. 1–15, quoting one version of Yang's original preface.

32. W. J. F. Jenner uses *Luoyang qielan ji* as a main source of information on Luoyang, aiming to "marry a modern European view of the origins, history, function, and nature" of Luoyang with a truncated translation of Yang's account. Jenner, *Memories of Loyang*. While agreeing that Yang's writing is a valuable source of information on Buddhist images in China before the mid-sixth century, I disagree with Jenner's view that Yang Xuanzhi was anti-Buddhist.

33. This translation is based on that in Soper, *Literary Evidence for Early Buddhist Art in China*, p. 8. The original was published in Yang, *Luoyang qielan ji*, pp. 72–78. This tale was omitted by Jenner, *Memories of Loyang*, pp. 169–70.

34. Yang, *Luoyang qielan ji*, p. 74.

35. Yang, *Luoyang qielan ji*, p. 29. This was a common criticism of females in history.

36. Wei Shou, *Weishu*, pp. 225–7, pp. 1111–22, pp. 1935–78.

37. Yang, *Luoyang qielan ji*, p. 20.

38. Yang, *Luoyang qielan ji*, p. 51.

39. Yang, *Luoyang qielan ji*, pp. 399–401.

40. Wang Zhenguo, "Tangsong Luoyang fosi, mingceng shiji gouchen," in his *Longmen shiku yu Luoyang Fojiao wenhua* (Zhengzhou: Zhongzhou guji, 2006), pp. 188–237, p. 223.

41. Wei Shou, *Weishu*, p. 2023. While the initial cost of labor (*yonggong*) between 500 and 520 CE was given as 802,366, it is unclear whether this represented the total workdays involved, the number of laborers, or some other form of expenditure calculation depending on how one interprets the term "gong."

42. Wei Shou, *Weishu*, p. 2022; see also Jenner's translation, *Memories of Loyang*, pp. 253–4.

43. According to Jenner, p. 267, probably at the Shaikhan Dheri site near Chārsadda.

44. Yang, *Luoyang qielan ji*, pp. 384–5.

45. The Gandhāra connection played a renewed role in the appreciation of Longmen in the nineteenth century among those elites who saw the world, in the age of modernity, as a place with shared cultural and artistic roots. Jenner, *Memories of Loyang*, p. 265, places Gandhāra in the valley of the Kābul running from Jālālābad to the Indus, possibly extending to the upper Jhelum valley in today's Afghanistan and Pakistan.

46. The Qi and Lu were major players in the warring states era, whereas the Zhu and Ju—small states located near the Qi and Lu—were annihilated. Yang, *Luoyang qielan ji*, p. 222; Jenner, *Memories of Loyang*, p. 215.

47. Yang, *Luoyang qielan ji*, p. 222.

48. These Shang descendants were forcibly moved there during the Western Zhou dynasty.

49. Yang, *Luoyang qielan ji*, pp. 342–5.

50. See below for more information on foreign communities in Luoyang during the Tang dynasty, based on new archaeological evidence from the Nestorian burial niches at Longmen.

51. Yang, *Luoyang qielan ji*, pp. 235–7, p. 235.

52. Zhang Xinglang (1881–1951), *Zhongxi jiaotong shiliao huibian* (Beijing: Zhonghua shuju, 2003), 4 vols., 1st ed. 1930 in 6 vols. Yang Zuolong and Mao Yangguang, eds. *Luoyang kaogu jicheng: Qinhan Weijin Nanbeichao juan* (Beijing: Beijing tushuguan chubanshe, 2007), 2 vols., vol. 1, pp. 108–43, maps.

53. Yang Chaojie, "Longmen Shiku funü zaoxiang ji xiangguan wenti," pp. 40–7.

54. Abe, *Ordinary Images*, p. 101. Ishimatsu Hinako , "Ryūmon Koyōdō shoki zōzō ni okeru chūgokuka no mondai,"*Bukkyō geijutsu* 184 (May 1989): 49–69.

55. Sima Guang, comp., *Zizhi tongjian*, vol. 3, p. 2529.

56. Zhang Naizhu, "Wenhua renleixue shiyu xia Yiluohe yan'an de Tangdai huren buluo: yi Longmen Shiku xinfanxian de Jingjiao yiku wei yuanqi," 2 parts, in *Shikusi yanjiu*, ed. by Zhongguo guji yizhi baohu xiehui shiku zhuanye weiyuanhui and Longmen shiku yanjiuyuan, part 1, no. 5 (December 2014), pp. 154–74; part 2, no. 6 (January 2016), pp. 255–99.

57. Caves and images carved in the manner of Huayan, Chan, the Pure Land, Esotericism, the Dharmalakṣaṇa school (Yogacara), Daoism, and other traditions can be seen at Longmen. Besides the temple caves, Longmen also has burial caves for high-ranking monks. Luoyang defang shizhi bianzuan weiyuanhui, *Luoyang shizhi*, vol. 15, p. 143. Emperors such as Xiaowen were equated with the incarnation of the Tathāgata Buddha who represented the eternal essence of being, beyond all coming and going. Alongside this, the grand entrance arch of the Huoshao Cave from the Northern Wei contains a relief of the Daoist immortals, the Queen Mother of the West and the King Father of the East, riding on dragons amid auspicious clouds. Amy McNair, *Donors of Longmen: Faith, Politics, and Patronage in Medieval Chinese Buddhist Sculpture* (Honolulu, Hawaii: University of Hawaii, 2007), p. 65. During the Western Han dynasty (206 BCE–8 CE), the image of the Buddha was absorbed into existing Chinese religious and burial practices, similar to rites featuring native deities like the Queen Mother of the West. Clunas, *Art in China*, pp. 90–1. More examples can be seen in Christine Mollier, *Buddhism and Taoism Face to Face: Scripture, Ritual, and Iconographic Exchange in Medieval China* (Honolulu, Hawaii: Hawaii University Press, 2008).

58. In 1999, a 13 × 8 centimeter dragon stone relief was discovered, below a small niche in the Shuangshi Cave, the first complete stone image of a dragon found at Longmen and a figure rarely seen in cave temples, according to Zhang Naizhu of the Longmen Research Academy. Zhang cautiously suggested a link between this relief and the role of dragon and the name of Longmen (the Dragon gate) in ancient history, but was unwilling to relate it to the Chinese-foreign divide. *Luoyang ribao*, August 9, 1999, p. 1.

59. N. Harry Rothschild, *Emperor Wu Zhao and Her Pantheon of Devils, Divinities, and Dynastic Mothers* (New York: Columbia University Press, 2015), p. 12.

60. Sir James George Frazer, *The New Golden Bough* (New Jersey: Phillips, 1965), p. 132.

61. Known in Japan as Haku Rakuten, Bai was buried near the Xiangshan Monastery.

62. Li Bai, "Qiuye su Longmen Xiangshan Si," written in 730 on his way to Xi'an, according to Lu Chaolin, comp., Xue Ruize and Xu Zhiyin, proofed and annotated, *Luoyang Longmen Zhi jiaozhu* (Jinan: Shandong huabao chubanshe, 2018), manuscript provided by Xue Ruize, p. 69. Min Jing, *Li Bai yuju Anlu shiwen xuanzhu* (Wuhan: Huazhong shifan daxue chubanshe, 2008), p. 37. Luoyangshi difang shizhi bianzuan weiyuanhui, *Luoyang shizhi*, vol. 15, p. 394.

63. Not the temple that houses the esoteric Buddha Vairocana today, the old Fengxian Monastery was located in what is today Weiwan Village at the south end of the Longmen Hill.

64. This is my own translation. Han Chengwu and Zhang Zhimin, *Dufu shi quanyi* (Shijiazhuang: Hebei renmin chubanshe, 1997), p. 1. Luoyang difang shizhi bianzuan weiyuanhui, *Luoyang shizhi*, vol. 15, p. 395.

65. Luoyang defang shizhi bianzuan weiyuanhui, comp., *Luoyang shizhi*, vol. 15, p. 395.

66. Zhu Yu, "Ti Shikusi," in Gong Songlin, *Luoyang xianzhi*, vol. 22, 9b. The poem is also titled "Ti Shiku Si Xiao Wendi suozhi." Some researchers believe the poem was written about the Yungang Grottoes, some believe Longmen, while others believe it refers to Gongxian's Grottoes near Luoyang. Xue Ruize, *Luoyang Longmen Zhi jiaozhu*, p. 126. The 35 poems mentioned in the text can be seen in Luoyang defang shizhi bianzuan weiyuanhui, *Luoyang shizhi*, vol. 15, pp. 392–8.

67. Bai Juyi, "Bai Juyi xiu Xiangshan Si ji," in *Bai Juyi ji*, proofed and punctuated by Gu Xuejie, Beijing: Zhonghua shuju, 1979, pp. 1441–2. A full but slightly different translation of Bai's note can be found in McNair, *Donors of Longmen*, p. 158.

68. It was later used by Monk Puming as a gathering place for Sima Guang's literary society, Lu Jilu and Wei Xiang, comp., *Luoyang xianzhi*, vol. 22.

69. Bai Juyi, "Xiangshan Si 'Baishi Luozhong ji' ji," in Xue Ruize, *Luoyang Longmen Zhi jiaozhu*, p. 122.

70. Bai Juyi, *Bai Juyi ji*, vol. 37, p. 844.

71. Halperin, *Out of the Cloister*, p. 36, fn 67 on p. 256. Ch'en, *The Chinese Transformation of Buddhism*, pp. 184–239; Sun Changwu, "Bai Juyi de Fojiao Xinyang yu shenghuo taidu," in Sun Changwu, *Tangdai wenxue yu Fojiao* (Xi'an: Shaanxi renmin chubanshe, 1985, pp. 102–25; Burton Watson, "Buddhism in the Poetry of Po Chü-i," *Eastern Buddhist* 21, 1 (Spring 1988): 1–22.

72. Bai Juyi, "You Wuzhen Si shi," 814, see Gu Xuejie, *Bai Juyi ji*, p. 121. The Tang poet Li Shangyin (circa 812–circa 858) also made a similar positive analogy between the Buddha's hairstyle and the spiral shell in his "Jinglan." Peng Dingqiu (1645–1719), et al., comp., *Quantang shi* (Zhengzhou: Zhongzhou guji chubanshe, 2018), vol. 540, pp. 2794–808, no. 55.

73. An early group of pieces devoted to Bai's thoughts on life from a Buddhist perspective probably dates from 804. Buddhist-themed prefaces and short religious pieces for miscellaneous occasions can be found in Bai Juyi, *Bai Juyi wenji jiaozhu* (Beijing: Zhonghua shuju, 2015 reprint, 1st ed. in 2011), proofed and annotated by Xie Siwei, 4 vols., pp. 104–12. Bai's writings also contain strong Daoist elements. For Bai's collected poems, see Bai Juyi, *Bai Juyi shiji jiaozhu*, proofed and annotated by Xie Siwei (Beijing: Zhonghua shuju, 2006), 6 vols.

74. Today, the massive groups of Buddhist stone images and caves on the West Hill are clearly visible from the Xiangshan Monastery. They were described as *mi ru fengchao* [as dense as beehives] by Luo Zhenchang, brother of Luo Zhenyu, in 1911. Luo Zhenchang (1875–1942), *Huanluo fanggu youji* (Zhengzhou: Henan renmin chubanshe, 1987), 1st ed. in 1936 by Yinyinlu shudian in Shanghai, p. 152. Bai described the Buddhist images and ceremonies performed in the scripture hall in "Bai Juyi Xiangshan xinxiu cangjingtang ji," Lu Chaolin, *Luoyang Longmen zhi*, vol. 8 of *Zhongguo fosi congshu* (Yangzhou: Guangling shushe, reprint 1996), pp. 67–70, also in Xue Ruize, *Luoyang Longmen Zhi jiaozhu*, pp. 54–5. Constructed in 516 CE and

probably destroyed in the late Yuan dynasty, during the Tang dynasty the Xiangshan Monastery was located at the south end of the East Hill and the southeast end of the nine Leigutai caves. Thus visitors to Longmen would have been able to see stone images at almost every point of their journey by boat and raft coming from the north. The Xiangshan Monastery that exists today was built in 1707 on the foundations of the Qianyuan Monastery, which dated from the Tang. Wen Yucheng, "Luoyang Longmen Xiangshan Si yizhi diaochao shijue," *Kaogu*, no. 1 (1986): 40–3. Wang Zhenguo, "*Tangsong Luoyang fosi, mingceng shiji gouchen*," p. 224.

75. Sun Qinliang, "Beiwei de Longmen he da Tang de Longmen," in *Jingdian Luoyang*, ed. by Qi Yongchang, Hong Kong: Zhongguo wenhua chubanshe, 2007, p. 91.

76. Bai Juyi, "Wangui Xiangshan Si," *Changqing ji*, in Lu Chaolin, *Luoyang Longmen zhi*, annotated by Xue Ruize and Xu Zhiyin, p. 111.

77. Gong Songlin, and Wang Jian, comp., *Luoyang xianzhi* (u.p.: 1924 reprint), based on 1745 ed. Lu Chaolin, comp., *Luoyang Longmen zhi* (1870/1887), private ed., pp. 73–4.

78. According to Wen Yucheng, Longmen's ten ancient temples are the Xiang-shan, Fengxian, Baoying, Qianyuan, Tianzhu, Puti, Guanghua, Jingshan, Yuquan, and Shengshan monasteries. Yang Xuanzhi's *Luoyang qielan ji* describes the Puti Temple located at Muyi li, the central and south Asian quarter of South Luoyang, but it is uncertain whether this was the same structure as Longmen's Puti Temple. Wen Yucheng, "Tangdai Longmen shisi kaocha," in Longmen wenwu baoguansuo and Beijing daxue kaoguxi, comp., *Zhongguo shiku: Longmen shiku*, vol. 2, pp. 217–32. As pointed out, during the Tang dynasty, the Xiangshan Monastery was located at the south end of the East Hill at Longmen. This identification is clarified in Lu Jilu and Wei Xiang, comp., *Luoyang xianzhi*, u.p.: 1813, 60 vols., vol. 22, 14b.

79. For the limitations of genre conventions in texts about Luoyang produced during the Song dynasty, see Christian de Pee, "Wards of Words: Textual Geogra-phies and Urban Space in Song-Dynasty Luoyang, 960–1127," *Journal of the Eco-nomic and Social History of the Orient* 52 (2009), no. 1: 85–116.

80. Halperin, *Out of the Cloister*, p. 107.

81. Sima Guang's account of the Northern Wei and the Xiaowen emperor in Luoyang uses the chronology of Northern Wei's rival Han regimes in North and South China; see, for instance, *Zizhi tongjian*, vols. 2–3, pp. 1263–877.

82. In addition, Luoyang was also the prefectural capital of Henan Prefecture (Henanfu/Honanfu) and the seat of two counties in Henan prefecture, Henan County (Henan Xian) and Luoyang County (Luoyang Xian).

83. Toqto'a (1314–1356), et al., *Songshi* (Beijing: Zhonghua shuju, 1999), vol. 3, p. 31. See "Official promulgation of Taizu to prohibit local officials from collecting money and donations from ordinary people in the name of the imperial visit," in Gong Songlin, *Luoyang xianzhi*, vol. 12, pp. 8–9.

84. Li Tao (1115–1184), *Xu Zizhi tongjian changbian*, vol. 65, p. 116, http://www.guoxuedashi.com/guji/7050l/ (accessed on September 19, 2018). This exchange was omitted in Zhenzong's official biography, see Toqto'a, *Songshi*, vol. 7, p. 89. The content and style of *Songshi* are widely considered to be heavily influenced

by neo-Confucianism. Xu Song (1781–1848), comp., *Songhuiyao jigao* (Beijing: Zhonghua shuju, 1957), Li 52, Xunxing. For statistics relating to imperial visits to Buddhist and Daoist temples, see Wu Qingyang, "Song Zhenzong de Daojiao Xinyang yu qi chongdao zhence," *Laozi xuekan* 1 (2016): 109–16, p. 111–12. Zhang Xiangyun, *Beisong Xijing Henanfu yanjiu* (Zhengzhou: Henan daxue chubanshe, 2012), pp. 503–51.

85. Zhipan (?–? thirteenth century), *Fozu tongji* (Jinan: Qilu shushe, 1997 reprint), vol. 44. Zhipan's account ignores the fact that Zhenzong probably promoted Daosim for political purposes rather than for religious reasons in an attempt to balance native Daoism and foreign-derived Buddhism.

86. Gong Songlin, *Luoyang xianzhi*, vol. 13, pp. 18b–19a. There has been confusion over the authorship of the preface and inscription, some commentators taking Bai Juyi as the author. In addition to some minor discrepancies, *Shuosong*, compiled in 1716 by Jing Rizhen, contains two phrases that are missing from Gong's gazetteer assembled several decades later. They are: "秘等觉之真身, 刻大雄之尊像." Zhengzhou shi tushuguan wenxian bianji weiyuanhui, comp., *Songyue wenxian congkan*, vol. 3, reprint of *Shuosong*, vol. 25, p. 551.

87. The translation is from Christian de Pee, "Wards of Words: Textual Geographies and Urban Space in Song-Dynasty Luoyang, 960–1127," 85–116.

88. Li Tao, *Xu zizhi tongjian changbian*, vol. 65.

89. Lu Wei, "Beisong shiqi Longmen Shiku yichanyu guankui: Zhonggu yijiang Longmen Shiku yichanyu yanjiu zhiyi," *Shikusi yanjiu* 7 (2017): 97–149.

90. Mei Yaocheng (1002–1060), *Wanling xiansheng ji*, vol. 58, p. 6b, http://skqs.guoxuedashi.com/wen_3230w/74016.html (accessed on September 30, 2018). On Longmen's Buddhist temples during the Song and Tang, see Wang Zhenguo, "*Tangsong Luoyang fosi, mingceng shiji gouchen*," pp. 188–237.

91. Shao Yong, "You Longmen," in *Luoyang defang shizhi bianzuan weiyuanhui, Luoyang shizhi*, vol. 15, p. 400. Don J. Wyatt, *The Recluse of Loyang*, pp. 19–20.

92. Ouyang Xiu, "Song Chenjing xiucai xu," in Zhang Chengde, *Zhongguo youji sanwen daxi: Henan juan* (Taiyuan: Shuhai chubanshe, 2011, reprint, 1st ed. in 2004), pp. 36–8. Ouyang Xiu, annotated by Li Zhiliang, *Ouyang Xiu ji biannian jianzhu* (Chengdu: Bashu chubanshe, 2007), 8 vols. Liu Jinzhu, *Tangsong Badajia yu Fojiao* (Beijing: Remin chubanshe, 2004).

93. Sima Guang, "Longmen," in *Luoyang shizhi*, vol. 15, p. 401. To control flooding, Yu the Great is said to have organized large groups of laborers to dredge the riverbeds and open up the drainage channel that ran down the Longmen Hill.

94. Ouyang Xiu, *Jigu lu*, vol. 5, p. 14, in Ji Yun, et al., comp., *Qinding siku quanshu*, http://www.guoxuedashi.com/zj/jiucuo.php?id=264167k (accessed on October 27, 2018). Also see Lu Jilu and Wei Xiang, comp., *Luoyang xianzhi*, 1813, vol. 22, Mingsheng zhi, 16a–16b. Prince Li Tai (618–652), son of the Taizong emperor, sponsored the renewed construction of the Binyang South Cave to honor his late mother, Empress Zhangsun. For an excellent presentation of the stories and controversies surrounding Li Tai, see McNair, *Donors of Longmen*, ch. 4.

95. Su Guo (1072–1123), "Wuti," accompanied by Buddhist monk Qihui, in *Luoyang shizhi*, vol. 15, p. 402.

96. Su Guo, "Wuti."

97. Zhang Lei (1054–1114), "Sankan," in *Luoyang shizhi*, vol. 15, p. 402.

98. Sima Guang, *Zizhi tongjian*, vol. 148, pp. 1785–6.

99. Zhang Ziyu, "You Longmen fang Qianxi qingshe"; Wei Boxiao, "Longmen"; Yuan Haowen, "Longmen zashi ershou," in *Luoyang shizhi*, vol. 15, p. 403.

100. Zheng An, "Yique guanlan ting ji," written in 1461, see Zhang Chengde, *Zhongguo youji sanwen daxi*, pp. 49–52.

101. Sadula, "Longmen ji," in Zhang Chengde, et al., comp., *Zhongguo youji sanwen daxi*, pp. 41–2.

102. Sadula, "Longmen ji."

103. Tang Shu, "Yique shan ji," in Zhang Chengde, et al., comp., *Zhongguo youji sanwen daxi: Henan juan*, p. 47.

104. Peng Gang, "Ti Longmen shixiang," p. 764.

105. Wen Ruzhang, "Jiuri tong Lü Wenchuan su Longmen dongzhong," in Zhengzhou shi, *Songyue wenxian congkan*, vols. 3, *Shuosong*, vol. 31, *Fengshi* 4, p. 778. This poem, along with the one on the author's trip to Mt. Mang in the spring, can be found in Gong Songlin, *Luoyang xianzhi*, vol. 21, p. 58. For a brief biography, also see Gong, *Luoyang xianzhi*, vol. 7, xuanjǔ, pp. 32b–33a, and vol. 8, p. 48a.

106. Gong Ding, "Yique Longmen guan shixiang wushier yun," in *Longyang shizhi*, vol. 15, p. 404.

107. For an example of this attitude, see the four poems by Gu Sili (1669–1722), "Longmen sishou," in Xue Ruize, *Luoyang Longmen Zhi jiaozhu*, pp. 80–1.

108. Lu Jiluo, *Luoyang xianzhi*, 1813, devoted vol. 2 to Qianlong's visit.

109. Qianglong, "Ti Xiangshan si ershou," in Lu Jiluo, *Luoyang xianzhi*, vol. 2, p. 10; also in *Luoyang shizhi*, vol. 15, p. 405.

Chapter 2

Shaping Chinese Modern Identity

Antiquities in Public Opinion at the
Turn of the Twentieth Century

The Germans say that in an autocratic country (as in Germany, Austria, or Russia) the Press is not of so great consequence, but in a country like China its influence is everything.

—1913, Frederick McCormick
(1870–1951), American journalist[1]

This chapter examines Longmen's rebirth as evidenced in the discourse in both Chinese and foreign books and in over thirty newspapers and magazines about antiquities and historical sites from the late nineteenth to the early twentieth centuries.[2] How did notions of antiquities (*guwu*) as a form of national essence and tangible heritage emerge, persist, and/or change in modern China? A survey of public opinion reveals a heterogeneous and less straightforward historical process of transformation, in which disdainful attitudes toward stone Buddhas at Longmen as a symbol of abuse of power and boorish artisanship lingered on, while ancient objects were gradually defined, redefined, and expanded in meaning and scope. First, ancient sites and cultural objects were increasingly perceived in Chinese and international opinion as public property—rather than private assets—that national sovereignty hinged upon. Second, historical sites and stone sculptures together with other categories of antiquities were reclassified as cultural valuables that, therefore, deserved protection.

In this chapter, Longmen serves as an important example of how this historical process unfolded. We first look into the Chinese cultural settings and limitations of epigraphic studies, or *jinshixue*, the text-based study of epigraphy and calligraphy engraved into metal and stone. Section 2 discusses a two-volume collection as well as its sequel of literary and geographical accounts of Longmen compiled by Lu Chaolin (1843–1920) around 1870 and printed in 1887 and 1898. Section 3 focuses on the pronouncements of two key Chinese intellectuals and publicists in the modern history of Longmen: They are Kang Youwei (1858–1927), mostly known for his role in the aborted One Hundred-Day Reform of 1898, and Luo Zhenyu (1866–1940), a Qing loyalist whose extraordinary contributions to Chinese cultural reformation have been eclipsed by his political bearings, that is, his loyalism toward the Qing. Both Kang and Luo elevated Longmen's inscriptions and rock images—long derided by Chinese literati as vulgar and inferior—to a prestigious status that had awakened public recognition of Longmen as fine art and a national gem. The last section documents the emerging conception of antiquities as carriers of history, culture and civilization, public property, and national sovereignty in Chinese and foreign newspapers and magazines.

EPIGRAPHIC STUDIES AS AN INNER CULTURAL DYNAMIC: "ONLY FOCUS ON THE TEXT, BUT IGNORE THE IMAGE"[3]

Chinese reevaluation of Longmen is inseparable from the study of epigraphic inscriptions among Chinese literati who were immersed in a culture of primarily writing-based learning and hierarchy that looked down upon stone craftsmanship before the advent of modernity in China. In general terms, *jinshixue* is considered as the forerunner of archaeology in China. Popular in the Northern Song dynasty (960–1279), *jinshixue* developed into a method which privileged the visual investigation of material objects, rather than simply relying on the interpretation of ancient texts.[4] For a long time, Northern Wei dedicatory inscriptions, mounted next to the stone images at Longmen, were not highly regarded in general.[5] Many traditional gentry and antiquarians showed no respect for rock transcribers and artisans, whether known or anonymous, or for Buddhist adherents, who were long considered vulgar and lower class in the orthodox Confucian social and cultural hierarchy.[6]

Epigraphic studies reached their peak in the Qing dynasty, and a significant number of Longmen's stone inscriptions became the object of collection and investigation, but many literati still despised the "shoddy" work of the craftsmen (*jiang*) at Longmen. For instance, Wu Yi (1745–1799, also called Qiusheng), a Qing scholar and epigrapher, commented in 1765: "On the cliffs flanking the Yique [Longmen], most of the stone inscriptions have not been rubbed since the Northern Wei, Qi, and Tang dynasties. Curio-lovers regret [this]. This past January, two gentlemen, Tang Qinquan and Zhao Jiesan, made over twenty ink-squeezed rubbings [at Longmen] and sent them to me. The texts [the contents of the stone inscriptions], nevertheless, are mostly in vernacular or commoner's language with no preservation value."[7]

In contrast with Wu Yi's disparaging remarks about Longmen's memorial steles, a new intellectual and social trend—focusing on first-hand physical examination of the Longmen stone inscriptions, but not the stone images as the primary focus—became increasingly popular, probably from the late eighteenth century. This was partly a result of overall prosperity and corresponding intellectual development during the high Qing.[8]

In autumn 1796, dissatisfied with sending assistants to ancient sites to make rubbings, the great Qing calligrapher, epigrapher, painter, and official Huang Yi (1744–1802) embarked on a forty-day pilgrimage, along with two workers (rubbing-makers), to historical sites in Kaifeng, Zhengzhou, Xingyang, Gongxian, Songshan, and Luoyang. On November 7, 1796, Huang and his companions, including his friend Wu Yi,[9] crossed the Luo River and arrived at Longmen. As if to match the bumper crop harvested that same year in the Luoyang region, Huang's eight-day visit to the Longmen caves and the Xiangshan (the East Hill) alone added 300 rubbings to his collection. "Altogether there were over four hundred rubbings made in Songluo. I also received more than forty old rubbings. It would be an extremely happy thing (*da kuaishi*) to be able to send copies of these rubbings to friends like Tieqiao, Meicun, and Jinggu."[10]

The chief motivation for these scholarly trips to Longmen was to see the ancient inscriptions on the steles in situ, not the images that shared the site, although the images were noted to some extent. Besides a diary kept during his journey, Huang also painted a landscape album of twenty-four leaves with descriptive captions to memorialize his visits. The diary and the visual material were titled, respectively, the Diary of and Illustrations of "Visiting steles in the Song-Luo area." In his diary, Huang did praise the stone images in passing; he noted briefly that "The Buddhist sculptures in the Binyang Cave are solemn and profound (*zhuangyan boda*)."[11] Leaf 22 of the 24 in Huang's landscape album shows the entrance to the Laojun Cave and a smaller one nearby, with a number of small stupas on the cliffs above.[12]

In 1827, Fang Lüjian (1790–1831), an epigrapher and book collector, visited Longmen and stayed in Qianxi Temple for a month, making over 800 rubbings.[13] This interest in collecting primary texts was partially driven by the Qing Evidential School of Research during the Qianlong and Jiaqing reigns (1736–1820), which was concerned to base its findings on the different recensions of ancient texts rather than on the Song Neo-Confucian interpretation of canons.[14] Though constituting an important intellectual capital in Longmen's passage to the modern world,[15] epigraphic studies of Longmen had their limitations. In Luo Zhenyu's words, premodern Chinese literati overly emphasized the written text but ignored the images, and placed a high value on memorial vessels for state and other official use while neglecting mundane utensils.[16]

THE DISCOURSE OF LONGMEN: LU CHAOLIN
(1843–1920) AND HIS *LUOYANG*
LONGMEN ZHI (1870/1887)

In this section, I focus on the two-volume *Luoyang Longmen zhi*, a collection of historical, literary, and geographical accounts of Longmen by Lu Chaolin (1843–1920) compiled and edited around 1870 and printed in 1887. Distinctive perspectives emerge from the printed work left by Chinese scholar-officials over a period of more than two millennia. How did Lu's view of Longmen resemble or differ from earlier Chinese treatises on Longmen partly covered in chapter 1?

A Qing official, poet, painter, and calligrapher, Lu Chaolin had his *Luoyang Longmen zhi* published in 1887 in Wanxian, Sichuan Province, where he was posted at the time. Lu hailed from Bijie, Guizhou Province, and both his grandfather and father held Qing imperial degrees, the most distinguished rank of imperial China's civil service examination and one conferring the greatest privilege.[17] Lu himself received the imperial degree in 1876, first becoming magistrate of Wanxian and later promoted to the position of head-of-prefecture elect in Henan.[18] As a teacher and friend of both the Guangxu emperor (1871–1908) and Xu Shichang (1855–1939), president of the Republic of China (1918–1922), Lu Chaolin was well connected and widely appreciated for his skills in poetry and calligraphy by high-ranking officials and scholars.[19] Lu died in Kaifeng in 1920 at the age of seventy-seven. Like Kang Youwei and Luo Zhenyu, Lu was an imperial loyalist and lived a quiet life after the collapse of the Qing dynasty in 1912.

Fascinated by Luoyang, Lu Chaolin combed through voluminous historical sources and put together *Luoyang Longmen zhi*, a sprawling, two-volume book, probably the first in Chinese, devoted to Longmen. Lacking an index and a clear structure, it is an assortment of copied texts, fragments, and excerpts from official historical records, private notebooks, travel records, and geographical books, in addition to anecdotes, legends, poetry, and other miscellaneous texts. In 1898, Lu had a short sequel containing additional anecdotes, essays, and poetry printed in Kaifeng, Henan.[20] Together, these descriptions of Luoyang's Longmen—spanning over 1,500 years—provide an invaluable, albeit inconsistent and idiosyncratic, discourse on Longmen, comprising at least six intertwined themes inherited from the past: the legendary Yu emperor, Yu the Great (circa 2200–2101 BC); geomantic power; cultural inheritance, represented by Bai Juyi (772–846); literary treatment of mountains, valleys, rivers, streams, trees, the moon, and other natural features; visits by literati, monks, and female entertainers; references to Buddhist monasteries, stone inscriptions, religious practices, and broken rock statues that were intended to put the legendary emperor Yu the Great in a favorable moral, spiritual, and economic light and, by contrast, to condemn the prodigality of the Northern Wei and Tang leaders.

It appears that the Buddhist cave images—seen as a symbol of vernacular artisanship—had remained out of favor with mainstream scholar-officials such as Lu Chaolin in the late nineteenth century. To Lu, Bai Juyi, a famed poet and scholar-official (*wenren*), as discussed in chapter 1, was a "feather in the cap" of the district, adding some much-needed refinement to Longmen, despite Bai's own association with the vernacular. Bai, a devout Buddhist believer, in later life spent much time at the Xiangshan Monastery on Longmen's East Hill just across the Yi River from the most elaborately carved stone monuments on the West Hill. Bai fashioned the new vernacular movement to loosen the rigidity and exclusiveness of Tang literary tradition, although sharp criticism followed him.

Lu Chaolin's collection of literati accounts of Longmen intensified long-held negative attitudes toward Longmen's rock icons, although he honored all the political and cultural capital accumulated at that ancient site. His chief concern was the perceived excessive spending on those gaudy stone images that were chiseled into the hills, some of which were then even coated with gold or other colors for worship. Lu Chaolin duplicated the inherited tropes of beautiful scenery to honor the memory of Bai Juyi, but at the same time Longmen's prayerful patrons from the past would have left him cold. In his preface, Lu's disdain for Buddhism and the lowliness revealed by stone niches soon was evident:

When it comes to the scenery [in Luoyang], Longmen is the best. Among Longmen's attractions, the Xiangshan Monastery [where the poet Bai Juyi frequently stayed on the East Hill] tops the list. Bai Juyi of the Tang dynasty brought fame to this temple. . . . There used to be eight temples here, all ascribed to the empresses of the Northern Wei, who doted on Buddhism. Following bad advice, they were beguiled into supporting the Buddhist sculpture project, which has been regarded as a great folly ever since. If Bai Juyi had not lived there and sung its praises, Longmen would have amounted to nothing more than the flowery rhetoric of Buddhist priests.[21]

A QUIET REVOLUTION: LONGMEN
IN THE WRITINGS OF KANG YOUWEI
(1858–1927) AND LUO ZHENYU (1866–1944)

The Chinese modern reimagination of their antiquities, including Longmen, involved reclassification of its archaeological sites alongside the inclusion of stone images and inscriptions to form an integral part of ancient ruins, in alignment with the wider world.

The quiet revolution, led by Kang Youwei and some others before him, canonized the calligraphic and historical values of the stone-carved epigraphs at Longmen in order to reform Chinese heritage for the sake of tradition. By the very end of the nineteenth century, phrases like *Longmen sipin, shipin, ershipin, wushipin*, and *baipin* became popular.[22] The most widely accepted selection of the "best" inscribed stone steles at Longmen is *Longmen ershipin*, "the Longmen top twenty," devised by Kang Youwei and Fang Ruo (1873–?). The canonical list of these twenty inscriptions was wholly made up by stone works from the Northern Wei period, nineteen of which were originally mounted in the Guyang Cave and the other in the Cixiang Cave.[23]

A high-born prodigy, a Chinese Renaissance and Enlightenment figure, and a political ideologue and activist, Kang Youwei was instrumental in shaping modern Chinese taste for antiquities in general and Longmen in particular. Kang was best known as a radical and revolutionary reformist, a Confucian fundamentalist, an evolutionist, and a cosmopolitan Qing loyalist—indeed, a host of oxymora can be applied to him.[24] His involvement in the abortive One Hundred-Day Reform of June-September 1898 and his *Kongzi gaizhi kao* (a study of Confucius as a reformer) have often masked the other political and cultural typhoon that Kang created in 1891 through his questioning of the orthodox norms of calligraphy, aesthetic appreciation, and art theory. Repelled by the dogmatic interpretations of Confucian teachings current in his day, it was not until 1895 that Kang finally passed the imperial metropolitan examination to become a holder of the highest degree, following five failed attempts between 1871 and 1894. While in Beijing for the civil service examinations between 1888 and 1895, Kang tried six times to get his memoranda for reform delivered to the Guangxu emperor (r. 1875–1908), eventually succeeding in 1895.

Kang's intellectual inheritance reflected the spirit of the Renaissance[25] and the Enlightenment,[26] and included Chinese, foreign and, most importantly, humanistic elements:

> I gathered the deep and more abstruse statements in the classics and other philosophic works, examined hidden meanings in Confucianism and Buddhism, studied new ideas developed in China and in the West, traced the evolution of man and nature, compared the tenets of various religions, pored over maps of the world, reviewed the present and the past in order to see the pattern of the future.[27]

Kang became committed to "seeking the truth" from classical empirical "facts," rather than from the orthodox interpretations offered by Song and Ming Neo-Confucianism and metaphysics.[28] Earlier scholar-officials, including Ruan Yuan (1764–1849) and Bao Shichen (1775–1855), had laid the groundwork for Kang in cataloguing and differentiating the Northern and Southern schools in terms of calligraphic styles, ink and brush techniques, forms, typology, and the determination of masterpieces. Kang synthesized, expanded, and systemized the work of his predecessors, but developed a decided preference for the Northern Wei–style of calligraphy on stone slabs. In line with his ideology of change and progress—akin to the forward-looking European Enlightenment movement—Kang worked with tradition but at the same time pioneered new ways of thinking. For Kang, the world, mankind, politics, culture, antiquity—considered from an international perspective—all served a single purpose: to vindicate his desire for change, because "change is the law of nature."[29]

Kang Youwei raised the "vulgar," Northern Wei stone inscriptions, of unknown workmanship, onto a lofty cultural plateau, thereby creating a major turning point in Longmen's modern history. As we have seen, in 1888, Kang sent his first petition for reform to the emperor, but his letter was blocked from reaching the throne by court conservatives. Returning home to Guangdong, Kang threw himself into his work, transcribing rubbed copies of stone epigraphs and reading books in Chinese translation from the outside world. According to Kang, his preparatory work for his book *Guangyizhou shuangji* [Better paired oars for the boat of art] was conducted during 1888–1890, and the volume was first printed in 1891.[30] Kang's book became an instant bestseller, and had already run to eighteen reprints by September 1898 when the Qing court ordered that the printing plates be destroyed. Kang's influence extended as far as Japan—six editions of the book appeared in Japan before his death in 1927.

In accordance with his evolutionist leanings, Kang's Longmen aimed to reflect a genuine Chinese classical heritage, summed up in the term *xionghun*—vigorous, firm, virile, rustic, and simple. In his words, it exemplified the unpretentious Longmen style, *Longmen ti*, without affectation.[31] But Kang's Longmen was imagined: Like most Chinese literati, Kang had done no fieldwork in Luoyang until 1923, four years before his death, and based his research on ink rubbings of the inscriptions, detached from the stone sculptures and the actual site of Longmen.

Kang Youwei's deficiency was addressed by other scholars, including Luo Zhenyu, another complex figure. Luo's discourse of Longmen points up the contradictions of China's modern turn. Despite his discomfort with Kang's tweaking of Confucius and the Confucian classics,[32] Luo Zhenyu, a Qing loyalist who served in the Japanese puppet government in Manchuria from 1931 to 1937,[33] was a reformer in the humanities, social sciences, and science. Growing up with the Chinese classics in an elite family, Luo gave up on the imperial examinations after failing twice at the entry level. Despite this setback, Luo believed that the old Qing imperial order was best for China.

"During the past two decades [since the Xinhai Revolution in 1911], the people have been plunged into the abyss of misery. This was all caused by the change from the imperial system to the republic."[34] The chaos and civil wars that followed had arisen because "everybody wants to become the president," and at any cost. The revolution had also led to the "flourishing of Communism," and the "harm done by the dictatorship of violent mobs [which] was far worse than monarchical autocracy."

On the other hand, Luo was a pioneer in Chinese archaeology and agricultural studies whose extraordinary scholarly contributions to the theory and practice of the modern Chinese humanities include his expansion of paleography (epigraphic studies) to include *gu qiwuxue*—the writing-based study of a wide variety of ancient artifacts, including Buddhist stone sculptures, along with field surveys—the prototype of modern archaeological methods.[35] Luo classified ancient artifacts into fifteen categories: ritual vessels; musical instruments; horse-drawn chariots and horse ornaments; ancient weaponry; weights and measures; coins, seals and tallies; household items and clothing; tomb objects; antique jades; ancient ceramics, bricks and roof tiles; ancient casting molds; stone reliefs from the Han dynasty; and Buddhist images.[36] Although long understudied in our own contemporary scholarship, Luo set the agenda in the public sphere for antiquity protection and preservation, as seen in the next section.

Luo Zhenyu visited Longmen on May 16, 1915 on a sentimental fifty-day tour to Shandong including Confucius' hometown Qufu and Henan such as Anyang where the oracle bones were discovered.[37] By then, Luo had been in exile in Japan for three years following the 1911 Revolution. In addition to his own writing, Luo Zhenyu learned a great deal from his brother, Luo Zhenchang, who had lived with him and his family for some time in Beijing and Japan. In the spring of 1911, Luo Zhenchang had spent thirteen days in Luoyang, from April 30 to May 12, as part of a two-month pilgrimage to see ancient sites and collect books, oracle bones, stone sculptures, mirrors, and other antiques in Henan.[38]

Luo Zhenyu's trip to Longmen is recorded in his essay "Wushiri menghen lu," to which he added an emotional preface on July 29, 1915, when back in Japan: "Reflecting on the visit, the mountains, rivers and places where I have been leap up vividly before my eyes, but they can all disappear in a flash. This is just like a dream."[39] The road to Longmen was notoriously rough: "All visitors to Longmen went there by sedan chair; I did not know about this in the beginning, so I went there by carriage. It was very bumpy all the way along, like a boat riding on wild waves." Arriving at Longmen's Binyang Caves, Luo found that soldiers were living there, who prevented him from entering the cave. After some lengthy negotiations, Luo was able to cross the threshold. "There are dozens of soldiers living there, sitting, lying, eating, and even cooking next to the stone images. The stone sculptures are blackened like ink." Next, Luo came to the Laojun (Guyang) Cave. "The stone stairs are steep and uneven. The guide helped me climb up. Most of the Buddha heads are missing. I heard that it was the antique assessor Zhu Xuzhai who hired beggars to come out late at night and chisel out the sculptures for sale to foreigners."[40] Luo was dismayed at the appalling state of the surviving ancient artifacts he found at Longmen and other sites.[41]

From the perspective of Chinese history, the turn of the twentieth century could be said to form a node around which China, acting both independently and interdependently, began to add new elements to its writing-based learning and practices at Longmen and other monuments. More importantly, this period also marks the time when China began to build something new from its epigraphic traditions, while at the same time absorbing ideas and practices from outside. A wide range of modern ideologies and approaches trickled into China, bolstering the government's strong political and social motivation to tackle the nation's problems. This mix of traditional Chinese and new foreign influences heralded the vigorous intellectual exchange that marked the decades following the foundation of the first Republic of China in 1912.

But this situation also allows us to consider the paradoxical complexity of the Qing loyalists, a political minority conventionally described as the reactionary "other," those "who chose the old system and resisted the new era and new ideas."[42] Mostly Han Chinese, their affiliations with the Qing dynasty disguised the fact that, poised on the cultural frontier of modern China with the wider world, many of the Qing loyalists made trailblazing contributions to reclassifying and reviving Chinese tradition and civilization as its organizers, guardians, and interpreters. Compared to iconoclasts (such as Chen Duxiu and Lu Xun), Kang Youwei, Luo Zhenyu, and other dissenting cultural pathfinders were largely ignored by history textbooks until relatively recently.

NEWSPAPER AND MAGAZINE COVERAGE OF CULTURAL ARTIFACTS AS PUBLIC PROPERTY, NATIONAL HERITAGE, AND SOVEREIGNTY

In the late nineteenth century, Chinese elites began to redefine their national heritage in a way that placed the local within the global while speaking to the past. The modernization of ancient sites in China refashioned and ultimately reconciled tradition and modernity. On the other hand, Chinese public discussion about antiquity protection emerged in the early twentieth century displayed the eternal race between and simultaneously mixed four tendencies—resistance, conformance, nationalism, and universalism. As an indicator of the public mood, the discourse of Longmen in the early twentieth-century China not only pointed up differences to stoke national sentiment but also promoted commonality and alignment among nations and cultures with the intent to create positive change—aspects which have been given less attention than they deserve.

In forming their political and cultural agendas, both Kang and Luo Zhenyu perceived differences and commonalities across cultures and nations. The "Other," be it Japan, Europe, the United States, Egypt, India, or anywhere else, was a source of inspiration for learning and self-criticism.[43] In 1904, to escape from the Qing government's prosecution, Kang went on a tour to eleven European countries. Seeing the stone sculptures and other beautifully preserved ancient heritage in Rome, Kang kept on commenting that "it all deeply shames (*shenkui*) the Chinese."[44] In a treatise on the protection of ancient artifacts published in 1913, Kang made a scathing comparison: "European thieves can even treasure cultural sites and ancient objects. Our Chinese emperors and officials, however, cannot preserve cultural sites and ancients. Is it not a shame? . . . [W]e Chinese cannot be compared to the Europeans, and even the Persians or Indians are far better than us!"[45]

Similarly, to Luo Zhenyu the foreign way of dealing with ancient sites and artifacts was worth learning. Luo argued that Western approaches to art and iconography should be incorporated into Chinese epigraphic studies and the study of Buddhist metal casting and stone carvings:

> Since the advent of the School of Images [Buddhism] during the Yongping years [58–75 CE] of the Han dynasty, during the Six dynasties and up till the Tang, metal casting and stone carving carried on uninterrupted. Such work reflects continuities and changing fashions in the ancient fine art. This branch of art studies is very popular in Europe, the United States and Japan. But in China, scholarship focuses solely on the text, and has now reached this area. One ought to adopt both methods in order to preserve [Chinese] art.[46]

Making the case for change in China, Kang Youwei emphasized humanistic commonalities in inventing and reinventing the written language. "How is the written script created? They [scripts] arose from human wisdom. . . . China is not the only one that has it. India has it; Europe has it; the Blacks in Africa have it, and the natives in Australia have it too . . . Human intelligence invents the written language, so it cannot be a question of just one stroke for all. The human spirit cannot control an individual—thus it is destined to change."[47]

In early Republican China, domestic and foreign discussions about antiquity and protection featured at least six interrelated themes. Nontraditional objects like stone sculptures at Longmen were appreciated more than ever before: first, public discussion in many newspapers and magazines denounced the destruction and loss of cultural objects, blaming negligent Chinese. Up till the late Qing dynasty, antiquities were generally considered more as private property than as a symbol of a culture, civilization, and nation. Therefore, ordinary people had no sense of responsibility toward historical sites and artifacts. One commentator wrote that it was not a surprise that China had coal, iron, gold and silver, but foreigners discovered them. "Ancient books, classics, and calligraphic works are unique valuables of China, and the Chinese invented them but do not care much about them. It is only when foreigners value them the Chinese start to treat them as valuables."[48]

Second, some profit-seeking Chinese colluded with foreigners to steal and sell ancient objects. Commercialization of Chinese antiquities came with cruel destruction of historical sites and relics. One newspaper reported: "West Henan is abundant in imperial catacombs and ancient tombs . . . Profiteers had workers dig up those tombs, steles, and forests. They stole and sold to foreigners bronze utensils and other items buried in the tombs. They only seek profit with no conscience to protect ancient objects."[49]

Third, political instability in China was to be blamed as well:

Our ancestors' spirit and fine art have gone through tens of thousands of catastrophes, with less than one billionth surviving. However, only few of them disappeared in natural selection. Instead, countless ancient artifacts were destroyed in man-made turmoil; every one hundred years witness one large upheaval and small-scale ones every several decades. Since the 1911 Revolution, we cannot tell how many scenic spots and historical sites have been ruined in wars, and to this day the painful history is still repeating itself.[50]

Fourth, ancient artifacts were linked to Chinese civilization, culture, and modernity in the age of industrialization. "Since antiquities concern Chinese culture, national sovereignty and industry, those who care about public welfare have the responsibility to preserve them. We hope that they can come up with measures to save [our cultural objects] to the utmost of their abilities."[51] One article in *Shenbao* commented: "Since the One Hundred-Day Reform of 1898 the idea of preserving antiquities has faded. Historical books, vessels, and epigraphs flowed into foreign countries, and it is getting even worse in recent years."[52] Bu Tao, a famous journalist, also publicized his views on the importance of antiquities to Chinese culture: "China is one of the five ancient civilizations, but its culture is retreating, and the country is having a harder and harder time."[53]

Fifth, public expressions urged to learn from the West and Japan to protect cultural artifacts through establishing public showrooms and museums. "Open-minded westerners all place the importance on cultural relic protection."[54] Again, Kang Youwei took the lead in sharing his travel experiences in Europe and Japan while shaming his own fellow countrymen: "I passed through European countries such as Britain, Germany, France, Austria, and Italy. Museums can be found in every small city. They collect their local arti-facts, things used by their ancestors, pieces of writing, clothes and anything else left by dignitaries, famous scholars and poets."[55] In contrast, Kang wrote, "China boasts its etiquette and civilization while despising foreigners as sav-ages. . . . However, we have no museums and only few libraries in such a vast country. We cannot even be compared with a village and a town in Europe and North America. Yet we claim ourselves as being cultured and cultured. What a disgrace!"[56]

Kang noted that Chinese did not treasure ancient items because they found no utility in those old objects and ancient sites. But national treasures "can enlighten their countrymen, touch their heart, make them nostalgic, sharpen their aesthetic sensitivity, and refine their way of life. Therefore, they are of huge significance."[57]

Sixth, consensus on saving Chinese antiquities, especially stone sculptures and other fine art, gradually formed among progressive Chinese elites. One report in *Shenbao* cited the minister of foreign affairs, Lu Zhengxiang:

> Lu . . . cherishes things from the past, and feels the pain every time Chinese cultural relics end up overseas. Before the New Year, he specially wrote to the Ministry of Education urging them to set up museums to collect ancient epi-graphic inscriptions and fine art, and suggesting that they work with Chinese Customs to make regulations to restrict export of antiquities. In this way our cultural relics from thousands of years ago would not be lost. His words were full of grief.[58]

Today very few people are aware that Longmen's stone Buddhas played a large part in this reappropriation and protection of antiquities and stone sculp-tures. Modern Longmen was a place where Chinese and foreign interests met, for good, bad, or ugly purposes. In 1913, Frederick McCormick (1870–1951), secretary of the China Monument Society and of American Asiatic Institute, dispassionately informed the world of the vandalism committed by both Chinese and foreigners at Longmen and urgently called for the complete control, protection, and preservation in China of Chinese art and antiquities. In the autumn, the increasing devastation and theft of Chinese antiquities led McCormick to bring the matter to the newspapers, the general public, and even Yuan Shikai, President of the Republic of China through Wellington Koo. On October 7, 1913, McCormick's letter to the editor of *North-China Daily News* was published under the heading, "Desecrating the Caves of Lungmen: Increasing Vandalism. The Need of Protection": With the emi-nent Charles Lang Freer and other collectors as a key advocate of Longmen, McCormick relayed disturbing information from Paris according to which some dozen or more stone heads from Longmen were exhibited:

Many of them showing recent fractures, and one most important life-sized relief of North Wei times, clearly showing where it had been cut from the rock, all of which had come to Paris within two years . . . In the view of competent judges, China is the most beautiful and valuable archaeological field in the world, and none of its ancient treasures are held in more esteem than those of Lungmen . . . They [Longmen's treasures] are situated in a limestone mountain defile about ten miles south of Honanfu, at the southern entrance to a valley through which flows a river with roads on either side. Along the valley lies the site of a once prosperous and populous city, Lolang [Luoyang], one of the finest of the capitals of ancient China, now almost completely obliterated. The few things that remain to tell the story of this ancient world suggest that great wealth and artistic talent were lavished upon places and temples, and the remains of this work at Lung-men are in danger of complete destruction.[59]

Frederick McCormick's letter of November 29, 1913 to President Yuan and its translation appeared in multiple media in China, Europe, and the United States including the influential German magazine *Ostasiatische Zeitschrift*[60] that was aimed at European scholars, connoisseurs, and professionals dealing with Asian art, culture, and history.

An American journalist in China mostly during the 1910s, Frederick McCormick, born in Brooksville, Missouri, was a well-respected, even-headed correspondent and contributor in East Asia in 1900–1922 for *Harper's Weekly*, *The London Graphic*, Reuters, the Associated Press, *The North China Herald*, *The Central China Post*, *The London Times*, *The New York Times*, and other printed press and radio broadcasts.[61] He covered the Boxer Rebellion and the Russo–Japanese War embedded with the Russian forces. Throughout his China years, McCormick authored several perceptive books based on first-hand experience, including *The Tragedy of Russia in Pacific Asia* (1907), *China's Monuments* (1912), *The Flowery Republic* (1913), and *The Menace of Japan* (1917). Knowing how to command the attention of major news channels, Chinese and foreign, while in China, McCormick was prominently framing public interest and China's early legal framework of antiquities protection, while capturing a powerful audience among Chinese leaders and intellectuals (Figure 2.1).[62]

McCormick was both a product and a shaper of the global and imperial outlook of America's "Pacific Era," as President Theodore Roosevelt called it.[63] On account of America's geographical position, the United States aimed to take the lead in East Asia and the Pacific Rim on its west. In correspondence, American diplomatic policy in China was to sustain the support of European powers "for the peace and safety of China . . . and Asiatic civilization," against Japan's efforts at destruction.[64] Geoculturally, this kind of strategy honored "those who established American science and research on the soil of Eastern Asia. Until now the country regarded Asia as being to the

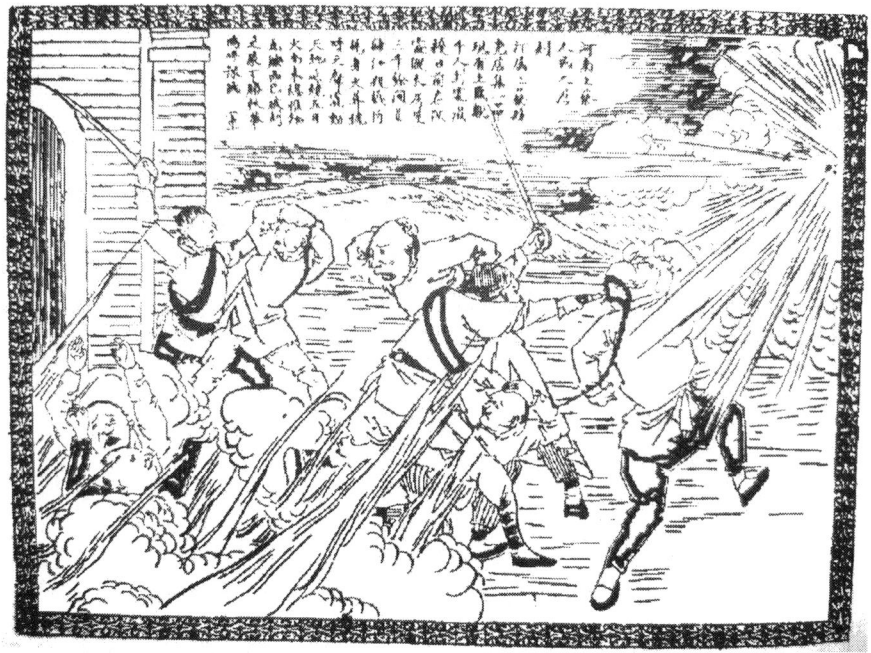

Figure 2.1   Cartoon, "Fighting Bandits in Honan."
Source: Frederick McCormick, *The Flowery Republic* (London: John Murray, 1913).

east of Europe instead of on its western frontier, and turned always to the sources of its civilization in Southern Europe with hardly a thought of its responsibilities and interests as a center."[65]

Geopolitics and national mood in the United States had an immediate effect for their "foot soldiers" in China. In 1908, owing to the increase of vandalism and theft of antiquities in China, especially those acts traceable to foreigners, McCormick founded the China Monuments Society in Beijing to promote the preservation of monuments, sculptures, tablets, and other cultural relics.[66] He worked with organizations of similar missions and peoples such as The American School of Oriental Archaeology in Beijing organized by Charles L. Freer for archaeological work and research in China.[67] The Society received support from the British, Russian, French, Spanish, and American ministers to China, missionaries, and other elites, such as Sir John Jordan, B. N. Kroupensky, Paul W. Reinsch, A. R. Conty, Aki Hioki, and Ludovico di Giura. And it took donations from Bishop James W. Bashford, Francis Davis Millet, Bishop William White, William Phillips, John Gardner Coolidge, and E. G. Meyerstein.[68]

The introduction of railways in China brought modern convenience as well as irreparable damage to antiquities.[69] This applied to Longmen's treasures too. "Vandalism ought to be ranked with evils like war, slavery, and opium," McCormick wrote of such a joint Chinese foreign concern:

> Shortly after the visit of Chavannes to that holy place in 1908 acolytes came out to meet foreign visitors with chisels in their hands and offered for pennies to shear off anything from the reliefs there that were desired. . . . In the markets of Europe and America, and in secret store-houses in China are to be found unusual art objects, especially Chinese sculptures, whose presence there nobody but the criminals who thieve or vend them, or their ultimate possessors can explain, and about which almost nothing seems to be known by the public or by Western Governments and the authorities in China, whose possessions under the circumstances could be illegal. . . . The antiquities in China are unprotected. At the same time there are no doubt responsible persons everywhere in China who, for a day's supply of food would sell any god or shrine, or break any sculpture. The co-operation of foreigners in their atrocious and revolting barbarism is essential to its completeness and it is receiving that co-operation.[70]

In McCormick's letter to Yuan, McCormick explicitly offered two ideas which were taken up instantly in China: first, McCormick advocated state ownership and state guardianship, which could also generate income for then poverty-stricken China. The "antiquities of a country belong to the people and are the immediate property of the State. The contents and property of the temples belong to the people and are the proper care of the State, which should be the final trustee. The antiquities of China are the richest in the world, and their value is that of a cash income to China, possible to be made equal to that of China's revenue from almost any other single source."[71]

Second, McCormick stated that European countries were hypocritical plunderers and criminals in Asian countries, and thus he put the United States on the high moral ground:

> Countries of European civilization have regularly plundered various countries of Asia of their antiquities, until now China is the only remaining country of Asia to plunder in this way. The work of filching and destroying antiquities from China has begun and is now an industry of both European and Asiatic nations. Acts of vandalism and theft of antiquities are crimes in all countries of European civilization and in Japan. This fact was recognized by France in 1902 . . . when she restored to Peking astronomical instruments taken in 1900–1901. Furthermore this kind of felony was fully recognized and abhorred by the United States when in 1903 imperial jade tablets from the T'ai Miao, found within the territories of the United States, were returned to China by the Smithsonian Institution.[72]

Third, it was fully justifiable for the Chinese government to defend the human rights of its own people and expect the "governments of all self-respecting nations of the world to return to China all unlawfully acquired Chinese antiquities in their national museums, or under national ownership; and also that they will now and hereafter forbid the entry and shelter in any national public building of any recently broken or otherwise suspicious Chinse sculptures, or immorally obtained antiquity or other archaeological, historical, or art work from china that has been or is the property of the State (China) in accordance with the inextinguishable rights of the Chinese black-haired people."[73]

McCormick's publicized opinion received immediate attention at all levels of Chinese society. By the early 1910s, it was widely accepted that China should take legal measures and effectively control exports to protect artifacts. In June 1914, a presidential order admitted that "it is said that recently many Chinese ancient objects are exported and sold overseas without supervision. If we do not repeat and implement the export bans, how can these antiquities sustain forever?"[74]

In the printed media in Chinese, public education in China about Longmen, the Yungang caves, and other historical sites were widely promoted, in tune with the above developments and changing perceptions. Spread of basic knowledge reflected Chinese initial efforts to study Longmen as art, cultural legacy, and most importantly as a serious scientific subject.[75] Unlike premodern China, attention was given to Longmen's caves, the style and number of stone Buddhas, and epigraphic inscriptions.

Physical surveys and tourism were popular despite rampant banditry at Longmen. It was reported in July 1916 that Longmen had 476 intact large Buddhas, 180 large but damaged stone Buddhas, 89,375 small Buddha icons in good condition, and 7,275 damaged small Buddhas. Altogether there were 97,306 stone Buddhas found at Longmen, which were grand and impressive to visitors.[76] Observers also made a comparison between Longmen and Yungang in appearance, size, style, cave structure, stone quality, imperial visits, and number of epigraphs. Yuan Xitao, who visited Longmen in August 1919, noted that most images at Longmen came with inscribed epigraphs, an enormous number of donor inscriptions in stone, and other texts inscribed on the same stone side by side with the hewn rock images to which they refer. According to Yuan, this level of epigraphic activity is largely absent at Yungang due to the culture and coarse-grained granite in the latter.[77] Today we know that the Northern Wei produced almost 3,000 "slabs" containing more than 300,000 characters at Longmen.[78]

CONCLUSION

The influence of public opinion, as expressed the Chinese and foreign press in the late Qing and the early Republic of China, cannot be underestimated in transforming politics and people's mind. American journalist Frederick McCormick witnessed its effect:

> The power of the Press in China was something truly startling in the end, the most comprehensive demonstration of that power which the Press has ever had. In the West the Press has been of slow growth, but in China it may be said to have arisen in a day, equipped like a giant. It brought on the greatest experiment in constitutional government ever attempted, and in five years it aroused and overturned an Empire and subverted a Dynasty.[79]

In theory, public opinion refers to "an aggregate of the individual views, attitudes, and beliefs about a particular topic, expressed by a significant proportion of a community."[80] According to W. Phillips Davison, scholars generally agree that, in order for a phenomenon to count as public opinion at least four conditions must be satisfied: first, there must be an issue; second, there must be a significant number of individuals who express opinions on the issue; third, there must be some kind of a consensus among at least some of these opinions; and fourth, this consensus must directly or indirectly exert influence.

In early twentieth-century China, the discourse of antiquities had a direct impact on the making of Chinese laws on cultural relics as well as on the institutionalization of protection agencies in the first half of the twentieth century—the focus of chapter 6. During the 1910s–1930s, the stealing and selling of the former Qing imperial household belongings in Rehe and Beijing, due to financial difficulties, Japanese invasion and other factors, also sparked a fierce debate over how to handle those royal inheritances. Later, the controversy over Swedish Sven Hedin's expedition to Northwest China further sharpened Chinese assertion of heritage sovereignty and gradually helped move forward the nationalization of ancient sites and relics including buried underground and exposed to the surface as public property in China.[81]

The evolving conception of Longmen and other antiquities at the turn of the twentieth century manifested the promise of modernity while China's modern identity took shape in a new human and universal—rather than merely national, or regional, or even global—cultural milieu. As part of the worldwide shared experience, modern China, too, was to a considerable extent built around the reappropriation of antiquity that brims with tradition and thrives on modernity.

The dilemma of modernity was on full display in the case of antiquities. The contradictions between the individual's aspiration for goods to save Chinese cultural artifacts and the reality of their limited choices in the market economy became discernible among important figures in the modern history of Longmen. McCormick had many admirers in China, who hailed him as a foreign hero for his activism on behalf of Chinese antiquities protection, but he himself, in reality, assumed a double, somewhat contradictory, role as a middleman for art collectors.

Kang Youwei and Luo Zhenyu could not escape public scrutiny either. In autumn 1923, Kang was invited to tour Luoyang en route to Xi'an to give lectures. While in Xi'an, besides some Buddhist images and other ancient objects, Kang allegedly walked away with the only copy of a Buddhist scripture from the Song dynasty in the Wolong Temple. Kang instantly became a thief in the eyes of public opinion, a perception that continued even after he was forced to return the scripture.[82] In 1909, Luo Zhenyu urged the Qing government to establish museums to house ancient objects, expressing concerns that more and more Europeans and Americans were studying sinology, "whereas our own national learning is dwindling. Ignorant merchants sell national treasures to foreigners just for immediate profits. It is deplorable."[83] However, following the outbreak of the 1911 Revolution, Luo Zhenyu, a political minority, moved to Japan at the end of November and lived in Kyoto for eight years until 1919. Together with four other households—the family of Wang Guowei, Liu Jiying, Luo Zhenchang, and Dong Kang—he brought along his family and a large quantity of rare books, manuscripts, and other ancient items. He confessed that he had to make a living there by selling his extremely fine collections of Song and Yuan books, rubbings, and paintings at a much discounted price.[84]

Yet human fallacies and the complexity of modern life did not stop people from pursuing age-old dreams for one-world community (*datong shehui*), standing above the nation, that combined the humanistic engagement with the world of both the Chinese and foreign intelligentsia. A one-world community that knew no borders, no classes, no races, no genders, no families, no personal possessions, and particularly no nation-states that overcame these very root causes of human violence and incessant wars, imagined by Kang Youwei in 1894.[85] From the late nineteenth century on, European, American, and Japanese elites also confronted the problem of modernity for different political, cultural, and personal reasons. The rise of archaeology in the search for human origins placed the human self at the apex of evolution and endowed modernity with iconoclasm, an inclination to destroy false interpretations of tradition, and unearth the authentic truth about one self and others around the world. And modern Longmen was part of that story.

NOTES

1. Frederick McCormick, *The Flowery Republic* (London: John Murray, 1913), Chapter 41, "The Chinese Press," p. 376. Here McCormick emphasized the power

of the Chinese press in regime change, which ushered in the Republic of China (1912–1928) replacing the Qing (1644–1912), the last dynasty in Chinese history.

2. Recent relevant publications include: Aida Yuen Wong, *The Other Kang Youwei: Calligrapher, Art Activist, and Aesthetic Reformer in Modern China* (Leiden: Brill, 2016); Yang Chia-Ling and Roderick Whitfield, eds., *Lost Generation: Luo Zhenyu, Qing Loyalists and the Formation of Modern Chinese Culture* (London: Saffron Books, 2012); Shana J. Brown, *Pastimes: From Art and Antiquarianism to Modern Chinese Historiography* (Honolulu, Hawaii: University of Hawaii Press, 2011).

3. Luo Zhenyu, "Xuetang cang guqiwu mulu xu," in *Luo Zhenyu xueshu lunji* (Shanghai: Shanghai guji chubanshe, 2013), vol. 7, p. 3.

4. On the rise of *jinshixue* and its dissemination in Korea, Japan, and Vietnam, see Lothar von Falkenhausen, "Antiquarianism in East Asia: A Preliminary Overview," in *World Antiquarianism: Comparative Perspectives*, eds. by Alain Schnapp, Lothar von Falkenhausen, Peter N. Miller, and Tim Murray (Los Angeles, Calif.: Getty Research Institute, 2014), pp. 35–66. Dorothy Wong, *Chinese Steles: Pre-Buddhist and Buddhist Use of a Symbolic Form* (Honolulu, Hawaii: University of Hawaii Press, 2004). For the connoisseurship and evolution of ink rubbings in the nineteenth century, see Qianshen Bai, "Composite Rubbings in Nineteenth Century China: The Case of Wu Dacheng (1835–1902) and His Friends," in Wu Hung, ed., *Reinventing the Past: Archaism and Antiquarianism in Chinese Art and Visual Culture* (Chicago, Ill.: University of Chicago Press, 2010), pp. 291–319.

5. Luoyang difang shizhi bianzuan weiyuanhui, ed., *Luoyang shizhi* (Zhengzhou: Zhongzhou guji chubanshe, 1996), vol. 15, pp. 231–300. Amy McNair, "Engraved Calligraphy in China: Recension and Reception," *The Art Bulletin* 77, no. 1 (March 1995): 106–14.

6. Lu Jilu and Wei Xiang, comp., *Luoyang xianzhi*, n.p.: 1813, vol. 59. Also see Xin Wenfeng chuban gongsi bianjibu, comp., *Shike shiliao xinbian* (Taipei: Xin wenfeng, 1986), vol. 3, issue 29, pp. 489–511. One exception among the Longmen stone inscriptions, however, was the text composed by the court official Cen Wenben, handwritten by the great Tang calligrapher and court censor, Chu Suiliang (596–659), which was first recorded in the work of the anti-Buddhist scholar-official, Ouyang Xiu (1007–1072). Ouyang Xiu, *Jigu lu* (Beijing: renmin chubanshe, 2010). Some of Longmen's stone inscriptions were also preserved independently in Zhao Mingcheng's (1081–1129) *Jinshilu*, Yu Yizheng's (circa 1522–1566) *Tianxia jinshi zhi*, Gu Yanwu's (1613–1682) *Jinshi wenzi ji* (written between 1657 and 1682 and published between 1682 and 1722), *Huanyu fangbeilu* (written in 1802) by Sun Xingyan, et al., Wang Chang's *Jinshi cuibian* (in 1805) and, more extensively, in *Luoyang jinshi lu*, compiled by Lu Jilu and Wei Xiang in 1813. Zhao Mingcheng, corrected by Jin Wenming, *Jinshilu jiaozheng* (Guilin: Guangxi shifan daxue chubanshe, 2005). Gu Yanwu personally visited steles scattered throughout Jiangsu, Zhejiang, Shandong, Hebei, Shanxi, Shaanxi, and Henan including Longmen in 1679. See Yu Dan, *Gu Yanwu Jinshi Wenzi Ji yanjiu*, Huadong shifan daxue, Masters' thesis, 2009.

7. Lu Chaolin, comp. and ed., *Longyang Longmen zhi* (1887), vol. 8 of *Zhongguo fosi congshu* (Yangzhou: Guangling shushe, reprint 1996), p. 207.

8. Normally the high Qing refers to the late seventeenth to the eighteenth centuries of Qing China. Visiting steles in person was practiced by some literati such as Gu Yanwu, Wang Shu (1668–1743), and Wu Yijin (1698–1773) in the Qing. Lillian Lan-Ying Tseng, "Retrieving the Past, Inventing the Memorable: Huang Yi's Visit to the Song-Luo Monuments," in Roberts S. Nelson and Margaret Olin, eds., *Monuments and Memory, Made and Unmade* (Chicago, Ill.: University of Chicago Press, 2003), pp. 37–58. For a somewhat different explanation of the reasons behind the flourishing of epigraphic studies during the early to mid-Qing dynasty, see Chen Xingcan, *Zhongguo shiqian kaoguxue yanjiu, 1895–1949* (Beijing: Zhongguo shehui kexue chubanshe, 2007), ch. 1. More details are below.

9. On Huang Yi's friendship with Wu Yi, see Lillian Lan-Ying Tseng, "Retrieving the Past, Inventing the Memorable." Huang's biography can be found in Zhao Erxun, et al., *Qingshi gao* (Beijing: Zhonghua shuju, 2013), 1928 1st ed., vol. 486, p. 13420.

10. Huang Yi (also known as Huang Xiaosong), *Songluo fangbei riji,* including a prologue, written in 1796, in Xin Wenfeng, *Shike shiliao xinbian*, vol. 3, no. 29, p. 603. Weng Fanggang (1733–1818), "Ti Songluo fangbei tu," in Xin Wenfeng, *Shike shiliao xinbian*, vol. 3, issue 29, pp. 591–93. In 2017, Huang's handwritten diary *Songluo fangbei riji*, along with a few notes and letters, were auctioned in Hangzhou, Zhejiang, for 2.07 million CYN, http://p549472027.key.shuoqian.net/ (accessed on June 7, 2017).

11. Huang Yi, *Songluo fangbei riji*, p. 601.

12. The Laojun Cave is better known today as the Guyang Cave, where allegedly the founder of Daoism Laojun (Lao Zi) practiced alchemy. Huang Yi's twenty-four-leaf album, *Songluo fangbei tu*, is held at the Imperial Palace Museum in Beijing. A reproduction of it can be found in Zhongguo gudai shuhua jiandingzu, comp., *Zhongguo gudai shuhua tumu* (Beijing: Wenwu chubanshe, 2000), vol. 23, pp. 234–7.

13. For a brief biography of Fang, see Zhao Erxun, et al., *Qingshi gao*, vol. 486, p. 13422. Sun Guanwen, "Longmen zaoxiang tiji jianjie," in Longmen shiku yanjiusuo, ed., *Longmen shiku yanjiu lunwenxuan* (Shanghai: Shanghai renmin meishu chubanshe, 1993), pp. 109–42.

14. Gong Songlin, appointed as magistrate of Luoyang county in 1742 and the main compiler of *Luoyang xianzhi* (The Luoyang gazetteer), which he published in 1745 with Wang Jian, organized the movement to erect tomb steles (*libei*) in an attempt to categorize them and prevent the numerous tombs on Mt. Mang in Luoyang from being plundered or turned into agricultural land. Luo Zhenchang (1875–1942), *Huanluo fanggu youji* (Zhengzhou: Henan renmin chubanshe, 1987), 1st ed. in 1936 by Yinyinlu shudian in Shanghai, pp. 127–33.

15. A comprehensive catalog and review of Longmen's "steles" and inscription-collecting is found in Guan Baiyi, *Yique shike tubiao* (Kaifeng: Henan bowuguan, 1935), 2 vols. Guan himself had surveyed Longmen in person and made ink rubbings of Longmen's stone inscriptions. Other investigators, who by the early twentieth century had made extensive collections of Longmen's stone inscriptions, included Liu Xihai, Lu Weiting, Miu Quansun (before 1898 through ink rubbings made by Wang Hequan), Édouard Chavannes in 1904, using ink rubbings made by Zong Huanpu in Xi'an, Luoyang's magistrate Zeng Bingzhang in 1915, and Qian Wangzhuo in 1934.

16. Luo, "Xuetang cang guqiwu mulu xu," in *Luo Zhenyu xueshu lunji*, vol. 7, p. 3. The original reads: "重文字而略图像，贵鼎彝而忽任器." A similar expression can be seen later: "只看见文字，未看见造像," [Only see the text, not the image] in Xiong Bingming (1922–2002), *Zhongguo shufa lilun tixi* (Beijing: Renmin meishu chubanshe, 2017), p. 215, 1st ed. in 1985 by the Hong Kong Commercial Press.

17. In 1867, Lu Chaolin's father Lu Huang was appointed as magistrate of Luoyang. For more detailed information on the Lu family, see Lu Chaolin, comp. and ed., Xue Ruize and Xu Zhiyin, proofed and annotated, *Luoyang Longmen Zhi jiaozhu* (Jinan: Shandong huabao chubanshe, 2018), manuscript, pp. 3–14.

18. Lu Chaolin's other works include *Lushi zhangfang zupu* (1895), *Lu Huang shendaobiao* and *Hong'eguan shichao*.

19. Lu was also Xu's uncle-in-law. Lu was also associated with Zeng Guofan, Li Shuchang, a diplomat and prose writer, and Huang Pengnian, a confidant of Zhang Zhidong, Tian Zhongyu, and Chen Huanzhang.

20. Lu Chaolin, comp. and ed., *Luoyang Longmen zhi xuzuan* (Kaifeng, 1898), reprinted in *Zhongguo fosi congshu*, vol. 8, pp. 263–81.

21. Lu, *Longyang Longmen zhi*, preface.

22. This phrase refers to Longmen's "four best" stone epigraphs, top four best pieces of Longmen's stone epigraphs (*zaoxiang tiji*). *Shipin* means top ten pieces, *wushipin* top fifty, and *baipin* top one hundred.

23. Kang Youwei, *Guangyizhou shuangji* (Guilin: Guangxi shifan daxue chubanshe, 2016), facsimile of the jingdong bieshu version, handwritten and unpunctuated, *yulun*, ch. 19, vol. 4, p. 269. Fang Ruo, *Jiaobei suibi* (u.p.: Huazhang shuju, 1922), 6 vols., in vol. 2, no. 17, pp. 12452–3.

24. On the rise of Confucian radicalism, see Peter Zarrow, *China in War and Revolution 1895–1949* (London: Routledge, 2005), ch. 1.

25. In *Qingdai xueshu gailun*, originally drafted in 1902, the ingenious Liang Qichao (1873–1929), a student of Kang Youwei, compared Qing academia to the European Renaissance, claiming that the key difference between them was the underdevelopment of fine art and literature in the Qing—although whereas the Qing intelligentsia were seeking to restore the spirit of the ancient *northern* Chinese civilization of the river plains, which had been weak in fine art, the Renaissance sought to return to the Greek civilization, which was exemplified by stone marble sculptures. Liang Qichao, *Qingdai xueshu gailun* (Beijing: Zhonghua shuju, 2015, 5th printing, 1st ed. in 2010), proofed and annotated by Zhu Weizheng, ch. 31, pp. 153–5.

26. The notion of one-world community was fully expressed in Kang's *Datong shu* (Beijing: Zhonghua shuju, 2nd ed. 2012), Zhou Zhenfu and Fang Yuan, proofed and punctuated, 1st ed. 1956.

27. Kang Youwei, *Kang Nanhai zibian nianpu*, 1895, in *Wuxu bianfa*, vol. 4, p. 117–18. The translation used here is from Jonathan D. Spence, *The Gate of Heavenly Peace: The Chinese and Their Revolution* (New York: Penguin Books, reprint 1987), pp. 34–5, 1st ed. 1981.

28. Besides Kang, the great essayist, reformer, and thinker Liang Qichao in 1904 also used the concept *shishi qiushi* to characterize Qing intelligentsia and scholarship. This term has been widely used by the Chinese Communist Party and others later on. See Liang Qichao, *Qingdai xueshu gailun*, Liang's self-preface, written in 1920, p. 3.

29. Kang Youwei, *Guangyizhou shuangji*, yuanshu, ch. 1, p. 32.

30. Critiques of *Guangyizhou shuangji* include Aida Yuen Wong's *The Other Kang Youwei*; Zhang Jianhua, "Beixue de fayang: Kang Youwei "Guangyizhou shuangji" jiqi shuxue sixiang yanjiu," PhD dissertation, Zhongguo meishu yanjiu yuan, 2012.

31. Kang Youwei, *Guangyizhou shuangji*, Yulun, ch. 19, p. 169.

32. See Luo Zhenyu's summary of the strengths and weaknesses of Qing scholarship, "*Benchao xueshu yuanliu gailüe*," written in 1930, in Luo Zhenyu, comp. by Wen Mingguo, *Luo Zhenyu zishu* (Hefei: Anhui wenyi chubanshe, 2014), pp. 252–3.

33. Wang Qingxiang, "Luo Zhenyu de zhengzhi shengya he xueshu chengjiu," *Shehui kexue zhanxian*, no. 5 (2002): 152–61.

34. See Luo's autobiography written in 1931, *Jiliao bian fulu sanzhong*, in Luo Zhenyu, *Luo Zhenyu xueshu lunwenji*, ed. by Luo Jizu, Shanghai: Shanghai guji chubanshe, 2013, vol. 11, pp. 78–9.

35. On Luo's contribution to the development of Chinese archaeology in the 1920s, see Denis Thouard and Tao Wang, "Making New Classics: The Archaeology of Luo Zhenyu and Victor Segalen," in Sarah C. Humphreys and Rudolf G. Wagner, eds., *Modernity's Classics* (Berlin: Springer-Verlag, 2013), ch. 11, pp. 231–60.

36. This is an incomplete list, in Luo Zhenyu, "Yu youren lun guqiwu xueshu," in *Yunchuang mangao*, see *Luo Zhenyu xueshu lunzhuji*, vol. 9, pp. 144–50. According to archaeologist and oracle bone scholar Dong Zuobin (1895–1963), Luo played a major role in the preservation of historical sources relating to the Ming and Qing cabinets; research on oracle bones; the organization of the Dunhuang files, inscribed wooden slips from the Han and Jin dynasties; and research on ancient tomb artifacts. In recent years, the growing interest in Luo Zhengyu and his paradoxical role in modern China have been documented in a number of books: Chia-Ling Yang, *Lost Generation*; Brown, *Pastimes*; Lin Zhihong, *Minguo nai diguo ye: Zhengzhi wenhua zhuanxing xia de Qing yimin* (Beijing: Zhonghua shuju, 2013), 1st ed. by Lianjing in Taiwan in 2009, p. 333.

37. Luo Zhengyu left Kobe, Japan, and arrived in Shanghai two days later on April 12, 1915. Luo Zhenyu, *Luo Zhenyu zishu*, pp. 93–122.

38. The Luo brothers were in regular correspondence during the 1911 trip to Henan. The Longmen Grottoes material is found in Luo Zhenchang, *Huanluo fanggu youji*, pp. 143–57. In his travel account, Luo Zhenchang did not disguise his dislike for his experience in Luoyang, which in the early twentieth century was plagued by poverty, banditry, deception, and chaos. On the other hand, the construction of the Longhai railway between Luoyang and Kaifeng in 1904–1909, and later westward between Luoyang and Guanyintang and eastward between Kaifeng, Shangxiu and Xuzhou in 1912–1915, made Longmen more accessible to Chinese and foreigners alike. Luo Zhenchang's book contains drawings of ancient objects.

39. Luo Zhengyu, "Wushiri menghen lu," preface, in Luo Zhenyu, *Luo Zhenyu xueshu lunwenji*, vol. 11, p. 153.

40. Luo Zhengyu, "Wushiri menghen lu," pp. 177–78.

41. Preserving ancient and scholarly texts seemed to offer some consolation. Several months later, in winter 1915, Luo edited, with a note for future research,

Chang Maolai's (1788–1873) *Luoyang shike lu*, a catalog of stone inscriptions, mostly from Longmen. See Xin Wenfeng, *Shike shiliao xinbian*, vol. 1, no. 27, pp. 20635–49.

42. Robert E. Harrist, Jr., *The Landscape of Words: Stone Inscriptions from Early and Medieval China* (Seattle, Wash.: University of Washington Press, 2008).

43. For a difference take on this in ancient Chinese history, see Mingming Wang, *The West as the Other: A Genealogy of Chinese Occidentalism* (Hong Kong: Chinese University of Hong Kong, 2014), pp. 7–12.

44. Kang Youwei, *Ouzhou shiyiguo youji erzhong*, in Zhong Shuhe, comp., *Zouxiang shijie* (Changsha: Yuelu shushe, 2nd reprint 2011, based on 2nd ed. in 2008), vol. 10, p. 110, p. 129, pp. 131–2, and more.

45. Kang Youwei, "Baocun Zhongguo minji guqi shuo," *Buren*, June 1913, no. 3, p. 12.

46. Luo Zhenyu, "Yu youren lun guqiwu xueshu," in Luo Zhenyu, *Yunchuang mangao*, a collection of short essays and correspondence compiled by Luo himself in 1920; see *Luo Zhenyu xueshu lunzhuji*, vol. 9, p. 148. Further examples of "speaking to the world" can be seen in Luo's preface to *Mingsha shishi yishu* and to *Liushan zhuijian* in *Luo Zhenyu zishu*, pp. 141–4.

47. Kang Youwei, *Guangyizhou shuangji, yuanshu*, vol. 1, pp. 19–22.

48. Leng, "Zhongguo guwu," *Shibao*, October 21, 1909, p. 3.

49. "Henan baohu yuxi gudai lingmu," *Shenbao*, August 8, 1914, no. 14905, p. 7. "Shoushi Longmen shifo cansheng ji," *Shenbao*, March 23, 1916, no. 15483, p. 6.

50. Cheng, "Du Jiaoyu huiyi baocun guwuan ganyan," *Zongsheng huizhi* 1, no. 5 (1913): 10–11.

51. "Yuren baocun tiaojinjiaobei zhi zhuojian," *Shenbao*, December 31, 1912, p. 6.

52. "Kaogujia jiqi tuzhi," *Shenbao*, January 28, 1913, no. 14354, p. 7.

53. Bu Tao, "Baocun guwu tan," *Shenbao*, November 26, 1914, no. 15015, p. 7.

54. "Yibao guji," *Shenbao*, January 29, 1913, p. 6.

55. Kang, "Baocun Zhongguo minji guqi shuo."

56. Kang, "Baocun Zhongguo minji guqi shuo."

57. Kang, "Baocun Zhongguo minji guqi shuo." Also see, "Lunshuo: Baocun guwu," *Shizheng tongbao*, 1914, no. 74, pp. 1–3.

58. "Waijiaozhang zhuyi baocun guwu," *Shenbao*, January 21, 1913, no. 14337, p. 3.

59. Letter of October 4, 1913 from Frederick McCormick, secretary of China Monuments Society, to the editor of *North-China Daily News*, October 7, 1913.

60. Frederick McCormick, "Representations made to China by the 'China Monuments' Society (Peking)," November 29, 1913, *Ostasiatische Zeitschrift*, Heft 1, April/June 1914, p. 103.

61. "A Compliment for McCormick," *Service Bulletin of the Associated Press* 18 (June 15, 1908), p. 13. Also see *Service Bulletin of the Associated Press* 2 (October 15, 1904), p. 7.

62. Frederick McCormick, "China's Monuments," *Journal of the North China Branch of the Royal Asiatic Society* 43 (1912): 129–88.

63. Theodore Roosevelt, "The Awakening of China," *The Outlook*, November 28, 1908, pp. 665–6.

64. Frederick McCormick, *Treaty of Peace with Germany: Statement of Mr. Frederick McCormick in Regard to Shantung* on August 29, 1919, Committee on Foreign Relations United States Senate, First Session, Sixty-Six Congress, 1919 (Washington: Government Printing Office, 1919). Frederick McCormick, *The Menace of Japan* (Boston: Little, Brown, and Company, 1917).

65. Unknown author, "Treasures of Archeology in China," *Journal of the American Asiatic Association* 13, no. 1 (1913): 5–6.

66. "The Prevention of Vandalism in China," *Art and Progress* 1, no. 1 (November 1909), Notes: 42–43.

67. Also named as the American School of Oriental Archaeology. Unknown author, "American School of Archelogy in China," *Journal of the American Asiatic Association* 13, no. 1 (1913): 6–7. Also see Box 232, Folders 1–3, "American School of Archelogy in China," Charles Lang Freer Papers, the Smithsonian Institution. Chapter 2 of Kin-Yee Ian Shin's doctoral dissertation "Making 'Chinese Art': Knowledge and Authority in the Transpacific Progressive Era," Columbia University 2016, examines the American Asiatic Institute, a related organization founded by Frederick McCormick in 1912 in Beijing.

68. Shin, "Making 'Chinese Art'," p. 43. "The Prevention of Vandalism in China," p. 43.

69. Frederick McCormick, "Representations made to China by the 'China Monuments' Society (Peking)."

70. Letter of October 4, 1913 from Frederick McCormick, *North-China Daily News*, October 7, 1913.

71. McCormick, "Representations made to China."

72. McCormick, "Representations made to China."

73. McCormick, "Representations made to China."

74. "Celing," *Shenbao*, June 16, 1914, p. 2.

75. "Shoushi Longmen shifo cansheng ji," *Shenbao*, March 23, 1916, no. 15483, p. 6, reprinted in *Dongfang zazhi* 13, no. 7 (July 10, 1916): 13–14.

76. "Shoushi Longmen shifo cansheng ji." For a summary of pre-1980 research on Chinese Buddhist stone temples including Longmen, see Su Bai, *Zhongguo Fojiao shikusi Yiji: san zhi ba shiji Zhongguo Fojiao kaoguxue* (Beijing: Wenwu chubanshe, 2010), pp. 1–6.

77. Yuan Xitao, "Luoyang Yique shiku foxiang ji," *Dongfang zazhi* 17, no. 23 (December 19, 1920), p. 88.

78. In 1964, two statues, a head of the Buddha weighing nearly half a ton from Longmen and a standing Bodhisattva, were among the exhibited artifacts from China and Central Asia at Columbia University. Isabella Drew applied physical tests and scientific techniques to analyze these two Longmen figures to supplement older sources of knowledge and connoisseurship of stylistic analysis, literary texts, and surface examination. She found that Longmen's limestone consists of tiny spherical to ovoid bodies (called oolitee), which are brownish. The thick-bedded limestone of the Longmen formation has undergone extensive recrystallization and conversion to dolomite. Later work on Longmen specimens helped Drew further identify the limestone or fragments from Longmen found in distant Chinese and global markets.

Jane Gaston Mahler, "An Assembly of Lung-Men Sculpture," *Archives of Asian Art*, vol. 24 (1970/1971): 70–75; Isabella M. Drew, "Limestone from Rock-cut temples at Lung-men in Honan, China," *MASCA Newsletter* 3, no. 1 (May 1967), Applied Science Center for Archaeology, The University Museum of Pennsylvania. Neutron activation analysis and X-ray diffraction suggest that Longmen's rocks have three distinct sources: the northern, middle, and southern zones of the West Hill. "The northern zone is a very hard dolomitic limestone that workers found ideal for carving niches and statues. . . . The middle zone consists of a calcite limestone that could still be worked to produce excellent results. However, the southern zone was found to fracture easily and its use was limited. By the time of the Tang dynasty suitable locations for carving were no longer available." The northern zone ranges from the Qianxi Temple to Moya Three Statues, the middle from the Wanfo to Huoshao Cave, and the southern from the Huoshao to Jinan Cave. Jian Zhu, Michael D. Glascock, Changsui Wang, Xiaojun Zhao, Wei Lu, "A Study of Limestone from the Longmen Grottoes," *Journal of Archaeological Science* 39 (2012): 2568–73.

79. McCormick, *The Flowery Republic*, p. 378.

80. W. Phillips Davison, "Public Opinion," *Britannica Online Encyclopedia*, https ://www.britannica.com/print/article/482436 (accessed on August 10, 2019).

81. Cai Yaming, "Cong yulun jiaodu kan jindai wenhuayichan renzhi de zhuanbian," Master's thesis, Shanghai University, 2019.

82. "Kang Youwei huanjing li Shan," *Shenbao*, January 18, 1924, no. 18283. Two conflicting recollections of the incident given by Ma Lingfu and Liu Anguo can be seen in Xia Xiaohong, comp., *Zhuiyi Kang Youwei* (Beijing: Sanlian shudian, 2009), pp. 358–62.

83. Luo Zhenyu, "Yonglu rizha," (Xu), *Guocui xuebao* 54 (1909), p. 6.

84. Luo Zhenyu and Wang Guowei, proofed and annotated by Wang Qingxiang and Xiao Wenli, *Luo Zhenyu Wang Guowei wanglai shuxin* (Beijing: Dongfang chubanshe, 2000), pp. 498–9.

85. Kang Youwei, *Datong shu*, first conceived in 1894, first partially (Parts A and C) published in 1913, and in its entirety in 1935, eight years after Kang's death. During the public debate over auctioning Imperial Palace holdings, some critics proposed to open them completely to the world (*shijiehua*) to make everybody a stakeholder. "Gugong de guwu," *Huanian* 1, no. 21 (1932), p. 405.

Chapter 3

Voices of Silence

European Discovery of Longmen

> We are well informed about the reasons behind the grottoes and the
> sculptures that adorn them from the numerous inscriptions still visible
> on Longmen's rock faces. From their dedications we learn that they are
> works created to either secure somebody's good luck in this world or
> the next, or, more often, to benefit the soul of a deceased, who would
> thus escape the misery of temporal existence by leaving the cycles of
> birth and death.
>
> —Édouard Chavannes, 1908[1]

Despite the prominent role assigned to France in making Chinese Buddhist
stone images and epigraphy known to the world,[2] existing scholarship remains
empirically elusive about the historiographical content of such a contribution.
The French sinologist and archaeologist Édouard Chavannes, for instance,
has been characterized as "the first all-round talented sinologist,"[3] but still
little is known about how he brought those long-neglected Chinese rock
temples to the attention of so many people both inside and outside China.[4]

This chapter seeks to offer the first comprehensive analytical account
of the French engagement with Longmen in early twentieth-century North
China—then dilapidated but today a state-of-the-art UNESCO World
Heritage site. In what follows, I shall first examine the historical context
for Longmen's French connection before zooming in on Philippe Berthelot,
Édouard Chavannes, Victor Segalen, and André Malraux in their scrutiny
of Longmen. I conclude that these French figures discovered an alternative
source of authoritative inspiration from lands afar: their ideas of rational and
empirical epistemology, universalistic spirituality, and existential reflexive-
ness found expression at Longmen. Thus, through sinology, art, and comparative religion, Longmen's French ties profoundly influenced the emergent

human sciences in Europe, China, Japan, and the United States more than a century ago.

EUROPEAN HISTORICAL INTEREST IN THE EAST

This section locates the origins of Longmen's French connection within a broader context of European historical interest in the East. I venture the notion that the rise of engineering, industrial production, and scientific norms and practices in France, Britain, Germany, the United States, and Japan by the late nineteenth century encouraged North Atlantic elites to mine new knowledge of humanity from all parts of the world in a rational, secular, empirical, and dispassionate manner, although nationalism, imperialism, colonialism, and geopolitical expediency loomed large in the background.

European notion of the Orient changed radically over time as an imagined geographical, religious, and historical space, shifting from the Holy Land to Turkey, Egypt, Persia, Arabia, India, China, and Japan. This impermanence began, in the view of many, with the Crusades of the eleventh century and Europe's long political interaction with the Ottoman Empire,[5] which cast Western Christendom as a force—"combining universalist claims with a missionary dynamic" in opposition to Islam—that unified, balanced, and legitimized the papal and imperial rule in the Middle Ages.[6] In addition to enmity, the Orient also fascinated Europe, causing it to absorb and subsume elements of Oriental culture to form a fond of shared European imaginings.

Interest in the Orient during the European Renaissance and the Enlightenment turned toward the Far East and was greatly facilitated by the presence of the Society of Jesus in Beijing from 1601 to 1805 and their voluminous correspondence with European scholars. China and Japan provided examples to emulate: Europe's despots and depravity were attacked indirectly through references to Chinese and Japanese ills and wrongs, while improvements in Europe, often challenging doctrines and power of clergy and monarchs, were obliquely proposed by praising Oriental wisdom and ingenuity.[7] India, Central Asia, and the Arabic world added layers to these multivalent European fancies.

During the eighteenth century, the political decline of Europe's Holy Roman Empire of German Nation awakened nationalistic, unifying desires inspired by the Orient.[8] Although German nationalist trends sought their roots in the German people and in German language, German nationalist thinkers dreamed of one world experienced through the nation: Johann Gottfried von Herder (1744–1803), for example, was at pains to focus on the universally *natural* rather than *divine* origin of language,[9] and romantic poet Novalis (Friedrich von Hardenberg, 1772–1801) saw the Orient as a metaphor of poetic transfiguration, by which the poet understood himself through the Oriental other; the poet regarded the nation as a glimpse of the universal.[10] At the turn of the nineteenth century, many German and other European thinkers invoked the Orient as a metaphor that stood in contrast to Europe's Christianity and the Hellenic-Roman classicism in order to achieve universal, pure, and untainted insight, as a fresh perspective on the world. In line with this, European intellectuals took interest in the archaeology and ethnology of the near East and the textual evidence from Indian, Central Asian, and Chinese civilizations that at the time were widely imagined to predate Greco-Roman antiquity.[11] This is evident in the emerging scholarship on Eastern languages and translations of Oriental classics, scholarship encouraged by the popular fervor of romanticism in the nineteenth century.

The East, accordingly, by the nineteenth century was a firmly established object of scientific, rational, dispassionate, and secular analysis of empirical evidence from archaeology, textual research based on comparative philology, evaluation of aesthetic styles, and comparative studies of religion. Increasing contacts through trade, war, and Christian mission caused discordance between the imagined Orient and the existing reality to arise, so the exploration of the history of Oriental civilizations stood high on the agenda. Napoleon's grand expedition of "savants" (scholars) to Egypt set in motion a new wave of European scholarship to study Eastern languages—in addition to the scholarship on Pharaonic monuments and hieroglyphs, the research on Sanskrit pioneered in India by William Jones (1746–1794) and the systematic study of Chinese by Jean-Pierre Abel-Rémusat (1788–1832).

The dominant tenor in contemporary research, however, is largely to deplore the false consciousness of European Orientalism which underpinned unequal relations in the capitalist world.[12] Marie-Paule Ha, by contrast, reveals that in colonial literature there was a clear sense of the complex and ambiguous relationship between colonizers and colonized, and the existential problems that the relationship entailed, as mentioned in the Introduction of this book.[13] Different from contemporary scholarly consensus, I argue that the French connection by the first half of the twentieth century had vested a metaphorical, epiphanic power in Longmen's stone images and inscriptions, by subjecting them and their history to rational scrutiny. In early European findings, cave temples at Longmen and some other places in North China represented universal spirituality and transcending beauty, demonstrating multidirectional, cultural, and religious transmissions between India, Greece, and China.

A SINOLOGICAL BREAKTHROUGH AT LONGMEN:
PHILIPPE BERTHELOT AND ÉDOUARD CHAVANNES

Philippe Berthelot (1866–1934), an amateur researcher and later top French diplomat, Édouard Chavannes (1865–1918), and others gave voices to Longmen where they found universal spirituality and a common human community—a one-world ideology in vogue in the decade or so before World War One. Through extensive fieldwork, Berthelot and Chavannes were convinced that parallel civilizations in ancient China, India, the Eurasian core, and the Greco-Roman world mutually influenced each other through direct human contact probably starting in the first century CE. To them, those silent Indic-Greek/Egyptian-Chinese stone Buddhas and deities at Longmen testified to the manifold links across Europe, Africa, and Asia.

In the early twentieth century, traveling to Longmen, even from the center of the city of Luoyang (then Honanfu, today the Old City District of Luoyang), was no easy task. Robberies and murders committed by bands of brigands with headquarters near Longmen were only part of the trouble to deal with during a day trip or a stay at Longmen. The presence of half a dozen armed guards with rifles was nothing unusual for visitors to Longmen. Further, the road conditions were poor and the means of transportation challenging—a cart with two-mule tandem and sometimes sedan chairs were a luxury for the privileged few.[14] Travelers would have to cross the River Luo southward on a scow before an around 10-kilometer bumpy journey to Longmen.

Despite these difficulties, Philippe Berthelot visited Longmen during his travels between 1902 and 1904. He later described the Central Binyang Cave at Longmen, where two bas-reliefs, one of a male and the other of a female procession of sculptures evoked a striking "impression of sacerdotal Egyptian figures mixed with Italian renaissance refinement, gracious manners, an expressive beauty of the gestures, equally distant from the Hindu taste as from the Chinese make."[15] He observed:

> Yet the seeming identity [between Egyptian and Chinese statues/bas reliefs] is a conjecture that emanates from imaginings rashly jumping across centuries. Critical scrutiny may one day make evident the uninterrupted history of reciprocal influences between Occidental and Oriental art through the ages.[16]

Berthelot's words echoed the one-humanity dream of late nineteenth- and early twentieth-century science.[17] He speculated on the reciprocity and perhaps shared origin of East and West, and implied that Egypt—the original *Orient* of Napoleon's *savants* almost exactly a century earlier—belonged to the Occident. Jean Babtiste Joseph Fourier opened his historical preface to a scientific report on the findings from the French expedition to Egypt with a radical shift of perspective on classical antiquity. He placed Egypt at the center, not only as a precursor but also as a founder of and as the location that spawned the early achievements of the Hellenic and Roman civilizations.[18]

Berthelot thus seemed to share the conviction of his time that the Occident consisted of Western civilization as defined by its classical Roman and Hellenic roots; France was seen to have conceptually integrated ancient Egypt into the Occident, as a contiguous extension of the classic world, even though Egyptian social, ethnic, and political realities remained "Oriental." Berthelot's coupling of Chinese and Egyptian statues and bas-reliefs was indicative of modern man's will to imagine cultural correlations across ancient civilizations. At the same time he articulated a strong urge to rationally prove the historical linkage.

Berthelot's comments on Longmen represented amateur French research of his age, in which intelligent field observations mixed with erudition. Berthelot's description of the Central Binyang Cave and photographs from 1899 provided by the globetrotting French engineer Felix Leprince-Ringuet (1873–1958) were valuable background for Édouard Chavannes' twelve-day visit to Longmen on July 24–August 4, 1907.[19]

Chavannes was indeed well prepared for his long visit to Longmen in 1907. Upon receiving Felix Leprince-Ringuet's photographic plates from Longmen, he had searched for detailed textual material, and by 1902 he had published an in-depth account of the grottoes and their historical background. During his first stay in China he already researched Chinese statues, in particular Han dynasty bas-reliefs from Shandong. He followed in the footsteps of his predecessors Jean-Pierre Abel-Rémusat (1788–1832) and Stanislas Julien (1797–1873) who had, respectively, translated the travelogues of Faxian and Xuanzang, the Buddhist monks who went to India and returned with holy sutras. Chavannes himself recounted the life of the monk Yijing who traveled to India via Southeast Asia and Ceylon and upon translating hundreds of sacred scriptures returned to Luoyang under the rule of Empress Wu Zetian and became closely associated with Longmen.[20]

In 1918, Henri Cordier (1849–1925), Édouard Chavannes' mentor, summarized Chavannes' intellectual character in remembrance of the latter. Cordier[21] wrote a fifty-page obituary of Chavannes in the prominent *T'oung Pao*.[22] In addition to paying homage to a deceased friend, protégé, and scholar, Cordier emphasized how Chavannes' upbringing shaped his modern scientific vocation and mindset. Chavannes was born into a French protestant family who settled in Lausanne (Switzerland) to escape religious prosecution. His grandfather had been a noted botanist, and his father, after being educated as an engineer in Lausanne, was the technical director of a cutting

edge factory for rolling stock in Lyon. Chavannes spent much of his child-
hood with his grandmother in Lausanne. He received his secondary education
in Lyon and passed the preparatory class for the philosophy program at École
Normale Supérieure (ENS) in Paris. Chavannes' background and subsequent
career fit Weberian ideal-type modernity: Protestant, bourgeois, international,
scientific, technological, meritocratic—in short, rational.

Chavannes' choice of specialization was carefully considered and strategic. ENS director Georges Perrot advised him to focus on China and Henri
Cordier encouraged him to develop the nascent field of Chinese history.
Chavannes took classes in classical and modern Chinese at two different
institutes in Paris. But soon Perrot, along with the minister of public instruction René Goblet, secured him a post as attaché at the French Legation in
Beijing, allowing him to study language and conduct research starting from
early 1889. Chavannes began translating Sima Qian's *Shiji* and remained in
China until he was appointed to a chair at Collège de France in 1893.

During his time in Beijing, Chavannes was unlikely to have known about
Longmen. In the nineteenth century, the Longmen rock icons, long neglected
or derided by many Chinese literati, had only roused limited curiosity among
foreigners, though they were, for example, described in Ferdinand von Richthofen's monumental geography of China published in 1882.[23]

Henri Cordier, in a speech at the closing session of the Congress of the
Learned Societies of Paris and the Departments held at Sorbonne on April 24,
1908, in the presence of minister of public instruction and later president of
France Gaston Doumergue (1863–1937), extolled Chavannes' archaeological
travel to Manchuria and North China as producing among most important
advances in French research:

> Our compatriot [Chavannes] passed the site of the first Buddhist temple ever
> built in China, and made a twelve-day stay in Henan, at the Longmen ravine,
> famous for its sculptures carved in the sixth century by the Wei, who had arrived
> from Datong, and in the seventh and eighth centuries by their Tang successors
> . . . [He] then went up north to . . . Datong, where he carried out a comprehensive
> study of the Yungang bas-reliefs, which, although heavily restored, still provide
> some good specimens of northern Wei art from the fifth century of our era. It
> was there that Mr. Chavannes discovered the curious personage reminiscent of
> the Greek Hermes and the many sculptures that allow us to stake out the route
> along which Greco-Buddhist art spread from northwestern India to Japan.

Cordier then commented on the historical significance of Chavannes' visit to
Luoyang and Datong:

> This trip is a landmark in the history of research on China, for it is the first time
> that a sinologist, who also is an archaeologist with strong training in classical

culture, went, after long and skillful preparation, to check on the spot the authenticity of the ancient annals of the ancient Chinese empire. The great honor of doing so fell on a French scientist, a worthy follower of the tradition started by Abel Remusat and continued by Stanislas Julien.[24]

Chavannes was also invited by Alfred Charles Auguste Foucher (1865–1952) to examine Chinese inscriptions found in India, and by Charles-Eudes Bonin (1865–1929) to translate rubbings of Chinese inscriptions from Central Asia.[25] Due to Sir Marc Aurel Stein's excavation of ancient Khotan, Stein (1862–1943) asked Chavannes to scrutinize thousands of Chinese inscriptions found on the Dunhuang Limes. So Chavannes must have been aware of Aurel Stein's and since 1907 Paul Pelliot's effort to secure the treasure trove of original Buddhist texts and text fragments from a 235-year period starting in 100 BCE, which had been discovered at Dunhuang. Thus, Chavannes had, without ever visiting Longmen, exceptionally good first-hand knowledge of all historical texts, as evidenced in his 1902 publication,[26] and had fully up-to-date information on their context.[27]

Chavannes' magisterial report based on his visit in 1907 speaks for itself:

I will directly move on to the examination of the Buddhist sculptures that are found partly fourteen kilometers west of Datong in northern Shanxi and partly fifteen kilometers south of Henanfu [Luoyang], in a ravine that . . . carries the very common name *Longmen* "Dragon Gate." In both cases we find rock walls where grottoes and niches of widely diverse dimensions have been made, some of less than the size of a person, and others raising their ceiling about thirty meters high, yet all with their walls decorated with figures of divinities, some minute, others colossal.

Chavannes then based his discussion on the inscribed votive texts in company of those images:

From their dedications we learn that they are works created to either secure somebody's good luck in this world or the next, or, more often, to benefit the soul of a deceased, who by this good deed would escape the misery of temporal existence by leaving the cycles of birth and death. The devout spenders were highly diverse. Some were emperors, empresses or princes, thanks to whom we have the gigantic Buddhas that demand many years of work and considerable disbursements. Others were people of a lesser status, who often declared that they spent all they have and even joined together to bring about a statue of medium size. Yet others contented themselves with a humble donation of a statuette that did not even match the greatness of their devotion. The rock walls of the grottoes are thus covered by sculptures that confirm the intensity with which all classes of society believed in Buddhist dogmas, from the ruler down to the commoners.[28]

A rapid flow of discoveries in the early twentieth century confirmed what had throughout the nineteenth century taken root among Orientalists and scientists alike. The French study and translation of Buddhist texts revealed cultural links between South, East, and Southeast Asia and awakened a broad interest in Eastern spirituality. The findings by Alfred Charles Auguste Foucher (1865–1952), Sir Marc Aurel Stein, and Édouard Chavannes that became widely known between 1902 and 1908 changed the worldview about the human shared past. The northward diffusion of Buddhism from India through Central Asia, along various routes through Dunhuang, Turfan, and Datong (Yungang) to Luoyang (Longmen), and further through China to Korea and Japan, was manifested in unearthed ancient cities, statues, bas-reliefs, paintings, inscriptions, manuscripts on bamboo sticks and other objects. These finds linked the transmission of Buddhist influences in Greece as well as of Hellenic influences in Gandhāra.[29]

LONGMEN: GRECO-BUDDHISM

During the early twentieth century, Chinese stone images at Longmen were considered a testimony to Greco-Buddhism, an important topic among some Orientalists. While Berthelot, in 1902, saw Egyptian traits at Longmen, a few years later Chavannes considered them to be Hellenic. Speaking of stylistic features, Chavannes attributed the Longmen cave temples broadly to Greco-Buddhist art, an influential term publicly used by Alfred Foucher since 1905. Chavannes published in 1896 his translation of five Chinese inscriptions photographed and rubbed by Foucher during his research in India.[30] So he must have had first-hand knowledge about Foucher's work. He wrote:

> One finds this among the statues of Gandhāra, of which at least one was brought to Turfan. So here we have the proof that the Northern Wei art was inspired by Gandhāra, i.e., the art that was born in Peshawar north of the Indus and was transmitted across Central Asia to Turfan, where the Wei must have got to know it as their military success brought them into contact with the peoples in eastern Turkestan.[31]

At Longmen's older sister site, the Yungang Caves, Chavannes saw clear mixed Indic, Chinese, and Greek influences:

> In other niches at Datong, the upper frame consists of a dragon that terminates at both ends with a rising head. The seven Buddhas who already appeared in the world are lined up under the dragon. . . . It is not only the characteristics of the art that differ so much, the persons [depicted] are totally new, so the sight of them yields unexpected surprises. Take for example, what is reproduced in

figure 7: doesn't he have the wings of Mercury on his helmet? Doesn't he hold Neptune's trident [three-pronged spear] in his left hand and isn't the object resting on his right shoulder Bacchus' thyrsus? Isn't he one of those divinities called pantheons that combine the attributes of several gods? Whatever he is, this enigmatic god can hardly have been conceived by a sculptor without knowledge of the works of Greco-Roman art which during the first centuries of the Common Era spread across Asia and exercised a real and profound influence on the art in Gandhāra.[32]

The phrase Greco-Buddhism was allegedly coined by Gottlieb Wilhelm Leitner in 1871 in Lahore.[33] It was, according to art historian Stanley Abe, an intellectual innovation at the time:

> The extent of Greek influence is here dramatically expanded to incorporate Buddhism as a whole and Leitner positions such influence as a natural part of a Universal History in which East-West exchange was symmetrical and mutually beneficial. The reversal in the direction of influence that Leitner identifies, however, is of no small significance. Early Orientalist scholars going back to William Jones had understood cultural influences in the main as flowing out of India. From the mid-nineteenth century onward, India was to be increasingly presented as recipient of foreign influence.[34]

Although the spread of Buddhism had been well known, not until around 1900 were the material evidence and the concrete geographical paths scientifically determined by, among others, Sir Aurel Stein and Édouard Chavannes. The scholarship in the early 1900s argued that not only India but also China was a recipient of Greek cultural influence. To them, Longmen was a spectacular example of the cultural diffusion from the ancient heartland of India to the cradle of Chinese civilization, Luoyang on the central North China Plain.

Chavannes studied the Tang dynasty (618–907), which saw the second flowering of Buddhist carvings at Longmen under Empress Wu Zetian. Empress Wu took up residence in Luoyang and played a key role in promoting Buddhism. Chavannes reported with comparison:

> In the grottoes of the Tang era, i.e., the seventh and eighth centuries, we see two or sometimes four persons that never appeared in the grottoes of the Wei period. These are imposing colossuses that stand by the sides of the opening as if to protect the entrance. These celestial kings charged with subduing the demons are, without any doubt, the successors of the Vajrapāṇi that serve as protectors at the sides of the Buddha on the bas-reliefs at Gandhāra. Their presence gives rise to an interesting archaeological question, for it forces us to explore which influence between the Wei and the Tang contributed to the appearance of these persons. Since the Tang period, they have persisted either in pairs or in groups of four in Buddhist art, and they are the ones we still in our time find at the

entry into major temples in China. They are also found in Japan where their Chinese origin is evident in monuments like in Longmen. Nothing resembles the celestial kings of the *Todaiji* [Temple] in Nara more than the colossuses that flex their powerful muscles at the entrance to one of the grottoes in Longmen.[35]

Then, Chavannes introduced the three Binyang Caves, especially the low reliefs, in the central grotto that quickly became much sought-after in world markets as discussed in chapter 6:

> The three largest Longmen grottoes date from the Tang period; they were completed in 642 by King Tai of Wei in memory of his mother, an empress who died in 636. The gigantic Buddhas that occupy the far end are in my view not remarkable. However, in the central grotto,[36] one finds some curious bas-reliefs on a wall in front of the statue. The best preserved are those mid-range that represent, on the one hand a procession of men . . . and on the other, a procession of women; these are apparently the person who donated the work and his wife with each their followers. These bas-reliefs are interesting for the study of costumes and hair-dress in seventh-century China.[37]

The narratives of Greco-Buddhist communication and Chinese history are deeply intertwined in Chavannes' analysis of Longmen. Despite its flaws, he carefully applied the knowledge presented in Chinese dynastic histories and other original sources and combined it with his personal evaluation of material evidence in a rigorous, critical process of scientific exploration. Longmen implied an important symbolic claim that Hellenic artistic elements affected an important site of Chinese civilization. French scholars accommodated these perceptions and inserted themselves into mainstream science and discourses with a European universal claim. To this day, the Chinese by and large have no issues with this conclusion, unlike their Japanese counterparts in history as shown in chapter 4.

LONGMEN: UNIVERSAL SPIRITUALITY AND MODERN CHRISTIANITY

The discovery of Longmen as an important place on Buddhism's route across China and on to Korea and Japan reflected a turning point in Euro-American discourses about the East between 1870 and the turn of the century, in the American Gilded Age and most of the European Belle Époque. The diverse and scattered interests and ideas that had emerged since the early eighteenth century gradually converged in a search to address existential questions, the answer to which could not be found in existing religious faiths, national cultures, or in the pan-European classicist tradition. The expanding knowledge of Semitic cultures in the near East and the pharaonic and Babylonic civilizations stretched the classicist ideals, while new impulses resulting from knowledge of India, China, and Japan demanded holistic new visions about the world and the human past.

Longmen bore relevance to two intertwined dimensions within these intellectual contexts. First, comparative philology began to explore the origin of languages explaining similarities between Sanskrit, Greek, Latin and many dead and living languages of Europe; the "standard" languages of classical antiquity were reduced to cases of linguistic evolution. Second, the main branches of Christianity came under pressure to explain history, defend rituals, and accommodate modern phenomena. The exclusive claim to the universal truth by each religion was questioned.

Christian clerics and missionaries were influenced by secular historical and natural science explanations as history and philology shattered their periodization and beliefs in their biblical worldview; nonbelievers sought new spiritual homes. For linguists, Indo-European and Semitic language evolution promised a distant convergence in a shared original language, a universal proto-language, an ideal of almost religious dimensions. For what other could it be than the universal language shared by Adam and Eve?

Such change was evident in British Protestant missionary Joseph Edkins (1823–1905), who was active in China from 1848 to 1905. He made it part of his life-work to promote the search for the original universal proto-language and seek the shared moral roots for great civilizations. With an undiminished conviction in saving the souls of nonbelievers,[38] he strove to vindicate the unified biblical origin of humanity and achieve the Christian aim of universal Christianity. The study of Chinese religions served his proselytizing cause, while the study of language, in his view, would justify the aim of Christianity as universal humanity.[39]

The search for the universal origin was justified within Christianity, although it broke church dogmas and introduced an essentially secular form of reasoning. Edkins wrote:

From whence then did the moral sense clearly displayed in Chinese, in Hindu, and in Greek literature, originate? It was not an invention of poets and historians. Plutarch did not create his heroes. He simply described their heroic deeds that posterity might know what brave men had done in Greece and Rome. The moral sentiments which make life beautiful and nations happy came by inheritance from an earlier age. The identity of moral sentiments in countries so far apart as Greece and China points to an earlier age when God spoke to man in the Mesopotamian plains, and inspired patriarchs gave instruction to their fellow-countrymen in religion and morality. This was before the Hindus and Persians had separated from the Teutons and the Greeks. It was in what we may call antediluvian times, before the days of Shem and Heber, when Semitic and

Aryan speech were both in the womb of the future. This is shown by identity of moral sentiment and monotheistic belief.[40]

Similarly, German-born Orientalist and linguist Max Müller (1823–1900), a professor of comparative philology at Oxford University (1868–1900), asserted:

> It was Christianity which first broke down the barriers between Jew and Gentile, between Greek and barbarian, between the white and the black . . . The idea of mankind as one family, as the children of one God, is an idea of Christian growth; and the science of mankind, and of the languages of mankind, is a science which, without Christianity, would never have sprung into life. When people had been taught to look upon all men as brethren, then, and then only, did the variety of human speech present itself as a problem that called for a solution in the eyes of thoughtful observers; and I, therefore, date the real beginning of the science of language from the first day of Pentecost.[41]

Edkins' and Müller's search for a rational understanding of Christianity as a universal, superior religion was, of course, not the only approach of the time. Léon de Rosny (1837–1914), the initiator of the International Congresses of Orientalists in 1873 and a specialist in Indian Buddhism,[42] moved far beyond that perspective in using "eclectic" Buddhist elements as a template for a universal religion. Rosny published in 1894 two works[43] that represented what Bernard Faure terms "positive Orientalism," a "modernized Buddhism" turned into a "religion of reason"—in short, a hasty reduction of Buddhism to its philosophical content, a mere "Buddhology."[44]

Edkins' and Rosny's disparate efforts coincided with the popularization of Buddhism in the United States and interreligious exchange[45] in the wake of the Chicago Parliament of Religions in 1893. Besides "sanitized" Buddhism, theosophy, which some called occultism, also became popular. Theosophy was established by Helena Blavatsky and Henry Olcott,[46] who strove toward a union of all religions:

> Therefore, in the end of the nineteenth century the same old Masters of Wisdom, who had founded Hinduism, who had founded Buddhism, who had founded Christianity, who had founded the other great religions of the world, have in these later days again initiated a spiritual movement to give further impulse to spiritual knowledge and to call men nearer to the home where alone their souls will find eternal peace.[47]

Distilling the divine elements of Christianity into spiritual ideals of supreme ethics and human universalism neither served popular needs for belief nor prevented the universal ideal from being used to legitimize partisan interest.

The ideological striving manifested itself in modern rationality, and at the same time was projected on to the stunning natural beauty of Longmen's ravine, the serenely trans-substantiated Buddhist rock images that had long lost their devotional meaning. Longmen became a symbol of the melting pot of cultural forces from Indian, Hellenic, Chinese, and other places right in the center of the Northern Wei dynasty's bygone civilization, all in marked contrast to the poor and harsh lives of the locals in Luoyang. This dilemma can also be found in a self-contradictory turn through Victor Segalen and André Malraux.

DISSENTING VOICES OF SILENCE AT LONGMEN:
VICTOR SEGALEN AND ANDRÉ MALRAUX

Victor Segalen (1878–1919) and André Malraux (1901–1976), each in their own way exhibited the imagined meaning of Longmen's statues in modernity. In the twentieth century, Longmen as an icon of modern ideas about universality was challenged by Segalen, a French physician, poet, archaeologist, novelist, and inveterate Sinophiliac, who claimed that Longmen lacked Han Chinese cultural purity. For Segalen, Longmen did not belong to the discussion of Chinese art. Even so, ironically, he extensively explicated its significance in the Chinese context.[48] Seen from the perspective of Segalen's wider literary work, the rock monuments at Longmen entailed a fundamental conundrum: the outside judgment of the pristine destroyed the authentic Other. In other words, the *knowledge* of the East soiled it. This philosophical riddle of the twentieth century reminds us of Heisenberg's uncertainty principle as represented by Erwin Schrödinger's metaphorical cat.

Marie-Paule Ha points out Segalen's fundamental self-contradiction, which was to demand pristine authenticity of the Chinese Other while at the same time wanting to penetrate and possess it. Originally due to Segalen's "acute sense of incomprehensibility"[49] of China, he tended to seek its authentic core through an archaeological process; in the search for pure authenticity he had to metaphorically work his way through thick layers of dirt.[50]

Segalen's search, with reference to Cervantes' *Don Quixote*, deferred the pleasure of revealing the Other since the moment of disclosure dispels the mystery surrounding the Other. His posthumously published novel *René Leys*[51] involved the narrator (Segalen) and his Chinese language teacher René Leys in a double narrative. Segalen kept a diary in which he confided how he, with the aid of Leys, was able to gain insight into (penetrate) the otherwise impenetrable "inner" Beijing; he himself lived in the outer part where foreigners had much privilege. The character Leys was a Belgian born in China and fluent in Mandarin. Leys could move freely in and out of inner Beijing

and told Segalen of his experiences inside the Forbidden City. The narrative
Segalen penned in his diary involved the most astonishing secrets, including
Leys' insinuated homoerotic relationship with the Regent,[52] Leys' promotion
to high posts including the chief of the secret police, and his "night of love
in the Palace" with the empress,[53] narrated with intimate detail. Leys lived
out the desires of Segalen, or rather, upon being questioned by Segalen about
details of his exploits, came back with stories fulfilling Segalen's cravings,
down to the smutty details from trash literature which had inspired Segalen.
Marie-Paule Ha observes:

> The novel ends with the narrator's refraining from "answering my doubt about
> myself and finally pronouncing: *yes* or *no*." By thus refusing to comment on the
> narrative's veracity, the narrator indefinitely suspends the moment of closure,
> which in turn enables him to maintain his impossible . . . quest . . . for the un-
> coverable Other.[54]

Victor Segalen, deeply aware of the difficulty associated with evaluating
the Chinese Other, faced the problem that, as an outsider, he would have to
judge what was authentic and what was not. His understanding of the Longmen statues was that they were alien, carriers of Buddhism, an anti-Chinese
heresy. However, their presence forced Segalen to afford them a chapter in
his work, one that might reflect both the need for a counterpoint in his story
to pristine Chinese sculpture, and reverence for Édouard Chavannes, without
whose pioneering work and example Segalen's posthumous book would have
been much more difficult to write. Segalen wrote:

> "Material deposits" [gisements] rather than monuments is the term deserved by
> such remains in stone: Vestiges full of piety, molded with faith, they are not
> temples; grazing an immense mountain face, they are not a facade, still less a
> "monumental" order; although of royal origin, they do not involve a palace or
> purely Chinese art; although they are covered with characters, they trace foreign
> forms![55]

Then, Segalen continued to denounce the stone statues at Longmen and
Yungang:

> When, at the end of the Wei, Longmen was in full vigor and the vast roofs, like
> tents, swelled with songs, flowers, incense and great breaths of universal hope,
> one could ignore the unfortunate effects of stereotypical statues. But even so,
> the orchestrated architecture did not justify that the statues were so ugly. These
> palaces, of which nothing remains, one may believe were powerfully ordained
> and honored to shelter masterpieces. But this book must treat—if not master-
> pieces—that great work: the Thousand Buddhas of Longmen and Yungang,
> some of which reached sixty feet, representing size, not greatness![56]

André Malraux,[57] the French minister of communication (1945–1946) and minister of culture (1959–1969) in Charles de Gaulle's government, confessed his fascination with Longmen's stone images and included them in volume two of his *Le musée imaginaire de la sculpture mondiale*:

> The problems that the imaginary museum of Chinese art poses us are of a different nature. Like it or not, Buddhism fills it. Buddhism dominates Chinese painting, which we shall not discuss here. In its sculpture, it plays a major role, despite recent discoveries, despite the tension given to the forms by the bronze sculptors of the oldest dynasties. The bronzes are objects, while the Buddhist caves are cathedrals; we know Chinese art as Americans know Gothic art. The great mask of the Shang dynasty is a masterpiece, but Longmen is a world.[58]

Born and raised in Paris, Malraux had received little formal education, but he developed literary and art criticism skills through booksellers, museums, and libraries, at first with a penchant for studying the surreal. He began publishing art criticism and literary works when only in his late teens. He was inspired by Friedrich Nietzsche and T. E. Lawrence, Lawrence of Arabia. Malraux's venture into Cambodia, then part of French Indo-China, in 1923 seemed driven by an existentialist urge to emulate Lawrence, to seek and face down the ultimate fate of life. Later, his restlessness might have had to do with the fact that the Great Depression had wiped out his family's wealth and that his father committed suicide in the face of ruin. Malraux fought in the Spanish Civil War, was active in anti-Fascist movements, and flirted with the Communist movement. He went to meetings in Moscow and got to know several Communist leaders, arranging for a round table in Paris with Leon Trotsky who was in exile for two years there in the early 1930s.[59]

Malraux's life was fascinating, for his beliefs, ideals, actions, rationality remain adumbrated, suggesting in a style that never drew the line between fact and fiction: his novels are felt to be autobiographic up to an uncertain level; his memoirs are "anti-memoirs," in which he presented his conversation with Zhou Enlai (see below), and struck a balance of suggestiveness, leaving it to the reader what he wanted to read into it.[60] Jacques Lecarme claimed that the dominant opinion among France's contemporary intellectuals is that Malraux was not a great writer, but an "imposter."[61] However that be, Malraux's ability to build a myth about himself was considerable, a feat in its own right.

Malraux developed an idiosyncratic view of art history.[62] He tirelessly presented a perception that portrayed the metamorphosis of art from being an object of mundane signification to becoming timeless and overcoming repressive forces that subdued life. Art became art through the detachment from original meanings and through its juxtaposition with other art, like in a museum. Not the museum as an artifact in itself, but as an act of juxtaposition and comparison, was thus liberating—the imaginary museum. This meant that for him putting together Gothic sculptures from the Cathedral in Rouen and from Longmen was not really a claim for historical-sequential origins, but one of aesthetic metamorphosis and existential liberation.

Malraux's affinity with the Longmen Grottoes was shown at several levels. He went to Longmen in 1965 during a state visit to China where he met Chen Yi, Zhou Enlai, and Mao Zedong, all senior Chinese top leaders.[63] Apart from Beijing, he only went to two other places: Luoyang to see Longmen, and Yan'an, the erstwhile revolutionary base area of the Chinese Communists after the Long March. Was it a sentimental journey? His novels *Les conquerants* (1928) and *La condition humaine* (1933) both depicted early stages of the Chinese Communist revolution, in particular the role of the Chinese Communist Party. Zhou Enlai, then the Premier of the PRC, is regarded by many (allegedly even by Zhou himself) as the model for one of the protagonists in Malraux's novels. Longmen had equal mythological and iconic importance for Malraux as Yan'an. The statues were a topic in his various books on art, an example of the metamorphosis, the very abstraction from context that he saw as the source of sublime beauty and as revenge on the hostile universe.

Seeing Longmen in person at the height of the Cold War, Malraux wrote that:

> [The Buddhist caves of Longmen] are now protected by glass, and the statues there seem like they are in shop windows. Above, some statues have lost their heads ("It's the Americans," says the guide). In the amphitheater, the crowd mills round at the feet of the Grand Buddha, surprisingly Indo-Hellenistic, while the sculptures of the Wei grottoes are less so. At the sides, the protecting giants symbolize the cardinal points. One of them tramples a pitiful little dwarf with his medieval boot . . . The colossal Buddha was sculpted for lovers under the orders of the Empress. Around the holy rock crying chickens compete with chirping crickets, while the radio receiver of a nearby inn intermittently blasts Beijing programs.[64]

Longmen and its Greco-Buddhist art also had a deeper, more personal meaning for Malraux. His struggles against depression and adversity in his own life contributed to his attempt in 1923 to sever and make off with heads of statues from the temples of Angkor in Cambodia, an act for which he was arrested and sentenced to three years in prison (later commuted to one, and never served). Later, he purchased severed sculpture heads in Afghanistan, which he exhibited in Paris in 1932 as Gothic-Buddhist art, in parallel with the Greco-Buddhist sculptures of Gandhāra. The public display with a deliberate surreal ambience and mythical adumbration that, in spite of the severed heads' authenticity and legal provenance, elicited a sense of incredulity in the media. Visiting the icons of Longmen, many of which had been decapitated, gave him an opportunity to connect with an important trope of his art theory and his personal life.

André Malraux detached works of art from their original context and meaning, and sought to conquer reality. Imaginatively, he restated art as a myth of human victory over existential constraints, yet he never overcame the problem of the individual versus the universal, or for that matter of the East and West.

CONCLUSION

In the early twentieth century, cultural forces for rationality, abstraction and a principled, modern scientific epistemology gathered in Longmen's French connection. "Where the different branches of Orientalism agreed on one and the same goal, it was to retrace the history of the spirit of humanity. Furthermore, they alone were able to do it," P. Rabault-Feuerhahn has written.[65] The French ties with Longmen imagined the shared roots of spirituality and humans common past, and did so not only within a framework of rationality but also with a liberalism that went beyond individual distinctions to a quintessentially modern ideal of the good. Such humanistic visions did not stand in the way of scientific practice, for they were two sides of the same coin: On the one hand, there was the vision of a unifying humanity and eliminating all barriers created by castes, races, and cultures. On the other hand, there was the imperative of a rational, impartial, and rigorous practice that allowed modernity to distinguish charlatans from scholars by evaluating their evidence and research methods.[66]

Located in the heart of early Chinese civilization, Longmen incorporated in aesthetic immediacy its Buddhist transubstantiation, its inherent role as signifier, and its history of early trans-civilizational diffusion, the core elements of such a human ideal. The encounter between stone Buddhas at Longmen and the French persons enabled humanism to find many voices. As a result, they articulated some of the most fundamental existential concerns among humans, which suggested that one can learn much from other societies, "not just those that dominate the present but also those that flourished in the past."[67]

Paradoxically, the story of Longmen and historical Orientalism represented an inherently contradictory modern effort to create a unified world from a divided reality. From the historical Orientalist perspective, Longmen in the backwater of modern China became a new spring of inspiration for modernity as well as a new source of modern capitalist consumption.

Underneath this modern, symbolic use of stone Buddhas, one senses its dilemma. The moment when stone Buddhas become modern universal reality is similar to the fleeting reality of the divine often referred to as "transubstantiation"—like the bread and wine becoming the flesh and blood of Jesus. Superimposing, even subconsciously and symbolically, the modern quest for universal human unity on to the moment of reaching Buddhahood and on to the true vision of the Eucharist ironically hinges modernity on mysticism: the Buddhist farewell to the treadmill of the material world is equated with the Christian sign becoming the material reality of God. Segalen's demand for the authenticity of the Other, and Malraux' imaginary museum played with this underlying tension without articulating its religious overtones; one keeping the suspense forever, the other turning it into an ongoing existential condition.

Finally, moving from the sublime to the grubby, it should be pointed out that, aside from being inspired, the French visitors to Longmen also brought capitalist modernity to Longmen. Their attention to the monument, like that given to many other long-neglected historical sites, was a disturbingly double-edged sword. Longmen's rock sculptures and other objects rapidly became tradeable merchandise with tagged values in the private and open markets around the world. As discussed above, the Central Binyang Cave, which caught the eye of the French travelers, was where the two bas-reliefs "Emperor Xiaowen and His Court" and "Offering Procession of the Empress as Donor with Her Court" originally belonged. However, during the 1930s, the two bas-reliefs were removed and then sold to their current homes, the Metropolitan Museum of Art in New York City and the Nelson-Atkins Museum in Kansas City, respectively. Having long been left alone in situ in desolation or peace, these two bas-reliefs gained a high value probably around the time of the publication of the 1905 article by the French diplomat Philippe Berthelot.[68] The severance of the two low reliefs from their authentic birthplace, and the removal of other artifacts, altogether showcased the cruel contradiction of the many voices of silence in Longmen's French connection. Or, was their displacement a further iteration of the Malruvian metamorphosis, a material incarnation of the imaginary museum?

NOTES

1. Édouard Chavannes (1865–1918), "Voyage archéologique dans la Mandchourie et dans la Chine septentrionale," *T'oung Pao* IX, 4 (1908): 513–14.

2. A small sample of works that manifests the enduring impact of French intellectuals especially Édouard Chavannes on the field of Chinese art history are Stanley K. Abe, *Ordinary Images* (Chicago, Ill.: University of Chicago Press, 2002); Dorothy

C. Wong, *Chinese Steles: Pre-Buddhist and Buddhist Use of a Symbolic Form* (Honolulu, Hawaii: University of Hawaii Press, 2004); Amy McNair, *Donors of Longmen: Faith, Politics, and Patronage in Medieval Chinese Buddhist Sculpture* (Honolulu, Hawaii: University of Hawaii Press, 2007).

3. Zhang Guangda, "À propos d'Edouard Chavannes, le premier sinologue complet," https://www.youtube.com/watch?v=YCd6grzkYMU, published on *Cap33 WebTV* on August 30, 2014, accessed on July 3, 2018. Norman J. Girardot, *The Victorian Translation of China. James Legge's Oriental Pilgrimage* (Berkeley, Calif.: University of California Press, 2002), p. 8 and p. 430.

4. Editorial, *The Guardian*, July 4, 2018, https://www.theguardian.com/commentisfree/2018/jul/04/the-guardian-view-on-world-heritage-in-the-beginning-was-the-dream (accessed on July 12, 2018).

5. Paul Rich, "European Identity and the Myth of Islam: A Reassessment," *Review of International Studies* 25, no. 3 (1999): 435–51.

6. Rich, "European Identity," p. 438.

7. Nathaniel Gilmore and Vickie B. Sullivan, "Montesquieu's Teaching on the Dangers of Extreme Corrections: Japan. The Catholic Inquisition, and Moderation in *The Spirit of the Laws*," *American Political Science Journal* 111, no. 3 (2017): 460–70; Jeffrey D. Burson, "Chinese Novices, Jesuit Missionaries and the Accidental Construction of Sinophobia in Enlightenment France," *French History* 27, no. 1 (2013): 21–44; Jeffrey D. Burson, "Unlikely Tales of Fo and Ignatius: Rethinking the Radical Enlightenment Through French Appropriation of Chinese Buddhism," *French Historical Journal* 38, no. 3 (2015): 391–420.

8. Tuska Benes, "Transcending Babel in the Cultural Translation of Friedrich Rückert (1788–1866)," *Modern Intellectual History* 8, no. 1 (2011): 63–64. Benes in particular refers to Rückert's influential translations of Middle Eastern and South Asian literature into German.

9. Johann Gottfried Herder, *Abhandlung über den Ursprung der Sprache* (Berlin: Christian Friedrich Voß, 1772).

10. Elena Pnevmonidou, "Veiled Narratives: Novalis' Heinrich von Ofterdingen as a Staging of Oriental Discourse," *The German Quarterly* 84, no. 1 (2011): 21–40; Novalis [Friedrich von Hardenberg], *Heinrich von Ofterdingen. Ein nachgelassener Roman von Novalis* (Berlin: Buchhandlung der Realschule, 1802); Vishwa P. Adluri, "Pride and Prejudice: Orientalism and German Indology," *International Journal of Hindu Studies* 15, no. 3 (2011): 253–92.

11. Suzanne L. Marchand, "The Rhetoric of Artifacts and the Decline of Classical Humanism: The Case of Josef Strzygowski," *History and Theory* 33, no. 4 (1994): 106–30.

12. Prasenjit Duara, *The Crisis of Global Modernity: Asian Traditions and a Sustainable Future* (Cambridge: University of Cambridge Press, 2015), p. 89. Marnia Lazreg, *Foucault's Orient: The Conundrum of Cultural Difference, from Tunisia to Japan* (New York: Berghahn Books, 2017); Mingming Wang, *The West as the Other. A Genealogy of Chinese Occidentalism* (Hong Kong: The Chinese University Press, 2014).

13. Marie-Paule Ha, *Figuring the East: Segalen, Malraux, Duras, and Barthes* (Albany, N.Y.: State University of New York Press, 2000).

14. For example, Charles Lang Freer in late October and early November 1910 wrote about his travel to Longmen from the city of Luoyang: "The ponies and mules turned out better than they looked, for they dragged their heavy loads through miles of mud, over rocks and boulders, through hundreds of ruts and through the wide Lo Ho (Luo) River at the crossing place, with a patience and determination befitting their veteran years." Charles Lang Freer's travel journal, October 29, 1910, Charles Lang Freer Papers, Freer and Sackler Gallery of Art Archive, Smithsonian Institution in Washington, DC.

15. Philippe Berthelot, "Note sur des inscriptions arabes, persanes et chinoises du Chen-Si, du Ho-Nan et du Chan-Toung," *Comptes rendus des séances de l'Academie des Inscriptions et Belles-Lettres* 49, 2 (1905): 186–204, p. 194.

16. Berthelot, "Note sur des inscriptions arabes," p. 204.

17. J. A. Moritz, "Darwin's Sacred Cause: the Unity of Humanity," *Theology and Science* 13, no. 1 (2015): 1–3.

18. Jean Babtiste Joseph Fourier, "Préface historique," in *Description de l'Égypte ou recueil des observations et des recherches qui ont été faites en Égypte pendant l'expédition de l'armée française.* Tome prémier. Deuxieme édition (Paris: Imprimerie de C. L. F. Panckoucke, 1821), i–clv.

19. For details of Chavannes' use of Berthelot's observations and Leprince-Ringuet's photos, see Édouard Chavannes, *Mission archéologique dans la Chine septentrionale* (Paris: E. Leroux, 1913–1915), vol. 1, part 2, 320, fn. 2. Chavannes' study based on Leprince-Ringuet's photos and extensive documentary evidence from Chinese historical sources was published as Édouard Chavannes, "Le défilé de Long-men dans la province Ho-nan," *Journal Asiatique*, Juillet-Août 1902: 133–59. For a broad account of Chavannes' travels in China, see Numa Broc, "Les voyageurs français et la connaissance de la Chine (1860-1914)," *Revue Historique* 559 (1986), 117–18.

20. I-Tsing (635–713, Tripitaka Dharma Master Yijing), *Les religieux éminents qui allèrent chercher la loi dans les pays d'Occident. Mémoire composé à l'époque de la grande dynastie T'ang* (Paris: Ernest Leroux, 1894).

21. An untiring Orientalist networker across Europe, Cordier left a legacy that is still felt in sinology and China studies. With limited knowledge of the Chinese language, he was exceptionally fluent in English in addition to his native French, and was, in 1872, appointed librarian of the North China Branch of the Royal Asiatic Society. He established and edited academic journals, perhaps most famously in 1890 *T'oung Pao* (still in operation), gave leadership to scholarly associations, edited collections of archival source materials, and published annotated bibliographies, conference volumes, as well as synthesizing overviews on topics related to China and Japan.

22. Henri Cordier, "Édouard Chavannes," *T'oung Pao*, XI/18, 1/2 (1918): 197–248.

23. Ferdinand von Richthofen, *China. Ergebnisse eigener Reisen und darauf gegründeter Studien* (Berlin: Verlag von Dietrich Reimer, 1882), vol. 2, *Das nördliche China*, p. 505.

24. Henri Cordier, "Séance de clôture," *Bulletin historique et philologique du comité des travaux historiques et scientifiques*, 1908: 122–50, p. 142; Chavannes'

dual competency as both sinologist and archaeologist is also emphasized by Broc, who credited him with the invention of the "original method" of corroborating ancient geographical and historical accounts in Chinese with the physical evidence from China's past. Broc, "Les voyageurs français," p. 117.

25. Édouard Chavannes, *Dix inscriptions de l'Asie central d'apres les estampages de M. Ch.-E. Bonin* (Paris: Imprimerie Nationale and Librairie C. Klincsieck, 1902).

26. Chavannes' sources mainly came from the official dynastic records of the Wei and Tang dynasties, Sima Qian's *Shiji*, as well as various local histories like the *Henan Tongzhi* and geographical treatises. Chavannes, "Le défilé de Long-men."

27. On the other hand, the full significance of the ancient manuscripts in Dunhuang's Mogao caves was yet to become clear as Chavannes traveled to Luoyang, see Cheuk-woon Taam, "The Discovery of the Tun-Huang Library and its Effect on Chinese Studies," *The Library Quarterly: Information, Community Policy* 12, no. 3 (July 1942): 686–705. On Dunhuang, see the extensive materials made available on the International Dunhuang Project website (http://idp.bl.uk).

28. Chavannes also commented on the social hierarchy shown at Longmen and Yungang in Datong, Shanxi: "It is however obvious that, although the fervor may have been the same among all, the richest and mightiest gave the most, and once they had opened the largest grottoes and erected the most beautiful statues, the lesser worshipers crowded in. The emperors ranked among the highest. That is how we can explain why the two groups [Longmen and Yungang] of sculptures we talk about are found in the immediate vicinity of cities that at the time when the grottoes were carved out functioned as capitals where the emperors and their courts lived." Édouard Chavannes, "Voyage archéologique dans la Mandchourie et dans la Chine septentrionale," pp. 503–28, 513–16.

29. On Sino-Indic multifaceted interactions before the fifteenth century, see Tansen Sen, *Buddhism, Diplomacy, and Trade: The Realignment of India-China Relations, 600-1400* (Lanham, Md.: Rowman & Littlefield, 2nd ed. 2016), 1st ed. 2003.

30. Édouard Chavannes, *Les inscriptions chinoises de Bodh-Gayâ* (Paris: Ernest Leroux, 1896); Stanley K. Abe, "Inside the Wonder House: Buddhist Art and the West," in Donald S. Lopez, Jr., ed., *Curators of the Buddha: The Study of Buddhism under Colonialism* (Chicago, Ill.: University of Chicago Press, 1995), pp. 63–106.

31. Chavannes, "Voyage archéologique," pp. 518–20.

32. Chavannes, "Voyage archéologique," pp. 518–20; Abe, "Inside the Wonder House."

33. Gottlieb Wilhelm Leitner, "Graeco-Buddhistic Sculpture," *The Imperial and Asiatic Quarterly Reviews and Oriental and Colonial Record* 7, nos. 13–14 (1894): 186–89; Michael Falser, "The Graeco-Buddhist Style of Gandhara—a "Storia Ideologica," or: How a Discourse Makes a Global History of Art," *Journal of Art Historiography* 13 (2015): 13–15.

34. Abe, "Inside the Wonder House," pp. 73–5.

35. Chavannes, "Voyage archéologique," pp. 516–24.

36. Chavannes erred due to his overreliance on the stone inscriptions on site when referring to the Binyang trio cave chapels. The construction of the three Binyang Caves (North, Central, and South) all began in the Northern Wei dynasty (386–534);

the Central and South Binyang Caves started in 500 and the North Binyang Cave was added between 508 and 511. Only the Central Binyang Cave was, for the most part, completed in 520 during the Northern Wei; the other two caves were unfinished. The North Binyang Cave chapel was largely constructed between 650 and 683 during the Tang dynasty, whereas renewed work on the South Binyang Cave was conducted probably between 616 and 673; the main figures and niches were completed then. Reading the famous commemorative text inscribed on the slab, authored by Cen Wenben of the Tang and dated 641, mounted outside on the outer wall between the entrances to the Central and South Binyang Caves, Chavannes mistakenly assigned this entire trio to the early seventh century during the Tang dynasty.

37. These are identical to those mentioned by Philippe Berthelot. Chavannes, "Voyage archéologique," pp. 516–24.

38. Joseph Edkins, *Religion in China: Containing a Brief Account of the Three Religions of the Chinese, with Observations on the Prospects of Christian Conversion amongst That People* (London: James R. Osgood and Company, 2nd ed. 1878).

39. Edkins' book *China's Place in Philology* opened with a bold declaration: "To *show* that the languages of Europe and Asia may be conveniently referred to one origin in the Mesopotamian and Armenian region, is the aim of the present work." Joseph Edkins, *China's Place in Philology: An Attempt to Show that the Languages of Europe and Asia Have a Common Origin* (London: Trübner & Co., 1871), xi.

40. Joseph Edkins, *The Early Spread of Religious Ideas Especially in the Far East* (London: Religious Tract Society, 1893), p. 111.

41. The origin of one humanity and universality was seen by many Christians as their *mission* bequeathed by the Apostles who had received it at Pentecost. Max Müller, *Lectures on the Science of Language Delivered at the Royal Institution of Great Britain in April, May, & June, 1861* (London: Longman, Green, Longman, and Roberts, 1862), p. 123. Lourens P. van den Bosch, "Language as the Barrier between Brute and Man. Friedrich Max Müller and the Darwinian Debate on Language," *Saeculum: Jahrbuch für Universalgeschichte* 51, no. 1 (2000): 57–89.

42. Léon de Rosny also led *Société d'Ethnographie de Paris*, founded in 1859 originally known as *Société d'Ethnographie Américaine et Orientale* (Society for American and Oriental Ethnography). Société d'ethnographie de Paris, *Comptes rendus des séances de la Société d'Ethnographie Américaine et Orientale* (Paris: Challamel Aîné, 1860). The organization claimed to advance the morals of the peoples of the world, and to eradicate racial prejudice and conventional borders. A polymath and winner of the prestigious Volney price for his essay on the Chinese language in 1861, Rosny was appointed chair of Japanese at the École des Langues Orientales in 1868. A formidable communicator, he had prolific scholarly publications. He was made a Knight of the Legion of Honor in 1884. Bénédicte Fabre-Muller, Pierre Leboulleux, and Philippe Rothstein, *Léon de Rosny (1837–1914). De l'Orient à l'Amerique* (Villeneuve d'Ascq: Presses Universitaires du Septentrion, 2014).

43. Léon de Rosny, *Le bouddhisme éclectique. Exposé de quelques-uns de principes de l'école* (Paris: E. Leroux, 1894); Léon de Rosny, *Les origines bouddhiques du christianisme* (u.p.: Vve Krüsi, 1894).

44. Bernard Faure, *Double Exposure: Cutting across Buddhist and Western Discourses* (Stanford, Calif.: Stanford University Press, 2004), pp. 4–5. See also David L. McMahan, *The Making of Buddhist Modernism* (Oxford: Oxford University Press, 2008).

45. Thomas A. Tweed, *The American Encounter with Buddhism, 1844–1912: Victorian Culture & the Limits of Dissent*, with a new preface (Chapel Hill, N.C.: University of North Carolina Press, 2002), 1st ed. in 1992. Thomas Albert Howard, "'A Remarkable Gathering': The Conference on Living Religions within the British Empire (1924) and Its Historical Significance," *Journal of the American Academy of Religion* 86, no. 1 (2018): 126–57.

46. Bernhard Faure, *Double Exposure*, p. 4. Henry Steel Olcott, *The Buddhist Catechism* (London: Theosophical Publishing Company, 1915, 1st ed. in 1881), 44th ed.; Henry Steel Olcott, *Le bouddhisme selon le canon de l'église du sud, sous forme de catéchisme* (Paris: Publications Théosophiques, 1905).

47. Annie Besant, "Theosophy is a System of Truths Discoverable and Verifiable by Perfected Men," in Theosophical Society, ed., *The Theosophical Congress at the Parliament of Religions, World's Fair of 1893, at Chicago, Ill., September 15, 16, 17. Report of Proceedings and Documents* (New York: American Section Headquarters, Theosophical Society, 1893), pp. 24–8.

48. Victor Segalen, *Chine. La grande statuaire. Les origines de la statuaire en Chine* (Paris: Collections Bouquins, Editions Robert Laffont, 2nd ed. 1995), 1st ed. 1972, ch. 7, "L'hérésie bouddhique," esp. p. 77 and p. 81.

49. Ha, *Figuring the East*, p. 25.

50. Ha, *Figuring the East*, p. 28.

51. Victor Segalen, *René Leys* (Paris: Georges Crès et Cie, 1971), 1st ed. 1922.

52. The novel covers the period February 28 to November 22, 1911, the final nine months of the Qing dynasty. The Regent (Zaifeng, 1883–1951) was taking care of state matters on behalf of the infant Xuantong Emperor Puyi.

53. Empress Dowager Longyu, widow of the Guangxu emperor.

54. Ha, *Figuring the East*, p. 44, emphasis in original, only the English translation of the quote has been rendered here.

55. Segalen, *Chine, La grande statuaire*, ch. 7.

56. Victor Segalen, *Chine, La grande statuaire*, ch. 7.

57. For a biography, see Olivier Todd, transl. by Joseph West, *Malraux. A Life* (New York: Alfred A. Knopf, 2005).

58. André Malraux, *Le musée imaginaire de la sculpture mondiale, vol. 2: Des bas-reliefs aux grottes sacrées* (Paris: La Galerie de la Pleiade, 1954), pp. 55–8.

59. Robert S. Thornberry, "A Spanish Civil War Polemic: Trotsky versus Malraux," *Twentieth-Century Literature* 24, no. 3, Andre Malraux Issue (autumn 1978): 324–34. Malraux wrote about his meeting with Trotsky for a weekly newspaper in late April 1934.

60. André Malraux, *Antimemoires* (Paris: Gallimard, 1967), pp. 510–18.

61. Jacques Lecarme, *Malraux et Sartre lecteurs de Michelet, ou la vérité d'un mythe*. In: *La France des écrivains: Éclats d'un mythe (1945–2005)* [online] (Paris:

Presses Sorbonne Nouvelle, 2011), http://books.openedition.org/psn/519 (accessed on October 3, 2019), pp. 15–16.

62. For a study of Malraux' oeuvre and impact on the art world, see Walter Grasskamp, transl. by Fiona Elliott, *The Book on the Floor. André Malraux and the Imaginary Museum* (Los Angeles, Calif.: Getty Research Institute, 2016).

63. The geopolitics of the 1960s was a most interesting backdrop. The French challenge to the U.S. dominance, its nuclear armament program, and its independent stance on NATO were pursued by de Gaulle in the Fifth Republic. France had, in 1964, established diplomatic relations with the PRC, and in early 1965 sent André Malraux on a state visit to China. To add more complexity, France's left-wing intellectual elite of the 1950s–1960s lost faith in Soviet-style communism between the events in Budapest 1958 and in Prague 1968. Led by sentiments against the U.S.–Vietnam War and intrigued by the Chinese Cultural Revolution, many turned Maoist, as recorded by Richard Wolin, *The Wind from the East. French Intellectuals, the Cultural Revolution and the Legacy of the 1960s* (Princeton, N.J.: Princeton University Press, 2nd ed. 2018), 1st ed. 2010.

64. Malraux, *Antimemoires*, pp. 508–9.

65. Pascale Rabault-Feuerhahn, "'Les grandes assises de l'orientalisme.' La question interculturelle dans les congrès internationaux des orientalistes (1873–1912)," *Revue Germanique Internationale*, 12 (2010), p. 54.

66. Louise Schwab, "Le parlement des religions à Chicago," *Bulletin de la Société d'Ethnographie*: 36/78 (1894): 165–72.

67. Richard Madsen, William M. Sullivan, Ann Swidler, and Steven M. Tipton, eds., *Meaning and Modernity: Religion, Polity, and Self* (Berkeley, Calif.: University of California Press, 2002), xv.

68. Berthelot, "Note sur des inscriptions," p. 194.

Chapter 4

"An Influence of the Souls of These Stone Saints"

Early American and Japanese Recognition, between Universalism and Nationalism

At Lungmen [Longmen], near Honan fu [Luoyang], there was discovered the most beautiful example of Chinese art that remains. It consisted of several hundreds of cave chapels, dug out of the solid rock on the cliff above the river. And here there were hundreds of thousands of carvings made out of the rock itself in the period from the fifth to the seventh centuries. There were not merely curios but things of real beauty.

—An interview with Langdon
Warner (1881–1951), 1914[1]

Preceding chapters suggest that, over a century ago, a worldwide search for lost or loosened human connections was expressed in recognition of antiquities in China, including Luoyang's Longmen on the North China Plain, as a source of spirituality and modernity. This was an important dimension of modern history that has mostly escaped the attention of commentators, who have thus far associated the modern scramble for Chinese artifacts across the Atlantic and the Pacific primarily with art collecting and connoisseurship.[2]

Corresponding to the European scene, stone Buddhas in North China also became an object of fascination among many influential and wealthy Americans and Japanese. As new precious commodities, they found their way on to the world markets, and at the same time awakened imaginings of cultural bonds spanning continents. In the imagination driven by

115

variegated individual, national, imperial, and cosmopolitan factors, stone Buddhas came to symbolize the urge to resume long lost human connections and the union across Asia and between America's European and Asiatic heritage.

This chapter seeks to explore early American and Japanese advocacy for Longmen's cave temples, rock sculptures, reliefs, and inscribed stone tablets around the world. In 1910, Charles Lang Freer (1854–1919)—an American industrialist, connoisseur, and founding donor of the Freer Gallery of Art, owned by the U.S. government and known mainly for its comprehensive collection of American and Asian art—stayed in the Qianxi Temple at the northern entrance of Longmen for two weeks from October 29 to November 14. In his journal, Freer wrote: "Lung-men [Longmen] is interesting as no other cave temples are interesting. Its power to interest almost overwhelms me. Its grip upon me constantly increases, it makes me almost feverish—an influence from the souls of these stone saints."[3]

Sixty-two pages in his normally brief travel diary recorded details of this trip, as well as the emotions and speculations sparked by this first and only visit to the site. Nothing similar to the spontaneous insights expressed here can be found elsewhere in his papers.[4] Longmen—more than any other ancient site—captivated Freer. In 1911, he asserted with foresight: "The workmen had to cut through obstacles, not around them. They hewed their way through the rocks; there was no short cut. The result of the efforts of these great workmen is absolutely neglected today, but some day it will be cherished by the world and the world will protect it."[5] Longmen, alongside many other ancient monuments, has been a true creation of modernity—a site of mental projection, a symbol of timeless perfection, and an object of scientific classification and analysis.

How did Longmen—a run-down place at the turn of the twentieth century—emerge as a source of fresh spiritual inspiration for important American and Japanese opinion-shapers such as Ernest Fenollosa (1853–1908), Okakura Kakuzō (1862–1913), Charles Lang Freer (1854–1919), and Langdon Warner (1881–1955) who were interlinked with each other? What impact did their affinity with ancient sites in North China have across the Pacific? To answer these questions, this chapter first investigates the social conditions that led ancient Chinese sites to become an inspiration for some leading American and Japanese intellectuals and connoisseurs who sought to reform their own traditions. Then, I zoom in on Freer at Longmen and the circle of people who influenced him and fine-tuned America's cultural taste. The following section argues that Freer's epiphany about Longmen manifested part of a movement bound by the common advocacy of Asia, but driven by different purposes and by heterogeneous groups represented by Japanese scholar, nationalist and pan-Asianist Okakura.

EASTERN TRADITION AS A SOURCE OF
INSPIRATION IN THE UNITED STATES

By the turn of the twentieth century, three major sociocultural develop-ments—anxiety over industrialization, the increase of overseas travel, and an expanded knowledge of Europe and Asia—had led to a strong conviction among many influential and wealthy Americans that, in the emerging field of Asia studies, art and aesthetics, "the two great streams of European and Asiatic practice, held apart for so many thousand years, have, at the close of the nineteenth century, been brought together in a fertile and final union."[6]

First, from around 1860, in reaction to industrialization and the rapid growth of a modern society, Americans—including the Boston Brahmins[7] and other industrialists, philanthropists, and antiquarians—had embraced Chinese classical art with one eye on America's future role in the Asia Pacific and the rest of the world. This trend can also be explained by America's aspirations to gentility, grandeur, and a sense of destiny, as reflected in the collecting of Chinese artifacts in Europe. At the same time, admiration for Chinese culture blossomed in new forms among Japanese, Chinese, French, Swedish, British, and German elites. Such a movement, where cultural homogenization and cultural heterogenization occur simultaneously, has been characterized by some as cultural globalization.[8] America's interest in (re-)discovering East Asian ancient ruins and traditions may have been partly inspired by transcen-dentalism, not only breaking with Puritan intolerance but also articulating inherent sympathy with Oriental thought and spiritual values.[9]

American appropriation of Chinese historical monuments may also have grown out of a desire to allay the anxieties inherent in modernization and industrialization or, conversely, anxiety about being left behind in the rapid march of modernization and industrialization. In sociology and Freudian psychology, anxiety involves both conscious and unconscious mechanisms of externalization[10] and internalization, a paradox reflecting both the obdurate and malleable aspects of personality and culture.[11] Externalization refers to the notion that individuals crippled by anxiety project their internal character-istics on to the outside world, particularly on to other people. Internalization, on the other hand, is the outcome of a social process of symbolic interaction, a transformation and conversion of the self whereby one learns to see oneself from the perspective of others. In this quasimystical way of thinking, ancient sites enkindle mystical moments of exaltation, illumination, and self-trans-formation when "the two become one entity; time and space are abolished": The perfect structure of these artifacts brings the mind to a state where the self becomes one with the spirit of humankind.[12]

Second, from the beginning, American society had been deeply influenced by the European tradition of *Bildungsreise*. Traveling to Europe, ingesting culture and the arts in France, Italy, Greece, and other European countries formed a part of the passage to adulthood among the privileged classes of the Eastern seaboard of the United States. Together with the popular commentary it inspired, touring abroad "influenced conceptions of national identity and formed part of a public debate about how the United States should behave in the world."[13] The large body of foreign travel literature produced by the American literati, including James Russell Lowell (1819–1891), Henry James (1843–1916), and Mark Twain (1835–1910), expressed both a vision of the world and outcomes ranging from a fascination with the Anglo-Saxon myths to a reverence for foreign civilizations.

Third, American knowledge of Asia and the world during this period had historical antecedents. Commencing in 1784, private trade and the U.S. naval presence in the Asia Pacific, especially during the Jackson years,[14] brought Chinese porcelain, paintings, and furnishings into American homes on the East Coast. In 1831, Nathan Dunn (1782–1844), a Quaker missionary and merchant who lived in China for twelve years, shipped back to the United States what was the largest collection of Chinese artifacts in the world at the time. In 1838, Dunn's China objects were exhibited in the "Chinese Museum" in Philadelphia, in space provided by the Philadelphia Museum Company. The exhibition attracted 100,000 visitors and an equal number when it moved to London in 1842.[15] Early American maritime traders who had traveled to China also bequeathed a literary legacy to the country.[16]

Post-bellum America spawned new waves of foreign travel. A modernizing Japan increasingly charmed many young Americans, who embraced new ways of looking at the Asia Pacific.[17] One of them was Charles (Charley) Appleton Longfellow (1844–1893), a Harvard Law School dropout and eldest child of the popular American poet Henry Wadsworth Longfellow (1807–1882).[18] The introduction of regular commercial steamers between San Francisco and Yokohama in 1867, the transcontinental railways that spanned the United States, and the opening of the Suez Canal in November 1869 all made travel to the Asia Pacific easier. Charley Longfellow was well-traveled, fond of yachting, and born into a leading New England family whose home had been the headquarters of George Washington. His mother, Frances Elizabeth Appleton, left him a considerable inheritance following her tragic death in 1861. Growing up in a privileged literary family in the Boston area certainly opened up a wider world of social and cultural capital. Charley Longfellow knew Bayard Taylor and Lt. George Henry Preble, the *New York Tribune* correspondent and a relative by marriage, who had been on Commodore Mathew Perry's expedition to Japan in 1853. Richard Henry Dana, Jr., an author who visited Japan for two weeks in 1860, was the Longfellows' next-door neighbor in Cambridge, Massachusetts. *Across America and Asia: Notes of a Five Year Journey around the World and of Residence of*

Arizona, Japan, and China, by Raphael Pumpelly, one of the first American geologists and mining engineers hired by the Japanese and Chinese governments, was read in the Longfellow home as well.[19] In June 1871, planning to stay for only a few weeks, Longfellow sailed for Japan from San Francisco for what became a twenty-month visit, so enchanted was he by the country. Like many American sea travelers of his day and even today, Longfellow's sojourn in Japan took him on to China, in his case for nineteen days from March 13 to April 2, 1873, on his journey home. He went first to Shanghai, then on to Hankou, Beijing, Nanjing, Fuzhou, Xiamen, Hong Kong, Canton, and Macau.[20]

Conditioned by the above three factors—the effects of industrialization, the ease of sea travel, and an expanding knowledge of Asia—by the late nineteenth century, the ancient monuments and artifacts of China and Japan were increasingly being regarded as legitimate forms of art, as sources of inspiration in America's attempts to modernize its own traditions—a mirrored parallel in modern world history. Ernest Fenollosa (1853–1908), an instrumental guide to Freer on Japanese and Chinese antiquities, observed in 1907: "It is not too much to say that the thousand and one innovations, the freer technique, and the generally increasing breadth of view of our recent generations, are either the direct or indirect results of this contact [with the Asia Pacific]."[21] He commented on the lack of awareness of Japanese and Chinese Buddhist art in Europe and the United States, as well as in Japan and China themselves, before the middle of the nineteenth century: "before oriental examples opened our eyes, few of our artists even suspected [their] existence." Around 1860, however, "Japanese art . . . began its course of freeing our Western practice from a narrow realism of long tradition."[22]

CHARLES LANG FREER (1854–1919) AND OTHER SHAPERS OF AMERICAN CULTURAL ORIENTATION

This section discusses early American affinity with Longmen through the lens of Charles Lang Freer, probably the first American who went to that historical site, and the circle of people who influenced him and helped redefine American cultural taste. The late nineteenth and early twentieth centuries witnessed a significant number of Americans who, like Freer, went to China with the intention of seeking connectedness and inspiration from the Eastern past, wherever it might be encountered. This paralleled a similar historical experience in which American missionaries reached out and tried to save the world but ended up changing America itself.[23]

More than any other ancient ruins, Longmen in China's interior captivated Freer, who lived nearly twenty thousand kilometers away. Born in Kingston,

New York, to a poor family of six children, Freer lost his mother at the age of fourteen. He was forced to drop out of school in grade seven to work in a cement factory. With the assistance of Frank J. Heckler, who recognized the young man's bookkeeping and organizational skills and later became Freer's business manager, Freer went on to make a fortune in the railway, automobile, and investment industries.[24] He was a self-made person who exemplified the American dream. Freer was diagnosed with neurasthenia, a nervous condition common among the upper classes in the United States at that time. Part of the cure involved encouraging sufferers to rest and spend time in the wilderness. Living in an industrialized society which valued material extravagance, Freer found peace and satisfaction in nature and the purity, simplicity, beauty, and harmony of artworks from all cultures and periods that expressed his own coherent aesthetic vision. His ideas and collecting were permeated by certain key themes, which he compared over a wide range of examples.

One of these themes was tonalism. Represented chiefly by George Inness and James McNeill Whistler, tonalism emerged in American landscape paintings in the 1880s, introducing an emphasis on mood and shadow; it frequently manifested in pervasive washes of color suggestive of atmosphere or mist. Between 1880 and 1915, dark and neutral hues, such as gray, brown and blue, or yellow and olive, dominated the compositions of many American artists, tonalities shared by the unknown stone carvers of the Longmen caves. In a journal entry written on the train from Beijing to Luoyang, Freer praised the healing power and beauty of his favored color palette and the subtle natural hues of the North China Plain, as yet untouched by industrialization. He also expressed a yearning for tranquility and simplicity amid the hustle and bustle of an industrialized age:[25]

> All day through a continuous garden of farms, pale green, yellow green, onion green and the green of recently sown grain, gray & corn colored grasses—deep reddish purple of the shrub from which small brooms are made—Furrowing the land for seed planting with two circular stones fixed to an axle—shoveling sand through sieves and piling in heaps resembling American haycocks—bricks making in foot mounds,[26] thrashing and winnowing grain, ploughing steel and wood—and harrowing the soil, stone rollers—women picking cotton, persimmon trees in fruit, digging sweet potatoes—During afternoon mountain range at West. Camels laden with sweet potato vines, carts loaded with baled cotton.

Despite his lack of formal training in Buddhism and foreign languages, Freer, then in his mid-fifties—what were to be the last few years of his life—and well-traveled, gave himself over to the study and appreciation of the stone icons at Longmen. To Freer, Buddhism, like other world religions, offered healing power to deal with the pressures and spiritual needs of the modern world: "All earthly existence is full of sorrow, and . . . the only deliverance from sorrow is the renunciation of the world and eternal rest. Seclusion from the world and the active business of life was obviously the first essential of the saintly life of Buddhism, as of all ascetic forms of religion."[27]

"For those with the power to see beauty, all works of art go together, whatever their period," wrote Freer.[28] The Buddhist stone icons at Longmen—especially those carved during the Northern Wei dynasty prior to the seventh century—struck a chord with Freer, who rejoiced in recognizing the linkages between the Hellenic and Chinese civilizations: "Here Greek power and intellectual predominance shown in the hundreds of huge figures are softened by dreamy ideals born of the Buddhist belief in the knowingness of all existence . . . The story of the beauty of these temples from which forever a stream of joy flows."[29]

This tendency for commonality across traditions was deliberately cultivated by a group of American public intellectuals. As early as 1907, Fenollosa, a close friend and adviser to Freer, suggested that attention be paid to the distinctive unity of the Freer collection of American and Eastern art objects, "which is destined to play a great part in developing the future art of America."[30] Even before he had concentrated his energies on collecting early Chinese Buddhist sculptures, Freer was seeking out elements of synthesis and kinship in the three divisions of his collection: the pictorial work of James NcNeil Whistler; glazed pottery from Egypt, Babylonia, Persia, India, China, Korea, and Japan; and Chinese and Japanese paintings. These three groups were interrelated, first through the ideal of historical completeness, where the paths of the world's advance could be seen. Second, their kinship was established through "the mysteries of light-play in the composition of these tones," the "secret chord" that pulls even the later dark limestone sculptures and pebble-like stones from Longmen into a "harmonic scheme" of green, gray, brick-red, and stone-brown, yellow, olive, and azure.[31]

Besides Fenollosa, Freer also formed deep association with four talented American painters, James McNeill Whistler (1834–1903), Dwight William Tryon (1849–1925), Abbott Handerson Thayer (1849–1921), and Thomas Wilmer Dewing (1851–1938). Together, they had a profound effect on Freer's collecting habits, both of Eastern artworks and Western painting:

> It was these late 19th century American paintings and the men who created them that had helped develop Freer's initial artistic vision. They enriched his predilection for subtlety with their own sense of refinement, and this cultivation of taste enabled Freer to appreciate Fenollosa's standards and to play a major part in the enhancement of the public's appreciation of art.[32]

Freer's imagery of Longmen was forged through studying, seeing, and comparing. In the series of lectures he gave in 1908 about Mt. Mihintale, the ancient cities of Anuradhapura and Polonnaruwa, Sigiri, Buddhist rock temples, and other monuments in Ceylon, and later around 1911 on Longmen (Lung-men) itself, Freer attributed the origins of cave sculpture and the selection of sites for Buddhist monuments to India:

> In most of the hill ranges of India and its borders, caves were occupied by holy men who soon learned to excavate them, while the face of the rock invited the earliest efforts of the sculptor. In addition to the selection of a rock suitable for excavation, the Buddhists, like the monks of the West, seem to have been influenced in the choice of a site, not only by such practical considerations as accessibility, the presence of a good water supply, and proximity to trade routes, but also by a keen appreciation of natural beauty. Magnificent scenery has a more intimate connection with the subject of Buddhism than appears at first sight. . . . In China, Java and Japan, the same principle has guided the selection of sites, with a distinct preference for the neighborhood of mountain streams.[33]

By his own choice, Freer spent the two weeks from October 29 to November 14, 1910, at Longmen only in the company of Nan Mingyuan, his Chinese business associate, and some Chinese guards and workers. He was among the very few privileged Caucasians, and perhaps the first American, to have ventured to Longmen, a fact which "means much to American art and scholarship," as an interviewer wrote in 1911.[34] Freer played a major role in an international effort to classify early Chinese Buddhist sculpture as art, and in some cases superior to their counterparts produced by any other civilization: "With what has been discovered by Chavannes, the French investigator sent to China by the French academy three years ago, and what I found myself there is absolutely no question that an art did exist in ancient China. And it was an art that, in my opinion, equals or exceeds in value that which is known to the world at present."[35]

Longmen appealed to Freer for two main reasons, both reflecting his identity as a discriminating and sophisticated pioneer of the arts in an age of industrialization in the United States. First, to Freer, the craftsmanship and artistry of the unknown sculptors of Longmen bridged temporal and regional divides and invited him to enter into a quasisymbiotic union with their creators. He yearned to converse with the inner soul of historical ruins. Despite not having begun to collect artworks until the 1880s, as a late starter, Freer practiced "intelligent travels," to use his own words, going far beyond mere sightseeing and the dilettantish purchase of works of art.[36] His imagination and distillation of what he saw as the inner life of art gave a distinctive character to Freer's patronage and generosity to artists and the public alike. In 1911, introducing Longmen to a wider group of audience in Japan, Freer stated:

Little is known of the details of the wonderful craftsmanship of these early sculptors, but of course their cutting was done with metal tools. One can see that there is a marvelous skill of and in the strong and delicate modeling; a miracle of training in the designs that surround many of the niches; and in the almost imperceptible figures cut in very low relief which decorate the back of many of the niches; also in the lotus dias found in the center of the ceilings of many of the large temples . . . To do work of this kind is to have perfect foresight and perfect skill; is to be both craftsman and artist. It is, first of all, to be a composer, a draftsman and then, as a crowning grace, to be a technician—a master of one's tools.[37]

Second, Longmen inspired Freer to envision a universal, monist world of unity and congruence expressed through a variety of authentic emotions, faiths, expressions, and relationships between men and women of different classes. This potent but somewhat neglected countercurrent of enlightened humanity stressed the possibility of creative relationships with humanity at large in a world of war, conflict, excess, and poverty. For him, the religious emotion felt in the strange light of the temples at Longmen symbolized the kind of relations which were "not merely the love of imitation but representative of genuine faith."[38] "In these sculptures one feels that the joy of work never departed from the workman; that he saw ever before him new pleasure in perfection of form and feeling."

This unitary vision extended to the complementarity of the sexes. The muscular lines of some of the Longmen figures were balanced by the spirit of femininity and "held together from end to end with a perfection of unity." It was the strength of feminine influence that molded the divinity of the Amida Buddha and his emanation Kwanyin into a gentler form. "To the Buddhists the true man was a combination of man and woman." To Freer, Longmen's caves manifested perfection of human creativity:

Wandering before the thresholds of these grottoes, many of which are grass-covered and all of which open outward to the clear, quickly flowing river and then through their lines and masses of unending sculpture above, below and on all sides of you, if, indeed, an unusual experience and the impression left upon the mind is far finer than those experienced in the renowned temples of India, Java or Japan. Here one sees much greater variety in size, form and decoration, to say nothing of mystery and environment.[39]

This combination of ideals also derived partly from Freer's experience of the World's Columbian Exposition, held to commemorate the 400th anniversary of Columbus' voyage to America, which opened in Chicago in May 1893. Over 200 World Congresses or Parliaments of anthropology, labor, medicine, temperance, commerce and finance, literature, history, art, philosophy, religion, and science were held in conjunction with the Chicago exhibition. Refinement, knowledge, and care of the soul were the values most cherished by Freer,[40] connecting him with Longmen and others of kindred spirit. At the time, the World's Parliament of Religions was hailed as marking the "dawn of a new era of brotherhood and peace."[41] According to one contemporary observer, monist idealism sought to "secure from leading scholars, representing the Brahman, Buddhist, Confucian, Parsee, Mohammedan, Jewish, and other faiths, and from representatives of the various churches of Christendom, full and accurate statements of the spiritual and other effects of the religions which they hold upon the literature, art, commerce, government, domestic and social life of the peoples among whom these faiths have prevailed."[42]

OKAKURA KAKUZŌ (1862–1913) AND OTHER MOBILIZERS OF THE PAST

America's initial appropriation of Chinese culture and ancient sites was inseparable from Japan, a cultural and logistical bridge in modern history. Mention of monist idealism and transcendentalist spirituality evokes the figure of Okakura Kakuzō and modernity's dilemma that had motivated him to visit Longmen in 1893, one of the earliest visits by a foreigner in the late nineteenth century.[43] From the turn of the twentieth century, prominent members of the Japanese intelligentsia, including Sekino Tadashi (1867–1935), Tokiwa Daijō (1870–1945), Mizuno Seiichi (1905–1971), and Nagahiro Toshio (1905–2001), made expeditions to Longmen and other ancient sites in North China. Their research into the materials, style, age, and condition of the sculptures, in combination with their extensive use of textual evidence—drawn from Chinese historical records—illuminated the significance of Longmen as the finest and the most representative Buddhist site of its time.

Although Okakura and Freer had nothing in common at a personal level, both men were bound by modernity's dilemma and their common advocacy of Longmen and other things Eastern within a small, privileged circle with centers on the eastern seaboard and elsewhere in the United States. These complex relations largely arose from Japan's own anxiety about its new role in the modern world as a result of rapid industrialization, and also from the curiosity of the Boston Brahmins who sought spiritual fulfillment and mental solace in Catholic and Asian artifacts and ancient ruins. To Freer—a product of the rising United States as a new world powerhouse with aspirations for geocultural status—Longmen represented the purest and highest achievement of the Chinese civilization that spoke to the Hellenic past and thus ought to be assigned a new value. To Okakura, Longmen helped legitimize modern Japan as the heir to the glorious past of Eastern civilization and the unrivaled leader of Asia.

Okakura's achievements as a nationalistic intellectual and his ties with the city of Boston and Harvard University are indicative of his entangled agendas and roles, operating under different mantles. With views bordering on ultranationalism and racism which was generally tolerated by his American contemporaries,[44] Okakura devoted himself to placing Japan at the center of the modern world order in the Asia Pacific, while consolidating his ties with the closely knit group of Boston Brahmins during the last ten years of his life (circa 1903–1913). The spread of Japanism in Europe and the United States can be seen in the writings of Edward Sylvester Morse, William Sturgis Bigelow, and Percival Lowell, in addition to Charles Appleton Longfellow. Daisy Yiyou Wang and Satoko Fujita Tachiki emphasize antimodernism as the binding factor that connected Okakura and the Boston Brahmins. "In meeting Okakura, the Boston Brahmins, as spiritual seekers from another continent, found a kindred spirit." For Bigelow, Okakura was a "queer duck, but he knows a lot."[45]

Born into a samurai family in 1862 in the treaty port of Yokohama, Okakura began studying English at the age of six or seven in the home of American missionaries James C. Hepburn and S. R. Brown.[46] In 1880, he graduated from the University of Tokyo, then an English institution, where he studied philosophy, Darwinism, English literature, and Western analytical philosophy alongside Americans who included Ernest Fenollosa.[47] Fenollosa was a Harvard graduate who came to Japan in 1878 to teach Western philosophy; he soon became enthusiastic about Japanese art and its preservation and was later a curator at the Boston Museum of Fine Arts (MFA). Influenced by Fenollosa's belief in the dichotomy between traditional Japanese spirituality and idealism and Western materialism and realism, Okakura started his first job in the Ministry of Education as secretary for music education in the summer of 1880.

Throughout his life, Okakura campaigned for the *kokugaku* or Japanese national learning movement and championed the notion that "Asia is one." Asia, to Okukara, knew no political boundaries, and modernized Japan was its undisputed leader.[48] In the 1880s, wearing his other hat, and together with Fenollosa, Okakura pioneered a new art movement. In 1884, the pair formed a new organization called *Kangakai*, the art appreciation club, supported by William Bigelow, a wealthy Bostonian and a then personal friend of Fenollosa. This new Japanese art movement was designed to empower traditional Japanese Buddhist art in particular with new Euro-American art theory as a way of countering the mindless imitation of Western forms in Meiji Japan. From September 1886 to October 1887, the Japanese Ministry of Education financed Okakura and Fenollosa on a trip to study art education in the United States (Boston, New York, and Washington, DC), France, Italy, Spain, Austria, and Germany. In 1889, Okakura established and headed the Tokyo Fine Arts School while serving as director of the Imperial Museum. However, ten years later he was forced to resign as a result of opposition to his new Japanese art movement and his involvement with his boss Kuki's wife. Shortly after, in 1899, with seventeen followers, he set up the *Bijutsu-in* (Academy of Fine Arts) to "protest against two movements—the pseudo-classic and pseudo-European," claiming that "art must be national, and that we shall be lost if cut away from our traditions."[49] Okakura was clearly using Longmen and other Chinese sites to react against antitraditionalist excesses and total Westernization in modern Japan.

In 1896, when Fenollosa resigned from his position at the MFA in Boston following his scandalous affair with Mary McNeil Scott (whom he later married), William Bigelow, a leading trustee of the MFA, invited Okakura to fill the role, unaware that Okakura had been forced to resign following a similar transgression in Japan. Between 1906 and 1910, Okakura served as advisory director of the Japanese and Chinese department of the MFA, where he served as curator from 1910 until his death in 1913. His main responsibility was to catalog and purchase Chinese and Japanese art objects in Japan and, especially, in China.[50] During his last ten or so years, Okakura split his time between Boston and Izura, Japan. Okakura died on September 4, 1913, in Tokyo. A memorial service was held at Boston's Fenway Court on October 20, 1913. The tribute read at the memorial service included the words: "In a true sense he was an exemplar of the finest traditions of his land, a nationalist and yet a cosmopolitan—a choice and potent personality the like of which our times may hardly produce again."[51]

Between July 15 and December 7, 1893, Okakura visited China for the first time, traveling via Korea and Shanghai on his return route, shortly before the Sino–Japanese War broke out. This field trip was sponsored by the Japanese Ministry of Education and the Ministry of the Imperial Household. He traveled in company with his houseboy, helper, and photographer Hayasaki Kōkichi.[52] Some speculated that his trip to Beijing with an interpreter, Miwa Kōsaburō, had a covert intelligence-gathering purpose. In addition to his 1893 trip, Okakura visited China three more times: in 1906–1907, to purchase artworks for the MFA; in June–July 1908, when he stayed in Manchuria and Beijing for two weeks on his way back to Japan from Europe; and finally in May–June 1912, when he spent a month in Beijing and Manchuria.

To aid in the task of cataloguing Japanese artworks and writing a history of Japanese art, Okakura set out to investigate Chinese sites and objects with a view to establishing the origins of Japanese art, and finding Chinese parallels. In early August the pair arrived in Tianjin before moving on to Beijing.

Their explorations of Beijing's temples, ancient sites, and the antique markets of Liulichang, as well as the urgings of their Japanese and Chinese contacts, prompted them to make an unplanned detour, south to Henan through Hebei Province. After visiting the White Horse Temple, the first Buddhist temple in China, and other places in Luoyang, Okakura spent September 19, 1893, at Longmen.[53]

In his early years, Okakura had believed that Hellenism implied a dominant, Eurocentric role for Roman and Greek art in the development of the Gandharan and Chinese Buddhist art styles. The resultant view that Indian-Chinese Buddhist art was subsidiary to the Greco-Roman classical style was unacceptable to Okakura. Alongside Longmen, Luoyang, the Northern Wei capital, provided Okakura with clear evidence of the transmission of the Hōryūji style of Japanese Buddhist art directly from China, rather than from Greece and Italy. This discovery had important implications for Okakura's narrative of Chinese history, according to which the Yuan Mongols destroyed Chinese civilization, thereby promoting Japan—an equal to the West in the modern world order—to center stage in Asia, in place of a backward China. On the other hand, the stone sculptures and *apsaras* found in the Central Bin-yang Cave at Longmen, and dating from the Northern Wei, clearly pointed to Hellenic-Indian influence. This compelled Okakura to acknowledge Hellenism as one foreign factor, along with Assyrian and Egyptian influences. According to Jing He, Okakura's new understanding of the role of China in the transmission of Japanese art enabled him to argue for a pure, equal, and independent style of Japanese art before the coming of Hellenism. On the latter point, his 1893 field trip had proven that Okakura was wrong about the Hellenistic influence in Japanese art in the debate over Hōryūji, established in 607 and today a UNESCO World Heritage site.[54] It should also be noted that, on the relationship between the art of the East and the West, Okakura was inconsistent over the years and in different contexts. In 1887, he asserted that "art belongs to heaven and earth, and there cannot be a distinction between the East and West."[55]

In 1908, Okakura charted the influence of Bactrian Greece on China as a central element, spread by way of Greek Bactrians and Scythians to Gandhāra and North China.[56] Bactria (*daxia*) formed part of the Balkh region in Northern Afghanistan, as well as today's Uzbekistan and Tajikistan in Central Asia. The Greco-Bactrian kingdom existed from 250 to 125 BCE. Greco-Bactrians later expanded into the Indian subcontinent and established the Indo-Greek kingdom from 180 to 130 BCE. Situated in the northwestern corner of the Indian subcontinent and including Chinese Turkestan, the Gandhāra region linked Greco-Bactrian Buddhist stone sculptures with their Chinese counterparts. Fenollosa was probably wrong to place the influence of Greek-Bactrian art on China at a later period, the seventh and eighth centuries.[57] Besides influences stemming from western Asia, notably Persia and Bactria, Osvald Sirén considered Central Asia—through the intermediation of Scytho-Sarmatian art—as providing the main impetus for the Chinese animal sculptures of the Han dynasty. He argued that it was only toward the end of the sixth century that the "two currents [from central and western Asia] . . . flowed together and formed one great stream of artistic development. Then the animal and the religious sculpture became almost homogeneous in their artistic character; Buddhist art flourished into a more mature national product, swallowing all the foreign influences which had reached Chinese sculpture from time to time."[58] In any case, the timing of Okakura's discovery was crucial, as by 1908 the Hellenic-Indian Buddhist link had been a hot topic for at least ten years among European explorers and sinologists such as Charles-Eudes Bonin, Édouard Chavannes, and Aurel Stein. In my opinion, it is hard to avoid the impression that Okakura was reinterpreting existing research findings from Europe to suit his own agenda.

Japanese nationalism and its tension with other political ideologies were central to Okakura's relationship with Longmen, China, the United States, and Europe. The political agenda becomes more conspicuous when the journal entries he made on his tour of Europe in 1887 are considered.[59] The discovery of Longmen and other ancient monuments helped Japanese intellectuals to recontextualize their own religious and cultural heritage in order to deal with the competing claims of West and East more effectively. Okakura was an important promoter of Japan and Japanese art who made himself a leading authority on Japanese and Chinese art and art history among the Western audiences of his day.

Freer acknowledged Okakura's huge influence in the United States and Europe in a letter dated September 6, 1913, to Langdon Warner, a Harvard professor, another important figure in the modern history of Longmen:

> Yesterday's papers print a dispatch from Tokio dated September 4, announcing the death of Okakura. His unexpected calling will doubtless create considerable stir in Boston, especially in museum circles. Although it was my misfortune to find many defects in Okakura, I recognize that his efforts did very much universally to awaken interest in oriental art, and I shall always have genuine admiration for certain characteristics of the man. I often wish that I had known less of certain official and personal doings of the man.[60]

In reply, Warner's letter, dated Thanksgiving Day, 1913, and written from Peking, asked: "Was it not a generous thing of Doctor Ross to give his prize statue to the M.F.A. in memory of Okakura, whom he did not entirely like and never professed to understand? I think that Okakura's work there in making people's eyes see was greater than the man himself, and he was an extraordinary creature."[61]

CONCLUSION

The more I see of the Chinese people, the greater is my respect and esteem. Someday they will again be what they were centuries ago— world-leaders in many ways.

—Charles Lang Freer[62]

In the latter half of the nineteenth century, thanks to steamships and other technological improvements, some privileged Americans and Japanese, such as Ernest Fenollosa (1853–1908), Okakura Kakuzō (1862–1913), Charles Lang Freer (1854–1919), and Langdon Warner (1881–1955), passionately promoted Chinese culture and stone Buddhas at Longmen as a form of art but with disparate political messages. They imagined that they were able to communicate with the human past through visiting and comparing ancient sites. After experiencing historical sites in person, many participated more actively and intelligently in giving direction and added purpose to their own country's domestic and global relationships. Their dissonant, fin-de-siècle discourses about Longmen intersected and ultimately gave strengths to each other. Thus, seminal American and Japanese efforts helped spawn transcultural connections and borrowings that till today stimulate reverence for a common global heritage. Four additional observations can be drawn.

First, the geopolitical and geocultural message of the early American exploration of the Longmen site formed a sharp contrast with Japan's case. Freer's imagination reflected the global bent of America's Pacific Era of the early twentieth century, as President Theodore Roosevelt called it, which meant that "the commerce and the command of the Pacific will be factors of incalculable moment in the world's history."[63] Endorsing Freer's various China initiatives including the American Archaeological School in China, Roosevelt clamored for a universal world to "bring all nations into intimate and brotherly association," and this was America's destiny during the fierce race of nation-states in the Pacific Ocean where East and West finally becomes one:[64]

Our place as a nation is and must be with the nations that have left indelibly their impress on the centuries. . . . The Atlantic era is now at the height of its development and must soon exhaust the resources at its command. The Pacific era, destined to be the greatest of all, and to bring the whole human race at last into one great comity of nations, is just at the dawn. . . . We cannot escape our destiny if we would; we must face the performance of our duties to mankind. . . . It depends largely upon the present generation of American citizens to say whether our country shall keep in the van of this glorious work and win the chief triumphs for ourselves; or whether we shall supinely permit others to make the effort, to run the risk and to reap the reward.

In Roosevelt's new world order, "the awakening of China is one of the great events of our age," and it was urgent to grasp and command China for "the West to implant its ideals in the Orient, in such fashion as to minimize the chance of a dreadful future clash between two radically different and hostile civilizations."[65]

Second, epiphanies such as that experienced by Freer at Longmen revealed the unity of humanity, in the sense that ancient sites were converted into a modern narrative of the past as well as the future. According to Freer, what lay beyond the physical, material world was a reality that transcended history and almost had a will of its own:

> The effect of the work at Lung-men is so rich, so harmonious, so right in the relation of its parts and in the relation of the whole to its surroundings, that when I first saw it, I forgot for the time the stupendous schemes and designs lost in the overwhelming effect as a whole, it is all thrilling and living—with these strange figures in different planes of relief, bending with curve of niches and vault, gazing out into the faint grey stillness born of many centuries.[66]

Third, this new, transcendent understanding of history gave human beings a voice to articulate their sense of uncertainty and stress caused by industrialization as much as their vision for modern society. For example, urging that humanity be united on a higher plane, Freer yearned "to unite modern work with masterpieces of certain periods of high civilization harmonious in spiritual suggestion,"[67] albeit aware of the limitations inherent in the challenge. In 1895, Freer found solace on a visit to Amo-no Hashidate, one of the most scenic places in Japan, meaning "bridge in heaven," on the Tango Peninsula, northern Kyoto Prefecture, spanning the Miyazu Bay:

> If the Buddhist idea is correct and I am inclined to think it is, not one earthly existence alone is sufficient but several are required to develop an imaginative mind. Does not this then mean experience and does not intelligent travel bring experience?? . . . My present trip has brought me one valuable sensation at least of a long and welcome escape from high pressure American business life. Foreign business life is as nearly rapid as ours. So the influence I wish for exists not at Paris, Bombay, Calcutta, Hongkong, Shanghai, Kobe, Kioto, or any other large cities I have yet found. Kioto, Japan's old capital comes nearest to it, because of its excellent old time art, in many forms, beautiful surroundings and absence of large commercial enterprises.[68]

Fourth, the impact of early American and Japanese discovery of Longmen were compromised in two ways. The first limitation arose from the very nature of the loose confederation of organizations and individuals who were bound together only by their common advocacy of China and Asia typified by

Charles Lang Freer with a predilection for one humanity and Okakura Kakuzō with the addition of pan-Asianism. The second limitation can be seen in the contradiction between idealism and reality which confronted every visitor to Longmen in the early twentieth century—although some were oblivious to it, some were aware of it, while others were incapable of reconciling the contrarieties involved.[69] This dilemma was evidenced in the records left by two other visitors to Longmen. The first extract is a translation from the book in Swedish by Carl Gustaf Emil Mannerheim (1867–1951), who visited Longmen on June 8, 1907. Mannerheim was engaged in an undercover intelligence mission, traveling through Asia overland from St. Petersburg from July 1906 to October 1907. He was attached to a scientific expedition led by French archaeologist Paul Pelliot, with whom he traveled from Tashkent to Kashgar:

Early in the morning, I made an excursion to a mountain situated 25 *li* south of the city [Luoyang], which is called "Lung-men" [Longmen] (the Dragon Gate). . . . The mountain is divided by a broad ravine, at the bottom of which flows a branch of the Luo river. . . . The mountains are not tall, yet they are beautiful, with steep sections and with the bare cliff-face protruding everywhere. . . . The mountain walls on both sides of the river reveal a multitude of grottoes, beginning with niches so small that each one frames its own Buddha image and ending with domes measuring 12–14 m in length and 7–8 m in width. . . . Everything here is strongly reminiscent of the domes and traces of painting that can be seen in the Turfan region. But here each Buddha statue and every ornament has been carved into the cliff, in many cases very artistically. An unbelievable amount of work has gone into it. . . . Several of the domes are blackened by soot from fires and many sculptures have been deprived of their heads or one of their limbs. Primitive stairs worn smooth by use and railings carved into the cliff testify that in the distant past this place was a much-visited pilgrimage site. This is said to be no longer the case.[70]

The second is from a letter written from a Peking hotel by Langdon Warner to Charles Freer in April 1914:

In spite of the fact that I had come over here expecting the very best from the Chinese and recognizing that I was on the track of the very roots of all the things that I most valued and loved in the Orient—still I have been getting more and more disgusted with the <u>present</u> [emphasis in original] state of things and more and more discouraged with the Chinese themselves. . . . One could not be human and go through this country with his eyes entirely on the past, if it were possible he could build up a grand and altogether admirable idea of the people. But with the government on the edge of ruin and no honest Chinese stirring a hand to help it, with sickness and disease and cruelty as bad as they were in Marco Polo's time, with no attempts to clean up morals or minds or bodies I cannot regard the most fascinatingly interesting trip in the light of a picnic. Like Nelson at

Trafalgar "I wouldn't be elsewhere for thousands." But like Nelson I am scared to death; and I have no faith in the ultimate result for the country.[71]

These diverse voices, although seemingly dissonant, evidenced a yearning for a unity of meaning based on a universal spirituality for varied purposes. Mannerheim's sober prospecting, Freer's visionary ardor, Okakura's understanding of a cultural exchange between East and West, and Warner's lamentation of past greatness mirrored in present misery—all projected the monumental ancient certainties of Longmen on to the unsettling reality of technological and social change in the modern world. What in a distant past had been a place of pilgrimage like Longmen could still, over a century ago and even today, spark—as artifacts, as a site—intense emotions about life, nation, and the universal future. Indeed, these voices, redolent of modernity, still reverberate in today's heritage practices.

NOTES

A part of the title of this chapter is derived from Charles Lang Freer's handwritten travel journal with grammatical adjustment. The original reads: "the influence from the souls of these stone saints," November 14, 1910, Charles Lang Freer Papers (CLF Papers thereafter), Freer and Sackler Gallery of Art Archive, Smithsonian Institution in Washington, DC.

1. "China's Precious Relics," an interview with Langdon Warner, *Central-China Post,* March 28, 1914.

2. K. Ian Shin, "The Chinese Art 'Arms Race': Comsmopolitanism and Nationalism in Chinese Art Collecting and Scholarship between the United States and Europe, 1900–1920," *The Journal of American-East Asian Relations,* 23 (2016): 229–56; Karl E. Meyer and Shareen Blair Brysac, *The China Collectors: America's Century-Long Hunt for Asian Art Treasures* (New York: Palgrave Macmillan, 2015); Daisy Yiyou Wang, "Charles Lang Freer and the Collecting of Chinese Buddhist Art in Early-Twentieth-Century America," *Journal of the History of Collections* (2015): 1–16. For a different approach, see Dong Wang, "Internationalizing Heritage: UNESCO and China's Longmen Grottoes," *China Information* 24, no. 2 (2010): 123–47; Dong Wang, "Restructuring Governance in Contemporary Urban China: Perspectives on State and Society," *Journal of Contemporary China* 20, no. 72 (2011): 723–33.

3. Freer's travel journal, November 14, 1910, CLF Papers.

4. David Hogge, "Freer's Longest Trip to China 1910-1911," *Arts of Asia* 41, no. 5 (2011): 122–34.

5. Freer's lecture on Longmen in Japan during his homeward trip, 1911, CLF Papers, transcript provided by David Hogge.

6. Ernest Francisco Fenollosa, "The Collection of Mr. Charles L. Freer," *Pacific Era* 1, no. 2 (1907): 57–66, p. 59. Ernst F. Fenollosa, "The Coming Fusion of East and West," *Harper's Magazine,* December 1898, pp. 115–22.

7. The Boston Brahmins refer to the old aristocratic gentry in the Boston area which were interlinked through marriage, wealth and exclusive social circles, such as the Adam, Cabot, Boylston, Appleton, Dana, Forbe, Winthrop, and Peabody families. Daisy Yiyou Wang and Satoko Fujita Tachiki emphasize antimodernism as the binding factor that connected Okakura and the Boston Brahmins.

8. William H. Goetzmann, *When the Eagle Screamed: The Romantic Horizon in American Diplomacy 1800–1860* (New York: Wiley, 1966); Justin Jennings, *Globalization and the Ancient World* (Cambridge: Cambridge University Press, 2010).

9. Thomas A. Tweed documents late-nineteenth-century attitudes among Americans who variously criticized Buddhism, sympathized with it, or even converted to it. Thomas A. Tweed, *The American Encounter with Buddhism, 1844–1912: Victorian Culture & the Limits of Dissent* (Chapel Hill, N.C.: University of North Carolina Press, 2000, 1st ed. in 1992); Arthur Christy, *The Orient in American Transcendentalism: A Study of Emerson, Thoreau, and Alcott* (New York: Columbia University Press, 1932); Connie A. Shemo, "Imperialism, Mission, and Global Power Relations in East Asian Religions in the United States," *Oxford Research Encyclopedia of Religion*, August 2017, DOI: 10.1093/acrefore/ 9780199340378.013.403.

10. Patrick James, "Externalization of Conflict: Testing a Crisis-Based Model," *Canadian Journal of Political Science* 20, no. 3 (1987): 573–98; Joseph Sandler, *Projection, Identification, Projective Identification* (London: Karnac Books, 1988).

11. Charles Horton Cooley, *Human Nature and the Social Order* (New York: Charles Scribner's Sons, 1902); Herbert C. Kelman, "Compliance, Identification, and Internalization: Three Processes of Attitude Change," *Journal of Conflict Resolution* 2, no. 1 (1958): 51–60; Gary Alan Fine, "Symbolic Interactionism in the Post-Blumerian Age," in *Frontiers of Social Theory*, ed. by George Ritzer (New York: Columbia University Press, 1990), pp. 117–57; King-To Yeung and John Levi Martin, "The Looking Glass Self: An Empirical Test and Elaboration," *Social Forces* 81, no. 3 (2003): 843–79.

12. Kathleen Pyne, "Portrait of a Collector as an Agnostic: Charles Long Freer and Connoisseurship," *The Art Bulletin* 78, no. 1 (1996): 75–97.

13. Previous research has investigated the international perspective of affluent Americans through their travels to Europe. Christopher Endy argues that transatlantic travels and the "popular commentary it inspired influenced conceptions of national identity and formed part of a public debate about how the United States should behave in the world." Christopher Endy, "Travel and World Power: Americans in Europe, 1890–1917," *Diplomatic History* 22 (Fall 1998): 565–94.

14. Andrew C. A. Jampoler, *Embassy to the Eastern Courts: America's Secret Pivot toward Asia, 1832–1837* (Annapolis, Md.: Naval Institute Press, 2015).

15. John R. Haddad, "China of the American Imagination: The Influence of Trade on US Portrayals of China, 1820–1850," in *Narratives of Free Trade: The Commercial Cultures of Early US-China Relations*, ed. by Kendall Johnson. Hong Kong: Hong Kong University Press, 2011), pp. 57–82.

16. Their accounts include André Everard van Braam Houckgeest's two-volume *Voyage de l'Ambassade de la Compagnie des Indes Orientales Hollandaises, vers l'Empereur de la Chine, dans les Années 1794 & 1795* (published in 1797–1798 in Philadelphia); Amasa Delano's *Narrative of Voyages and Travels, in the Northern*

and Southern Hemispheres, Comprising three Voyages round the World; together with a Voyage of Survey and Discovery, in the Pacific Ocean and Oriental Islands (1817, Boston); and Robert Waln, Jr., *China: Comprehending a View of the Origin, Antiquity History, Religion, Morals, Government, Laws, Population, Literature, Drama, Festivals, Games, Women, Beggars, Manners, Customs, &c of that Empire* (1823, Philadelphia). In 1843, the *Journal of the American Oriental Society* was founded. The 1840s also saw the publication of Robert B. Forbes' *Remarks on China and the China Trade* (1844 Boston, Mass.) and Samuel Shaw's *The Journals of Major Samuel Shaw, the First American Consul at Canton* (1847, Boston, Mass.).

17. Masao Miyoshi, *As We Saw Them: The First Japanese Embassy to the United States* (Philadelphia, Pa.: Paul Dry Books, 2005, 1st ed. 1979), ch. 1. The first Japanese known to have lived in the United States was Nakahama Manjirō (John Mung), who was saved at sea in 1841 by an American whaleboat and later served in the first Japanese mission to the United States in 1860. Dong Wang "The United States, Asia, and the Pacific, 1815–1919," in Alan McPherson, ed., *The Society for Historians of American Foreign Relations (SHAFR) Guide: An Annotated Bibliography of American Foreign Relations since 1600* (Leiden: Brill, 2017), online.

18. Elisabeth Doucett, *Finding Aid: Charles Appleton Longfellow (1844–1893) Papers, 1842–1996* (Cambridge, Mass.: Longfellow National Historic Site, U.S. National Park Service, U.S. Department of Interior, 2006), pp. 19–20. Charley's sister, Alice Mary Longfellow (1850–1928), "Morituri Salutamus, or The Old Order Changes" and "Reminiscences of My Father" (very brief), Alice Mary Longfellow Papers, Longfellow National Historic Site archives, Cambridge, Mass., AML-B20-F13 and AML-B20-F15, transcribed by Amy Harlow in summer 2016. In *Longfellow's Tattoos: Tourism, Collecting, and Japan* (Seattle, Wash.: University of Washington Press, 2004), Christine M. E. Guth discusses the role of photographs, tourism and globe-trotters such as Charles Longfellow in defining U.S. home life, cultural authenticity and the taste for Japanese art and artifacts in the latter half of the nineteenth century.

19. While in Japan, Charley Longfellow received a letter from his sister Edith dated July 19, 1871: "I was eager to hear more about your voyage to Japan, for you know I have just finished the great [Raphael] Pumpelly and feel quite learned in that quarter." Christine Wallace Laidlaw, ed., *Charles Appleton Longfellow: Twenty Months in Japan, 1871–1873* (Cambridge, Mass.: Friends of the Longfellow House, 1998), p. 26. Raphael Pumpelly, *Across America and Asia: Notes of a Five Year Journey around the World and of Residence of Arizona, Japan, and China* (New York: Leypoldt & Holt, 1870), 2 vols.

20. Charles Appleton Longfellow (CAL), "Charles Appleton Longfellow China Journal," 13 March to 2 April 1873, CAL Papers Box 10, Folder 9, transcribed by Regine Thiriez in 2011. CAL Journal, January-June 1874, China and Southeast Asia, transcribed by Frances Ackerly in 2010, Longfellow National Historic Site archives, Cambridge, Mass.

21. Fenollosa, "The Collection of Mr. Charles L. Freer," p. 57.

22. Fenollosa, "The Collection of Mr. Charles L. Freer," p. 59. Nancy Gwinn details the role of the Smithsonian Institution, various learned and scientific societies, and the U.S. government in creating an international framework for the orderly

exchange of official government publications, particularly in the 1870s and 1880s. Nancy E. Gwinn, "The Library of Congress, the Smithsonian Institution, and the Global Exchange of Government Documents, 1834–1889," *Libraries and the Cultural Record* 45, 1 (2010): 107–22.

23. David Hollinger, *Protestants Abroad: How Missionaries Tried to Change the World but Changed America* (Princeton, N.J.: Princeton University Press, 2017).

24. Thomas Lawton and Linda Merrill, *Freer: A Legacy of Art* (D.C.: Freer Gallery of Art, 1993); Charles Lang Freer and James McNeill Whistler, *With Kindest Regards: the Correspondence of Charles Lang Freer and James McNeill Whistler, 1890–1903*, ed. by Linda Merrill (D.C.: Freer Gallery of Art, Smithsonian Institution Press, 1995).

25. Freer's travel journal, October 19, 1910, CLF Papers.

26. This appears to refer to the kneading of clay brick mud as part of the traditional brickmaking process in China and elsewhere.

27. Freer lecture notes, no box numbers, CLF Papers, transcript provided by David Hogge.

28. Freer, quoted in the exhibition room downstairs in the Freer Gallery of Art, Washington, DC, as of March 2018.

29. Freer lecture on Longmen, circa 1911 in Japan, CLF Papers, transcript provided by David Hogge.

30. Freer's friendship with Ernest Fenollosa began in 1901, although they had met in the 1890s. See the preface by Fenollosa's wife Mary Fenollosa, who edited her husband's posthumous notes in Ernest F. Fenollosa, *Epochs of Chinese and Japanese Art: An Outline History of East Asiatic Design* (London: William Heinemann, 2nd ed. 1921), vol. 1, 1st ed. 1912.

31. Fenollosa, "The Collection of Mr. Charles L. Freer," p. 63; Aline Saarinen, *The Proud Possessors: the Lives, Times, and Tastes of some Adventurous American Art Collectors* (New York: Random House, 1958).

32. Lawton and Merrill, *Freer*, chs. 5 and 6; Nichols Clark, "Charles Lang Freer: An American Aesthete in the Gilded Era," *The American Art Journal* 11, no. 4 (1979): 54–68; Fan Jeremy Zhang, "Asian Art for U.S. College Museums: Two Pioneering Collectors, Charles Freer and Dwight Tryon," in *The West in Asia and Asia in the West: Essays on Transnational Interactions*, eds. by Elisabetta Marino, and Tanfer Emin Tunc (Jefferson, N.C.: McFarland & Company, 2015), pp. 192–202.

33. Charles Lang Freer, Lecture manuscript on the Buddhist ruins in Ceylon, 1908, date is the author's inference, CLF Papers, transcript provided by David Hogge.

34. Charles Lang Freer, Interview, the press cutting published in *Detroit News Tribune*, after February 1911, date suggested by David Hogge.

35. Freer, Interview, 1911.

36. Freer's letter on a hand scroll to Dwight William Tyron on June 17, 1895 from Amo-no Hashidate (Amanohashidate), Japan, CLF Papers, provided by David Hogge.

37. Freer's lecture on Longmen in Japan, 1911.

38. Freer's lecture on Longmen in Japan, 1911.

39. Freer's lecture on Longmen in Japan, 1911.

40. Charles Lang Freer's letter to Dwight William Tryon, July 27, 1893, CLF Papers.

41. Charles C. Bonney (1831–1903), a Chicago lawyer, judge, teacher, and orator, was president of the World's Congress at the World's Columbian Exposition of 1893. The *New York Times* Obituary of Charles C. Bonney, August 24, 1903. Among the prevailing harmony at the event, Bonney also sensed a "note of discord": "This is not surprising, for differences of opinion on every subject must exist; but it is remarkable that most of the criticisms have come from persons assuming to speak in the name of Christianity."

42. Bonney, Charles C. "The World's Parliament of Religions," *The Monist* 5, no. 3 (1895): 321–44, p. 330.

43. Among Longmen's Japanese visitors in premodern times was monk Enchin. In 855, Enchin had made a pilgrimage to the Pagoda of Śubhakarasiṃha at Longmen. Many people mistakenly regard Okakura as the first person to visit Longmen in the nineteenth century. But German geologist Ferdinand von Richthofen must have visited Longmen before 1882. Ferdinand Freiher von Richthofen, *China: Ergebnisse eigener Reisen und darauf gegründeter Studien* (Berlin: Verlag von Dietrich Reimer, 1882), vol. 2, p. 501.

44. Satoko Fujita Tachiki, "Okakura Kakuzo (1862–1913) and Boston Brahmins," PhD dissertation, the University of Michigan, 1986. On February 11, 1904, a few days after the outbreak of the Russo–Japanese War, Okakura and his students, Taikan Yokoyama, Sunso Hishida, and Shisui Rokkaku, boarded a ship for Seattle, Washington. Despite their misgivings about America's attitude toward the war, they were treated favorably by the American press: "Mr. Okakura, with the insight of the scholar and the fearless conviction of the erudite critic, reported that Japan had nothing to learn from the art of the Western world. On the contrary, it behooved the government to preserve Japan's priceless inheritance and enlarge upon it in the lines upon which enduring fame had been achieved." The *New York Times*, report, March 20, 1904.

45. Tachiki, "Okakura Kakuzo (1862–1913) and Boston Brahmins," p. 9 and p. 92.

46. F. G. Notehelfer, "On Idealism and Realism in the Thought of Okakura Tensin," *The Journal of Japanese Studies* 16, no. 2 (1990): 309–55.

47. In Japan, Fenollosa's annual salary was 4,500 yen (US$ 4,374), eight times Okakura's pay at the Ministry of Education and twelve times Fenollosa's salary at the Museum of Fine Arts in Boston. Tachiki, "Okakura Kakuzo (1862–1913) and Boston Brahmins," p. 19. The two men eventually fell out with each other.

48. Okakura Kakuzō, *The Ideals of the East: The Spirit of Japanese Art: The Spirit of Japanese Art* (New York: Cosimo, 2007), pp. 1 and 90–102, 1st ed. 1904.

49. Tachiki, "Okakura Kakuzo (1862–1913) and Boston Brahmins," p. 69.

50. *The New York Times*, September 1, 1913. Isabella Stewart Gardner (1840–1924) Papers, 1760–1956, Archives of Isabella Stewart Gardner Museum in Boston, Mass.

51. Okakura Yoshisaburo's letter to Isabella Gardner dated September 11, 1913, informed Mrs. Gardner of the passing of his brother Okakura Kakuzō: "While in full consciousness [just before his death] he mentioned your name and wanted me to send you his heartfelt gratitude for your long friendship." Okakura Yoshisaburo's Letter to Mrs. Gardner on September 11, 1913. Isabella Stewart Gardner (1840–1924) Papers, 1760–1956, Archives of Isabella Stewart Gardner Museum in Boston, Mass.

52. For a detailed itinerary and map of Okakura's trip, see his journal "Shina Ryokō Nisshi," published in Okakura Kakuzō, *Okakura Tenshin Zenshū* (Tokyo: Heibonsha, 1979–1981), vol. 5, pp. 120–6, p. 492.

53. Shaanxi and Sichuan were on Okakura's original itinerary.

54. *Okakura Tenshin Zenshū*, vol. 5, p. 28, p. 51 and p. 151. For information about the Hōryūji debate and the impact of Longmen on Okakura, see Jing He, "China in Okakura Kakuzō with Special Reference to His First Chinese Trip in 1893," PhD dissertation, the University of California at Los Angeles, 2006, pp. 35–43, pp. 169–75.

55. Okakura, "Kangakai ni oite," in *Okakura Tenshin Zenshū*, vol. 3, pp. 173–8.

56. Masako N. Racel, "Okakura Kakuzō's Art History, Cross-cultural Encounters, Hegelian Dialectics, and Darwinian Evolution," *Asian Review of World Histories* 2, no. 1 (2014): 17–45. Wang Yiyou, "The Loouvre from China: A Critical Study of C. T. Loo and the Framing of Chinese Art in the United States, 1915–1950," PhD dissertation, Ohio University, 2007, pp. 129–130.

57. Its core territories are in today's Afghanistan and Pakistan. Fenollosa, *Epochs of Chinese and Japanese Art*, vol. 1, pp. 73–89.

58. Osvald Sirén, *Chinese Sculpture from the Fifth to the Fourteenth Century* (London: Ernest Benn, 1925), pp. 26–7.

59. Okakura, "Ōshū Shisatsu Nisshi," in *Okakura Tenshin Zenshū*, vol. 5, pp. 281–448.

60. Freer, Correspondence: Warner, Langdon, September 6–December 25, 1913, CLF Papers, Box 25, Folders 18–22; Box 26, Folders 1–8.

61. Langdon Warner's letter to Charles Lang Freer on November 27, 1913, p. 8. Langdon Warner Papers (LW Papers thereafter), Harvard Houghton Library, MS Am 3138, Box 8, Folder 26, "American School of Archaeology Expedition, Freer, 1913–1914."

62. Freer's letter from Kaifeng, Henan, China, to his business partner Frank Hecker (1846–1927), October 24, 1910, CLF Papers, Box 10, Folders 26–34; Box 11, Folders 1–10, Correspondence: Hecker, Frank, J., Col., 1892–1917.

63. Theodore Roosevelt, "The Pacific Era," *The Pacific Era* 1, no. 1 (October 1907): 1–4.

64. Roosevelt, "The Pacific Era." Freer and Roosevelt correspondence, CLF Papers, Box 21, Folder 19, Correspondence: Roosevelt, Theodore, 1906–1913.

65. Theodore Roosevelt, "The Awakening of China," *The Outlook*, November 28, 1908, pp. 665–6.

66. Freer 1911 interview.

67. Freer's letter to Samuel P. Langley, December 27, 1904, CLF Papers, Box 235, Folder 7, Offer of Gifts and Bequests.

68. Freer's letter on a hand scroll to Dwight William Tyron on June 17, 1895.

69. Discussing what travel can do and cannot do for travelers, Joshua Fogel uses Okakura as an example of the latter. According to Fogel, Okakura was oblivious to the Chinese reality when promoting his "Asia is One" message, despite the fact that he had traveled in China. Joshua Fogel, *The Literature of Travel in the Japanese Rediscovery of China, 1862-1945* (Stanford, Calif.: Stanford University Press), pp. 85–90.

70. Carl Gustaf Emil Mannerheim, *Resa genom Asien: Fältmarskalken Friherre C. G. Mannerheims dagböcker förda under hans resa Kaspiska havet—Peking* (Stockholm: Lindfors Bokförlag A. B., 1940), vol. 2, p. 327. Flemming Christiansen assisted the present author with Swedish sources. A former general in the Russian imperial army, Mannerheim had served in the Russo–Japanese War, and was president of Finland from 1944 to 1946. Stig Jägerskiöld, *Mannerheim: Marshall of Finland* (Minneapolis, Minn.: University of Minnesota, 1986), ch. 4.

71. Langdon Warner's letter to Freer in April 1914, LW Papers, Box 8, Folder 26, "American School of Archaeology Expedition, Freer, 1913–1914."

Chapter 5

Longmen and Osvald Sirén (1879–1966)

Sirén, a pleasant young Swedish scholar of Italian Primitive . . . has an international reputation for sound scholarship. And it is particularly interesting to me that he is seriously thinking of turning his whole attention to Oriental art. He needs but another nudge to topple him over the line. For this reason I hope you may be able and willing to see him when he comes to New York this week and to fire him with some of your contagious enthusiasm. Since the death of Mr. Fenollosa we have no one with a decent training in Western art to apply scholarly methods on the Orient. He will be a great catch for our school.

—Letter from Langdon Warner to
Charles L. Freer, February 28, 1915[1]

Modernity gave birth to a new Longmen. Besides the aforementioned figures such as Kang Youwei, Luo Zhenyu, Édouard Chavannes, Victor Segalen, André Malraux, Okakura Kakuzō, and Charles Lang Freer, Longmen's high status today can also be attributed to Osvald Sirén (1879–1966), a Swedish intellectual and the first recipient of the Charles Lang Freer Medal in 1956. Joining the host of Longmen's admirers in the early twentieth century, Sirén promoted Longmen's rock temples and stone sculptures as works of art and human innovations, "fully equal, if not superior, to Western products of corresponding kind."[2] In fact, he even boldly contrasted Michelangelo's sculpture of Moses with certain representations of Buddhas or *arhats* at Longmen, which in Sirén's view embodied the deeper meaning of human life.

Place, for instance, the great Buddha of Lung Men [Longmen's Buddha of Vairocana] at the side of Michelangelo's Moses. . . . [A] figure in complete repose, strictly frontal, seated with legs crossed and arms close to the body.

139

. . . The quiet rhythm of the mantle folds which fall in a series of long curves over the broad chest serve to accentuate the reposeful harmony of the whole conception . . . It matters little whether we call it a prophet or a god, because it is a complete work of art permeated by a spiritual will which communicates itself to the beholder. A work like this makes us realize that all the individual differentiations which are so far pressed in the sculptures of the Renaissance are only ripples on the surface of the great waters which form the fountain of life.[3]

This chapter begins with a sketch of Osvald Sirén and his affinity with rock cave images at Longmen.[4] We then proceed to explore Sirén's role in turning Longmen's statues into an academic topic in historiography, and Longmen as a place where antiquity met modernity. The last section focuses on the limitations and legacy of Sirén seen through the prism of cultural interactions between Europe, the United States, Japan, and China in the conflicted age of modernity.

OSVALD SIRÉN: A SKETCH

Born in 1879 in Helsinki, Osvald Sirén was a Swedish scholar, antiquarian, curator, connoisseur, and a shaper of the modern fate of Chinese Buddhist cave temples, stone images, and, above all, the arts and crafts of China.[5] With an initial academic interest in Italian Renaissance art of the fifteenth-sixteenth centuries, Sirén quickly rose to prominence in the European and American academic field. He was a professor of fine arts at the University of Stockholm from 1908 to 1923, but was captivated by the Eastern especially Chinese art in 1915 and thereafter. Between 1926 and 1945, he worked as curator of painting and sculpture in the National Museum in Stockholm.

Widely connected throughout Europe, the United States, Japan, and China, Sirén was, during most of his adult life, affiliated with the Theosophical Institute headquartered in Point Loma, California, which was part of a global movement that espoused spirituality of the East and universal brotherhood. Reaching beyond industrial materialism, theosophy and spirituality played a role in Sirén's extraordinary contribution to the modern reappropriation of Chinese antiquity including those at Longmen.

In April 1918, after crossing the Atlantic, then following the usual route taken by many of his American associates and colleagues, via California, Japan and Korea, Sirén made his first trip to Longmen, Gongxian, and another ancient city Kaifeng. Sirén later returned to Longmen and also surveyed the White Horse Temple on December 9–14, 1921, in Luoyang on his way back from Xi'an.[6]

The Chinese perspective on Osvald Sirén[7] and his work involving Longmen highlights the unusual contributions made by him and a small circle of

Euro-American-Japanese intellectuals in the East Asia field.[8] However Chinese research on Osvald Sirén has been piecemeal at best. Thus far, of Sirén's many works, only *Walls and Gates of Peking: Researches and Impressions* has been translated into Chinese, a book that is gaining renewed popularity.[9]

Sirén struck a balance between competing ideas and between political ideologies. During his lifetime before the much wider diplomatic recognition of the PRC in the 1970s, he allegedly was the only leading scholar who gained admittance to both Communist China and Taiwan.[10] In 1957, the seventy-eight-year-old Sirén perceived himself as a conduit of understanding between the East and West and "between the extremes of radical anti-traditionalism and reactionary condemnation of everything new":[11]

I feel myself as a bridge-builder, not only between East and West but also between the two factions of the East [traditional China and radical Communist China]. I deplore that so much of noble old China is being swept away by ruthless reformers, but China has to make up for such lost time in the past and the Western nations have all a share of responsibility in the present uproar in the Eastern world.[12]

In his scholarship, Sirén's approaches paralleled his political and cultural proclivities. He not only strengthened a belief in the outstanding quality of Chinese stone images but, more importantly, also sought to define the aesthetic properties common to all cultures. Described as "a mixture of the bee and the fox,"[13] Sirén unified opposites in ways rarely seen—he combined monumentalism and care for detail, burning passion and calm analysis, incisive abstraction and thorough specifics. But, above all, one can sense the strong rationalism and dedication to critical observation that ran through his life and oeuvre. This distinct combination is visible in Sirén's daring characterizations of Michelangelo's Moses, the Slaves, or some of the female figures for Michelangelo's Tomb of Pope Julius II, as juxtaposed with the colossal Vairocana Buddha[14] and other stone statues at Longmen. Sirén wrote (Figure 5.1):

None of them [Michelangelo's sculptures] remain in a restful attitude; they are all deeply disturbed, represented in situations of extraordinary psychic effort or interior struggle which shakes their frames and strains every nerve. . . . The base note of Michelangelo's art is one of tragedy, and it could hardly be otherwise, as he drew the full consequences of the incompatibility of the Pagan and the Christian attitude towards the human figure.[15]

Sirén navigated the tension of modernity and modernism with the skill of a diplomat amid the irreconcilable positions of his time. He pursued, as we shall see in the following text, the secular and the spiritual, the authentic and the reproduced, epiphanic imagination and scientific precision, unicity and

Figure 5.1   Juxtaposition of Longmen's Vairocana Buddha and Michelangelo's Moses.
Source: (a) Osvald Sirén, *Chinese Sculpture from the Fifth to the Fourteenth Century* (London: Ernest Benn, 1925). (b) Photo by Westerdam. Creative Commons.

fragments, the universal and the distinct—all manifestations of modernity's contradictions. For Sirén, fine art and history, born of modernity, expounded modern persons' cultural disenchantment and reenchantment with modern life ingrained in the Protestant Reformation, the scientific revolution, the Enlightenment, romanticism, and other social and intellectual fluxes.

Unlike Kang Youwei who yearned for the precise, realistic portrayal of the real world in Western oil painting,[16] Osvald Sirén rejected the mundane European realism of his time as overbearingly constraining while identifying the "primitive" and "abstraction" as emerging aesthetics. Although highly sensitive to historical circumstance of art production, he was never sensitized to Walter Benjamin's notion of "art fetishism."[17] Nor did Sirén emphasize the irreconcilable pursuit of the authentic *Other*,[18] for he thought that it was possible to hone one's ability to sense the universal sublime.

Although a historical empiricist, Sirén emphasized the detached imagination of human creations which broke the bonds of mundane constraints. For him, the emotionally detached and observing flâneur of modernity had no interest, yet his career and comportment were discretely stage-set and he reticently narrated his observation rather than exalting his own impact. Among those who pioneered the use of photography in documenting history and art, he was never disturbed by the reproducibility of art. Sirén juxtaposed art works in innovative ways, a practice André Malraux later developed into the notion of an *imaginary museum*,[19] yet each pursued different effects in doing so. Sirén's interest in Longmen's stone Buddhas suggests that he cherished both epiphany and the full history of them as human artistic creations rather than the devotion they once had attracted.

CHINESE STONE ICONS AS A RESEARCH TOPIC IN HISTORIOGRAPHY

In his 1915 letter to Freer, Langdon Warner suggested how the burgeoning academic discipline of East Asian studies was attracting young and credible scholars like Osvald Sirén. Chinese antiquities, including Longmen's stone votive images, were becoming an integral component of this new cultural ferment.

Aside from archaeology, our contemporary understanding and appreciation of Longmen's specimens is largely derived from epigraphy and iconography, two of the separate branches of historical, art, and aesthetic studies that converged in the early twentieth century. Osvald Sirén consolidated the disjointed historical knowledge, enlarged it, and added new layers of critical experience. He deployed his cultural capital in the early 1920s while preparing his monumental four-volume *Chinese Sculpture from the Fifth to the Fourteenth Century*, a lavishly printed work where Sirén laid solid foundations for a subject which was scarcely known either in the West or the East and proved himself to be an important authority in the field.

During the latter half of the nineteenth century, foreign interest in China and Japan mushroomed, as did Chinese and Japanese interest in other countries. This was the age of economic development, oceanic steamers, electricity, the camera, and other great technological advances. Social change was tangible in the growing curio and antique markets that catered to foreign tastes in China's major cities. The earliest known foreign photographs of Qing China were published in 1873 by John Thompson (1837–1921), who provided his readers with a glimpse of the dealers and antiquarians active in Beijing at the time:[20]

> Like all foreigners who visit Peking [Beijing], I had been but one night in the metropolis when I found myself waited upon by half a dozen dealers in curiosities, introduced to my notice by a servant whom I had engaged at Tientsin [Tianjin] . . . There are shops of course in this street, as in all others, of the highest respectability, where a foreigner, conversant with the language, can purchase articles at their fair market value. Indeed, taken as a whole, and judging from my own experience, I believe that, in upright dealing, the shop-keepers in Chinese cities are not inferior to those of Europe.

The presence of diverse foreign powers and their citizens in China under the unequal treaty system may account for the fact that, from the outset, expertise and interest in China and Chinese objects had a strongly multinational, indeed international dimension. The looting of the Imperial Summer Palace in Beijing in 1860 by British troops launched an international market in Chinese antique art.[21] In the same period, foreign expertise in Chinese artifacts and history began to emerge in London, Paris, New York, Yokohama, Tokyo, Beijing, and Shanghai. These dynamic, interrelated foreign markets rapidly led to Chinese artifacts being placed on a par with classical European art objects, and in some cases even superseding them in trading. The rise of an intellectual authority within the art world beyond and above national borders generated the need for specialist arbiters like Sirén, who further developed practices of analogy and comparison where Chinese and Asian artifacts became a stimulus to and source of modernity.

Sirén was not alone in pursuing such a role. European American scholar Bernard Berenson (1865–1959)[22] and Sirén had followed similar paths to East Asia, both coming from a specialization in late medieval and Renaissance Italian art. Sirén met Berenson in 1902 on one of his annual visits to Italy. Berenson could at times be bowled over by Chinese paintings. In 1903, Berenson commented that in Chinese painting, "we feel an ecstasy of devotion and vision, here we behold a transubstantiation of body into soul, whereof we rarely get as much as a vanishing glimpse in our own art."[23] Although Berenson's approaches to Italian Renaissance art and his pioneering adoption of photography to art connoisseurship had inspired Sirén, Sirén was the one who used these methods systematically and consistently to identify the characteristics, rhythms, and forms common to all artistic creations, whether originating from the West or the East. And among the two of them, Sirén went on to become a more prolific and respected expert on Chinese art and antiquity.[24]

Sirén's first documented venture into Chinese antiquity was an article published in Swedish on primitive and modern art in 1915. Both following and departing from Berenson, Clive Bell, and Roger Fry, Sirén's broad-brush account of primitive and modern art[25] developed the idea that good art emerged in a creative exaltation of the artist, who used his mastery of materials and form language to give abstract expression to a feeling. Like Berenson, who used a Chinese Buddhist painting of Lohans as the stimulus, Sirén drew inspiration from two Chinese religious paintings from the twelfth century as excellent examples of emotional expressiveness in abstract form, as a creation "from within." "The artist reaches in meditation for the spiritual essence of the motive and integrates it in his expression: The line he draws speaks his soul."[26]

Sirén recalled when receiving the Charles Lang Freer Medal in 1956 how his understanding of East Asia had come to him four decades earlier, probably in 1915 or 1917, like a bolt of lightning, triggered by Denman Ross' comments and gestures in the MFA in Boston, Massachusetts. This became a starting point for his further speculation about the essentials of Chinese art. He recounted:

> I found myself in one of the old exhibition rooms of Chinese painting in the distinguished company of John Lodge and Dr. Ross. My actual knowledge of Far Eastern art was very slight, but I was on the trend of new discoveries and eager to arrive at a better understanding of the essentials in this art, which attracted me irresistibly. By my searching questions I was trying to draw out the secret from these gentlemen who did not lose their patience in explanations. Finally Dr. Ross opened his arms as if to embrace the view in front of him, then joining his fingertips on his breast, said, 'In Western art it is all like this'—illustrating by the gesture the artist's dependence on an outside view or motif. But then, as a second act, he moved his hands from the breast outward again, and said, 'In Chinese painting it is the opposite way'—illustrating by the gesture how something was growing from within, from the very heart or creative center of the painter, and then opening out into flowers of art. The gestures said more than the words and brought home to me a realization of the Chinese point of view in contradistinction to methods of representation common in Western art, and that gave me a starting point for further speculation about the essentials of Chinese painting.[27]

Sirén's memories testified to the birth of the avant-garde East Asian art discipline within the United States, France, Great Britain, Japan, Italy, Sweden, and Germany. By the early twentieth century, Buddhist stone statues at Longmen had become an academic topic, objects of art and commodities at the center of global exchange. And scientific knowledge and narratives of the Longmen relics gave them new meaning and value. The emergence of a shared transcultural, scientific recognition of the essential artistic qualities of Chinese historical ruins was fueled by nineteenth-century advances in philology and archaeology as rigorous, evidence-based sciences. These new academic disciplines examined regularities and patterns in the universal evolution of human societies and civilizations. East Asian artifacts therefore became part of a much larger and ever-expanding market for cultural experience in the modern age.

The vogue of treating Japanese and Chinese artifacts as objects of scientific study received additional momentum when foreign literati became involved. Longmen became a must-see amid the unstoppable urge and enthusiasm for travel and research in China. Okakura's exposition on the spirit of the East to question Western conventions of realism provoked deep changes in perception. His pan-Asianist formulation, "Asia is one," expressed in his short 1904 book *The Ideals of the East: The Spirit of Japanese Art*, was repeatedly cited in the ensuing three decades. It even became the opening phrase of lecture given by Laurence Binyon, one of the first recognizable figures in Anglo-American modernism, at Harvard University in 1933.[28]

Like Binyon, Sirén was a devoted follower of Okakura. Shortly before conducting fieldwork at Longmen in April 1918, Sirén completed the manuscript of a lengthy series of articles on Chinese and European paintings published in the 1918 volumes of *The Theosophical Path*. In the first installment, which appeared in the February issue, Sirén could not resist retelling Okakura's Daoist fable of Boya (Peiwoh, Pai Ya) and the taming of the harp in the Ravine of Longmen. Contrasting the attitudes of West and East toward art and life, Sirén noted that, to the former, a work of art "was primarily more or less a skillful representation of nature," an echo of a person's own moods, ideas, and personality. But, to the latter, the tenor of a work of art was humility, something deeper, displaying a readiness to listen to the message of nature and to learn from it.[29] "Heard melodies are sweet, but those unheard are sweeter," Sirén wrote.[30]

Besides Okakura Kakuzō, Sirén was also in regular contact with Charles L. Freer, who was a fierce promoter of Longmen but, according to Sirén, had no time for Okakura. Information about Longmen was by now widely disseminated in the international press: In 1911 *Art and Progress* announced the publication of *Academy Notes*, the bulletin of the Buffalo Fine Arts Academy, which reprinted "an account of ancient works of art discovered by Mr. Charles L. Freer in cities in the interior of China rarely visited by Caucasians." "Photographs of remarkable stone carvings, found in one of the many ancient temples at Lung-Men, have been lent by Mr. Freer as illustrations and are admirably reproduced."[31]

In July 1917, Sirén met Freer in Detroit, Michigan, studied his collections and sought his advice, joining him again in late November and early December that year. In December 1917, Freer, who was in poor health, was "overjoyed" when he learned that Sirén had decided to sail from San Francisco to visit Japan and China, especially since their mutual friend Langdon Warner would be out there, too. Sirén asked Freer to write letters of introduction to Freer's contacts in Japan and China. "While in China don't miss Lung-men and Yun Kan [Yungang]," Freer urged Sirén. "I wish I had the energy necessary to join you and Warner in the adventures ahead, but I must not chafe against restrictions! Have a look at every fine thing the gods permit, and think kindly of we absent sinners."[32]

The turn of the twentieth century marked a watershed in the recovery of Chinese historical sites, when international studies of the grottoes and iconography of Longmen began to appear in the disciplines of archaeology, sinology, religion, and East Asian art. Broadly speaking, scholars approached Longmen through one of the two avenues: text-based or image-based studies. The two important early publications that between them covered both approaches were *Mission archéologique dans la Chine septentrionale* (1909) by Édouard Chavannes (1865–1918)[33]; and Sirén's four-volume *Chinese Sculpture from the Fifth to the Fourteenth Century*. The meticulous studies produced by these two men remain key reference points for understanding Longmen as well as its modern development.

Chapter 3 demonstrates that sinologist, archaeologist, and historian Édouard Chavannes pioneered the text-based approach to Longmen's rock carvings and inscriptions. He has been credited with devising a method of corroborating ancient geographical, local, epigraphic, and other historical sources in Chinese with archaeological evidence, rather than relying solely on Confucian canonical texts.[34]

Besides Chavannes' eminent works, Sirén absorbed the research findings by Japanese scholars, receiving personal assistance from Sekino Tadashi and other leading Japanese scholars who had made their own expeditions to Longmen from the turn of the twentieth century. Heavily influenced by Euro-Atlantic methodology, their research on the materials, style, age, and condition of the sculptures, in combination with their extensive use of textual evidence—drawn from Chinese historical records—further bolstered the significance of Longmen as the "finest" and "most representative" Buddhist site of its time.[35]

Setting aside the many people who influenced him, what was Sirén's own role in the modern transformation of Longmen? The verdict delivered by Alexander Coburn Soper in 1970 still carries weight: "The beginning reader who takes Sirén seriously as a guide today will still learn a great deal to his profit. He will be occasionally misled, but not for long or (generally speaking) in very important matters."[36] Sirén painstakingly studied the changes in stylistic expression discernible in artifacts within a chronological framework. He applied the techniques of comparative stylistic-chronological analysis to the aesthetic interpretation of Longmen's sculptures, reliefs, and stone inscriptions, identifying the specific political and social contexts of their patronage.[37] Sirén had tremendous respect for the epigraphic evidence from Longmen presented by Chavannes, to the extent that he would sometimes compromise his own finely honed intuition and visual senses in favor of an erroneous interpretation by Chavannes based solely on stone inscriptions. In one case this led to confusions in assessing the style and the chronology of the important trio of imperial Binyang Caves of the Northern Wei dynasty (386–523).[38]

CHINESE STONE IMAGES AS WORK OF ART AND A SOURCE OF INSPIRATION

In his scholarship on Longmen's stone images, Sirén stood for a new type of epistemology, critically appraising the veracity, methods, and scope of the evidence at hand. In the case of historical monuments, he dissected the various elements that went into their creation.

In his 1907 article on Michelangelo's Medici funerary monuments in the new sacristy of the Church of San Lorenzo in Florence, Sirén began by examining the changing politics, financing, timing, and other conditions at the time, then moved onto the practicalities of space, proportion, and material (marble in this case). Then, refuting Dr. E. Steinmann, who claimed to have discovered the "secret" meanings of the Medici monuments,[39] he considered aesthetics, composition, and other factors not controlled by Michelangelo himself.

Sirén also looked at the philosophical and erotic inclinations of Michelangelo as expressed in the four allegorical figures of the monuments: Night [Natten], Day [Dagen], Evening [Aftonen], and Morning [Morgonen].[40] To Sirén, the true inherent meaning of artwork could only be revealed through empathic inspection and diligent empirical examination.

Further, he argued that the process of creation of Michelangelo's Medici monuments dominated all of the above elements: "During the process of the work, the idea expanded and he [Michelangelo] was not any longer interested in giving the figures [the four figures] any particular attributes or literary labels. They became simple, monumental expressions in human form for the multitude of universal forces that the master's imagination saw working in humans and in nature."[41] Sirén's meticulous research on Michelangelo's Medici monuments reflected how Sirén treated sculpture as an expression of a universal process of creation, while being precise about how the imagination was bound by specific historical, physical, philosophical, and financial influences.

Sirén incorporated in his analyses the sources and techniques available to him, including materials, inscriptions, historical records, archaeological findings and photography.[42] This is characteristically represented in his work of 1925, a milestone that primarily focused on the artistic side of Chinese sculpture from the fifth to the fourteenth centuries. For instance, unlike Édouard Chavannes' classification by historical sites, Sirén organized the material according to the evolution of style, which was divided into four stages: the archaic period, the transition period, the period of maturity, and the period of decadence and reflorescence.[43] Within his chronological framework, Sirén established subcriteria of provincial groups, which was a more systematic modern cataloguing. For example, in the section of his book on the period of decadence and reflorescence, he carefully explained all possible factors that led to the decline of large Buddhist stone carving activities at Longmen and other places in North China after the Xuanzong Emperor (685–762, r. 713–756) of the Tang dynasty. These factors included Xuanzong's personal interest in poetry, music, painting, and Daoism; the anti-Buddhist movements; the flourishing of Zoroastrianism, Manichaeism, Nestorianism, and

Mohammedanism in Tang's capital, Xi'an; the disappearance of fervid Buddhism in Central Asia and India; and so on.[44]

Sirén also brought the comparative approach to his methodological framework for Longmen studies that he had applied in his analytical catalog of Italian drawings in the National Museum in Stockholm. The major benchmarks he utilized were those signed Italian artworks that were fully documented, and which could be used for stylistic and other kinds of comparison. This empirical approach involved benchmarking, systematizing, and comparing, and had already gained ground in nineteenth-century science, for example, in diachronic studies of language evolution, in Darwinian evolutionary theory (standing on the shoulders of Linnéan taxonomy), and in archaeology. It gradually replaced older methodologies such as speculative constructivism. Sirén's style of scientific analysis relied on evidential hermeneutics based on the "work" in its own right, supplemented by circumstantial evidence, textual references, and inferences drawn from the artist's biography.

Indeed, Sirén saw forms such as monuments and artifacts as a whole across borders, nation-states, races and cultures, positing a modernity that, as evidenced in Longmen, unified all art. Sirén's approach counterpoised late medieval and Renaissance Italian monuments with the Longmen Grottoes and other Chinese historical monuments, seeing a systematic antithesis. Rhythm, forms, motifs, and creative processes associated with in-depth historical and geographical knowledge were core ingredients of his systematic cultural analysis, which one could term hermeneutic inversion.

Like Ernest Fenollosa's, Sirén's ingenuity lay in his ability to free the conventional approach to Western art from realism, from what he called "fidelity to nature," as the basis of appreciation:

> We Westerners have done our best to bind art down to the world of material phenomena, we have made fidelity of reproduction the highest virtue in painting and sculpture, and have considered that the perfection of art lay in the artist's power to create illusive imitations of nature.[45]

By contrast, rhythm functioned as both a structural and aesthetic device in Asian art. Rhythm reconstituted the Longmen Grottoes as a life organism; it was the "pulse-beat in a work of art," he wrote:

> The more intensely we feel the rhythm in a work of art, the more our aesthetic enjoyment is stimulated. It is through the medium of rhythm that we may enter into a work of art and experience something of the exuberance and glow which fired the artist to creation . . . Rhythm can be conveyed by means of relatively concrete as well as in abstract form; it can be expressed in line or tone, by the balance of cubic forms as well as by a reflex of light, plastically or pictorially.

But it cannot be achieved by a mechanical reproduction of outer form; it must be created from within, out of the union between the artist and his motif.[46]

The concepts of rhythm and form were central to Sirén's innovative theory, which precipitated a value shift in the appreciation of Longmen and other Buddhist ruins in China. Earlier development of these two key concepts can be found in his 1915 and 1917–1918 writings, which argued that true-to-life, realistic pictures of nice views and pretty faces lacked the unity of form and artistic emotion.

Sirén unfolded his understanding of rhythm and form, and its impact on Western art, in two stages. First, he put pre-Renaissance "primitive art" under the spotlight, reaching beyond its origins in Christian religious art and exploring its use of abstract form.[47] Second, he attributed the same creative power to modern art, focusing on the paintings of Paul Cézanne (1839–1906) as great art embodying classical harmony and meaningful form. Sirén predicted the innovative breakthrough in modern art toward "clean and expressive form."[48]

According to Sirén, rhythm and form were inherent in all human creations on earth. Spiritual qualities were revealed in the "harmonious relationship of soul and body, rhythm and form." And during the classical age of European antiquity, "this harmonious relationship was sought in the perfect proportions and the organic form of the ideal human figure." However, this spiritual immanence was lost in later times in European art when "it devoted itself to religious subjects. . . . It never found the path that leads beyond the differentiations of the material world and the limitations of space towards the great rhythm which blends manifested life with infinity." The problem with many of the most famous "religious" sculptures of the Renaissance, Sirén said, was that "they may exhibit a perfect knowledge of anatomical form and muscular movement, they may be startling revelations of dramatic pathos or sentimental reverie," but they fail to invoke an authentic sense of spirituality.[49]

In contrast, the votive stone images at Longmen constructed from the fifth to the twelfth centuries are transhuman, transreligious, transracial, and transcultural beings,

who have reached far above the human stage in their spiritual evolution. They may retain some outward resemblance to human beings, but their essential nature is not like that of ordinary men. They represent rather the unifying basic features of human nature than individual differentiations; they are lifted above all conflicting desires and the opposites of good and evil. Their postures and gestures symbolize spiritual states of consciousness, and their contemplation should lead to a deeper understanding of the inner realities of life. They are not to be worshiped as images, but simply to be contemplated as symbolic manifestations of the great guiding powers in nature and in the life of man.[50]

Endowed with the power of abstraction, Sirén dwelled on the inner, abstract qualities of the Longmen images. He thus elevated Chinese art to a level of universality, equal to the classical art of European antiquity, Renaissance art, and the emerging "modern" art of painters like Cézanne, when judged by the same standards of rhythm and form rather than by race, religion, or nation-state. At the same time, rather than engaging the controversial Greco-Buddhist paradigm of interpretation,[51] Sirén separated purely aesthetic expression of monuments from religious devotion, and gave such expression magisterial weight in his narrative of the "highly important" Longmen sculptures.

One might best characterize Sirén's approach to Longmen statues in terms of contrasting dyads. For his monumentalism was tempered by a strong sense of detail, his passion energized his calm analysis, and his grand vision typically took a back seat to meticulous scrutiny of objects. To him, Buddhas, Bodhisattvas, the lokapālas, and the dvārapālas displayed spiritual power that was beyond intellectual definition.[52] Facial composures, ornaments, garments and draperies of the figures, as well as the postures and positions of the hands (mudrās), legs, and feet, were crucial transmitters of the inner mood, and rhythm was expressed through lines and folds:

> The linear arrangement of their draperies recalls sometimes quite closely the conventions known from early Romanesque sculpture. It is perhaps most evident in some of the seated, cross-ankled figures at Yün Kang [Yungang] or in the Ku Yang tung [Guyang Dong] at Lung Men [Longmen], whose very flat and angular forms are vested in mantles with pleated folds which form a kind of curving wings at the sides of the feet."[53]

Sirén concluded that the Chinese had "infused new artistic significance" into the traditional Indian forms and symbols of Buddhist sculpture. And this idea of sinicization, whether one agrees or not, became a foundation for the study of Buddhism in China, especially its intersection with local society such as Luoyang—a research method critiqued in chapter 1.

How did Sirén penetrate the spirit of Longmen's rock chapels? Theosophy and Lomaland on the Point Loma Peninsula in San Diego, California, with its unusual facilities and environs, may also help us comprehend some motifs and linkages.[54] Also known as the Universal Brotherhood, the Theosophical Society was created in 1875 in New York City by Helena Petrovna Blavatsky, an aristocratic Russian immigrant to the United States, who believed that theosophy—which encapsulated fundamental, ethical, and metaphysical principles about the genesis of the universe and mankind—ran through all religions including Buddhism, Christianity, Confucianism, Daoism, Islam, and Zoroastrianism.[55]

The Point Loma Institute, one of the society's branches, was led by Katherine Tingley (1847–1929) of Newburyport, Massachusetts. Established in

Figure 5.2   Lomaland, San Diego, California, and the reconstructed Greek Theater.
Source: Photo by the author, March 22, 2018.

1897, the hilltop utopian community of Lomaland provided Sirén with a practical foothold. Sirén shared an interest with theosophy in the universal brotherhood of humanity without distinction of race, creed, sex, caste or color; in comparative studies of art, religion, philosophy and science; and in the inherent spirituality of nature and man.[56] Although Sirén appeared to have kept a careful scholarly distance from theosophy,[57] in 1923 he openly defended Tingley's Point Loma Institution as a refuge for dedicated individuals in literary, artistic and practical professions who were working for the "uplifting of humanity"[58] (Figure 5.2).

LIMITATIONS AND LEGACY

In 1956, while reflecting on East Asia art as an academic subject in Europe, Japan, and the United States for half a century, Sirén spoke magnanimously of his predecessors as well as his peers:

> We have to admit that many of their estimates, opinions or theories regarding Chinese painting are unacceptable in the light of a more exact historical knowledge and critical experience, but their wholehearted enthusiasm was of the creative kind and opened new avenues of approach; nor should we be too sure that our critical knowledge is sufficient to save us from illusions.[59]

The same principles should be applied to our assessment of Sirén's role in the emergence of Chinese stone sculptures as treasures and cultural innovations.

Figure 5.3   The Binyang Trio Caves.
Source: Photo by the author, June 25, 2017.

Sirén helped rescue those stone icons at Longmen and other ancient sites from neglect, chiefly as an industrious European and China art historian with some knowledge of Chinese, rather than a sinologist. Yet, his narrative of the Binyang trio caves at Longmen, under the influence of Édouard Chavannes, as noted earlier, is not free of misconception and inchoateness (Figure 5.3).

As pointed out in chapter 3, the construction of all three Binyang Cave chapels (North, Central, and South) began in the Northern Wei dynasty; the Central and South Binyang Caves started in 500 and the North Binyang Cave was added between 508 and 511. Only the Central Binyang Cave was, for the most part, completed in 520 during the Northern Wei; the other two caves were unfinished. The North Binyang Cave chapel was largely constructed between 650 and 683 during the Tang dynasty, whereas renewed work on the South Binyang Cave was conducted probably between 616 and 673; the main figures and niches were finished then.[60] Reading the famous commemorative text inscribed on the slab, authored by Ceng Wenben and dated 641, mounted outside on the outer wall between the entrances to the Central and South Binyang Caves, Édouard Chavannes mistakenly assigned this entire trio to the seventh century during the Tang dynasty. But Sirén's sharp eyes told him that the Central Binyang Cave was made in the Northern Wei at least a century earlier. So Sirén ended up deferring to Chavannes' dating of the three Binyang Caves but indicated with his own visual judgment: "Yet the main stylistic features of the sculptures, discernible in the arrangement of the mantle folds and in the ornamental motives, are still those of the Northern Wei period."[61]

A limitation of a very different kind that beset Sirén and many of his colleagues arose from an historical predicament: Longmen's stone icons captured the world's imagination in the early twentieth century, but Sirén and other privileged scholars from abroad were so taken by their beauty that they did not appear to be disturbed by the harsh everyday life faced by people in China then. Joshua Fogel relates that Okakura was oblivious to Chinese reality when promoting his "Asia is one" mantra, despite having been to China.[62] Sirén's zealous search in China for the beauty lost by Western modernity was likewise a dilemma. And while heaping praise on the great Buddha of Vairocana at Longmen, Sirén and Chavannes composed photographs with their coolies—half-naked in the summer heat in Chavannes' case—at the foot of the giant Buddhas (Figure 5.4).

Moreover, Sirén was planning to carry out excavations in Anhui, Shaanxi and other places when he ventured to China again, this time for over a year in 1921–1922. Although his plans were aborted due to scheduling problems and the disapproval of the Chinese authorities, Sirén corresponded with his compatriot Orvar Karlbeck, who was working as a railway engineer in Bengbu, Anhui, and had developed a strong interest in trading in Chinese artifacts and in excavations.[63] In one letter, Karlbeck told Sirén that, for his forthcoming trip, he would first have to lodge in a Chinese inn and find "not very comfortable" "quarters with a farmer."[64] However, Karlbeck added, on the positive side, recent heavy rains were causing severe flooding, and "it is mostly after heavy rains that important finds are made, so let us hope the same will be the case this year." Karlbeck indicated that with their crops ruined and facing numerous difficulties, the local farmers "will probably be willing to part with their land at a reasonable rate"—archaeologists would routinely buy land they wished to be excavated. In his next letter, Karlbeck wrote:

We have been visited by the worst flood within the memory of living man. About 8,000 square miles have been under water, and it is only recently that the water started dropping. . . . Conditions are of course awfull [*sic*] up in this region now and is [*sic*] gradually getting worse. We are in for a very bad famine probably accompanied by typhus and other diseases. For that reason you may have some unpleasant experiances [*sic*] while up in this part. On the other hand the opportunities for picking up bronzes ought to be very good. There have [*sic*] been a great deal of land slips probably exposing a number of ancient graves and loose objects. Only the other day a friend of mine, who had been travelling up there showed me a sword which he had picked up along the shore of the river. It was of bronze and with fine decorations.[65]

Figure 5.4   Coolie and Longmen's Buddhas (Moya sanfo).
Source: Édouard Chavannes *Mission, archéologique dans la Chine septentrionale*. Plates (Paris: Ernest Leroux, 1909).

Such was the lack of sensitivity to suffering that the search for beauty could beget.

The aesthetic reevaluation of Longmen in modern times, like many other long-neglected historical sites, was an insoluble aporia.

CONCLUSION

Sirén assumed a position in historiography premised not only on superb dispassionate scholarship and tenacity but also on passion for art and impartiality. With an international career in neutral Sweden, and pointedly agnostic yet spiritual, well-trained in art history and versed in the use of up-to-date methods and tools, his important place in Longmen's modern history was warranted for two reasons. First, Sirén's grounding in the "old masters" of the Italian Renaissance, so to say the old gold standard of art appreciation, gave credence to the more universal standard, both new and at the same time of greater antiquity. Another was the decontextualization of art, both geographically distant and outside the realms of known rivalries and contestation, yet knowable through science.

Second, Buddhist icons depicted the hope of release from the cycles of rebirth, the elevation to a supreme state of being. In other words, transubstantiation of body into soul brought to mind in the mystery of the Eucharist and by implication religious conflicts that modernity was at pains to leave behind. But Sirén's interpretation of Longmen's stone carvings sought further to achieve the universal, the ultimate abstraction of life.

What does the story of Longmen and Osvald Sirén tell us about the world of the early twentieth century? First, Sirén's universalizing gaze at Chinese stone Buddhas was in tune with a geohistorical impulse of the time, which whetted the cultural appetite for Central Asia and the Far East. "No professional or human education is complete without a stay in the far east," Berthelot declared.[66] Such a belief, popular among Euro-American elites, defined the global pursuit to understand China, its culture, religion, and historical sites as part of world geohistory.

January 25, 1904, was a founding moment of geopolitics as a field of study, when Halford John Mackinder (1861–1947), a British academic and politician, read his influential polemic, "The Geographical Pivot of History," to the Royal Geographical Society. Mackinder presented two major themes of world history in a pithy formulation. First, during the post-Columbian age, "every explosion of social forces . . . will be sharply re-echoed from the far side of the globe." Second, he stressed the central importance of what he regarded as the global heartland, the core expanse of Euroasia, in the "life of world organism."[67]

Global exploration of and competition for unexplored territories such as Central Asia precipitated many new expeditions, yet Mackinder's rational, strategic analysis annihilated the taken-for-granted racist supremacy of the West and pointed at the possible ascendance of non-Western powers.[68] The rise of modern geopolitics and human sciences demanded a spirituality that knew no borders and a belief in art that put individuals in touch with higher, more universal principles. Meanwhile, art became an object of research and rational scrutiny; it needed scientific explanation and analysis to understand the links between different cultures. Sirén responded to this modern turn toward conceiving humanity as one and toward rational, scientific approaches by elevating the Chinese stone Buddhas to sublime art.

Second, Oswald Sirén stood atop a transcultural wave—the global quest for new inspirations in China in order to revitalize what some influential intellectuals, in the face of modernity at the turn of the twentieth century, regarded as moribund occidental traditions. Where modernity inclined toward the natural, materialistic, secular, rational, technological, systematic, universal, and by implication explicable, its countermovement tore asunder its progress, justice, fairness, morality, authenticity, even beauty and the universality.

Sirén's work on the ancient Chinese stone Buddhas reflected these developments and offered them a point of convergence. He wrote about "a characteristic expression of the scientific culture of the West which has a general tendency to confuse ends and means":

> We have lately been forced to recognize that this culture suffers from serious inner defects; but it cannot be made over again by outer means. Its regeneration must be accomplished naturally as a result of inner growth. Much that may be of use in this direction may be learned from the culture of the ancient nations of the East.[69]

Sirén's style of suasion arose from both spirituality and rationality; he had his epiphany in 1915 or 1917, and the above quote is almost programmatic, published in 1918 during his first journey to China. He soon profoundly influenced the way in which Chinese artifacts were appreciated and understood, reconstituting the meanings of ends and means.

Third, modernity involved a social reorientation from status hierarchies based on descent to meritocracy and material wealth in an industrialized age. Art, cultural knowledge, and philanthropy for educating the masses were refashioned as important symbolic markers of social status. Knowledge, self-restraint, and aesthetic experience replaced self-expression articulated by means of religious devotion, the ostentatious display of wealth, or sheer hedonism. Abstract, conceptual art forms gained ground as tasteful, while naturalistic, decorative, and functional art products were decried as increasingly vulgar. This, in turn, strengthened new forms of social exclusion. Appreciation of Chinese antiquity alongside modern comfort became symbolic of high taste and exclusivity. This was ceremonially endorsed, for instance, by the Swedish Crown Prince Gustaf Adolf and American President Theodore Roosevelt in their support for archaeology and their national collections of Chinese art.[70]

In a major work, *The Rise of American Civilization*, published in 1930, Chinese art was ascribed a categorical value on a par with the best of classical European art: Buddhist images were mentioned in the same breath as Michelangelo's Moses.[71] This echoed Sirén's bold comparison, made a few years earlier, of Longmen's Vairocana Buddha and Michelangelo's Moses. Comparison did change perceptions.

The promotion of Chinese artifacts as inspiration testified to the dream of a human culture in Europe and the United States, a metamorphosis of historical human creations into timeless beauty, going hand in hand with a belief in soul, body, and harmonious spirituality. As a cruel corollary, the modern gaze at the votive stone Buddhas arguably triggered a wave of destruction and division. This was seen in the controversies over the removal of artifacts from their original homes and their appropriation through commercialization and new technologies that superseded the promises of the modern, rational, spiritual, and harmonious. Thus, a new chapter of sin and redemption was to be written as the twentieth century marched on.

NOTES

1. Charles Lang Freer Papers (CLF Papers henceforth), Freer and Sackler Gallery of Art Archive, Smithsonian Institution in Washington, DC, Box 25, Folders 18–22; Box 26, Folders 1–8, Correspondence: Warner, Langdon, undated.

2. Osvald Sirén, "Professor Sirén's Address," in Freer Gallery of Art, *First Presentation of the Charles Lang Freer Medal* (D.C.: Freer Gallery of Art, Smithsonian Institution, 1956), p. 18 and p. 10.

3. Osvald Sirén, *Chinese Sculpture from the Fifth to the Fourteenth Century* (London: Ernest Benn, 1925), vol. 1, p. 20. A contradictory view of the Longmen statues was voiced by Victor Segalen (1878–1919), as discussed in the previous pages, in Victor Segalen, *Chine, La grande statuaire* (Paris: Collections Bouquins, Editions Robert Laffont, 2nd ed. 1995, 1st ed. 1972), chapter 7, "L'hérésie bouddhique," in especially pp. 77 and 81.

4. *Enchanted by Lohans: Osvald Sirén's Journey into Chinese Art* (Hong Kong: University of Hong Kong Press, 2013), by Minna Törmä, solidly accounts core facts of Sirén and China, but does not address the significant place that Sirén occupied in cultural heritage, international relations, and the historiography of Longmen.

5. For an introduction to Sirén and his oeuvre, see Törmä, *Enchanted by Lohans*.

6. For an additional summary of Sirén's travels, see Törmä, *Enchanted by Lohans*.

7. Letter of November 30, 1921, from Feng Yuxiang to Sirén, Östasiatiska Museet in Stockholm, Sirénarkiv, A2: 1921–1929.

8. Wen Yucheng, preface, "Zheren weixiao, qiangu miaodi," in Longmen shiku yanjiusuo, ed., *Longmen liusan diaoxiang ji* (Shanghai: Shanghai renmin meishu chubanshe, 1993), p. 1.

9. Osvald Sirén, *Walls and Gates of Peking: Researches and Impressions* (London: John Lane Ltd., 1924). The three Chinese translations are Xi Renlong, transl. Xu Yongquan, *Beijing de chengqiang he chengmen* (Beijing: Yanshan chubanshe, 1985); Xi Renlong, transl. Deng Ke, *Beijing de chengqiang he chengmen* (Chengdu: Sichu renmin chubanshe, 2017); Xi Renlong, transl. Song Xibing and Xu Yongquan, *Beijing de chengqiang he chengmen* (Beijing: Beijing lianhe chubanshe, 2017).

10. William Watson (1917–2007), obituary of Osvald Sirén, 1966, "Professor Osvald Sirén," *The Burlington Magazine* 108, no. 762 (September 1966): 484–85.

11. Kristin Stapleton, *Fact in Fiction: 1920s China and Ba Jin's Family* (Stanford, Calif.: Stanford University Press, 2016), p. 16.

12. Letter from Iverson L. Harris (quoting Sirén) to Osvald Sirén. Sirénarkiv, December 5, 1957.

13. Watson, "Professor Osvald Sirén."

14. See the Introduction. For a description and debates over the Vairocana Buddha, see ch. 6 of Amy McNair, *Donors of Longmen: Faith, Politics, and Patronage in Medieval Chinese Buddhist Sculpture* (Honolulu, Hawaii: University of Hawaii Press, 2007). On Empress Wu's use of folklore, Confucian, Daoist, and Buddhist deities and goddesses to legitimize her own authority, see N. Harry Rothschild, *Emperor Wu Zhao and Her Pantheon of Devils, Divinities, and Dynastic Mothers* (New York: Columbia University Press, 2015). Works on Buddhism and Longmen include Wang Zhenguo, *Longmen Shiku yu Luoyang Fojiao wenhua* (Zhengzhou: Zhongzhou guji chubanshe, 2006).

15. Sirén, *Chinese Sculpture*, vol. 1, p. 20.

16. Aida Yuen Wong, *The Other Kang Youwei: Calligrapher, Art Activist, and Aesthetic Reformer in Modern China* (Leiden: Brill, 2016), Introduction.

17. Elizabeth Mansfield, "Art History and Modernism," in Elizabeth Mansfield, ed., *Art History and Its Institutions: Foundations of a Discipline* (London: Routledge, 2002), ch. 1.

18. Victor Segalen's discussion of "exoticism" could not resolve the unknowability of the "authentic other," for the other was but a reflection of the own imagination. Marie-Paule Ha, *Figuring the East. Segalen, Malraux, Duras, and Barthes* (New York: State University of New York Press, 2000); Victor Segalen, *Essay on Exoticism: An Aesthetic of Diversity*, transl. and ed. by Yaël Rachel Schlick, with a foreword by Harry Harootunian (Durham, N.C.: Duke University Press, 2002); Victor Segalen, *René Leys* (Paris: Gallimard, 1972).

19. Malraux (and/or his assistants) borrowed ideas and observations from Sirén for his work on the imaginary museum, in most cases without or only with scant acknowledgment of his sources, see Walter Grasskamp, transl. by Fiona Elliott, *The Book on the Floor and the Imaginary Museum* (Los Angeles, Calif,: Getty Research Institute, 2016), ch. 3.

20. John Thomson, *Illustrations of China and Its People: A Series of Two Hundred Photographs with Letterpress Descriptive of the Places and People Represented* (New Delhi: India Isha Books, 2013), 4 vols., vol. 4, plate 11, nos. 28–29,1st ed. 1874 by Sampson Low, Marston, Low, and Searle in London.

21. James L. Hevia, *English Lessons: The Pedagogy of Imperialism in Nineteenth-Century China* (Durham, N.C.: Duke University Press, 2003).

22. Born in 1865 in the Vilna Governorate of the Russian empire, Berenson migrated with his parents to the United States in 1875. A Harvard graduate, Berenson was a prominent and controversial (because of the exceptionally high commission fees he charged for his expertise) figure when it came to influencing the prices of and American taste for Renaissance art.

23. Bernard Berenson, "A Sienese Painter of the Franciscan Legend," *Burlington Magazine* 3 (1903): 3–35, 171–84. For more on Berenson and a series of inner struggles surrounding the *Burlington Magazine*, see Helen Rees Leahy, "'For Connoisseurs': The *Burlington Magazine* 1903–1911," in Mansfield, ed., *Art History and Its Institutions*, pp. 231–45.

24. Carl Brandon Strehlke, "Bernard Berenson and Asian Art," in *Bernard Berenson: Formation and Heritage*, eds. by Joseph Connors and Louis A. Waldman (Villa I Tatti, 2014, pp. 223–4), implies a negative assessment of the reception of Sirén's

scholarship on Italian painting in the United States, unlike the positive judgment evident in the letter from Langdon Warner to Charles L. Freer in February 1915 (quoted above).

25. Osvald Sirén, "Primitiv och modern konst," *Ord Och Bild*, no. 47 (1915): 35–47. Gratitude is expressed to Flemming Christiansen for his help with Swedish sources. The first appearance of China in Sirén's scholarly writings was followed by a series of articles in English on Chinese and European painting published in 1918. Osvald Sirén, "Studies of Chinese and European Painting," *The Theosophical Path* 14–15, nos. 2–6 and 1 (February–July 1918): 163–77, 229–48, 336–43, 431–52, 530–50, 56–65. Clive Bell and Roger Fry were both prominent English exponents of modern art in the first decades of the twentieth century who shaped the development of modernism and new aesthetics.

26. Sirén, "Primitiv och modern konst," pp. 41–2, fn 1.

27. Sirén, "Professor Sirén's Address," pp. 19–20. Minna Törmä offers several possibilities for when, where and how Sirén was "converted" to Chinese art in her book *Enchanted by Lohans*, especially chapter 3.

28. Laurence Binyon, *The Spirit of Man in Asian Art* (Cambridge, Mass.: Harvard University Press, 1935), Charles Eliot Noten Lectures, 1933/34; Laurence Binyon, *Asiatic Art in the British Museum (Sculpture and Painting)* (Paris: Brussels, G. van Oest, 1925). John Hatcher, *Laurence Binyon: Poet, Scholar of East and West* (New York: Oxford University Press, 1995). Okakura Kakuzō (Okakura Tenshin), *The Ideals of the East: The Spirit of Japanese Art* (New York: Cosimo, 2007), 1st ed. 1904.

29. The two versions of the tale have minor spelling variations. Osvald Sirén, "Studies of Chinese and European Painting," *The Theosophical Path* 14, no. 2 (February 1918), pp. 171–2. Kakuzō Okakura, *The Book of Tea* (New York: Dover Publications, 1964), pp. 42–3, 1st ed. 1906.

30. Osvald Sirén, "Studies of Chinese and European Painting," p. 172.

31. "In the Magazines," in *Art and Progress* 3, no. 1 (November 1911), p. 405. Freer's account of Longmen was published originally as an interview in the *Detroit Free Press*. Shortly afterward, Freer donated six photographs of the Longmen sculptures to the Cleveland Museum of Art. *The Bulletin of the Cleveland Museum of Art* 1, no. 2 (July 1914), p. 4.

32. Letter from Freer to Sirén, December 17, 1917, CLF Papers, Box 22, Folder 1, Correspondence: Siren, Osvald, 1917–1918.

33. Édouard Chavannes, *Mission archéologique dans la Chine septentrionale* (Paris: E. Leroux, 1913–1915), 2 vols.

34. Henri Cordier, "Séance de clôture," *Bulletin historique et philologique du comité des travaux historiques et scientifiques*, 1908, p. 142. Numa Broc, "Les voyageurs français et la connaissance de la Chine (1860–1914)," p.117.

35. Tokiwa Daijō (1870–1945) and Sekino Tadashi (1868–1935), *Shina bunka shiseki: kaisetsu* (Tokyo: Hōzōkan, 1939–1941), vol. 2, p. 7. Sekino Tadashi, and Tokiwa Daijō, *Shina Bukkyō shiseki* (Tokyo: Bukkyō shiseki kenkyūkai, 1925–1928), 5 vols. In *Chinese Sculpture*, Sirén used Sekino's plan drawings of Yungang and Longmen. Sekino was an architecture historian and archaeologist, a pioneering figure carrying out field research in Korea and China. Tokiwa was a prominent Japanese

historian of Buddhist studies who conducted early multiple field trips in China mostly throughout the 1920s.

36. Alexander Coburn Soper, "Review of *Chinese Sculpture from the Fifth to the Fourteenth Century*," *Artibus Asiae* 32 (1970): 336–38.

37. Sirén's solid skills in systematic cataloguing and critical annotation were evident in his early work documenting Italian drawings. See *Italienska handtecknin-gar från 1400–och 1500–talen i Nationalmuseum: Catalogue raisonné* (Stockholm: Bröderna Lagerströms Förlag, 1917).

38. See details later in this chapter.

39. E. Steinmann, "Hemligheten i Mediceergrafvårdarna," cited in Sirén, "Michaelangelos Medici-grafvårdar," p. 418.

40. Osvald Sirén, "Michaelangelos Medici-grafvårdar," *Ord och Bild* 16 (1907): 417–35.

41. Sirén, "Michaelangelos Medici-grafvårdar," p. 435.

42. Sirén's early use of photography tends to be associated with his photographs in *Den gyllene paviljongen: Minnen och studier från Japan* (Stockholm: P.A. Norstedt and Söner, 1919), *The Walls and Gates of Peking* (1924), and *Imperial Palaces of Peking* (1926), all deriving from his travels in 1918 and in 1921, and before that juxtapositions in *Rytm och form* (Stockholm: Bröderna Lagerström, 1917) and "Studies of Chinese and European Painting." See Minna Törmä, "Osvald Sirén's Encounter with the Arts of China and Japan," in Shigemi Inaga, ed., *Questioning Oriental Aesthetics and Thinking: Conflicting Visions of "Asia" under the Colonial Empires* (Kyoto: International Research Center for Japanese Studies, 2010), pp. 83–90. Sirén's use of photography in *Chinese Sculpture* (1925) stood out in its time due to its exuberant infusion of photographs, analysis, and contextual narrative. It had a broader and analytical vision than Alfred Salmony's *Die chinesische Steinplastik* (Berlin: Verlag für Kunstwissenschaft, 1922, vol.1), a valuable and large photographic catalog of the rich collection held by the Museum for East Asian Art in Cologne as of the early 1920s. See also the discussion of photography of Chinese sculptures in Grasskamp, *The Book on the Floor*, ch. 3.

43. Though in hindsight Sirén's periodization oversimplified matters, this chapter focuses on its historical significance in the early twentieth century.

44. Sirén, *Chinese Sculpture*, pp. 111–14.

45. Osvald Sirén, *Essentials in Art*, London, 1920, p. 1.

46. Sirén, *Chinese Sculpture*, p. 17.

47. Sirén, "Primitiv och modern konst," pp. 43–4.

48. Sirén, "Primitiv och modern konst," p. 47.

49. Sirén, *Chinese Sculpture*, p. 19.

50. Sirén, *Chinese Sculpture*, p. 15.

51. Joseph Beck, "Greco-Buddhist Sculpture," *Bulletin of the Metropolitan Museum of Art* 8, no. 6 (June 1913): 133–6; Ernest F. Fenollosa, *Epochs of Chinese and Japanese Art: An Outline History of East Asiatic Design* (London: William Heinemann, 1912), vol. 1, chs. 5–6.

52. Although Sirén did not directly invoke any sense of contemporary Buddhist faith in his analysis, the contemporary imagination was palpable: The impact of

Buddhism in Europe and the United States in the nineteenth and twentieth centuries was significant, as a "world religion" (after the Parliament of World Religions in 1893) and practiced faith, an intellectual current early on inspired by translations from Sanskrit and Chinese, in particular the tale of Buddhism's transmission to China, later followed by a flood of tropes in literature and themes in psychoanalysis. Sirén focused exclusively on ancient Buddhist art. Bernard Faure, *Double Exposure: Cutting Across Buddhist and Western Discourses* (Stanford, Calif.: Stanford University Press, 2004).

53. Sirén, *Chinese Sculpture*, 1925, p. 21.

54. Overlooking the Pacific Ocean, Point Loma is the historical landing place of the first European explorers to present-day California. It was also the launching point for Charles Lindbergh's sailplane, a Bowlus "Model A," in January 1930. Lomaland, the estate of the Theosophical Society Point Loma, is today the campus of Point Loma Nazarene University.

55. Helena Blavatsky, *The Secret Doctrine: The Synthesis of Science, Religion, and Philosophy* (London: Theosophy Publishing Company, 1888); Nicholas Goodrick-Clarke, *The Western Esoteric Traditions* (Oxford: Oxford University Press, 2008); Iverson L. Harris, "Reminiscences of Lomaland: Madame Tingley and the Theosophical Institute in San Diego," *The Journal of San Diego History* 20, no. 3 (summer 1974). http://sandiegohistory.org/journal/1974/july/reminiscences-lomaland-madame-tingley-theosphical-institute-san-diego/ (accessed on January 8, 2017).

56. The Raja Yoga School was established to provide instruction from the primary grades through advanced graduate studies for the 500 or more residents and families living at Point Loma. The premises also had a refectory, bakery, stables, carpentry shop, smithy, machines shop, orchards, vegetable gardens, and a publishing house. It was closed in 1940 due to financial difficulties. In addition, the Lomaland campus had a Greek theater constructed in 1901, the first open air theater in the United States.

57. The Theosophical movement depended on its prominent figures to comport themselves in a scientific and dispassionate manner in order to gain public credibility, much in line with Sirén's character and his own intention to be seen as international, secular, and spiritual. Responding to his Point Loma–based friend Iverson Harris, who urged him to put his weight more strongly behind the Theosophical cause, Sirén stated that "I am following a line of work which may serve the *cause* even without the theosophical label. Such is my hope" (back-cited in Letter from Iverson Harris to Sirén, December 5, 1957).

58. Sirén also wrote that "the spiritual inspiration in the life at Point Loma is much closer to the teachings of Jesus than any form of Hinduism." Osvald Sirén, "Mrs. Katharine Tingley och Point-Loma-Institutionen," *Hufvudstadsbladet*, no. 230, 6, August 29, 1923.

59. Sirén, "Professor Sirén's Address," pp. 11–12.

60. These dates have been estimated using the data presented in the chronicles of Longmen carvings and events, my field work photographs, and Wen Yucheng, "Longmen Tangku painian," in Longmen wenwu baoguansuo and Beijing daxue kaoguxi, comp., *Zhongguo shiku: Longmen Shiku* (Tokyo/Beijing: Heibonsha/Wenwu chubanshe, 1992), vol. 2, pp. 172–216. For epigraphic texts at Longmen and analysis, see the two-volume *Longmen Shiku beike tiji huilu*, comp. by Longmen

shiku yanjiusuo, Liu Jinglong, and Li Yukun (Beijing: Zhongguo dabaike quanshu chubanshe, 1998).

61. Sirén, *Chinese Sculpture*, vol. 1, p. 47, Text, pp. 24–5 and p. 123.

62. Joshua Fogel, *The Literature of Travel in the Japanese Rediscovery of China, 1862–1945* (Stanford, Calif.: Stanford University Press, 1996), pp. 85–90.

63. Letter from Feng Yuxiang rejecting Sirén's request to excavate in Xi'an, November 30, 1921, Sirénarkiv, A2: 1921–1929. Valérie A. M. Jurgens, *The Karlbeck Syndicate 1930–1934: Collecting and Scholarship on Chinese Art in Sweden and Britain*, PhD thesis, School of Oriental and African Studies, University of London, 2010, pp. 85–6.

64. Letter from Orvar Karlbeck to Sirén, July 17, 1921, Sirénarkiv, A2: 1921–1929.

65. Letter from Orvar Karlbeck to Sirén, Sirénarkiv, October 11, 1921.

66. Words ascribed to Philippe Berthelot: "Il n'y a pas de formation professionnelle ni humaine complète sans un séjour en Extrême-Orient." See Pierre Morel, "Français en Chine, d'aujourd'hui et de toujours," *Revue des deux mondes*, July-August 1999, p. 18.

67. H. L. Mackinder, "The Geographical Pivot of History," *The Geographical Journal* 23, no. 4 (April 1904): 421–44. Over the past decade or so, this geostrategic worldview has become popular again especially as China continues to grow and push forward its Belt and Road Initiative.

68. Imre Galambos and Kitsudō Kōichi, "Japanese Exploration of Central Asia: The Ōtani Expeditions and Their British Connections," *Bulletin of School of Oriental and African Studies* 75, no. 1 (2012): 113–34.

69. Sirén, "Studies of Chinese and European Painting," Introduction, p. 166.

70. King Gustaf VI Adolf (1882–1973, Crown Prince 1907–1950, r. 1950–1973) had a lifelong interest in art history and archaeology, and gave strong support to the East Asian collection of the Swedish National Museum. President Roosevelt, by "vigorous means," secured the acceptance in 1906 of Charles L. Freer's art collection as a donation to the U.S. federal government. Letters from Freer to Roosevelt, December 23, 1912, and January 6, 1913; letter from Roosevelt to Freer, December 30, 1912, CLF Papers, Box 21, Folder 19, Correspondence: Roosevelt, Theodore, 1906–1913.

71. Charles A. Beard, and Mary R. Beard, *The Rise of American Civilization* (New York: The Macmillan Company, 1930), vol. 2, p. 248.

Chapter 6

Blighted Beauty

Longmen and Cultural Heritage Law in Early Twentieth-Century China

Who destroyed ancient objects of the Central Plain?
All points to the United States of America.
They not only stole the tri-color glazed horses from the Tang tombs
But also Longmen's apsarases and Buddhas
Hacking the stone walls is despicable
How could one be barefaced unrepentant
Alan Priest is but a plunderer
Boston is a sordid graveyard for the spoils
The friezes must be returned to whence they came
To redeem the world depends on the populace

—Guo Moruo, 1959[1]

The recognition of Longmen in the early twentieth century as a treasure trove embodied both the promise and dilemma of modernity. "There followed a revival of interest in the arts of Eastern Asia, and the purchases of collectors, who began to visit the country [China] in numbers, and bought things never before known to possess cash value, fostered the trade."[2] As Chinese antiquities especially stone sculptures and stupas were assigned economic value in the markets across the world and in China, the destruction and removal of artifacts from their original sites escalated dramatically. Appreciation and commercial vandalism—wanted and unwanted attention—to this day pit money-making, scientific pursuit, aesthetic marvel, moral conscience, and legal judgment against each other in an eternal, uneasy contest.

Early curators of East Asian art in many world most famous museums, leaders of key institutions as well as progenitors of China studies, including Langdon Warner (1881–1955), Laurence Sickman (1907–1988), and Alan Priest (1898–1969), also strongly influenced the modern fate of Longmen's artifacts. Chinese anguish at foreign possession and trading of their

165

antiquities[3] highlighted the intertwined role foreigners, their Chinese associates, and foreign legal regimes played in the complex history of Chinese antiquities. Foreign ways of dealing with antiques served and still serve as reference points for Chinese approaches.

Three legal aspects are interrogated. I shall first explore cultural relics (*guwu* and *wenwu*) in Chinese legal history, highlighting the issues of antiquity territorialization and nationalization chronologically from the 1910s to the 1940s.[4] The second section is devoted to precedence and parallel trends in foreign legal frameworks and the Chinese historical take on heritage protection. Then we examine different records in Chinese and English on the removal of two bas-reliefs from Longmen. The chapter ends with an argument that two pairs of binary legal principles, private versus public ownership and national ownership versus world humanity ownership, manifested an iron cage of modernity in Chinese and world history.

GUWU (WENWU) IN CHINESE LEGAL HISTORY: TERRITORIALIZATION AND NATIONALIZATION, 1910S–1940S

It was not until the nineteenth century that art as "imaginative expression" was distinguished from art as "skill," "industry," and "utility."[5] At the turn of the twentieth century, leading Chinese cultural reformers Luo Zhenyu and Kang Youwei championed adding Buddhist stone sculptures to fine art (*meishu*) and antiquities for appreciation and protection. Indeed, similar to the situation in many other countries, the establishment of a legal regime of cultural property in China involved definition and redefinition of art and antiquities, and the classification of private collections as public or state property. How did stone Buddhas become antiquities in China? How were Chinese antiquities categorized? Why should one own them? What heritage institutions were established to accommodate the needs?

This section fleshes out regulatory frameworks and historical trends in Chinese domestic laws on antiquities. Prior to and with the creation of national ownership legislation, most source nations relied on export controls to stop the trade in looted artifacts. This was the case in China as well. In the early twentieth century, the Qing government commenced classification of movable and immovable antiquities and gradually expanded the scope of protection and measures. The territorialization of artifacts warranted government ownership. Each province was ordered to establish their own inventory of antiquities including archaeological artifacts. Provincial rules on lawful excavation, detecting and reporting archaeological artifacts diverged in many ways, but public pressure gradually generated a consensus. Both Chinese and foreign activities and opinions forced the national Beijing government and later the Nationalist government to intervene, thereby giving birth to modern Chinese national museums and other agencies of cultural heritage. This four-decade process was from the outset fragmented and fragile but progressed toward safeguarding cultural property, to a great extent comparable with European countries, the United States, and Japan.

Some scholars view institutionalized measures against smuggling and illegal trade as part of nation-building and the expansion of state power. Philip Thai shows that law-making and law-breaking evolved antagonistically, recursively, as well as symbiotically in modern China. And law-breaking was a transformative agent in extending state capacity,[6] also in regard to antiquities laws in China.

The meaning and scope of antiquities defined cultural objects as linked directly to Chinese cultural essence, national spirit, and morality. Foreign countries were emulated, visible in the alignment with international standards and practices in China. Professional and social organizations were concurrently formed to preserve Chinese antiquities and archaeological artifacts, and the media consistently reported on foreign countries' interest in and possession of Chinese treasures. A consensus emerged to the effect that sharing, public ownership was perceived the best form of protection.

Public discussion on antiquities law-making contributed to four waves of change: First, in the beginning, the Qing government's attention to and promotion of things from the past was criticized as a waste in light of country-wide poverty and suffering, as a wrong priority in domestic affairs. Second, Chinese and foreign joint efforts in 1913–1914 prompted further change for antiquities protection. Longmen's Buddhist ravine (*fogu*) featured prominently in this heritage protection movement.[7]

Third, legislation and public discussion during the 1920s gravitated more toward the existential issue of national ownership arising from the selling of Qing imperial collections. Protecting antiquities had added urgency and been equated to patriotism, which reflected rising Chinese nationalism and anti-imperialism in the 1920s, the anti-Christian movement, and the nationalization of Christian schools. Fourth, there was stronger opposition to foreign participation in excavation during the 1930s.

Regulatory Framework of Antiquities: Genesis in the Late Qing

The early Chinese legal regime of cultural relics (*guwu*) commenced in 1906 and continued through the 1930s, the profusion of illegal and legal Chinese antique markets only tapering off in the late 1940s after World War Two and the founding of the PRC.

In heritage modernization, Qing China took inspiration from foreign countries such as Japan. In 1888, the Meiji government organized the first investigation of cultural antiquities in Japan with the participation of Okakura Kakuzō (1862–1913) and Ernest Fenollosa (1853–1908). It took nearly ten years to establish an inventory of 215,000 pieces of antiquities in the national registry, which became the foundation for later protection efforts. Approximately two decades later, as part of its modernization platform, the Qing government started to build institutional capacity to deal with heritage protection. In 1905, the *Xue bu* (the Ministry of Education) was established and also included the remit of antiquities protection. The following year, *Minzheng bu* (the Ministry of the Interior)[8] was formed, under which the *Yingshan si* (the Building Department) was charged with "supervising, managing and auditing (except for the Beijing area) official civil engineering projects and expenditure reimbursement while being charged to protect historical sites and surveying temples."[9] *Xue bu* and *Minzheng bu* were the earliest protective agencies of cultural property in modern China.

In 1909, the Qing promulgated the first regulations, Implementation Measures for the Preservation of Antiquities (*Baocun guwu tuiguang banfa*), emphasizing the need of investigation and protection. Interestingly, stone relics topped both lists of six investigation and five protection groups of ancient objects because they were "key to fine arts and especially precious compared with epigraphic inscriptions."[10] This was a sharp departure from Chinese literati's conventional preference for calligraphy—the handwritten script—and paintings. These "new" classes ranked antiquities in the order of steles, stone stupas, stone plaques, statues, stone carvings, ancient paintings, cliff inscriptions, calligraphy, etc. since the Zhou and Qin dynasties; stone objects from the past (*shizhi guwu*); frescos of dignitaries and fine sculptures; ancient imperial mausoleums and tombs of legendary sages; memorial temples for people of note; and epigraphic inscriptions (*jinshi*). Local governments were ordered to report to the Ministry of Interior on the location, types, content, physical conditions of these antiquities.

The Ministry of Education was tasked with carrying out surveys of antiquities, and in 1910 notified local governments to survey, report, and to protect ancient sites.[11] Under the wing of the Ministry of Education, in 1909 the Metropolitan Library was founded. There were also proposals to form the Antiquities Preservation Association.

The last few years of the Qing dynasty witnessed the formation of legal and institutional frameworks responsible for the preservation of cultural relics, all unprecedented in Chinese history. On the other hand, definition and selection criteria for antiquities remained loosely imprecise, which called for improvement.

Ordinances of Relics and Objects of Art:
The Beijing Government (1912–1928)

In 1912, China became a republic and the last emperor of the Qing, the Xuan-tong emperor abdicated. The new Ministry of Internal Affairs (*Neiwu bu*) replaced the Ministry of the Interior responsible for antiquities matters. Under the Ministry of Internal Affairs, the Building Department of the Qing was replaced by *Lisu si* (Department of Rituals and Customs) in charge of protecting, investigating, and managing temples and other antiquities.[12] *Jiaoyu bu* (The Ministry of Education) continued the jurisdiction of its predecessor in managing museums and libraries. Local governments, such as Xi'an Prefecture, were more awakened to the issue of antiquities:

> Shaanyuan's Stele Forest houses calligraphy of various kinds such as the seal script and cursive script since the Wei and Jin Dynasties. Since the Shuori Revolution last September, military troops have been stationed in schools and the Stele Forest is left unguarded. It is a pity that the nation's thousand-year precious quintessence is slowly disappearing. Yesterday, Xi'an Prefecture requested the approval of the governor to dispatch former educational instructors and officials in Xi'an Prefecture to attend to the Stele Forest. This would preserve antiquities while mitigating poor economic conditions of government personnel. Indeed it would be like killing two birds with one stone.[13]

As discussed in chapter 2, news reports in the early 1910s on the destruction and loss of Longmen's artifacts raised grave concerns in public sphere. Besides Chinese newspapers' wide distribution of McCormick's letter, the Ministry of Internal Affairs forwarded McCormick's letter to its branch office in Henan Province, ordering local officials to prohibit troops stationed at Longmen from causing further damage to the Buddhist caves, and to go to the site together with the magistrate to examine the situation and establish a registry of all the stone sculptures. It instructed Luoyang's officials to designate nearby monks to take care of Longmen and allow them to charge a fee from visitors for their own keep, and the magistrate to have staff inspect the site frequently.[14]

The Longmen correspondence fell silent until the Ministry of Internal Affairs followed up nearly three years later in 1916: "For over two years we have not heard back from you yet about how you handle the situation. Please reply immediately: How many Buddhist stone sculptures were there before? How many there are now? Have there been incidents that incurred damage and desertion? How do you intend to preserve them? Have Detailed Regulations been made for special care?"[15]

Two weeks later, Henan governor Tian Wenlie responded and complied by issuing eight-clause rules, terse to the bones, for a review to be made by

Luoyang's magistrate Wang Xiling along with commissioner Liu Xu. One clause was to award those who captured the robbers and vandals, regardless of color and race, twenty taels. Another clause was for the responsible monk to collect twenty dimes (*wen*) as his own stipend. A list of the images at Longmen was also submitted to the Ministry of Internal Affairs, dividing stone carvings into two groups of large and small stone Buddhas on the Longmen Hill (West Hill), the Yishui, Westshore (*xi'an*), and the Yi River banks, with a rudimentary table of damaged artifacts.[16]

At the end of 1913, a decree for the protection of antiquities, alongside the by-laws for the Institute of Antiquity Exhibition [Guwu chenliesuo][17] and the Association for the Preservation and Promotion of Antiquities, was set to start museums in China: "Countries in the East and the West all collect rare and precious objects, and establish specialized institutions. This is to showcase both their high-level production of goods and the development of fine arts. They especially pay attention to items from the past, keep them safe forever so that their countrymen can go see them on display. This intends to promote academic innovation as well as industrial growth."[18] The rise of the modern henceforth served the formation of national heritage as a mobilizing concept.

Modernizing efforts were also carried out through popularizing antiquity, which stressed both state and individual interest at stake didactically: Protecting antiquities "concerned educated people, but is the responsibility of the state."[19] Meanwhile, honorary leadership positions in the Association for the Preservation and Promotion of Antiquities were open to Chinese and foreigners alike. This shows that in the early years of heritage modernization, the general atmosphere in China was rather liberal about both international and national ownership of antiquities.

During the Beijing government era (1912–1928), attempts at export control over antiquities did not move very far beyond bureaucratic agencies. Internal communications between the two government branches disclosed barriers of coordination and application in regulation/law-making, on the one hand, and on the other the efforts by Chinese and foreign traders to push the legal boundaries: Although there was a consensus that antiquities embodied national essence (*guocui*) and should not be allowed for export, neither the Chinese Customs nor the Ministry of Internal Affairs enforced the export ban. This was because foreigners and their Chinese compradors argued that since there had never been tariff regulations on antiquities, there should be no ban on antiquities export.

Moreover, foreign ministers to China demanded that no tariffs be levied on antiquities, claiming that those antiquities to be transited overseas were for museum displays and not for sale. Long-standing precedents of tax exemption on cultural artifacts made that the Chinese Customs had no basis for rejecting foreign claims. "Consequently, antiquities were in recent years exported in bulks, tens of crates at a time. We can neither forbid it, nor can we collect tariffs," wrote the Chinese Customs in a letter of December 27, 1913 to the Ministry of Internal Affairs. The Chinese Customs requested the Ministry of Internal Affairs to forward previous regulations on antiquities protection, but was told to wait until all provisional regulations were publicized.

The situation did not get any better even with a presidential decree and provisional measures. In 1914, President Yuan Shikai repeated the ban on antiquities export and private art dealings between Chinese and foreigners. The same decree also ordered the Ministry of Internal Affairs to coordinate with the Chinese Customs (*Shuiwu chu*), which—foreign-led due to the treaties and agreements signed between China and foreign countries—was in charge of drafting regulations on restricting antiquities export.[20] In March 1916, the Ministry of Internal Affairs, citing McCormick's letter and pointing at Longmen as the finest among Chinese antiquities, again ordered all heads of the provincial departments of interior to heed the obligation to prevent the export of ancient objects and protect historical sites. "Chinese antiquities cannot even be protected by their own country, while it is the foreigners who are making an effort to do so. This is a peculiarly improper aspect of our national system."[21]

In 1916, the Ministry of Internal Affairs enacted the "Provisional Measures for the Preservation of Antiquities," ordering all provincial governors, military governors (*dutong*), and county officials to urgently take stocks and make an inventory of antiquities.[22] The importance and urgency to protect antiquities in China was by this time fully understood by all involved.

The "Provisional Measures for the Preservation of Antiquities" consisted of five articles that were built on and continued the efforts made in the Qing dynasty. Article One stipulated that by the end of the year, local governments must provide evidence to the Ministry of Internal Affairs that local officials of the Qing had protected imperial mausoleums and tombs of cultural sages. Article Two regulated that ancient city walls, passes, barriers, caves, buildings, memorial temples, terraces, pavilions and towers, dikes, bridges, lakes and ponds, wells, and so on must be safeguarded. Article Three demanded that documents surrounding the local methods of protection for tablets, statues, frescos, cliff inscriptions, and historical monuments be submitted for scrutiny. No rubbings, selling and transporting overseas were permitted. Article Four added ancient trees, for instance locust trees from the Qin dynasty and pine trees from the Han,[23] to the protection list. Article Five specified that all provinces must select and keep in a safe place fine epigraphic inscriptions, bamboo and wooden utensils, ceramics and embroideries, and famous calligraphy works and paintings. Private collections should be abolished lest they be sold to foreigners without authorization, if they could not be purchased by the government.[24]

The "Provisional Measures for the Preservation of Antiquities" defined the concept of "antiquities" (*guwu*). Antiquities, movable and immovable, referred to ancient objects, historical sites (*guji*), and precious old trees in five groups. The task of protection fell within the jurisdiction of local officials, who could delegate the responsibility to public organizations, men of good standing, temple priests, and other groups and individuals:

> All remains of ancient items are the forerunner of a nation's cultures . . . Every country East and West exerts itself mightily to preserve their antiquities. The ancient city of Pompeii, Egypt's obelisks, Greco-Buddhist stone carvings, and the ruins of the Japanese shrines: each of them is embellished for the sake of prominence and each is great on its own account. Museums are built to collect rare and unique treasures and classify them. Exhibitions of ten thousand wonders abound for the sake of national quintessence. What can surpass the first blooms on China's vast and well-endowed lands handed down to us as ancient treasures? But only less than one percent of the few and scattered were preserved by the public due to all the catastrophic destruction . . . Officials report that in recent years unscrupulous profiteers sold them to foreign merchants so that they flowed out overseas in great numbers. If we fail to protect them, they are doomed to perish.[25]

The 1916 interim measures were not formal legislation, mainly because the situation of the legislature under Yuan Shikai who claimed emperorship in December 1915. Its approach to cultural relics was unsystematic and incomplete, for it only stipulated the scope of protection without detailing specific methods, institutions, and coordination plans needed for implementation. Nevertheless, in this stymied process of creating rules and legal frameworks, separation between private collecting and public collecting, Chinese and foreign ownership took shape, even though foreign ways of antiquities preservation served as the model.

Despite general public awakening, support and its legal significance that ultimately led to the first piece of Chinese legislation in 1930, the Beijing government's provisional measures were either ignored or treated with indecisiveness in practice. At the end of 1925, the Chinese Customs corresponded with the Ministry of Internal Affairs that the Beijing Chamber of Commerce (*Jingshi zongshanghui*) conveyed a complaint made by the Beijing Association of Antiquities (*Jingshi guwan shanghui*): "There has never been any fixed taxation rules on antiquities. Lately all newly excavated items receive hefty dues. This interferes with trade. We therefore plead for tax exemption in order to encourage export."[26]

Knowing the clear ban on selling antiquities to foreigners, the Chinese Customs still asked for advice from the Ministry of Internal Affairs on how to distinguish different classes of cultural relics so as to limit the export volume.

The Ministry of Internal Affairs replied that the ban on antiquities export was absolute before an official law of antiquities became available. At the end of its life, the Beijing government was still sending letters to provincial governors of Henan and Shanxi about the large, frustratingly unstoppable effluence of Longmen and Yungang statues abroad.[27]

The Nanjing National Government: Asserting the Nation, 1928–1949

> In recent years, foreigners coming to Luoyang marveled at and wrote about this treasure trove. Those who liked to display art objects then approached the villagers for purchase. Seeing this as profitable, villagers for their own gain cut off the Buddha heads one after the other. And some even hacked the entire body. The damage has over the years grown—a catastrophe of our national historical sites. When we this time went to inspect . . . we heard that the Buddha head robbers were mostly Muslims. In Wai'ao Village (also called Weijia'ao Village) south of Longmen all stonemasons have the stealing of stone statues as their common occupation. Working together with bandits, they brought high ladders and flashlights to carry out their nightly destruction. Bandits also arrived from the south, wreaked destruction and fled back south after they were done.[28]
>
> —A field investigation report, *Shenbao*, 1937

In 1928, the Nanjing Nationalist government was established. Based on the organizational and legal foundation left by the Beijing government, the antiquities protection movement veered further toward the centralization of power during the Nanjing government era. The administration for antiquities protection fell under the Affairs Department of Rituals and Customs, in the Ministry of Internal Affairs, with three offices (*ke*) handling matters concerning the management and registration of monasteries, surveying and preservation of historical ruins, historical sites, imperial tombs, special temples, and public exhibitions.[29]

Meanwhile, the new, centralized government organs drafted laws and guided provincial and county-level offices dealing with cultural relics and monuments. In 1928, at the suggestion of the Minister of Education Cai Yuanpei, the Nationalist government announced the "Amendment to the Organizational Law of the Council of Higher Learning (Daxueyuan) of the Republic of China." Under the Council of Higher Learning, various special commissions were set up, one of which was the Antiquities Stewardship Commission (*Guwu baoguan weiyuanhui*). As China's first special agency of its kind, the Committee was specialized in the management of matters concerning custody, research, and excavation of historical sites and antiquities throughout the country.[30]

The Antiquities Stewardship Commission, under the leadership of Zhang Ji, consisted of between eleven and twenty of the most prominent cultural men of China. Its first members were predominantly scholars with overseas experience, who simultaneously held responsibility for protecting the National Palace Museum.[31] The Committee was instrumental in drafting the law for antiquities protection. When the Council of Higher Learning was disbanded in 1929, the Antiquities Stewardship Commission fell directly under the jurisdiction of the Ministry of Education.

In 1930, the Nationalist Government in Nanjing promulgated the Antiquities Preservation Act (*Guwu baocunfa*), the first national cultural relic protection law in Chinese history and the prototype for a series of later legal initiatives. Some note that both the Chinese Antiquities Preservation Law and the concurrent Implementation Regulations for the Antiquities Preservation Act were mainly modeled upon the Japanese National Treasure Preservation Act of 1929 (*Guobao baocunfa*) and the enactment decree and guidelines for implementation. More comprehensive, the Antiquities Preservation Act of 1930 specified the scope, preservation institutions, and reporting rules for antiquities. First, antiquities were defined as "all archaeological, historical, paleontological and other cultural artifacts."[32] Second, the 1930 Act reorganized and designated the Central Antiquities Stewardship Commission (*Zhongyang guwu baoguan weiyuanhui*) as the agency to determine the scope and types of antiquities.

The 1930 Act included fourteen provisions that recognized private ownership of antiquities. It ruled that "privately-owned antiquities cannot be transferred to foreign outsiders" to prevent the outflow of cultural relics; that excavated relics, that is, "those buried underground or exposed from the underground belong to the state"; that persons with new finds must report them to the local government immediately; and that those who hid and refused to report them would be punished as "thieves." Ancient objects should be unearthed by central or local academic institutions that were approved by the Central Antiquities Protection Committee and held a license from the Ministry of Education and the Ministry of Internal Affairs. Unlicensed excavations of antiquities were to be equated to theft and thus subject to criminal prosecution. Foreigners were allowed to assist in surveys. Antiquities could only leave the country with a special passport, and they must be returned to their Chinese home within two to three years.[33]

The 1930 Law also clarified two important principles. First, all antiquities, buried underground or exposed on the surface, belonged to the state as the property of the Chinese nation, a stipulation that did not challenge private ownership of items in existing collections. Second, the circulation

of antiquities was limited to domestic territory, so they were not to be transferred to foreigners or/and transported overseas without authorization.

The following year, the nineteen-clause Detailed Regulations on Implementing Antiquities Protection was issued. Besides requiring registration
of both publicly and privately owned antiquities, the Detailed Regulations
specified that while antiquities were limited to domestic distribution only,
they could leave the country for academic research, under the condition that
designated personnel must accompany them on the trip with a permission
issued by both the Ministry of Education and Internal Affairs. Violators faced
financial penalties and criminal prosecution.[34]

In July 1934, the Central Antiquities Stewardship Commission was officially formed with offices in Beijing and Xi'an. The following year, the Central Antiquities Protection Committee fell under the Ministry of the Interior
to continue to play a key role in determining legal matters.[35] The Committee,
in 1935, grouped antiquities according to three main criteria: (1) antiquities from antiquity; (2) rare antiquities; and (3) antiquities with scientific,
historical, or artistic value. And twelve categories of antiquities were also
established: (1) paleontological objects, (2) prehistoric relics, (3) buildings,
(4) paintings, (5) sculptures, (6) epigraphic inscriptions, (7) books, (8) currency, (9) clothing, (10) weapons, (11) utensils, and (12) miscellaneous items
that did not belong to the above categories.[36] The meaning of antiquities was
continuously reappropriated by the Nationalist government; the coverage
expanded from instrumental objects to archaeological materials and historical sites, classified in what was at the time considered a more detailed and
scientific manner.

Translating foreign laws and regulations was another significant work
conducted by the Central Antiquities Stewardship Commission. In 1935, for
example, it compiled and published the Compilation of Antiquities Preservation Laws of All Countries. This publication introduced different nations'
path to the protection of historical buildings such as in Italy, France, Belgium, and the United Kingdom. As a standard reference for China to make
and implement laws of cultural heritage, it also assembled regulations on the
export of antiquities in France, Switzerland, Egypt, Japan, the Soviet Union,
and the Philippines.

Besides the central expansion of bureaucratic and professional institutions,
provincial and county branch offices, corresponding organizations and regulations were created. Between 1930 and 1932, for instance, Henan Province,
the home of the Longmen Grottoes, had its first organizational rules for museums, and the Henan Association for Historical Monuments was formed in
conjunction with the National Central Research Academy. Luoyang County
had its Antiquities Preservation Committee with an eleven-article charter
confirming trade in artifacts with foreigners and assistance in transporting

antiquities abroad was an offense. Unauthorized excavation and possession of objects exposed to the ground were criminal theft that would be punished.[37]

All these first steps, albeit in many ways ineffective, became the sources and historical capital for legislation and expansion of cultural heritage institutions during the era of the PRC.[38] Contemporary Chinese laws on heritage protection are becoming more comprehensive and systematic. In 1961, the central government issued the Provisional Regulations of the Protection and Management of Cultural Heritage (*Wenwu baohu guanli zanxing tiaoli*). Two decades later, the 1982 Law replaced the 1961 provisional regulations, with its first revision in 1991, the second in 2002, the third in 2007, the fourth in 2013, and the fifth in 2017.[39]

Among all PRC's legislation concerning cultural heritage, the 1982 and 2002 laws are most significant, with the former laying the founding principles.[40] The Regulations for the Implementation of the Law of the PRC on the Protection of Cultural Heritage are based on the 2003 version with its first revision in 2013, the second in 2016, and the third in 2017. The 80-article 2002 Law of the PRC on the Protection of Cultural Heritage and 2003 Regulations for the Implementation essentially provide the bulk of the present legal framework and content in China.[41] In line with international law, cultural relics/heritage in China are items of historical, artistic, or scientific value dating from various historical periods; significant items related to more recent or contemporary major events, revolutionary movements or famous individuals (Article Two of the 2002 Law). Immovable cultural relics are protected at the national, provincial, and municipal or county level depending on their importance and value. Movable cultural relics are divided into valuable cultural relics and ordinary cultural relics, and valuable cultural relics are further divided into three grades (Article Three of the 2002 Law).[42]

ANTIQUITIES PROTECTION IN INTERNATIONAL LAW

Besides domestic legal measures, China has also been participating in international legal regimes and active in multilateral and bilateral cooperation with other counties to crack down on the theft and smuggling of cultural objects. As of January 2019, China has signed the mutual agreement of understanding with twenty-one countries including the United States, Peru, India, Italy, the Philippines, Greece, Chile, Cyprus, and others. For instance, in January 2009, after ten-year negotiations, China and the United States signed an agreement on the United States restricting the import of Chinese archaeological materials and ancient sculpture and frescos of more 250 years old.[43] With a five-year term limit, this bilateral agreement has been extended twice respectively in 2014 and 2019.

Seen from above, Chinese legislation on antiquities has been hugely influenced by foreign countries including the United States, Japan, Greece, and Italy, and international laws. As a main receiving country of Longmen's artifacts, the United States, alongside France, Germany, Japan, the Netherlands, Switzerland, and the United Kingdom, remained a principal market for stolen cultural goods in the twentieth century. It is therefore useful to trace the global legal history of antiquities, or cultural heritage or objects or relics.[44] Attention focuses on the coexistence of mutually overlapping principles of ownership (a) private/individual ownership versus public/state ownership and of (b) domestic/native place versus foreign ownership. This concerned and concerns the case of Longmen and many others such as the fight over the Parthenon Acropolis/Elgin Marbles between Greece and Great Britain.[45]

Private ownership versus public/state ownership, and domestic/origin or market country ownership and foreign/receiving country ownership stands out as a set of persistent dilemmas. Held sacred as individual right to the enjoyment of possessions in Roman law, principles of private property find many specific and deeply ingrained expressions and interpretations in contemporary law, being fundamental to the legacy societies and economies of the Enlightenment: Amendment V to the 1787 U.S. Constitution, ratified in 1791, stipulated that private property shall not be taken for public use without just compensation.[46] The French Civil Code of Napoleon conferred to the owner the absolute right to lawfully enjoy a property and to dispose thereof. Expropriation, deprivation of private possessions, and interference with individual ownership could only be done by law and with compensation.[47]

Broadly speaking, national and international laws of cultural heritage tend to address antiquities as tradeable and protected objects. Although largely ineffective in practice, many national and international regimes of antiquities patrimony laws in peacetime and during armed conflict have existed since the nineteenth century.[48] Their scope and impact have expanded since the twentieth century, and even more so in the twenty-first century, often in the face of predation and destruction, and reflecting the rise of nationalist sentiments.[49] Before the UNESCO conventions, Italy took the lead in 1820 to enact the first legislative decree, a code to protect historical objects and artworks, followed by France in 1840 to protect historical buildings, Great Britain in 1882, and Japan in 1897. El Salvador claimed all cultural property for the state in 1903, allowing the export of artifacts existing in duplicate. Starting in 1906, the United States issued a series of legislation on preserving historical sites and national parks. At the suggestion of President Theodore Roosevelt in 1904, the Hague Convention (IV)—Respecting the Laws and Customs of War on Land—and its annex—Regulations concerning the Laws and Customs of War on Land (The Hague, October 18, 1907)—was enacted in 1910. Section III of the Hague Convention IV of 1907 required that, in military conflict, "the occupying state must safeguard the capital of these properties, and administer them in accordance with the rules of usufruct."[50] Since World War One under President Woodrow Wilson, U.S. alien property custodianship has also formed an important chapter in the history of global antiquities.

In the 1930s and later, both national laws and international treaties on cultural property progressed. Under a Greek law of 1932, all antiquities that were discovered in Greece belong to the government, demanding registration of collectors and dealers and only allowing the trade of multiples. In 1935, an international treaty, the Roerich Pact, also known as the Treaty on the Protection of Artistic and Scientific Institutions and Historic Monuments was signed in Washington, DC by the United States and twenty-one countries in the Americas. The Roerich Pact not only promotes legal protection of cultural heritage but also represents a philosophical vision for world peace through culture.[51] Italy, in 1939, claimed all cultural property of over fifty years old for the state but allows the export of declined items. Japan, in 1950, promulgated the Law for the Protection of Cultural Properties (*Bunkazai hogohō*) while under reconstruction after World War II. The Chinese drew lessons that in Japan's case cultural heritage protection conformed to efforts to develop national identity and independence.[52] Egyptian antiquities, according to Egyptian Law 117 in 1983, were owned by the Egyptian government. In the same year, Turkey enacted new legislation that required dealer registration and the state to claim all man-made or natural items of cultural, geographic, and other value. Switzerland largely has no antiquities control, and is therefore a favorite place for antiquities smuggling.[53]

Two important regimes of international treaties deal with cultural property disputes. Three of the most representative conventions are the 1954 Hague Convention for the Protection of Cultural Property in the Event of Armed Conflicts together with two protocols; the UNESCO 1970 Convention on the Means of Prohibiting and Preventing the Illicit Import, Export and Transfer of Ownership of Cultural Property and the 1995 Convention on Stolen or Illegally Exported Cultural Object of the International Institute for the Unification of Private Law (UNIDROIT).[54] Not retrospective, these two international legal regimes address three sources of cultural property disputes and possible restitution and repatriation: the domestic and global black market of billions of dollars for antiquities exported in violation of the domestic law of origin states; many valuable antiquities not stolen or removed in violation of domestic law, but demanded by origin states for return; many antiquities looted or destroyed in war. The 1970 UNESCO Convention only deals with claims made by nation-states, whereas the 1995 UNIDROIT Convention only handles claims by individual private owners, and the "possibility for group claims is therefore limited."[55]

The 1954 Hague Convention and its two protocols obligated belligerents to avoid targeting cultural property and to protect it when possible. It also required states at peace to take measures to safeguard their own cultural property against foreseeable wars.[56] The 1970 UNESCO Convention allows source nations, believing their cultural property to be threatened by looting or pillage, to request assistance in the form of immediate import restrictions from market nations. UNESCO also created the World Heritage Committee, an intergovernmental group to keep inventories of all cultural and natural heritage items and receive request for international assistance. The main purpose of the 1970 UNESCO Convention is to halt illicit trade in art and artifacts through import control of cultural property that was either illegally exported or stolen. Many market nations, foremost the United States, objected to labeling all trade as unlawful due to domestic laws of origin states and, as a result, significantly amended this provision to fit within their individual jurisprudence before ratification.[57] As an instrument of public law "in that it deals with matters by action between national administrations,"[58] the 1970 UNESCO Convention nations urged signatories to enforce cultural property protection according to their national laws. In 1983, the U.S. Convention on Cultural Property Implementation Act (CPIA, CCPIA) was enacted. Customarily the U.S. domestic law does not recognize foreign legal principles, so that the United States in CPIA subscribes to the basic rule that a foreign country's law, declaring export to be illegal, does not make import into the United States illegal without United States' law declaring the same.[59]

Historically, cultural property protection fell into the class of public goods. In "cultural nationalism," a viewpoint common to source nations including China, the relationship between an artifact and its country of origin is most significant and the retention of national heritage trumps worldwide heritage. Most market nations including the United States, however, tend to argue for "cultural internationalism," whereby cultural property is viewed as subject to the common interest of mankind and that efforts should focus on the free flow of tradeable objects and protection by those with best resources.[60] Eric Posner argues against international treaties and UNESCO conventions of cultural property on the grounds that they have been a "failure" and that "[t]he distinct features of cultural property do not justify the existing treaty regimes or proposals to strengthen them."[61] "The treatment of cultural property would improve, even during wartime, if the current regime of international regulations were abolished."[62]

On the other hand, public opinion has corresponded to the legal orientation in the twenty-first century in the United States and Europe, with the center of gravity moving toward stronger cultural artifacts protection. This was before the age of Trump when popular nationalism is on the rise again. In a 2000 Harris Poll, 90 percent of the surveyed Americans thought laws should prevent importing artifacts from a country that does not want them exported.[63] Court cases displayed similar tendencies. About eight in ten (84 percent) say laws should prevent the general public from removing rock art.[64] The withdrawal of the United States from UNESCO, founded in 1945, in December 2018 overshadows the financial and key policy orientation, considered by some as a step backward for global cultural cooperation but by others as saving money from wasteful spending, call for reforms and a protest against UNESCO's anti-Israel bias.[65]

THE FOREIGN "OTHER": SINNERS AND REDEEMERS. AN ETERNAL RACE BETWEEN HERITAGE NATIONALISM AND COSMOPOLITANISM

Historical trends in China were comparable to the global legal movement toward stronger heritage protection while attempting to balance domestic versus foreign and private-public trade and ownership of artworks and antiquities. The three major waves of Chinese legislation and institution building over the course of 1900s–1930s were gradually taking effect and matched by appropriated and reappropriated cultural and social function of antiquities. The foreign "Other" was an indispensable, conspicuous component to this transition in China. The removal of Longmen's artifacts, especially the two low reliefs from the Central Binyang Cave, not only was a sad chapter in the legal history of Chinese antiquities but also encapsulated the situation of a civil war-torn and impoverished interior China in disorder.

This section zooms in on the double or hybrid role that foreign ways of dealing with and in cultural relics played, both exemplary and erring with reference to the same ideals. This points to a perennial interaction between state control and private trade in artifacts, heritage nationalism, and cosmopolitanism in law-on-books, law-in-action, custom and social norms.[66]

The Foreign "Other" as Savior

First, foreigners and their handling of their own antiquities and historical monuments by the early twentieth century informed and helped shape Chinese laws and social norms of antiquities, rules, and ideas considered synonymous with civilization, culture, and national essence in China. As covered in chapter 2, Frederick McCormick, an American journalist in China, was a foreign hero to the Chinese public through his activism for Chinese antiquities protection, even though he himself, in reality, assumed a double, somewhat counteracting, role as a middleman for art collectors. He explicitly recommended to Chinese presidents and high offices that China should make legal recognition of its monuments and antiquities as its own national property. An object of universal sympathy, China had the moral support of all mankind and the political support of all self-respecting nations.[67] McCormick's idea was well taken and implemented by the Chinese authorities.

Chinese intellectuals and officials who visited Japanese Buddhist temples in the flesh also drew sentimental lessons. In 1926, Zhou Zhaoxiang, president of the Chinese Painting Association and the Beijing Buddhist Association, summarized his Japanese trip in a letter to the minister of internal affairs: Having seen so many Buddha heads from the Longmen and Yungang caves in the houses of rich Japanese families, Zhao chatted and learned from Saeki Jōin (1867–1952), the Dharma-character School abbot of Hōryūji in Nara, that Saeki specially made a proposal to the Chinese delegates attending the East Asian Buddhist Conference in Tokyo in 1925 to protect Longmen and Yungang. It was a deep regret that the proposal was not materialized in China, Zhou lamented.[68] "I have witnessed Japan's respect for the Dharma and its protection of fine arts nearly consistent nation-wide. The wooden elephant of the Tianping Temple, the Buddhist paraphernalia passed down to Japan from China's Sui and Tang dynasties, and a series of [our] national treasures, on which the [Japanese] government expends great effort and care to protect appropriately."[69]

Besides Europe, the United States, and Japan as the admirable models, Egypt and many other developing countries were also for China to emulate in the Chinese media. In 1936, the central Chinese news agency in company of the Chinese delegation at the World Sports Games in Egypt filed a report with *Shenbao*:

> The museum in Egypt was built in 1900 and is now only thirty-six years old. It contains all the antiquities related to Egyptian culture. These cultural objects were, before the museum was constructed, stored in an old museum. The new museum, a one-story building, is magnificent and upon entering our first impression was its good order. No police guards were seen at the entrance, for after all Egypt has never experienced thefts or loss of antiquities. The Egyptians really regard their antiquities as the national essence, the crystallization of their national culture. Nobody aspires selfishly to appropriate them as their personal treasure. On paying the entrance fee of five piasters, one enters through a small door on wheels. The antiquities are on neat and orderly display, allowing the visitors to inspect them systematically.[70]

The Foreign "Other" as Plunderer

The other or concurrent function of the foreign "Other" as perceived in Chinese heritage history of the early twentieth century was that they were rascals, villains, robbers, and thieves who colluded with greedy Chinese merchants to steal and destroy Chinese antiquities and historical monuments. An incomplete list from 1993[71] identified sixty-two objects that were removed from their original site in Longmen and kept in world-renowned museums and by individuals. One-third of them found their home in the United States. Today's visitors to Longmen will find that more than 85 percent of the Buddha heads are missing. Most scandalous of all incidents was the removal of the two low reliefs from Longmen's Central Binyang Cave by eminent figures in the modern historiography of Chinese art and antiquities, such as Langdon Warner, Laurence Sickman, and Alan Priest.

Originally, the two dark gray limestone murals, Emperor Xiaowen and His Court (*Huangdi lifo tu*) and the Offering Procession of the Empress as Donor with Her Attendants (*Huanghou lifo tu*) were mostly carved onto the east wall with a small portion at the east corner of both the north (the former) and south (latter) walls of the Cave.[72] Although by the nineteenth century, Longmen's rock icons had long been neglected or derided by many Chinese literati and had only attracted limited curiosity among foreigners, only tersely described in Ferdinand von Richthofen's monumental geography of China published in 1882,[73] the two bas-reliefs won sudden attention in 1905. In that year, French diplomat Philippe Berthelot reported on a visit to Longmen, describing the Binyang Cave at Longmen, where a "fresco" of a male and a female procession of sculptures evoked a striking "impression of sacerdotal Egyptian figures mixed with Italian Renaissance refinement, gracious manners, expressive beauty of the gestures, equally distant from the Hindu taste as from the Chinese make."[74]

The story of how the two Longmen low reliefs—most prized and "comparable in Chinese art to the Parthenon or Chartres"[75]—ended up at their current homes, respectively at the Metropolitan Museum of Art in New York City and the Nelson-Atkins Museum in Kansas City during the mid and late 1930s is relatively clear when both English and Chinese accounts are cross-examined. It should be noted that most of the Chinese account to this day at both academic and popular levels either holds Alan Priest (Pu Ailun) and Yue Bin (1896–1954), the Chinese dealer in Ta-erh Hutong and Liulichang in Beijing, solely responsible for the destruction and stealing of the two friezes, or is vague about what happened to the Empress low relief. The two cases were rather different, and the Chinese account appears to ignore that it was Laurence Sickman (Shi Kemen), his mentor and instigator Langdon Warner (Hua Shana), the German art dealer based in Beijing, Otto Burchard, and others who were behind reassembling the broken smithereens of the Empress frieze that appeared in the markets of Beijing and Shanghai as well as its eventual departure for the United States.[76]

Between 1931 and 1935 through hushed-up, camouflaged deals, involving a small circle of Chinese and foreign dealers and maritime customs officials in Beijing, Tianjin, Shanghai, and their agents in Luoyang and other places, the two murals were hacked from the cliff face and broken into pieces, and then secretly shipped out of China to the United States. It is well-documented that Warner, Sickman, Priest, and Yue Bin knew what they were doing was, so to say, audacious.

China connoisseurs, scholars, and art and antiquities dealers were well informed that the Chinese government had already for several decades subjected them to transaction and export controls. The American School of Oriental Archaeology files contain a 1913 clipping of the *Government Gazetteers* (*Zhengfu gongbao*) with a translation of the ordinance of the Ministry of Interior which ordered the governments of different provinces "to preserve with care all the relics and objects of art which have been in Confucian and Buddhist temples or in any public places, as well as the temples thereby."[77] Upon return from the 1931 shopping trip to China for the Nelson Gallery, Warner wrote to the German dealer, W. A. Bahr:[78] "Just back from China and Japan . . . Stone sculpture cannot be exported without endless corruption of officials, which I am not prepared to undertake. Work up country has come to an absolute stop for anyone but grave robbers and hunghutze [i.e., outlaws]—but, as you know, all China seems to have joined those two groups."[79]

In autumn 1909 while in Japan with regular training from Okakura Kakuzō, Langdon Warner, a young Harvard graduate, first became exposed to the "Honan business," Longmen in Okakura's words. In a letter to his father, Warner recounted his first education about Longmen given by Okakura:

Honan [Henan], or rather Loyang [Luoyang] in the province of Honan in China, is a mountain-side pieced with hundreds of rock-cut Buddha temples containing tens of thousands of sculptures dating from 516 and stretching along to the 13th century or probably later. . . . Of course in Honan and the nearby provinces the place is famous but beyond that even Chinese have seldom heard of it for Confucian scholarship has so overload [*sic*] everything else that there is not even any literature on the subject beyond a casual mention in the poets and the fact of the Empress Hu having begun it.[80]

Then, he showered the paired Emperor and Empress Processions reliefs with praise in comparison to Greek masterpieces:

By the photographs I am sending you now you can see what classical Chinese sculpture was in its prime. Look at the procession of figures—it is well composed as the Parthenon frieze, and for line I have never seen it beaten . . . Sensei [Okakura] considers it very important that this mine of top notch Chinese sculpture should become accessible to the West—it is an unopened Parthenon or rather the whole Acropolis of Athens waiting to be studied.[81]

Warner played a crucial role in helping the new Kansas City's Nelson Gallery acquire the Empress Procession low relief at Longmen. Warner lived and lives on in the hagiology of the Japanese as a "protective angle," who saved Kyoto and Nara from bombing in World War Two, and in the demonology of the Chinese as a cultural robber (*wenhua qiangdao*) and a plunderer of antiquities (*wenwu daoqiefan*) who stole over ten pieces of frescos from no. 328 Cave of color sculpture and other places in Dunhuang.[82] He himself visited Longmen in 1914 and 1923, on the former occasion financed by Charles Lang Freer, who went there in 1911 and was infatuated with it as well.

In 1931, Warner accepted a profitable advising appointment to the trustees of the yet unbuilt William Rockhill Nelson Gallery in Kansas City, and went on an acquisition trip to China in 1931 for the Gallery. For the whole month, he made purchases from dealers in Beijing accompanied by his favorite student, Laurence Sickman, who studied in Beijing from 1930 to early 1935 on a Harvard-Yenching fellowship which Warner had helped Sickman secure. Young, driven and enthusiastic, Sickman instantaneously impressed and received guidance from John Ellerton Lodge (director of the Freer Gallery of Art), Paul Pelliot, Warner, and many other professionals in the field. When Warner left Beijing for home in 1931, he left Sickman a few thousand U.S. dollars deposited in the Chase Manhattan Bank in Beijing for Sickman to acquire works on Warner's approval. Sickman became acquainted with the cloak-and-dagger business world in the antiquities market. On Warner's recommendation, Sickman was contracted to make purchases for the as yet unformed Nelson collection, mainly from the market in Beijing and to a lesser degree in Shanghai, but still in consultation with Warner for major acquisitions.[83]

Sickman visited Longmen three times, first in December 1931 when the Empress relief was largely intact, March 1933 accompanied by a local official and Wilma and John Fairbank finding that a large section of the empress relief and several isolated heads were gone, and last in 1934 when he found the bas-relief of the empress and her court was almost completely gone (Figure 6.1):[84]

> My inquiries disclosed the fragments of the empress relief were not concentrated in the hands of one owner but were scattered, some in Peking, others in Cheng-chou, Kaifeng, and Shanghai. Later one fragment was found in Germany. Since the relief not only was gone from its proper site but was in danger of being completely dispersed and lost forever as a unified composition, we decided that the best course would be to assemble as many of the fragments as possible and attempt to reconstruct the sculpture. Some of the fragments had been put together by the dealers into relatively large sections, but much was in the form of chips of varying sizes.[85]

Figure 6.1   Laurence Sickman in Luoyang, China, 1932.
Source: Laurence Sickman Papers, MSS 001, The Nelson-Atkins Museum of Art Archives, Kansas City, Missouri.

In early 1934, instigated by Warner and approved by Edward Forbes and the Nelson Gallery, the plan for the Harvard Fogg Museum and Nelson Gallery to sponsor the pursuit of the Empress relief was carried out by Sickman and Burchard who assembled the chips. The down payment for acquiring most of the pieces was US$ 13,000. In May 1934, two large restored sections were shipped out of Shanghai with the aid of Jim Plumer at Chinese customs. Sickman wrote in a letter of May 2, 1934 to Plumer who was asked to destroy it upon reading:

> I was then a happy artless young man, I am now gray and bent, and my mind none too clear, but I have the complete relief of the entire procession. From here and there, from shop after shop, from K'ai Feng (Kaifeng), from Cheng Chou [Zhengzhou], yes, from Shanghai. I have collected bit by bit, half a head here, a sleeve there, a hand from Hsia, hundreds and hundreds of small fragments. . . . Three months to put it together. Little boys sit all day long trying this piece and that. Where does it go, how does it fit? Is it an eye or a bit of ruffle?[86]

The reconstructed Empress frieze was made public in 1941 at the Nelson Gallery. According to Sickman, it took several years to gather the many fragments that could be found, and not until the winter of 1939–1940 that the reconstruction began in Kansas City, Missouri with the assistance from the sculptor Wallace Rosenbauer of the Kansas City Art Institute. But still the reconstructed Empress bas-relief "is rather like a person who has suffered a very severe accident. The skill of the facial surgeon may make him recognizable to his friends, but he is never quite the same."[87] Sickman concluded: "Works of art throughout history have often had eventful and frequently tragic careers. . . . And yet, all who are concerned with the cultural tradition of China would far rather wish that the relief of the empress were still in far-off Honan province, an integral part of the Pin-yang [Binyang] Cave for which it was made."[88]

The frenzy over stone sculpture and other artifacts at Longmen reached a climax in the equally cruel removal of the Emperor frieze in 1935. The main culprits in China were Alan Priest and Yue Bin. A Harvard graduate, a member of the 1924 Harvard Fogg Museum Expedition, and a student of Langdon Warner, Priest served as the Metropolitan Museum of Art's (MET) second curator of Far Eastern Art from 1928 to 1963, before retiring to Kyoto, Japan. Equally determined to get Longmen's objects for the MET, Priest went back to China in 1934 and joined the race.[89] While in Beijing, Priest learned, through Yue Bin, about the secret chain of Otto Burchard, John Ferguson, Laurence Sickman, Langdon Warner, and Kansas City.[90] The pressure was on. On November 27, 1934, Priest and Yue Bin signed a contract for Yue Bin to deliver a total of nineteen pieces at the price of Chinese currency 14,000 yuan within five years (Figure 6.2).

On the day of signature, Yue Bin gave Priest six pieces of stone heads (*pingxiang rentou*) from the Emperor frieze—the chips of which were allegedly assembled by Yue Bin and his apprentices at his shop Binji[91]—and received four thousand Chinese yuan. The remaining thirteen pieces of heads

Figure 6.2   Yue Bin in the late 1930s, first from the left in the back row.
Source: Public Domain, unknown source.

were to be delivered altogether, or in two or four phases, and paid in install-ments.[92] Allegedly, Yue confessed that he himself went to a Luoyang local scoundrel named Ma Tulong (also nicknamed Ma Longzi) in Dongguan in today's Chanhe district of Luoyang and asked Ma to have the work done at the price of 5,000 Chinese yuan. Ma went to a group of bandits in Yanggou Cun near Longmen to browbeat their own village's three stone cutters to hammer the frieze off the Central Binyang Cave walls.[93]

Born into a poor village family in Tongxian, Hebei Province in 1896, Yue Bin, also named Wenxuan, received two years private schooling. At the age of fourteen, Yue followed a fellow villager, who collected antiquities in

Beijing, to Beijing's Longfu Temple and Liulichang as an apprentice. Yue quickly learned to train his eyes, and later started his own antique business. Within two decades, he became a rich dealer in antiquities, dealing also with French, Japanese, American, and other clients.[94] In 1952 during the political movement of Three-Antis and Five-Antis (*Sanfan Wufan*), officials went to Yue's residence in Tan'er Hutong to check the financial books of his antique shop that was closed in 1950. Since he stopped doing business back in 1950, Yue assumed he was safe with the movement that targeted economic corruption, tax evasion, and stealing of state resources. He casually turned in his old books for inspection. Paging through financial records, the official saw the contract inserted in one of the notebooks. One week later, Yue was summoned by the court. The physical evidence and testimonies by a few informants revealed Yue's dealings with Alan Priest and Longmen's low relief were disclosed. Later at Yue's home, the authorities found two leftover crates of broken stone pieces that could not be puzzled together in the early 1930s and over 500 pieces of artifacts.[95] Soon, 300 intellectuals jointly signed a petition demanding the government impose harsh penalty on Yue. Yue was sentenced to death, suspended for two years, and he died just before the lunar New Year in 1954 (Figure 6.2).[96]

There has been speculation on whether the pair friezes at the Nelson and MET museums are authentically original, and whether Yue kept the originals and sold his forgeries. We may never know.[97] We may never know, either, how Yue Bin would have defended his Faustian pact to himself. In May 1935 when the reassembling of the Empress was completed, Sickman defended his action: "I feel that we have done something for the art of China and for the world the value of which can only be estimated in future generations."[98] Priest's 1944 book recorded the "present history of the reliefs of the Pin Yang Tung":

In 1933 and 1934 the heads and bits of drapery of the two series of donors, male and female, and other fragments from this particular cave temple began to appear on the Peking market. This was the way the things were raped: the little village near Lung Men stands watch, but from across the river men waded armpit-deep and chipped fragments from the surface at night. These they took down to Chengchow [Zhengzhou], where agents of the Peking dealers bought them. In Peking, the fragments were assembled, and with zeal copies were made from photographs and rubbings. . . . Two museums, both in the United States, have sought to save the reliefs—the fragments of the frieze of female donors is [*sic*] on view in the William Rockhill Nelson Gallery in Kansas City, and the Metropolitan Museum has the wreck of the male donors. . . . These two reliefs . . . are a lost thing—nothing more wicked has ever happened to a great monument of a race. They are gone—we have only these pathetic fragments to show.

But there are photographs and the rubbings, which is, I think, the best shadow of what was there.[99]

In April 1947, Langdon Warner wrote to Liang Sicheng, a foremost Chinese architect and architect historian, who was visiting the Department of Fine Arts at Yale University, requesting a formal rehabilitation of his and other names in China:[100]

My purpose in writing is to ask if something cannot be done by dealers and collectors in America to mend the rather touchy situation in regard to the export of antiquities and works of art from China, which is satisfactory to neither sides. . . . I am well aware that I am considered a criminal for fetching a clay statue and three fragments of wall painting from Tun Huang. And yet I cannot regard the matter as being anything but a beneficent action of preservation because the local priest was engaged in collecting funds to repair the ancient walls and substitute new clay statues for the old. . . . However that may be, rather than add to our difficult international problems, I would cheerfully advise Harvard College to return the statue and the fragments to a proper Government authority if they really desire it. . . . However, it should be remembered that the 'loss' of examples from Tun Huang may conceivably be more than compensated by the presence in America of such beautiful and appealing examples of Chinese culture. Without such original works of art our laudable attempts to give Americans a sense of kinship and comprehension of Chinese history and accomplishment must fail. You, as an art historian, realize as well or better than I that photographs and replicas fail to impress students, and at best can be used only to help recall experiences we have personally undergone. I am, from this point of view, very glad that China, like Greece and Rome and Italy, is so well represented over here.

Then Warner went on to stress the necessity of reconciliation and an official statement from China to clear his and other people's name:

Without such missionary works of art, Americans would be even more ignorant and unsympathetic than you have found us. . . . This double interest—that China shall not feel robbed and aggrieved and that the West shall comprehend China's culture—are [*sic*] not incompatible. . . . We (and as many dealers and collectors as will join us) would welcome some direct statement from the Academia Sinica [emphasis in original], or other appropriate body, as to what they wish to do in this matter. They must realize first, however, that the New York dealers, like the American collectors, do not usually know of the existence of works of art until they have been offered for sale on the open market. Further we do not wish to resort to any such obvious legalism as to claim that starving Chinese peasants are to blame for robbing graves and stone grottoes. . . . However to adjust matters I do not know, but I do know well that we in America cannot afford to lose Chinese friendship over a small matter of money or even a large matter of cultural treasures useful to create good understanding.[101]

Modern eastward engagement with China and Longmen manifested many levels of insoluble contradiction. And the biggest contradiction is that votive monuments such as Longmen were in premodern society not meant for sale at all. Capitalist markets added value to them so that everybody became a captive of modernity and double dealing—aspiring for the public good while submitting to one's own interest. Longmen's stone Buddhas would have continuously been left largely in solitude, had not railway lines, the core of industrialization and modernization, been built in the early twentieth century. "Cruelty and art are not as strange bedfellows as critics make it sound. Great patrons of art could also be whimsically cruel. Patronage showed not only taste but also power."[102]

More subtle and diverse opinions about foreigners in Chinese history of antiquities have emerged in the last seven years or so. How do the rising scholarship of young art historians in mainland China[103] and nonspecialists of their generation appraise the broken Longmen of today? Some Chinese admire the great stone craftsmanship that "shook their souls," while feeling upset about the "stealing" of 85 percent of the Buddhist heads, a "true regret of our country."[104] Calmer than Guo Moruo's epigraphic poem, some young Chinese appreciate the depth of history and imperfect beauty:

> We finally came to this place [Luoyang] that witnessed so many winners-take-all vicissitudes of life to experience the only known divine capital of China. . . . The [Longmen] cave shrines have gone through the baptism of thousands of years of history, many were already destroyed, and some are even empty, leaving later generations with impaired beauty and sentiments.[105]

CONCLUSION

This chapter documents the emergence and development of a particular area of Chinese law that focused on items and monuments passed down from the past associated with culture and civilization. Before modern times, traditional Chinese literati treasured mainly comprised calligraphy, paintings, and bronze or stone steles. At the turn of the twentieth century, the parameters of antiquities (*guwu*) expanded to include the long-ignored stone sculptures, ancient temples, and ancient trees, etc. Moreover, cultural relics were redefined in the development of peoplehood, and in doing so articulated a classic legal justification for Chinese culture- and nation-oriented argument to antiquities.

Classical ownership theory tends to overlook the possibility of non-owners exercising stewardship over tangible and intangible goods.[106] However, what arose from the controversy over the two bas-reliefs at Longmen was the relational vision of antiquities that in reality honored the legitimate interests of both original owners and non-owners, in furtherance of various human and social values. In an effort to exonerate himself and some other scholars, collectors and connoisseurs, Langdon Warner argued subtly for the cultural commons approach to antiquities. Access to original Chinese artifacts provided Americans a sense of one-world community and understanding of Chinese civilization.[107] There is of course an element of self-justification and apologetics here. But Warner's view sits well with critiques of cultural patrimony both at the extreme and moderate sides of cultural commons, open access, and cultural good for humanity.[108]

In earlier history, the Longmen caves were expressions of devotion and belief. A Janus-faced modernity channeled the past into a universal but blighted beauty. The more modernity appropriates the past, the more opposite direction it needed and regressed in order to sustain. Both sin and redemption were irresistible sociocultural swirls. Through examining the origins and content of antiquities protection laws promulgated in the three different periods of the Qing, the Beijing, and the Nationalist governments, it is clear that the Chinese definition of cultural relics constantly veered toward expansion while the legal and institutional capacity was enhanced for better management. I argue that the modernist dilemma, as in the case of Longmen, was rooted in the insoluble conflict of modernity. One can see this in our own contemporary example in the last few years: nationalism is on the rise, and surely it is being countered by a counter movement, the resurgence of cosmopolitanism.[109] However, it is not a rarity today that Chinese scholars and intellectuals indicate that Longmen belongs to the world and that Longmen is Luoyang's Longmen and the world's Longmen. Whatever it means to different people is another matter.[110]

Passions and interests involved from a legal historical perspective on Longmen do reveal that the theme of antiquities in domestic and international law has found a way to develop through alignment, clashes, compromises, and balancing. In the end, it all converges on one point, the unifying power of human creations, as one Luoyang local author puts it: "When we visited the Longmen Grottoes, we met a tourist group of over one hundred people. It did not seem that they were speaking English; some said that they seemed to be French, while others said they appeared to be German. No matter whether one is French or German, to them the Longmen caves denote one common language—art does not distinguish national boundaries!"[111] The laws for culture protection will not work if the community does not display any interest and take actions in correspondence. But here again, alas, do we end up where we began, and we have to ask ourselves whether there *is* a point of convergence or whether we are dealing with the vanishing point as an artistic illusion of convergence, a reality or a perspectivistic technique.

NOTES

1. Guo Moruo (1892–1978), "Yuqinjin fanggu shiba shou," *Wenwu*, no. 8 (August 1959), p. 2. Among many of his cultural, political appointments, Guo was the first director of the Chinese Academy of Science and the Chinese Academy of Social Sciences.

2. Letter from Frederick McCormick, secretary of China Monuments Society, to the editor of *North-China Daily News*, October 7, 1913.

3. Descriptive, repetitive, and emotionally charged works in Chinese can be found in Guo Moruo, "Guan Longmen shiku chi meidi cuihui daoqie wenwu ershou: Fang Fengxian Si Shiku," *Wenwu*, no. 8 (August 1959), p. 2; Yi Ming, *Kangyi meidi lueduo woguo wenwu* (Beijing: Wenwu chubanshe, 1960); Zhang Zicheng, ed., *Bainian Zhongguo wenwu liushi beiwanglu* (Beijing: Zhongguo lüyou chubanshe, 2001), on the loss of Longmen, the "collusion" between Chinese dealer Yue Bin (1896–1955) in Beijing and Alan Priest, see pp. 224–30; Zhang Jian, *Guobao jienan beiwanglu* (Beijing: Zhongguo lüyou chubanshe, 2000); Xu Senyu, ed., *Zhongguo jiawu yihou liuru Riben zhi wenwu mulu* (Shanghai: Zhongxi shuju, 2012); Sun Di, *Zhongguo liushi haiwai Fojiao zaoxiang zonghe tumu* (Beijing: Waiwen chubanshe, 2005); Wu Xiaoding, *Liushi haiwai Zhongguo Fojiao zaoxiang* (Tianjin: Tianjin renmin meishu chubanshe, 2001).

4. On the interchangeable terms for antiquity and cultural heritage, see Introduction.

5. Tony Bennett, *The Birth of the Museum: History, Theory, Politics* (London: Routledge, 1995), links museum and art objects with governance.

6. Philip Thai, *China's War on Smuggling: Law, Economic Life, and the Making of the Modern State, 1842–1965* (New York: Columbia University Press, 2018).

7. Important Chinese newspapers and magazines published the translation of Frederick McCormick's letter to President Yuan Shikai as well as of his interviews with American newspapers and of foreign coverage on the "stealing" of Chinese cultural objects. "Guanyu zhongguo guwu beidao zhi tanpian ji jisi," and "Lun Zhongguo gubei zhi beidao," both in *Dongfang zazhi* 10, no. 12 (1914): 34–36, and "Makemi jun baocun Zhongguo guwu banfa zhi hanjian," *Dongfang zazhi* 11, no. 6 (1914): 15–18.

8. The translation of terms of organizations follows H.S. Brunnert and V. V. Hagelstrom, transl. by A. Beltcheko and E. E. Morgan, *Present Day Political Organization of China* (Shanghai: Kelly and Walsh, Limited, 1912).

9. "Yini Minzhengbu guanzhi zhangcheng qingdan gongcheng yulan," Shangwu yinshuguan bianyisuo, comp., *Daqing Guangxu xinfaling: dier lei guanzhi yi. jingguan zhi* (Beijing: Shangwu chubanshe, 1909), vol. 3, p. 28.

10. The original reads: "美术所关，较之字迹，犹可珍宝," in Neizheng bu nianjian biancuan weiyuanhui, comp., *Neizheng nianjian 3* (Shanghai: Shangwu yinshuguan, 1936), p. 148.

11. "Tongchi chabao baocun guju," *Ta Kung Pao*, December 17, 1910.

12. "Neiwu bu tingsi fenke zhangcheng," (announced in August 1912) in Shangwu yinshuguan bianyisuo, ed., *Zhonghua minguo faling daquan* (Shanghai: Shangwu yinshuguan, 1913), pp. 51–5.

13. "Xi'anfu baohu Beilin," *Shen bao*, no. 14122, p. 6, June 16, 1912.

14. "Neiwubu wei tuoshan baohu Longmen guji yu Henan shengzhang gongshu wanglai wen," Correspondence no. 1: "Neiwubu zhi Henan minzhengzhang xunling" February 26, 1914, in Zhongguo di'er lishi dang'anguan, comp., *Zhonghua mingua dang'an ziliao huibian*, disanji, wenhua (Zhongguo di'er lishi thereafter, unless specified otherwise) (Nanjing: Jiangsu guji chubanshe, 1991), pp. 190–1.

15. Correspondence no. 2: "Neiwubu zhi Henan minzhengzhang xunling," October 2, 1916, in Zhongguo di'er lishi, p. 191.

16. Correspondence no. 3: "Henan shengzhang Tian Wenlie zhi Neiwubu," October 18, 1916, and two enclosures, "Baoshou Longmenshan shifo guitiao," and "Longmenshan dengchu zaoxiang shumubiao," in Zhongguo di'er lishi, pp. 191–6.

17. Founded in 1914, the Institute of Antiquity Exhibition is the first Chinese imperial and national museum of art. It was merged into the Imperial Palace Museum in 1948. https://zh.wikipedia.org/zh-hans/ (accessed on August 7, 2019).

18. Zhu Qiling (Minister of Internal Affairs), "Neiwubu ling (wei baocun guwu)," "Guwu chenliesuo zhangcheng," and "Baocun guwu xiejin hui zhangcheng," all issued in December 1913, *Tongsu jiaoyu zazhi*, no. 5 (1914): 2–8, citation in sequence on p. 2 and p. 3.

19. Nian Ming, "Quan dajia baocun guwu," in *Yanjiang huibian: Lousu gailiang*, no. 52, 1917: 53–65.

20. "Da Zongtong fabu xianzhi guwu chukou ling," June 14, 1914 in Zhongguo di'er lishi, p. 185.

21. Correspondence 4: "Neiwubu wei qieshi baocun qiandai wenwu guji zhi gesheng minzhengzhang xunling," in Zhongguo di'er lishi, p. 197.

22. "Baocun guwu zanxing banfa," in Zhongguo di'er lishi, pp. 198–9.

23. Qinhuai hanbo, that is, trees of the Gleditsia or Robinia genera.

24. "Neiwu bu dingding baocun guwu zanxing banfa," October 1916, *Faling daquan sanbian*, online database, vol. 3, 5th category: Neiwu, pp. 46–7.

25. "Neiwubu wei diaocha guwu liebiao baobu zhe ge shengzhang/dutong zi," in Zhongguo di'er lishi, pp. 199–200.

26. "Shuiwuchu zhi Neiwubu gonghan," December 14, 1925, in Zhongguo di'er lishi, p. 186.

27. Correspondence 9: "Neiwubu guanyu Yungang, Longmeng zaoxiang daliang wailiushi zhi Shanxi, Henan shengzhang zi," in Zhongguo di'er lishi, pp. 203–5.

28. "Yusheng guwu beidao shenduo, Yuan Tongli chakan hou baogao," *Shenbao*, January 14, 1937. This story was compiled by Rong Yuan as "Yusheng Luoyang Longmen Huixian wenwu duo beidao," *Yanjing xuebao*, no. 21 (June 1937): 292–94.

29. "Xiuzhen Neizheng bu gesi fenke guize," in Neizheng bu zongwusi dierke, comp., *Neizhengfa huibian* (Beijing: Jinghua yinshuguan, 1931), pp. 225–36.

30. Daxueyuan gongbao bianjichu, ed., *Daxueyuan gongbao*, no. 4 (April 1928): 31–32.

31. Daxueyuan bianjichu, ed., *Daxueyuan gongbao*, no. 4 (April 1928): 9–10. Founding members were: Fu Sinian, Cai Yuanpei, Zhang Renjie, Yi Peiji, Hu Shi, Li Siguang, Li Zongtong, Li Huangying, Gaolu, Xu Bingtui, Shen Jianshi, Chen yinque, Li Jishen, Zhu Jiaji, Gu Jiegang, Ma Heng, Liu Fu, Yuan Fuli, and Wen Wenquan.

32. *Sifa gongbao*, online database, 1930, no. 75, p. 12.

33. "Guwu chuguo huzhao guize," March 16, 1935, in Zhongguo di'er lishi, *diwuji, wenhua* 2, pp. 630–1. In the 1930 *Guwu baocun fa*, the time limit for cultural relics to travel overseas was two years.

34. Article 13, "Guwu baocun fa," and "Guwu baocunfa shishi xize," in Zhongguo di'er lishi, diwuji, wenhua 2, pp. 609–11, 622–5.

35. Neiwubu nianjian bianzuan weiyuanhui, comp., *Neizheng nianjian 3* (Beijing: Shangwu yinshuguan, 1936), p.165.

36. "Zhongyang guwu baoguan weiyuanhui disanci changwu huiyi jilu," in Zhongyang guwu baoguan weiyuanhui, ed., *Zhongyan guwu baoguan weiyuanhui huiyi shilu diyice*, 1935, p. 4. "Zanding guwu zhi fanwei ji zhonglei dagang," ed. by Zhongyang guwu baoguan weiyuanhui, *Zhongyan guwu baoguan weiyuanhui huiyi shilu diyice*, 1936, pp. 52–3.

37. "Henansheng wenwu guji baoguan yu yanjiu jigou zhangze," "Guoli zhongyang yanjiuyuan Henansheng zhengfu hezu Henan guji yanjiuhui banfa," "Luoyang xian guwu baocun weiyuanhui jianzhang," in Zhongguo di'er lishi dang'an'guan, comp., *Zhonghua mingua dang'an ziliao huibian, diwuji* (series no. 5), *wenhua* 2, pp. 584–8.

38. For an examination of heritage-related legal documents of the PRC, see Jocelyne Fresnais, *La Protection du Patrimoine en Répubic Populaire de Chine, 1949–1999* (Paris: Imprimerie Rey Villeurbanne for Éditions du comité des travaux historiques et scienctifiques, 2001). Guojia wenwuju, *Zhongguo wenhua yichan shiye fagui wenjian huibian (1949–2009)* (Beijing: Wenwu chubanshe 2009); Guojia wenwuju, *Zhongguo wenwu shiye liushi nian* (Beijing: Wenwu chubanshe, 2009); Xie Chensheng, "Xin Zhongguo wenwu baohu gongzuo wushi nian," in Peng Qingyun, ed., *Xie Chensheng wenbo wenji* (Beijing: Wenwu chubanshe, 2010).

39. Besides the actual substance, one can also infer this from the fact that the online English version of the 2017 revised versions of both the protection law and implementation regulations is the 2002–2003 ones, http://www.sach.gov.cn/art/200 7/10/29/art_1034_6944.html and http://www.sach.gov.cn/art/2007/10/29/art_103 4_6941.html (both sites accessed on February 8, 2019).

40. Peng Lei, "Wenwu fazhi jianshe zhong ying zhuyi de jige wenti," *Zhongguo wenwu kexue yanjiu*, December 15, 2015, pp. 28–32.

41. "Zhonghua Renmin Gongheguo wenwu baohufa," see Guojia wenwuju, http://www.sach.gov.cn/art/2017/11/28/art_1034_121351.html (accessed on February 8, 2019).

42. For an interesting take on the 2002 legislation and contemporary private collecting and antique markets in China, the United States, Sweden, South Korea and Hong Kong, see former reporter Zhou Ti, *Guwan shichang jinxi kao* (Hong Kong: Xianggang tianma chuban youxian gongsi, 3rd expanded ed., 2007), 1st ed. by Zhongguo wenlian chubanshe in 2001.

43. http://culturalheritage.state.gov/ch2009MOU.pdf; http://www.xinhuanet.com/culture/2019-01/15/c_1123989537.htm (accessed on March 7, 2019).

44. The 1995 UNIDROIT Convention uses "cultural objects." The 1954 Hague Convention and the 1970, 1972, 2001, and 2003 UNESCO Conventions use "cultural property."

45. Usually source nations argue that historical monuments symbolize a culture, a civilization, and they belong to their territorial physical birthplace. For market/receiving countries, they argue that cultural objects belong to the entire human museum of cultures, https://www.youtube.com/watch?v=J3MXPqYKKRM (Parthenon battle).

46. The Commission on the Bicentennial of the United States Constitution, *The Constitution of the United States with Index and the Declaration of Independence* (D.C.: Government Printing Office, 1992 18th ed.), p. 22.

47. Marie-Sophie de Clippele and Lucie Lambrecht, "Art Law & Balances. Increased Protection of Cultural Heritage Law Vs. Private Ownership: Towards Clash or Balance?" *International Journal of Culture Property* 22 (2015): 259–78.

48. Examples include Lieber Code: Instructions for the Government of Armies of the United States in the Field (April 24, 1863); the Japanese 1871 Plan for the Preservation of Ancient Artifacts (*Koki Kyūbutsu Kozonkata*); Brussels Declaration: Project of an International Declaration concerning the Laws and Customs of War (Brussels, August 27, 1874), Oxford Manual: The Laws of War on Land (Oxford, September 9, 1880); The 1899 Hague Convention (II): Convention (II) with respect to the Laws and Customs of War on Land and its annex: Regulations concerning the Laws and Customs of War on Land (The Hague, July 29, 1899).

49. Some legal scholars point out the counterbalance in the case of Belgium: "Belgian jurisprudence, influenced by recent decisions of the European Court of Human Rights, seems to counterbalance the trend towards increased heritage protection by taking into consideration the interests of the private owner, thereby confirming a dialectic movement between both interests. . . . These two considerations might open the way for the search of a new balance between private ownership rights and the general interest of cultural heritage protection." Marie-Sophie de Clippele and Lucie Lambrecht, "Art Law & Balances," pp. 260–1.

50. Articles 55–56, http://avalon.law.yale.edu/20th_century/hague04.asp (accessed on March 7, 2019).

51. Leslie Brenner, "Nicholas Roerich: Idealist and Visionary," *Foreign Affairs Journal* (April 1990), p. 17 and p. 20; Lewis R. Elbinger, "The Unifying Power of Art," *Foreign Service Journal* (April 1990), pp. 16–17. The same issue, pp. 17–18, contains the text of the Roerich Pact: Protections of Artistic and Scientific Institutions and Historic Monuments (Inter-American), http://afsa.org/foreign-service-journal-april-1990, all accessed on November 23, 2019.

52. Zhao Shanshan, "Wenhua yichan de falü baohu: Zhongri bijiao yu bentu xuanze," *Guowai shehui kexue*, no. 6 (2018): 25–33; Zhou Xing and Liao Mingjun, "Fei wuzhi wenhua yichan baohu de Riben jingyan," *Minzu yishu* 2007 (1): 26–35.

53. Alexi Shannon Baker, "Selling the Past: *United States V. Frederick Schultz*." https://archive.archaeology.org/online/features/schultz/, April 2002, last updated in June 2003 (accessed on February 5, 2019).

54. States are not bound by the conventions until they ratify or accede to it. Paris, November 14, 1970. For the 26-article Convention, see http://portal.unesco.org/en/ev.php-URL_ID=13039&URL_DO=DO_TOPIC&URL_SECTION=201.html (accessed on February 13, 2019). For its strengths and weaknesses, see the commentary by Patrick J. O'Keefe, *Commentary on the UNESCO 1970 Convention on*

the Means of Prohibiting and Preventing the Illicit Import, Export and Transfer of Ownership of Cultural Property (Leicester: Institute of Art and Law, 2007).

55. For an analysis of the loopholes in the 1970 and 1995 conventions, terminological definition, types and difficulties of disputes, see Kathryn Last, "The Resolution of Cultural Property Disputes: Some Issues of Definition," in *Resolution of Cultural Property Disputes*, ed. by the International Bureau of the Permanent Court of Arbitration (The Hague: Kluwer Law International 2004), pp. 53–84.

56. Article 3, The Hague, May 14, 1954, http://portal.unesco.org/en/ev.php-URL_ID=13637&URL_DO=DO_TOPIC&URL_SECTION=201.html (accessed on February 13, 2019).

57. Kelly Elizabeth Yasaitis, "National Ownership Laws as Cultural Property Protection Policy: The Emerging Trend in *United States v. Schultz*," *International Journal of Culture Property* 12 (2005): 95–113.

58. O'Keefe, *Commentary on the UNESCO 1970 Convention*, p. 13.

59. In the high-profile *United States v. Schultz*, Frederick Schultz was found guilty of conspiring to receive stolen Egyptian antiquities (that belonged to Egypt according to the Egyptian Law 117) in violation of the 1934 U.S. Federal National Stolen Property Act (NSPA) and was sentenced in June 2002. Many legal scholars note that "there is an unmistakable trend" in the United States cases whereby foreign cultural property ownership laws can be the basis for the prosecution of violators under the NSPA criminal statute. Similar to the NSPA, the United Kingdom enacted the *Dealings in Cultural Objects (Offences) Act 2003*, a criminal statute dealing with the "acquiring, disposing of, importing or exporting tainted [unlawfully excavated] cultural objects." Yasaitis, "National Ownership Laws as Cultural Property Protection Policy," p. 108. For criticism of the Schultz conviction, state ownership and restricted movement of antiquities, see Steven Vincent, "The Stake in the Schultz Trial," *Orientations* 33, no. 2 (February 2002), Commentary; Steven Vincent, "Schultz Convicted," *Orientations* 33, no. 4 (April 2002), Commentary. Paul M. Bator, "An Essay on the International Trade in Art," *Stanford Law Review* 34 (1982): 275–348. J. H. Merryman, "Two Ways of Thinking about Cultural Property," *American Journal of International Law* 80, no. 4 (1986): 831–53; J. H. Merryman, "Cultural Property, International Trade and Human Rights," *Cardozo Arts & Entertainment Law Journal* 51 (2001): 51–68.

60. J. B. Cuno, "Ownership and Protection of Heritage: Cultural Property Rights for the 21st Century: U.S. Art Museums and Cultural Property," *Connecticut Journal of International Law* 16, no. 2 (2001):189–96.

61. Eric A. Posner, "The International Protection of Cultural Property: Some Skeptical Observations," *Chicago Journal of International Law* 8, no. 1 (summer 2007), Article 12, pp. 213–31, https://chicagounbound.uchicago.edu/cjil/vol8/iss1/12 (accessed on February 5, 2019).

62. Posner, "The International Protection of Cultural Property," p. 215. Posner's point seemed to be proven: One study of seven major museums and individual antiquities collections for signs of looting and smuggling shows that about 75 percent of the 1,396 antiquities in those collections were of unknown origin, with many surfacing for the first time well after the passage of national antiquities regulations. See

Baker, "Selling the Past," under "The Numbers." Regarding China, some people believe that "100,000 looters are active in China. With more than 400,000 ancient graves robbed in the last 20 years alone," Lauren Hilgers in 2013, http://savingantiquities.org/a-global-concern/china (accessed on January 31, 2019).

63. Maria Romos and David Duganne, Harris Interactive, Society for American Archaeology, "Exploring public perceptions and attitudes about archaeology," February 2000, https://documents.saa.org/container/docs/default-source/docpublicoutreach/harris_poll1999.pdf?sfvrsn=8fefd9a4_4 (accessed on February 4, 2019), pp. 26–7.

64. de Clippele, "Art Law & Balances. Increased Protection of Cultural Heritage Law Vs. Private Ownership: Towards Clash or Balance?" pp. 260–1.

65. The United States contributed 22% of financial support for UNESCO. Like the United Kingdom, Singapore and South Africa, the United States left UNESCO before, in 1984 and rejoined it in 2003. Robin Coningham, http://theconversation.com/why-the-us-withdrawal-from-unesco-is-a-step-backwards-for-global-cultural-cooperation-85692 (accessed on February 5, 2019).

66. China historian Xiaoqun Xu defines custom as what people had been doing all along in the imperial era, whereas social norms refer to a moral normative of right and wrong. Xiaoqun Xu, "Law, Custom, and Social Norms: Civil Adjudications in Qing and Republican China," *Law and History Review* 36, no. 1 (2018): 77–104. Xiaoqun Xu, "The Rule of Law without Due Process: Punishing Robbers and Bandits in Early-Twentieth-Century China," *Modern China* 33 (2007): 230–57.

67. McCormick, "Representations made to China."

68. "Zhou Zhaoxiang zhi neiwu zongzhang cheng," in Zhongguo di'er lishi, pp. 204–5.

69. "Zhou Zhaoxiang zhi neiwu zongzhang cheng."

70. Feng Youzhen,"Shiyun daibiaotuan suizheng ji," (7) *Shenbao*, August 9, 1936, no. 22728. Tim Wright alerted me that these were most ludicrous statements ever made. Egyptian grave robbers made the Chinese look like amateurs.

71. Longmen shiku yanjiusuo, ed. *Longmen liusan diaoxiang ji* (Shanghai: Shanghai renmin chubanshe, 1993). Longmen objects housed in the Freer and Sackler Gallery of Art of the Smithsonian Institution in Washington D.C. are not included on this list. The list published by the same institution, now named the Academy of the Longmen Grottoes, in 2015 registered fifty-eight specimens from Longmen housed in museums around the world, of which about one-third are in the United States. Longmen Shiku Yanjiuyuan, ed., *Longmen baiwen* (Zhengzhou: Daxiang chubanshe, 2015), pp. 195–8. According to a newspaper report, the number of stolen or dispersed items from the Longmen Grottoes totals 626 stone sculptures of Buddha and Bodhisattva. Liu Jianxin, "Longmen shiwen," in *Luoyang ribao*, April 20, 2001, p. 2.

72. The Metropolitan Museum of Art gives the dimensions of 208.3 cm (H) and 393.70 cm (W) for the Emperor Procession frieze, and the Empress one is 203.2 cm (H) and 278.13 cm (W) according to the Nelson-Atkins Museum of Art. The Chinese description on site for both low reliefs is close to 2 meters high × 2.50 meters wide.

73. Ferdinand von Richthofen, *China. Ergebnisse eigener Reisen und darauf gegründeter Studien* (Berlin: Verlag von Dietrich Reimer, 1882), vol. 2, *Das nördliche China*, p. 505.

74. Philippe Berthelot, "Note sur des Inscriptions Arabes, Persanes et Chinoises du Chen-Si, du Ho-Nan et du Chan-Toung," *Comptes rendus des Séances de L'Academie des Inscriptions et Belles-Lettres* 49, no. 2 (1905), p. 194.

75. Alan Priest letter to Herbert Winlock, February 15, 1934, 35.146, Curatorial Files Far Eastern Art, Metropolitan Museum of Art, cited in Karl E. Meyer and Shareen Blair Brysac, *The China Collectors: America's Century-Long Hunt for Asian Art Treasures* (New York: Palgrave Macmillan, 2015), p. 97.

76. He Zhijun, "Luoyang Longmen shiku de lishi jienan he wenwu huigui," *Zhongguo wenwu bao*, July 27, 2018, p. 3; Zhao Zhenhuan, "Longmen shiku de daozao," *Jingdian Zhongguo shufa* 227, no. 3 (2012): 96–105; Luoyang difanshizhi bianzuan weiyuanhui, *Luoyang shi dashiji: 50,000 BEC–1990 CE* (Luoyang: Luoyang difang shizhi bianzuan weiyuanhui, 1991), p. 295, p. 353. Sickman was specified as the culprit in Plate 2 photo of the Empress relief but the main text was vague in this regard. See Kaogu yanjiusuo ziliaoshi, "Jielu Meidi yiguan lueduo woguo wenwu de wuchi zuixing," *Kaogu* 4 (1960): 1–10 and 8 plates. One rare exception is the essay in *Beijing ribao* that mostly copied directly from the translation of Myer 2015 and Cheng Chongyuan's works, Huang Jiajia, "Guibao yusui: Longmen shiku 'dihou lifo tu,' mengnan ji," *Beijing ribao*, February 6, 2018, two parts, p. 13 and p. 16. This essay has been recirculated in many digital and social media in China.

77. CLF Papers, The American School of Oriental Archaeology, Box 232, Folder 2, Clippings 1913. In close communication with Freer and as the founding director of the School, Langdon Warner went on an expedition financed by this organization, an offshoot of the Smithsonian Institution for the expedition from Boston to London, Paris, and then Russia through trans-Siberian train to Manchuria and Beijing 1913–1914, and 1915–1916 Japan. Langdon Warner Papers, Box 10, MS AM 3138: Warner's diary, Harvard Houghton Library. Warner's mentor and close collaborator, Okakura Kakuzō wrote a letter of May 1, 1912 from Peking to Warner suggesting where to go for Buddhist rock temples, see Box 2, Folder 30, Okakura, Kakuzo, circa 1906–1912, Houghton Library.

78. Osvald Sirén, Document Group 17, 1907–1957. "Lopnr. File no. 1–28, A: 1 (Box 1), Brev Och Document (Document) 1907–1919," Sirénarkiv, Östasiatiska Museets, 1907–1919. A: 2, Box 2, Files no. 29–221, 1920–1929.

79. Warner's letter of September 10, 1931 in response to Bahr's letter of August 25, Langdon Warner, Langdon Warner Personal Archive, 1881–1955, Harvard University Archives, Box 1, Folder: Langdon Warner Correspondence.

80. Langdon Warner, ed. by Theodore Bowie, *Langdon Warner through His Letters* (Bloomington, Ind.: Indiana University Press, 1966), pp. 32–3.

81. Warner, *Langdon Warner through His Letters*, p. 33.

82. A simple search at baidu.com yielded this result; however, as of March 2020, these Chinese search engine hits are no longer available in Germany. Warner, *Langdon Warner through His Letters*, preface by Bowie.

83. "Laurence Sickman in His Own Words," "Excerpts from the Address of Acceptance: The Charles Lang Freer medal," in Michael Churchman, ed. *Laurence Sickman: A Tribute* (Kansas City, M.O.: Nelson-Atkins Museum of Art, 1988), pp. 11–14, 23–7.

84. Meyer, *The China Collectors*, pp. 93–4.

85. Laurence Sickman, "The Empress as Donor with Attendants," *The Kansas City Star*, January 29, 1967.

86. Meyer, *The China Collectors*, p. 94. Sickman to Jim Plumer, May 2, 1934, RG 02, Series I, Sub-Series A, 5.18-5.19 "P" Nelson-Atkins Museum of Art. On Warner's recommendation, the Nelson Gallery appointed Sickman to the curatorship of Oriental Art in 1935, Warner, *Langdon Warner through His Letters*, pp. 146–9. During World War Two, Sickman served as a U.S. Army Intelligence Officer in China. After the Japanese surrender, he worked in the Arts and Monuments Division of the General Headquarters of the Supreme Commander of the Allied Powers (SCAP) in Tokyo, Japan. Among many honors and awards, Sickman was the 1973 recipient of the Freer Medal.

87. Sickman, "The Empress as Donor with Attendants."

88. Sickman, "The Empress as Donor with Attendants."

89. In his reminiscences on his fellowship at the MET from 1953–1954, James Cahill (1927–2014), a former professor of Chinese art at the University of California at Berkeley, commented that "Alan Priest was a crusty, malicious character modeled on the then-popular image of the lovable rogue who insults everybody (see "The Man Who Came to Dinner: etc) and played the part well." http://jamescahill.info/the-writings-of-james-cahill/responses-a-reminiscences/165-43-an-alan-priest-story (accessed on February 23, 2019); http://jamescahill.info/the-writings-of-james-cahill/responses-a-reminiscences/161-39-alan-priest-and-c-t-loo (accessed on February 2, 2019). John A. Pope, review of Alan Priest, *Chinese Sculpture in the Metropolitan Museum of Art* (Photographs by Tet Borsig), *College Art Journal* 4, no. 2 (1945): 118–20.

90. Meyer, *The China Collectors*, pp. 97–8. "A patriarch of Peking's American community" (John Fairbank) in the 1930s, John Calvin Ferguson (1866–1945) was an American missionary, dealer, collector, government adviser, and scholar who spent most of his adult life in China. Lara Jaishree Netting, *A Perpetual Fire: John C. Ferguson and His Quest for Chinese Art and Culture* (Hong Kong: Hong Kong University Press, 2013).

91. Chen Chongyuan (1928–2010), *Lao gudongshang* (Beijing: Beijing chubanshe, 2008) mainly features Yue Bin and related contemporary antique dealers; *Liulichang lao zhanggui* (Beijing: Beijing chubanshe, 2015), pp. 160–207. Chen worked as apprentice since the age of ten until the late 1940s at his uncle's antique shop, initially funded by Yue Bin, in Liulichang, the antiquities area of Beijing.

92. Wang Shixiang, "Ji Meidi sougua woguo wenwu de qida zhongxin," *Wenwu cankao ziliao* 7 (1955): 45–55, plus 34 plates. Kaogu yanjiusuo ziliaoshi, "Jielu Meidi yiguan lueduo woguo wenwu de wuzhi zuicxing," *Kaogu* 4 (1960): 1–10, plus 8 plates.

93. 2007 Chinese Central Television presented a documentary series, "Zhongyuan dafaxian," and the fifth episode features the thefts at Longmen (Longmen daoying). http://www.cctv.com/program/tsfx/topic/geography/C20322/20071228/104498_1.shtml (accessed on October 22, 2016). Zhao Zhenhua, "Longmen shiku daozao shi," in Li Zhengang, ed., *2004 nian Longmen Shiku guoji xueshu yantaohui wenji* (Zhengzhou: Henan renmin chubanshe, 2006), pp. 269–78.

94. Chen, *Liu Lichang laozhanggui*, pp. 160–203.

95. Chinese Central Television, "Zhongyuan dafaxian," Longmen daoying.

96. Chen, *Liu Lichang laozhanggui*, pp. 206–7; Chen, *Lao gudongshang*, ch. 30. Letter from Liu Kaiqu et al., and editorial, "Zhicai daomai wenwu de jianshang," *Renmin ribao*, December 16, 1952.

97. Liu Lianxiang, "Meiguo daduhui yishu bowuguan cang Longmen Beiwei huangdi lifotu kaobian," *Gugong bowuyuan yuankan* 165, no. 1 (2013): 120–31.

98. Meyer, *The China Collectors*, p. 94.

99. Alan Priest, *Chinese Sculpture in the Metropolitan Museum of Art* (New York: The Metropolitan Museum of Art, 1944), p. 26.

100. Warner's letter of April 11, 1947 to Liang Ssu-ch'eng, Box 5, Folder 15, "L"-2, 1937–1949, Langdon Warner Personal Archive, Harvard University Archives 1881–1955, HUG 4872.1010.

101. Warner's letter of April 11, 1947 to Liang Ssu-ch'eng.

102. Rajeshwari Ghose, posting on the Tamerlane Award at H-Asia on May 1, 2010.

103. Ye Gongping's "Er'shi shijie zaoqi Beijing de yishupin jiancang yanjiu," PhD dissertation, Nanjing shifan daxue, 2014, profiles Beijing and native Chinese, Japanese, American, and European China collectors and connoisseurs. Focusing on the Emperor and Empress friezes at Longmen and Gongxian, Jiao Lin argues that the pair murals were a special type of iconology of Buddhist devotees paying homage to the Buddha that consisted of a crowned protagonist on an outing with servants behind him or her. The appearance of the image of emperors and empresses in these low reliefs was significant and innovative in the Chinese history of fine arts. Jiao Lin, "Dihou lifotu yanjiu," PhD dissertation, 2015, Zhongyan meishu xueyuan. A CNKI search, conducted on February 21, 2019, yielded seventy-two hits on Laurence Sickman, and thirty-two on Alan Priest. The overwhelming majority of Chinese scholarship involving both figures was published after 2009 in art history and archaeology.

104. Baijiahao, blog, posted on April 7 (no year), https://baijiahao.baidu.com/s?id=1564006962066203&wfr=spider&for=pc (accessed on January 16, 2018).

105. Guilinren luntan, blog, originally posted on April 25, 2017. http://bbs.guilinlife.com/forum.php?mod=viewthread&tid=9026129 (accessed on January 16, 2018).

106. K. A. Carpenter, S. K. Katyal and A. R. Riley, "In defense of property," *Yale Law Journal* 118, no. 6 (2009): 1022–125.

107. Warner's letter of April 11, 1947 to Liang Ssu-ch'eng.

108. Michael Brown, *Who Owns Native Culture* (Cambridge, Mass.: Harvard University Press, 2003); Naomi Mezey, "The Paradox of Cultural Property." *Columbia Law Review* 107 (2007): 2004–46; Kwame Anthony Appiah, *Cosmopolitanism: Ethics in a World of Strangers* (New York: Penguin, 2006).

109. See articles on new nationalism and cosmopolitanism in *Foreign Affairs*, February 2019, https://www.foreignaffairs.com/issues/2019/98/2 (accessed on November 23, 2019).

110. Wen Yucheng, preface, in Longmen shiku yanjiusuo, ed. *Longmen liusan diaoxiang ji*, p. 3. Sun Qinliang, "Luoyang de Longmen he shijie de Longmen," in *Jingdian Luoyang*, ed. by Qi Changfa, Hong Kong: Zhongguo wenhua chubanshe, 2007, pp. 94–9.

111. Sun Qinliang, "Luoyang de Longmen he shijie de Longmen," p. 95.

Chapter 7

UNESCO's Longmen and Chinese Urbanization

Better City, Better Life?

The process of turning Longmen into to a Chinese and world heritage site had a long gestation. For over a millennium, the site was chiefly appreciated for its scenery, political and cultural heroes such as Yu the Great and Bai Juyi, and epigraphic inscriptions. Longmen's striking natural landscape (*shanshui*), rather than its stone niches and statues, was most often the center of attention. The turn of the twentieth century marked a watershed, when international studies of Longmen's caves and iconography began to appear in the fields of archaeology, sinology, religion, art, and East Asian studies. Since its founding in 1949, the People's Republic has carried on the historical legacy from the early twentieth century, although it was in a very limited fashion until the 1990s. The many voices from the past attesting to the significance of Longmen not only reflect its enduring attraction under varied circumstances but also demonstrate how far China has come in managing its heritage sites and learning to appreciate the value placed on the caves by the international community. Longmen would not have been today without the initial impetus given by international and Chinese recognition and systematic study. Toward the end of the twentieth century, new momentum emerged from China's desire to participate more actively in the post–World War Two world order.

On February 16, 2001, based on the report of the twenty-fourth session of its World Heritage Committee held from November 27 to December 2, 2000, in Cairns, Australia, UNESCO decided to add the Longmen Grottoes to the WHL of properties deemed to have outstanding universal value.[1]

Adopted in November 1972 at the seventeenth session of the UNESCO General Conference in Paris and ratified by 187 countries as of 2010, the Convention Concerning the Protection of the World Cultural and Natural

Heritage is intended to identify and protect cultural and natural sites that "merit recognition as part of the common heritage of humankind."[2] In China, measures taken to encourage sub-national factors favoring World Heritage (Shiyi) nomination, and resulting conservation efforts, have been growing in strength since it joined the World Heritage Convention in 1985. In tandem with Italy, China has as of August 2019 more World Heritage properties than any other countries in the world.[3]

This chapter examines how China during the past four decades aligned its aspiration for global prestige with urbanization in the case of Longmen from three angles: first, preparations that led to China's UNESCO listing and ensuing efforts to fulfill its World Heritage obligations have brought change to not only Longmen's but also Luoyang's physical environment. UNESCO's WHL has rapidly put down roots in the country in China's unceasing push for urbanization, widely considered modernity's synonym. Currently somewhat overlooked in scholarly debate over Chinese foreign policy, linking WHL with Chinese domestic agendas helps explain how China used the world order for its own benefits and influence around the world.[4]

Second, this chapter examines the mass mobilization and local workings of the Chinese political system in heritage governance, a synergistic style of interaction that aims to incorporate international, national, and local rules and norms rather than produce isolated and uncoordinated efforts. How did the city of Luoyang government establish legitimacy for itself in the realm of heritage governance? What light did the Longmen experience cast on the nature of political reality at the local level?

Third, UNESCO heritage management at Longmen has been integrated into Chinese official plans for urbanization. Although China did not announce any official urbanization policy until 2014, since the 1980s urbanization has been the core goal of China's forceful push for modernization and national rejuvenation. Chinese urban population by the official census count rose from 17 percent of the total population in 1979 to 56 percent in 2015, and it was 60 percent in 2019.[5] What has happened to the over 700 households of former villagers at Longmen, who are now urbanites in situ as a result of Longmen's new world status and Chinese urbanization?

NOMINATING LONGMEN FOR THE UNESCO WORLD HERITAGE LIST

China's transformative participation in the world heritage regime has furnished it with new concepts, techniques, and technology for domestic reform and for protecting its cultural treasures. The case of Longmen has been no exception. In this local version of modernity, a complex array of local, national, and international agencies and actors at governmental, intergovernmental, and nongovernmental levels formed a variety of hybrid coalitions aimed at conserving and refurbishing the site. Through various means, material and nonmaterial, political and cultural organizations combined their resources to mobilize the power inherent in national pride, antiquity, international institutions, and prevailing cultural norms.[6]

Since 1988 when Longmen was put on the internal possible nomination list, Luoyang's participation in the World Heritage regime had largely been directed by the state, which permitted the city authorities to coordinate its role in events with a complex mix of agents horizontally and vertically.[7] This approach corresponded to the prime role taken by nation-states as prescribed by the 1972 World Heritage Convention. Nation-states are entrusted with full powers in Article 4 of the Convention: "Each State Party to this Convention recognizes that the duty of ensuring the identification, protection, conservation, presentation and transmission to future generations of the cultural and natural heritage referred to in Articles 1 and 2 and situated on its territory, belongs primarily to that State."[8] The state, non-state, and interstate agents involved in the Longmen nomination included the UNESCO World Heritage Centre; the International Council on Monuments and Sites (ICOMOS); UNESCO Japan Funds-in-Trust; the Sino-Italian Cooperative Training Centre for Conservation and Restoration of Cultural Heritage; the Chinese State Administration for Cultural Heritage; the Henan Provincial government and its subordinate offices, such as the Henan Provincial Administration for Cultural Heritage; and the Luoyang municipal government including the Luoyang Administration for Cultural Heritage and other subordinate offices.

For the project to gain legitimacy, UNESCO required that government initiatives be cemented by regulations and political consensus, enhancing the ability of a regulatory regime to exercise authority over the structure and behavior of public and private entities alike.[9] International conventions, and national, provincial, and local statutes and rules provided important sources of leadership—the political mandate—for the Luoyang municipal authorities to make important decisions on heritage matters. A second-tier source of legitimacy was a series of Chinese national laws on land administration, urban planning and housing demolition, and statutes on the protection of cultural relics issued in 1982 and replaced by a more detailed law in 2002. Third, the project's legitimacy was also in part secured by the structure of provincial and local government in China. Urban governments are elected by and held accountable to local people's congresses.

Since 1996, measures taken to conserve the grottoes and upgrade their sur-
roundings have been driven by China's aspirations to have the site added to
the WHL in conformity with UNESCO's requirements for continuous moni-
toring of the conservation and management of cultural sites. When asked why
China should seek World Heritage status, Guo Zhan, then general secretary
of the Chinese National Committee of ICOMOS, replied:

> Being able to contribute to humanity through the World Heritage List is itself a
> new starting point, one which enhances the self-esteem, confidence and creativ-
> ity of the local people involved. When Nara in Japan was applying for World
> Heritage status and was asked why it was applying for the World Heritage List,
> people from all walks of life unanimously responded that it would be the driving
> force for social progress [in the region].[10]

The Luoyang city government and its Administration for Cultural Heritage
spent 1997 and 1998 developing a strategy and dispatching staff to study
existing World Heritage sites in Beijing, Dunhuang, and Chengde.[11] The
Institute for Longmen Grottoes Research (now the Research Academy of the
Longmen Grottoes) took responsibility for drafting a comprehensive nomination portfolio, which included audiovisual materials. In February 1999, the
Luoyang city government sought support from the Henan provincial government for its plans to apply for World Heritage status for Longmen.[12] In April
1999, at the third meeting of the Standing Committee of the 10th People's
Congress of Luoyang, new legislation was passed for the management and
protection of Longmen. One month later, it was approved by the 9th Congress
of Henan Province.[13]

The boundaries of two special protected zones—"inner" and "general"—
were demarcated. No buildings can be constructed within the "inner" protection zone—about 4.3 square kilometers, bounded by Yuziling to the east,
Erdaoqiaogou to the south, the Yiluo highway to the west, and Meiyaogou
to the north. In the general protection zone—9.5 square kilometers, bounded
by Shimagou in the east, Shuinichang in the south, Peijiayao in the west, and
Yuanlinchang in the north—construction is restricted and must conform to
relevant environmental regulations.[14]

Further to the passing of legislation at the national, provincial, and municipal levels—in compliance with the UNESCO criteria—the city of Luoyang
was also obliged to ensure adequate management and control mechanisms to
preserve the integrity of Longmen.[15] Two events were crucial for understanding the workings of the local municipal system at Longmen. These were the
massive environmental enhancement program from July 21 to September 5,
1999, and the demolition, relocation, and renovation project carried out at
Longmen's north entrance (February 19–April 15, 2000).

Longmen's poor infrastructure and dilapidated environment was the biggest hurdle for its nomination—the "most difficult, burdensome, demanding, yet essential task," as one document expressed it.[16] As a result, a complex environmental makeover was undertaken in the summer of 1999. The work was carried out in four stages—an initial publicity drive and mass mobilization (*dongyuan xuanchuan*, July 21–August 5) followed by a voluntary (*zixing zhili*, August 6–20) and mandatory (*qiangxing zhili*, 21–31 August) clean-up and inspection (*jiancha yanshou*, September 1–5) process.[17] The Luoyang municipal government allocated CNY (RMB) 1.7 billion (US$ 25.8 million), with additional discretionary funds of CNY 15 million and CNY 30 million from the state and provincial governments respectively, to restore the natural landscape of Longmen according to the requirements of international charters on the protection of cultural relics. The fast environmental clean-up started on July 20 and continued for fifty days until September 10, 1999.

In this process, "villains" and "heroes" did not fall conveniently along the state–society divide.[18] Often, actors—official, unofficial, or of hybrid status—were "culprits" and "heroes" at the same time: illegal buildings and other structures targeted for demolition or relocation had often been erected by private villagers or by village-, district-, and town-owned enterprises, but sometimes they were under the jurisdiction of the government or the army. In the inner and outer protection zones, for example, polluting factories—7 quartz sand plants, 538 stone quarries, 91 factories on the Yi River, and 92 lime plants—were owned not only by the "state" but also by "society."[19] In all, more than eighty structures in the protection zones were demolished or relocated, because they "severely damaged the natural landscape of the Longmen Grottoes, some . . . have caused visible pollution to domestic and foreign visitors and tarnished Luoyang's reputation, and some have threatened the conservation of the Grottoes."[20]

The city government dredged and removed riverbed sediments over an area of 30 hectares. The Jiaozhi railway line was moved 700 meters (0.43 miles) away from the site, and antivibration devices were mounted on the rail track. To protect the Longmen property from motor vehicles, the Luoluan and Luolin highways were relocated outside the protection area.

Behind-the-scenes coordination between governmental agencies was crucial to the sweeping environmental makeover at Longmen in the summer of 1999. During the clean-up campaign, six illegal buildings and other structures targeted for demolition or relocation fell under the jurisdiction of the province, while a further three belonged to the army.[21] To gather support for the campaign, the Luoyang city government made numerous requests to various provincial agencies.[22]

Properties belonging to the provincial authorities or the army included a movie complex, occupying an area of 2,000 square meters, 200 meters away from Longmen's caves; an earthquake observation station with twenty residential apartments, only 100 meters away from the site; cable tracks and six offices belonging to the Luoyang hydrological station; high power lines of 230 meters long; an oil depot of 2,114 square meters, belonging to the provincial mining and geology group; a satellite communication tower on Longmen's Xiangshan (East Hill); and a water supply station; and vacant but run-down barracks belonging to three army units.[23]

On August 15, 1999, "the Chinese dragon palace" (Zhonghua Longgong)—a hotel and entertainment complex consisting of a 158-meter-wide main building and four underground structures, with one of the structures on the "problem" list, was leveled to the ground in a series of controlled explosions by army engineers. Built in 1992, the complex—owned by the Longmen town government and erected at a cost of over CNY 10 million—had earned popular disapproval as its artificial, contemporary style was felt to be totally out of character with the Longmen Grottoes. To execute the demolition safely, the army first detonated explosives set on the eastern side of the "palace" so that the building would fall to the east away from the densely carved niches and caves of the West Hill. Half a second later, the blasting crew ignited explosives attached to two side columns, bringing the building down.[24]

In July 1999, the Longmen nomination dossier for the WHL was submitted to UNESCO by the Chinese government.[25] The National Commission of the PRC for UNESCO argued that Longmen met the criteria laid out in UNESCO's "Operational Guidelines for the Implementation of the World Heritage Convention," in addition to the required "test of authenticity."[26] Preserved in its original form, Longmen is one of the most significant "treasure houses of great classical art . . . in the world today," observed the Chinese UNESCO Commission. According to the official dossier, in contrast to the Dunhuang Mogao Grottoes in Gansu Province, noted for their painted sculptures and murals, and the "foreign-looking" Yungang Grottoes near Datong in Shanxi Province—strongly influenced by artistic traditions depicting Indian *gandharvas* (nonhuman beings) and by the Gupta (*Jiduo*) art—the Longmen Grottoes bear the witness to the sinification and popularization of Buddhism in China. Longmen is also synthetic in its iconography, encompassing a wide variety of Buddhist schools including the Dharmalaksana and Avatamsaka schools, the Three Stages and Pure Land sects, Tantrism, and even Daoism. The Chinese UNESCO Commission concluded its submission by noting that Longmen's caves were "products of imagery administered [*sic*] by the imperial court during the heyday of the Northern Wei and Tang Dynasty."[27]

Accepting the general thrust of these arguments, ICOMOS, the expert advisory body designated by UNESCO to evaluate the application, recommended that Longmen be added to the WHL on three counts:

Criterion One: The sculptures of the Longmen Grottoes are an outstanding manifestation of human artistic creativity. Criterion Two: The Longmen Grottoes illustrate the perfection of a long-established art form that was to play a highly significant role in the cultural evolution of this region of Asia. Criterion Three: The high cultural level and sophisticated society of Tang Dynasty China are encapsulated in the exceptional stone carvings of the Longmen Grottoes.[28]

On November 30, 2000, Longmen's addition to the list was officially announced. The city of Luoyang greeted the news with unrestrained euphoria. On the streets, cars carried streamers proclaiming "Warm Congratulations on the Success of Longmen's Application."[29] "Buddha Vairocana is smiling," the title of one article in the Chinese press, expressed the feelings of local people to a tee.[30] To celebrate the occasion, an official rally, entitled "Singing an Ode to Longmen," was held at the Fengxian Monastery on December 10, 2000 and attended by over 10,000 people.

The unprecedented environmental projects to elevate Longmen's international status showed that UNESCO devolved responsibility on each nation-state government with the power to override more divisive collectives at district, village, and regional levels and the ability to overcome the dialectic between the universal and the local.[31] This centralized multilateral fertilization process has brought about simultaneous interpenetration and interdependence which has borne fruit in a growing social pluralism.

HERITAGE AND URBANIZATION AT LONGMEN

This section sheds light on the integration of heritage management, modernity, and urbanization at Longmen. Among many meanings, modernity is about the dissemination of modern concepts of life, culture, and heritage. During the past three decades, there has been an explosion of information on the UNESCO World Heritage Convention and List which is easily accessible to ordinary people. A 40-hour TV documentary series, "World Heritage in China" (*Shijie yichan zai Zhongguo*), produced and broadcast by the Chinese Central Television (CCTV) in 2008, generated both interest and questions. In response to the series, one internet surfer asked: "Can World Heritage status adequately represent Chinese civilization?"[32] The website of the Chinese Academy of Agricultural Science published several full-length lectures on the WHL and its impact on China by Guo Zhan, then the general secretary of the Chinese National Committee of ICOMOS.[33]

The UNESCO listing has encouraged ordinary citizens to form coalitions to protect heritage properties and take part in the burgeoning social pluralism that is developing in inland China. Today's environmental movement is not only a "top-down" process but also a spontaneous grassroots phenomenon exhibiting the profound social transformation emerging in contemporary China. Studies of nongovernmental organizations (NGOs) in China point to three major aspects of involvement in environmental protection: the consolidation of connections between NGOs and other activist groups; collective action and the sharing of experience; and the growth of holistic community awareness.[34]

Similar kinds of social networking are developing elsewhere. Nanyan Guo teases out changing perceptions of nature and culture on the Ogasawara Islands in Japan by invoking the concept of "environmental culture" (*kankyou bunka*), that is, "the ideas, beliefs and customs that are shaped by a society's understanding of its natural environment, and are used to protect the environment."[35] People from all walks of life and organizations ranging from the Ogasawara Branch of the Tokyo Government, the Ogasawara General Office of the Japanese Government, the Ogasawara Wildlife Research Society, to the Village Office have joined forces to advocate biodiversity and ecotourism as the best way forward for the Islands.

In the case of Longmen, alert citizens were issuing constant warnings of the dire consequences of overdeveloping or exploiting historical relics with insufficient forethought and vision. They labeled such destructive practices as consuming "cultural fast food" (*wenhua kuaican*). One commentator claimed that less than CNY 100,000 out of the CNY 50 million gathered in admissions each year was actually spent on conservation work. Questions about continuing environmental crises along the Yi River have been repeatedly raised with the local and state departments of cultural heritage.[36] The five-star Dongshan Hotel, converted from a former retreat center for senior officials in the inner protection zone in 2003, was the focus of much public criticism for many years. Locals questioned the legality of the hotel, which is wedged between the Xiangshan Temple and Bai Juyi's grave—a space reserved for the Bai Juyi Memorial in the state and provincial plans for 1997.[37]

The imbroglio, involving a private development project in the general protection zone over ten years ago, showed that public input could be more than window dressing. Cyberspace has created an online community that allows the moral majority a voice. In early December 2008, internet surfers drew attention to the ongoing construction of twenty-nine "unidentified" villas, just 2 kilometers east of the Longmen Grottoes.[38] The media quickly followed up on the story, setting off a barrage of public outrage. It soon became known that the villas were being developed by Longxiang Villa Food and Beverages Ltd., a company operated by a group of cadres and villagers from Guofu Village who were reportedly granted land use and zoning permits by Yichuan County in November 2007, yet without construction permits.

Official investigations concluded that the developers had failed to follow procedures and that the apartments were 200 meters within the general protection zone. The problem arose in part from the change in administrative boundaries involving Guofu Village. Originally under the jurisdiction of Yichuan County, Guofu Village was allegedly transferred to the district of Luolong (part of the city of Luoyang) in May 2008. However, Luolong officials ruled that, as of September 2008, Guofu Village would fall under the jurisdiction of the Longmen Office run by the newly formed Management Commission for the Longmen Cultural and Tourist District in Luoyang.

On December 15, the city of Luoyang publicly announced disciplinary penalties imposed on nine officials from Yichuan County. Two days later, the twenty-nine villas were bulldozed by order of the municipal government.[39] Immediately prior to the outbreak of the villa story, a series of incidents involving other corrupt officials was also uncovered by net surfers and then taken up by the media—publicity which ultimately put pressure on the government to investigate. This unofficial network of checks and balances encouraged one reporter from the influential *People's Daily* to ask when the government offices responsible would get around to *proactively* identifying and exposing such problems, rather than simply responding to public pressure. "People have good reason to expect that the government will do more."[40]

Sometimes state and society can act together. The movement for the preservation of urban memories (*baocun chengshi jiyi*)[41]—integral to China's cultural rejuvenation and heritage movement—has been driven by both state and local actors, together connecting all parts of the system. In his keynote report to the seventeenth National Congress of the Central Committee of the Communist Party of China, then General Secretary Hu Jintao outlined the party's goals for cultural and international development: "The great rejuvenation of the Chinese nation will definitely be accompanied by the thriving of Chinese culture."[42] Compared with the negative historical evaluations of Longmen,[43] local officials, intellectuals, and ordinary citizens of contemporary Luoyang have mostly shown a marked pride in Longmen as their cultural heritage: in verbal and written testimony, they repeatedly stressed that the cultural heritage movement has "enhanced people's consciousness of protecting their cultural treasures, from the government to city-dwellers."[44] For them, the restoration of local heritage is inseparable from national development and national prestige

What does Longmen's World Heritage status mean for those people who have for generations been living at Longmen? During the major environment clean-up for Longmen's nomination for WHL in 1999–2000, the demolition, relocation, and renovation project at Longmen's north entrance involved the relocation of 716 households in Longmen Village within twenty days and construction of a new commercial street and public parking lot to replace the 10-hectare structures owned by twelve state and four community entities. Coordinated activities involving governmental, intergovernmental, and nongovernmental agencies were combined with traditional state-organized mass mobilization by way of persuasion and coercion.[45] In executing those ambitious plans for environmental enhancement, particular emphasis was placed on grassroot cooperation and participation. As a political assignment, each organization involved was required to provide a clear explanation of its work plan and provide compensation for affected work units and individuals, utilizing official resources. At the time, some villagers found it hard to move to a new residential area two or three blocks away from their old homes, although they did comply.

The rehabilitation of the landscape was given a tremendous buildup in the local press. The story of Fan Cheng—the head of the Weiwan Village committee in the town of Longmen, who kicked off the clean-up campaign by striking the water cistern of the village car shop with a large hammer—was one of many reports issued by the media.[46]

In August 1999 alone, *The Luoyang daily*, the city's major newspaper, published thirty reports about Longmen and the UNESCO World Heritage site, helping mold public opinion in favor of the project.[47] The newspaper also published a list of illegal buildings and structures including the chimney of the Longmen Research Institute's building, their owners, locations, and the improvements required.[48] This list included both public and private businesses owned by the state, the army, various municipal authorities, and individuals. Owners were persuaded to fulfill their duty through slogans such as "sacrificing the small family for the big family" (*xisheng xiaojia gu dajia*).[49] Grooming Longmen for the World Heritage nomination was a very challenging task, as the then mayor, Liu Dianli, saw only too clearly:

> Nominating Longmen for the World Heritage List is an obligation that weighs as heavily on us as Mount Tai. If the nomination succeeds, it will provide Luoyang with great spiritual wealth and lay a sound foundation for future development. If on the other hand it turns out to be a missed opportunity as a result of our poor preparation, we would be sinning against the nation and the people.[50]

It should be pointed out that rehousing the agrarian population near Longmen has also been part of the urbanization process in Luoyang. In the early 2000s, the development of vast peri-urban areas such as the new district south of the Luo River involved relocation of large numbers of villagers near their former home, including the eight peri-urban villages around the Longmen Grottoes in the newly created Luolong District.[51]

Those eight peri-urban villages have experienced urbanization in two major waves, in 1999–2000 and from 2012 onward, primarily driven by the changed status of Longmen, in concert with China's urban spread and New-Type Urbanization Plan. Tenacity, innovation, and flexibility are all qualities needed to negotiate the complex urban environment and deal with the Chinese authorities—situations that often have their fair share of drama. The same mechanisms are at work in Luoyang, too, where experiments designed to phase out the hukou system are being carried out by the authorities.[52] In the newly developed Luolong District, residents have formulated a range of strategies—including opening "bed & breakfast" hotels and constructing new floors or nooks on houses flagged for demolition in order to optimize the footage claimed for compensation—to deal with land expropriation.

In January 2011, out of curiosity my father and I paid a visit to Longmen Village, in our capacity as locals, to see how the villagers were faring. On a winter afternoon, we entered a convenience store and spoke with the owner, a friendly young woman, who had no other customers to keep her occupied. We learned that the villagers had all made a "fortune" from the relocation. Each farmer had also received 300–400 Chinese Yuan for every small tree on their property, and over 3,000 Chinese Yuan for a small, shallow family well drawing on the high water table at Longmen. "Now they live in spacious three-story houses, and they are happy," she said. Some middle-aged villagers were employed to do landscaping and cleaning work in the protection zone.[53]

We walked into Longmen Village, composed of blocks of buildings. We observed an old couple, the Lis, both in good health, attending to their small vegetable patch around their house. Both the man—aged eighty-one, a Korean War veteran—and his seventy-six-year-old wife told us that, as they had nothing to do at home, planting vegetables not only saved them money but also gave them regular exercise. When asked about their "new" living situation, the husband replied:[54]

> It has been 11 years now [since the relocation in early 2000]. We have four sons, and we used to live in 10 small rooms without running water. The government paid us 40,000 Chinese yuan for the move. We now have three houses equipped with running water, and just recently an additional house was built so each son now has his own home. Every month each villager receives 35 *jin* (17.5 kg) of rice and flour of our choice for free. . . . Now the village is clean and tidy. We don't have to work, nor do we have any worries about food and clothing.

Seven years afterward, in late April 2018, accompanied by local residents, I again visited Longmen Village for three consecutive days. The "village" is located in blocks of residential buildings, and it was rumoured that they were to be demolished for further development in the near future. Mrs. Li's convenience shop had already been removed in the second wave of development that got underway in 2011–2012 to widen the main thoroughfare, Longmen Avenue, and to construct an eco-zone in the northwest approaches to the grottoes. Now the owner of a beauty store, Mrs. Li had moved to a gated, urban-looking neighborhood called Longmen Neighbourhood's Tangyun Community, equipped with gas pipes for cooking and hot water, a few blocks away from her old neighborhood. A total of 154 households were relocated there from Longmen Village during the second wave of demolition.[55]

In contrast to what I saw during my 2011 visit, in 2018 the Longmen Village neighborhood was teeming with family-run hotels, social services such as purified drinking water distribution sites, convenience and grocery shops, restaurants, kindergartens, and primary and middle schools.[56] I was accompanied to Longmen Village by Mr. Liu, a local urbanite in his early thirties from nearby Du Village, a village close to the Longmen East High Speed Railway Station. Pointing out the numerous makeshift additions to the villagers' three- or four-storey houses, Mr. Liu explained that they were part of a strategy by established residents to maximize their compensation during the coming rounds of relocation. He noted that some villagers had already moved to the Tangyun Community, but renting out their houses in Longmen Village. Many other local people confirmed that, as soon as villagers heard about the development plans, they would rush to expand their homes by adding additional floors or internal structures in order to claim extra compensation from the developers. Many of those we spoke to emphasized that they regarded demolition and relocation as an opportunity to get rich, and they were ecstatic if they learned that their old houses were in the demolition zone.[57]

CONCLUSION

Over the past thirty-five years, the Chinese state has taken the lead in tapping the potential of the World Heritage Convention, making proactive use of the international system while melding multiple influences from the historical, political, social, and economic spheres into its urbanization process.[58] Such a process displays great variation in the different sectors that make it up. Whether one likes it or not, urbanization and China's use of the international order since 1979 resulted in a strengthened state on multi-levels under certain circumstances, although civil society flourished to some extent as well.

An increasing number of scholars from a variety of disciplines have approached the topic of cultural heritage in terms of management and the construction of identity, memory, and space. Perceived from political mobilization, there was coordination as a political metric task, but from purely professional managerial perspective of the West, this was problem-laden at Longmen, as Luca Zan and Sara Bonini Baraldi point out in their 2012 article.[59] Marina Svensson explicates the role of villagers in "engaging the state and other actors in the creation of partly new spatial identities" in post-reform Zhejiang Province.[60] The same process has taken place in other locales around the world. Mary Elizabeth Hancock connects the subject of heritage to themes of rural-urban migration, gender and the tourism industry, and cultural memory in South India.[61]

Diverging from the above angles, this chapter places the issue of cultural heritage in a new light by viewing Longmen as a site where antiquity meets modernity, where world heritage blends with urbanization in China, and where village, town, urban, provincial, national, and international organizations and local communities intersect. A human dimension is added to the evolving process of modernity, urbanization, and site management at Longmen as political tasks and human experiences.

Critics of the WHL have raised questions, inter alia, about UNESCO's assumptions regarding the existence of a homogenous national heritage in nominating a particular monument, building, village, town, landscape, or cultural tradition. The failure to add the town of Agadez in Niger in 2005, for example, shows how the nomination process could be torpedoed in a seething cauldron of colonial and postcolonial political, ethnic, administrative, and financial conflicts involving UNESCO, ICOMOS, the World Conservation Union (IUCN), the French embassy, Niger's Department of Patrimony and Museums and its Ministry of Culture, CRAterre (a French consulting firm specializing in clay architecture), the reigning sultan, and so on.[62] In contrast, at Longmen, the tensions between universal internationalism, particular nationalism, and diverse localism were reconciled through developments managed by the state and its subordinate governments.

From the foregoing chapters, we know that in modern history horrors of robbery and banditry filled the pages left by Longmen's admirers and visitors, both Chinese and foreigners. One observer, Cui Yingke, an intellectual, visited Longmen in 1928 at a time when political order had broken down, following the failure of the constitutional experiment that gave birth to the first Republic of China (1912–1928). During that period, Luoyang had been turned into a military training ground used by Yuan Shikai, the first president of Republican China, and Wu Peifu, a warlord of the Zhili Clique.[63] Just like some of the chief protagonists in this book, Okakura Kakuzō, Édouard Chavannes, Charles Lang Freer, Langdon Warner, Luo Zhenyu, Osvald Sirén and others, Cui recorded his visit for which he and his acquaintance, Mr. Xia, risked their lives:[64]

After an early breakfast, we took a risk and headed out . . . When we were stopped at the crossroads [by locals], I never uttered a single word; when questioned, Mr. Xia—a native of Henan Province—was able to show his local knowledge and avoid provoking the villagers, or local bandits who might have kidnapped us for ransom. We walked for about 30 *li* (15 kilometers) before reaching Longmen. After viewing part of the site, we had a bite to eat and hurried back. We were lucky to find a horse-drawn carriage for hire, but after 20 *li* the driver stopped, leaving 10 *li* of the journey still to do. He was worried about being spotted by the clerks from the magistrate's office, who would make him run errands for the army for free. We offered to pay extra, but he was utterly unmoved. It was nearing dusk as we alighted from the carriage. We dared not use the same route we had taken on our outward trip, so we made a detour for several *li*. Entering Luoyang through the southern gate, we groped our way in the dim, misty moonlight back to the military training headquarters in Xigong [a district in Luoyang where Cui was staying].

Ninety years later, the human story of Longmen continues to unfold but with new sets of conditions, concerns, and opportunities. Contemporary Longmen's villagers have turned into urbanites within a short twenty years, embodying the human quest for a better life across countries and cultures. The inner dynamics and multiple processes of the World Heritage listing and urbanization at Longmen generated such a possibility.

NOTES

Some of the ideas expressed in my two following articles have been updated and reformulated, alongside some printed and fieldwork materials. Dong Wang, "Internationalizing Heritage: UNESCO and China's Longmen Grottoes," *China Information* 24, no. 2 (July 2010): 123–47 and Dong Wang, "Restructuring Governance in Contemporary Urban China: Perspectives on State and Society," *Journal of Contemporary China* 20, no. 72 (November 2011): 723–33.

1. "Report of the 24th Session," UNESCO Archives, WHC-2000/CONF.204/21, also available online at http://whc.unesco.org/archive/repcom00.htm (accessed on August 11, 2007).

2. UNESCO, World Heritage Convention, the United Nations Foundation, and National Geographic, "World Heritage, 2008–2009." The complete text of the 1972 Convention can be seen at http://whc.unesco.org/en/conventiontext/ (accessed November 24, 2019). For the administrative and intellectual genealogy of the World Heritage Convention, see Sarah M. Titchen, "On the construction of outstanding universal value. UNESCO's World Heritage Convention (Convention concerning the protection of the world cultural and natural heritage, 1972) and the identification and assessment of cultural places for inclusion in the World Heritage List," PhD dissertation, Australian National University, Canberra, Australia, 1995.

3. For details, see Introduction.

4. Larry Diamond, and Orville Schell, et al., *Chinese Influence & American Interests: Promoting Constructive Vigilance* (Stanford, Calif.: Hoover Institution Press, 2018); Andrew Scobell, et al., *At Dawn of Belt and Road: China in the Developing World* (Santa Monica, Calif.: RAND, 2018).

5. Dong Wang and Flemming Christiansen, "The Pursuit of New Citizenship by Peri-urban Residents in China: Status, Rights, and Individual Choice," *China Information*, March 2019, pp. 1–20, https://doi.org/10.1177/0920203X19835455.

6. Conversation with Rüdiger Frank of the University of Vienna on September 17, 2009.

7. Interview with Wang Zhiqiang, director of the Administration of the Longmen Cultural Tourism Zone at Longmen on January 1, 2010.

8. http://whc.unesco.org/en/conventiontext/ (accessed on January 13, 2008).

9. UNESCO World Heritage Centre, "Operational Guidelines for the Implementation of the World Heritage Convention," March 1999, WHC-99/2.

10. "Geguo weihe zhongshi shenbao 'shijie yichan,'" *Zhongguo wenhua bao*, April 14, 2002, editorial. Gong Dazhong and Gong Wansong, "Zhenfen jingshen, jixu xiang 'shijie yichan minglu' jinjun," *Heluo chunqiu* 1 (2001): 19–23.

11. Lu Wei, "Jijin quzhe zhong kaiyan, xiaotan huihuang yin jinzhao: Longmen shiku shenbao shijie yichan jishi," *Heluo chunqiu* 1 (2001): 11–14.

12. Luoyangshi renmin zhengfu, "Guanyu jiang Longmen shiku shenbao wei shijie yichan de qingshi," signed by Zhu Guangping, the City of Luoyang archives, file no. 16, February 11, 1999.

13. Luoyangshi renmin zhengfu, "Guanyu tiqing 'Longmen shiku baohu guanli tiaoli (cao'an)' de yi'an," April 15, 1999, the City of Luoyang archives, file no. 41.

14. Luoyangshi renmin zhengfu, "Guanyu Longmen baohuqu huanjing zhili de tonggao," *Luoyang ribao*, August 2, 1999.

15. World Heritage Centre, "Operational Guidelines for the Implementation of the World Heritage Convention," February 1997, WHC-97/2, March 1999, WHC-99/2.

16. "Zuohao shenyi gongzuo, tisheng gudu xingxiang," undated document (written in 2008, my inference), manuscript provided by Lu Wei.

17. Luoyangshi renmin zhengfu, "Longmen shiku baohuqu huanjing zhili shishi fang'an," the City of Luoyang archives, file no. 75, July 26, 1999.

18. In social sciences debates, often the state is equated to "villains" and civil society "heroes." Here I argue that often the line between these two actors is difficult to draw clearly.

19. Luoyangshi renmin zhengfu, "Guanyu qingqiu jiejue Longmen shiku shenbao shijie yichan huanjing zhili zhong youguan wenti de qingshi," City of Luoyang archives, file no. 109, July 8, 1999.

20. Luoyangshi renmin zhengfu, "Guanyu yinfa Longmen shiku baohuqu huanjing zhili shishi fang'an de tongzhi," July 28, 1999, City of Luoyang archives, file no. 75. "Luoyang Longmen huanjing zhili zhihuibu gonggao," *Luoyang ribao*, August 5, 1999.

21. Luoyangshi renmin zhengfu, "Longmen shiku shenbao Shijie yichan neiwai huanjing zhilizhong sheji shengguan danwei he junchan qingkuang diaocha," City of Luoyang archives, file no. 109, July 8, 1999.

22. For examples, see the letter from the Luoyang city government to the Provincial Earthquake Bureau. Luoyangshi renmin zhenfu, "Guanyu xietiao chaichu gaizao Luoyang dizhentai jian(gou)zhuwu de han," City of Luoyang archives, file no. 141, August 15, 1999.

23. Luoyangshi renmin zhengfu, "Longmen shiku shenbao shijie yichan neiwai huanjing zhilizhong sheji shengguan danwei he junchan qingkuang diaocha," City of Luoyang archives, file no. 109, July 8, 1999.

24. Shi Hongtao, "Dichen yisheng xiang, 'julong' bian wali: Zhonghua longgong baopo ji," *Luoyang ribao*, August 17, 1999. Gu Kefeng (of Zhongxin press), "Luo-yang Longmen shiku jinqu baopo chaichu weizhang jianzhu," August 18, 1999, http://news.sina.com.cn/society/1999-8-18/6641.html (accessed January 13, 2009).

25. Two letters dated June 30, 1999, to Mr. Mounir Bouchenaki, Director, UNESCO World Heritage Center, from Yu Fuzeng, Secretary-General, the National Commission of the People's Republic of China for UNESCO. UNESCO Archives in Paris, World Heritage Centre, CLT/WHC/NOM542, China folder, Longmen Grot-toes, no. 1003.

26. The "Operational Guidelines" indicate that the cultural properties in the World Heritage List (WHL) must meet "one or more of the following criteria *and* the test of authenticity. Each property nominated should therefore: (a) (i) represent a mas-terpiece of human creative genius; or (ii) exhibit an important interchange of human values, over a span of time or within a cultural area of the world, on developments in architecture or technology, monumental arts, town-planning or landscape design; or (iii) bear a unique or at least exceptional testimony to a cultural tradition or to a civilization which is living or which has disappeared . . . *and* (b) (i) meet the test of authenticity in design, materials, workmanship or setting and in the case of cultural landscapes their distinctive character and components (the Committee stressed that reconstruction is only acceptable if it is carried out on the basis of complete and detailed documentation of the original and to no extent on conjecture); (ii) have adequate legal and/or contractual and/or traditional protection and management mechanisms to ensure the conservation of the nominated cultural properties or cul-tural landscapes. The existence of protective legislation at the national, provincial, or municipal level and/or a well-established contractual or traditional protection as well as of adequate management and/or planning control mechanisms is therefore essen-tial and, as is clearly indicated in the following paragraph, must be stated clearly on the nomination form. Assurances of the effective implementation of these laws and/ or contractual and/or traditional protection as well as of these management mecha-nisms are also expected. Furthermore, in order to preserve the integrity of cultural sites, particularly those open to large numbers of visitors, the State Party concerned should be able to provide evidence of suitable administrative arrangements to cover the management of the property, its conservation and its accessibility to the public." See UNESCO Intergovernmental Committee for the Protection of World Cultural and Natural Heritage Sites, "Operational Guidelines for the Implementation of the World Heritage Convention," WHC-99/2, March 1999, http://whc.unesco.org/archive/opgui de99.pdf (accessed January 1, 2009).

27. The State Administration for Cultural Heritage of the People's Republic of China (now National Cultural Heritage Administration), *World Heritage Convention, Nomination of Cultural Properties for Inscription on the World Heritage List: China, Longmen Grottoes*, UNESCO Archives, World Heritage Centre, CLT/WHC/NOM 542, p. 12.

28. "Report of the 24ᵗʰ Session," UNESCO Archives, WHC-2000/CONF.204/21, also available online at http://whc.unesco.org/archive/repcom00.htm (accessed August 11, 2007).

29. "Longmen shenbao shijie wenhua yichan shimo," http://travel.sohu.com/82 /37/travel_article15013782.shtml (January 25, 2009).

30. Cui Mingde et al., "Lu She Na weixiao le," *Zhongzhou guji*, no. 1 (2001): 4–7.

31. Charles A. Keller, "The Christian Student Movement, YMCAs, and Transnationalism in Republican China," in Dong Wang, ed., *Christianity as an Issue in the History of U.S.–China Relations*, The Journal of American-East Asian Relations 13 (November 2008): 55–80.

32. http://space.tv.cctv.com/podcast/sjyczzg, accessed January 2, 2009.

33. Guo Zhan, "Shijie yichan zai Zhongguo," http://www.gscaas.net.cn/bbs/d ispbbs.asp?boardid=8&id=223 (accessed January 3, 2009).

34. Fengshi Wu, "Environmental Activism and Civil Society Development in China," talk at the China Lunchtime Seminar, the Fairbank Center for Chinese Studies, Harvard University, May 12, 2009.

35. Nanyan Guo, "Environmental Culture and World Heritage in Pacific Japan: Saving the Ogasawara Islands," *The Asian-Pacific Journal*, vol. 7, issue 17, no. 3, Article ID 3130 (April 12, 2009). https://apjjf.org/-Nanyan-Guo/3130/article.html (accessed on March 6, 2020).

36. Gaoming, "Longmen shiku: kaifa yu baohu shuzhong?"

37. Unknown author, "Shui zhan le Bai Juyi de di?" http://yl.peoplexz. com/2273/2289/20081223105300.htm, posted December 23, 2008 (accessed January 13, 2009).

38. Qu Changrong, "Luoyang Longmen Xishan jingxian 29 tao shenmi bieshu!" *Renmin ribao*, December 10, 2008. Also see unknown author, "Henan Luoyang Shijie wenhua yichan Longmen shiku pang maochu bieshuqun," http://www.ha.xinhua .org/add/hnnews/2008-12/10/content_15140498.htm, posted on December 10, 2008 (accessed on December 26, 2008).

39. Xinhua wang, "Luoyang Longmen shiku Xishan bieshuqun chaichu wanbi, jiuming guanyuan bei zewen," http://www.ha.xinhuanet.com/add/2008-12/18/content_15211088.htm, posted on December 18, 2008 (accessed on December 26, 2008). Public announcement, *Luoyang ribao*, December 15, 2008.

40. Qu Changrong, "Luoyang Longmen Xishan jingxian 29 tao shenmi bieshu!"

41. Meng Guoqing, "'Tianzi jialiu:' jingshi faxian," *Luoyang wanbao*, December 22, 2008.

42. Beijing Review, "Charting Roadmap for China: Special Report, 17th CPC Congress," *Beijing Review* 50, no 43 (October 11, 2007).

43. Dong Wang, "Internationalizing Heritage: UNESCO and China's Longmen Grottoes."

44. Meng Guoqing, "'Tianzi jialiu:' jingshi faxian." Chen Xiaowei, "Longmen liusan wenwu huigui," *Luoyang wanbao*, October 25, 2005, p. 5. Luoyang guangbo dianshi bao, *Luoyang mudan huahui wanquan shouce, Luoyang guangbo dianshi bao*, no. 14, April 7, 2006. Sheila Melvin, "China Remembers its Lost Treasures," *International Herald Tribune*, October 22, 2010, p. 10. Interviews and conversations

with Wang Zhiqiang, Lai Xuezhai, Xu Jinxing at Longmen and Luoyang, on January 1–2, 2010, and July 16–20, 2007.

45. Alan Liu, *Mass Politics in the People's Republic: State and Society in Contemporary China* (Boulder, C.O.: WestviewPress, 1996). James R. Townsend, *Political Participation in Communist China* (Berkeley, Calf.: University of California Press, 1967).

46. Shi Hongtao, "Longmen shiku huanjing zhili zhanyi daxiang," *Luoyang ribao*, August 4, 1999. http://travel.sohu.com/82/37/travel_article15013782.shtml (accessed on January 25, 2009).

47. Zhang Yawu, "Nongmo zhongcai 'Longmen song,'" *Luoyang ribao*, April 4, 2008, special issue, T31.

48. "Luoyang Longmen huanjing zhili zhihuibu gonggao," *Luoyang ribao*, August 5, 1999.

49. "Xisheng xiaojia gu dajia, jiji xingdong zhua luoshi: Longmen shiku huaijing zhili jinzhan shunli," *Luoyang ribao*, August 7, 1999, editorial.

50. "Zuohao shenyi gongzuo, tishen gudu xingxiang."

51. They are Longmen Village, Gaozhuang Village, Sigou Village, Zhanggou Village, Weiwan Village, Guozhai Village, Dongcaodian Village, and Xicaodian Village.

52. Zhonghua Remin Gongheguo guojia fazhan gaige weiyuanhui, "Nongye zhuanyi renkou shiminhua anli," December 2016. http://www.ndrc.gov.cn/fzgggz/fzgh/zcfg/201612/W020161219342511160639.pdf (accessed on April 30, 2018), pp. 66–69. Continuous and locally specific changes have already made significant parts of the hukou system obsolete. The trend is to replace the system with a new registration system for permanent residents, while maintaining temporary residence for groups not meeting the criteria for social insurance and certain other entitlements.

53. Conversation with Ms. Li in her shop just outside the Longmen Grottoes, January 4, 2011.

54. Conversation with Mr. Li and his wife in Longmen Village, January 4, 2011.

55. "Xijia Houpianqu guoyou tudi cheqian pinggu," December 26, 2013, http://www.lmsk.gov.cn/news/show-570.aspx (last accessed April 24, 2018, no longer available).

56. Wang, "The Pursuit of New Citizenship by Peri-urban Residents in China."

57. Information provided by my sources on June 13, 2018 confirmed the profits, more than CNY 100,000 within five years, earned by villagers following the same strategy in Shijiatun Village in Luoyang.

58. Natarajan Ishwaran, "International Conservation Diplomacy and the World Heritage Convention," *Journal of International Wildlife Law & Policy* 7, issue 1–2 (January 2004): 43–57.

59. Luca Zan, and Sara Bonini Baraldi, "Managing Cultural Heritage in China: A View from the Outside," *China Quarterly* 210 (June 2012): 456–81. Luca Zan, Bing Yu, Jianli Yu, and Haiming Yan, *Heritage Sites in Contemporary China: Cultural Policies and Management Practices* (London: Routledge, 2018).

60. Marina Svensson, "In the Ancestors' Shadow: Cultural Heritage Contestations in Chinese Villages," working paper no 17, 2006, Centre for East and Southeast Asian

Studies, Lund University. For similar approaches, see Jun Jing, *The Temple of Memories: History, Power, and Morality in a Chinese Village* (Stanford, Calif.: Stanford University Press, 1996); Diane Barthel, *Historic Preservation: Collective Memory and Historical Identity* (New Brunswick, N.J.: Rutgers University Press, 1996); Peter Howard, *Heritage: Management, Interpretation, Identity* (London: Continuum International Publishing, 2003); Mayfair Mei-Hui Yang, "Spatial Struggles: Postcolonial Complex, State Disenchantment, and Popular Reappropriation of Space in Rural Southeast China," *Journal of Asian Studies* 63, no. 3 (August 2004): 719–56; Jing Wang, ed., *Locating China: Space, Place, and Popular Culture* (London: Routledge, 2005); Tim Oakes and Louisa Schein, *Translocal China: Linkages, Identities, and the Reimaging of Space* (London: Routledge, 2006).

61. Mary Elizabeth Hancock, *The Politics of Heritage from Madras to Chennai* (Bloomington, IN: Indiana University Press, 2008).

62. Marko Scholze, "Arrested Heritage: The Politics of Inscription into the UNESCO World Heritage List: The Case of Agadez in Niger," *Journal of Material Culture* 13, 2 (2008): 215–31. An examination of the failure of the UNESCO project to reshape American ideas about race can be found in Michelle Brattain, "Race, Racism, and Antiracism: UNESCO and the Politics of Presenting Science to the Postwar Public," *American Historical Review* (December 2007): 1386–413.

63. Li Jianren, *Luoyang gujin tan* (Luoyang: Shixue yanjiushe, 1936), pp. 234–47.

64. Cui Yingke, "Luoyang Longmen zhi zaoxiang," *Guoli Zhongshan daxue yuyan lishixue yanjiusuo zhoukan* 5, no. 55 (November 14, 1928): 9–11.

Conclusion

Slighted and denounced as a squandering of resources on gaudy frippery for centuries by many Chinese elites, today the large group of stone icons, decorated cave chapels, votive niches, walls, ceilings, inscribed steles, pillars, and floors at Longmen are appreciated by millions of tourists.[1] The century-long process of recovery and reevaluation of Longmen was led by a host of far-thinking individuals of different nationalities—American, British, Canadian, Chinese, Finish-Russian, French, German, Japanese, Swedish, and others—drawn from the fields of politics, history, art, archaeology, culture, antiquarianism, and connoisseurship. Through its rehabilitation, Longmen, alongside many other historical sites, became a creation of modernity—a monument of mental projection, a symbol of timeless perfection, an object of scientific classification and analysis and, most importantly, the focus of a shared determination to make sense of life.

Linking with a number of major themes in modern and contemporary China, this book advances three conclusions of historiographical significance. First, the modern Chinese experience of the world was far more comprehensive than the conventional dual storyline—the tired narrative of a century of national humiliation in Chinese historiography, twinned with the East-looks-to-the-West trope (*Xixue dongjian*, or the predominance of Western civilization over its Eastern counterpart) in *both* Chinese and Western historiographies.[2] Widely accepted, this narrative holds that after 1800, "because of their success, Europeans and their descendants in North America thought of themselves as too far advanced to find much of substantive value in a backward nation like China. China became a source of merely exotic interest because of its past and was no longer important as a source of current knowledge."[3] This book illustrates some counter-patterns of influence that have regrettably been all but eclipsed by these two master narratives of Chinese history-writing.

There is a further layer of complexity to this story. Ongoing efforts, spearheaded by the Chinese central government, are being made to recast history and China's role in the world, as evidenced by the establishment of the Research Academy of Chinese History (Zhongguo Lishi Yanjiuyuan) in January 2019 within the Chinese Academy of Social Sciences. Contemporary critics who are alarmed, if not overawed, by these developments have for the most part ignored the challenge that conventional Chinese historiography poses to the Chinese establishment's political project of an "alternative" history,[4] one which glorifies traditional Chinese culture, but contradicts China's long-standing position that the Chinese Communist Party emerged during the May Fourth era as an anti-Confucian, anti-traditional, and anti-imperialist political force.[5]

In *The Temple of Memories*, Jun Jing reminds us that historical landmarks evoke ideas and practices that are not mechanically retrieved from the past; rather, they are blended with cultural inventions, shaped by local experiences, and permeated by contemporary concerns.[6] In contemporary China, this process is clearly outlined in a recent piece by President Xi Jinping entitled "Strengthening cultural self-confidence, and building a strong socialist country of culture." President Xi's words dialectically echo a consensus reached in the public debate over antiquities a century ago: "Culture is the soul of a country and a nation."[7]

Second, while my discussion, spanning over two millennia, makes no claim to be an exhaustive treatment of an enormous subject, the story of Longmen is well worth telling. Today, even many senior China experts and journalists are unaware of the significant role that Longmen and other historic Chinese ruins played in helping shape European, American, and Japanese modernity at a time when scholarly attention has been focused on the radical Chinese intellectuals of the period who, at some point during their careers, blamed China's backwardness on its traditional culture. Consequently, the historical revaluation of Longmen and other historical sites and its contribution to constructing modern Chinese identity has been largely ignored.

The appreciation or appropriation of tradition and cultural heritage is a prerequisite for modernity shared by all mankind.[8] China is certainly no exception. In 1943, Cao Bohan published a lucid study of Chinese national learning (*guoxue*) for middle school students and general readers.[9] Espousing the integration of national learning with science and international academic disciplines, Cao's book discussed antiquities (*guwu*), paleontology, the excavation of the Yin ruins (Yinxu) of the Shang dynasty in Anyang, studies of oracle bones, antiquities and sociology, and antiquities and ancient texts, among other subjects.

A complex array of historical elements including self-criticism, nationalism, transnationalism, the market, politics, law, culture, attitudes to foreigners, and cosmopolitanism should, therefore, be taken into account in considering the shaping of relations between China and the world. The liminal space created by relations within and between China and other countries—between old and new, traditional and modern, divergence and convergence, for instance—is the exciting zone that cultural historians are now exploring, whether in detail or in more general terms. The dynamics of a more comprehensive history that is now being crafted originated in the interaction of influences from all over the globe—sometimes collaborative, sometimes contentious.

Third, over the past decade scholars have documented important global interconnections in the seventeenth century, as exemplified by Timothy Brook's discussion of Dutch genre paintings in his book *Vermeer's Hat: The Seventeenth Century and the Dawn of the Global World*.[10] Historical awareness of such global links can also be found in the various expressions of "This Neighborly World" in the first half of the twentieth century.[11] Champions of cosmopolitan "worldism" in China recognized human interdependence in a world made up of many parts, different races and competing opinions. To be sure, this vision also had its commercial counterpart. In 1937, Carl Crow (1883–1945), an American advertising agent based in Shanghai who published a book about China entitled *400 Million Customers*, told his American readers that a shrinking world "makes you a neighbor of the 400 millions of China."[12] Such perceptions validate contemporary scholarly efforts to reveal the common traits that run through religions and cultures. Recent books—such as *The Crisis of Global Modernity*, *History and Popular Memory* and *The Great Civilized Conversation*—have continued to explore this historical theme.[13]

Over a century ago, the search for lost or loosened human connections was expressed in the reappropriation of Longmen and other ancient ruins (*guji, lishi yiji*) in China as a source of transglobal spirituality and modernity—an important dimension of history that has for the most part escaped the attention of commentators.[14] In helping bring Longmen to the world's attention, French diplomat Philippe Berthelot (1866–1934) and Sinologist Édouard Chavannes (1865–1918)[15] saw in these remains a common humanity and universal connections that led them to conclude, in the words of Prasenjit Duara, that "many important and eventful changes in world history have in one way or another been tied to transcendent sources of imagination, inspiration, commitment and resolve."[16] Though trained in different professions, both Berthelot and Chavannes believed that parallel traditions in ancient China, Egypt, India, the Eurasian core, and the Greco-Roman world had developed not in isolation, independently, or endogenously, but had mutually influenced each other through direct human contact as early as the first century Common Era.[17] One product of these multidirectional influences was the Indic-Greek-Chinese Buddhas and deities of the Longmen cave chapels that were sculpted a few centuries later.

In seven chapters, this book explores the sinicization of religion; public discourse and historical artifacts in modern China; the European, American, and Japanese discovery of Longmen; law and cultural heritage; and the connections between UNESCO world heritage status and China's ongoing urbanization project, where Longmen and other historical sites are seen to act as a unifying force, bringing discordant elements together.[18] Longmen's stone Buddhas have revealed the potential for change and betterment in the human condition, even though this may mean very different things for different times and peoples. Each social or national group involved worked for its own political and cultural ends while using others to strengthen their own positions. Longmen shows how the demands of the modern state have shaped global affairs through mining the past, trading places, and ultimately, mirroring influence. Speaking to our own time through the people of the past, Longmen's story illuminates a path to reducing renewed great power rivalries among Russia, China, and the United States especially since 2016, whether in the geostrategic or in the geocultural arena.

NOTES

1. Its stone statues are considered the essence of the historical remains at Longmen.

2. For a critical study of the origins and role of the master narrative of national humiliation, see Dong Wang, *China's Unequal Treaties: Narrating National History* (Lanham, Md.: Rowman & Littlefield, 2005); Dong Wang, "Redeeming 'a Century of National Ignominy:' Nationalism and Party Rivalry over the Unequal Treaties, 1928–1947," *Twentieth-Century China* 30, no. 2 (April 2005): 72–100. David E. Mungello, *The Great Encounter of China and the West, 1500–1800* (Lanham, Md.: Rowman & Littlefield, 2nd ed. 2005), 1st ed. 1999.

3. Mungello, *The Great Encounter of China and the West*, p. 130.

4. Maximilian Mayer, "China's Historical Statecraft and the Return of History," *International Affairs* 94, no. 6 (2018): 1217–35.

5. This ongoing readjustment to the conventional historiography of the May Fourth Movement can be read between the lines in President Xi Jinping's remarks at the 14th collective study meeting of the CCP Politburo Committee on April 20, 2019, http://www.xinhuanet.com/2019-04/20/c_1124393835.htm (accessed on April 21, 2019).

6. Jin Jung, *The Temple of Memories: History, Power, and Morality in a Chinese Village* (Stanford, Calif.: Stanford University Press, 1996), p. 12.

7. Xi Jinping, "Jianding wenhua zixin, jianshe shehui zhuyi wenhua qian-guo," https://article.xuexi.cn/articles/index.html?art_id=10234064154315503061&st udy_style_id=video_default&pid=&ptype=-1&source=share&share_to=wx_feed&fr om=groupmessage&isappinstalled=0 (accessed on June 25, 2019). In April 2007, Lien Chan, honorary chairman of the Nationalist Party (Guomindang) in Taiwan, visited Longmen and other historical sites in Henan Province, stating that "Henan is home to the soul (*xinling*) of Chinese sons and daughters." Shi Baoyin, "Guoming-dang ronyu zhuxi Lian Zhan: Henan shi zhonghua ernü xinling de guxiang," April 17, 2007, http://tw.people.com.cn/GB/14810/5617855.html# (accessed on October 8, 2019).

8. Yang Chia-Ling, and Roderick Whitfield, eds., *Lost Generation*, p. 23. Mar-shall Berman, *All that is Solid Melts into Air: The Experience of Modernity* (London: Verso, 2010), 1st ed. 1982 by Simon and Schuster.

9. Cao Bohan (1897–1959), *Guoxue changshi* (Beijing: Zhonghua shuju, 2017, 12th printing), based on the 1947 ed. by Shanghai wenguang shudian. The 1st ed., where the author took the penname Cao Pu, was published by Guowen zazhishe in 1943.

10. Timothy Brook, *Vermeer's Hat: The Seventeenth Century and the Dawn of the Global World* (New York: Bloomsbury Press, 2008).

11. Carl Crow, *400 Million Customers: The Experiences—Some Happy, Some Sad of an American in China and What They Taught Him* (Norwalk, Conn.: EastBridge, 2003), p. 318, 1st ed. pub. 1937.

12. Crow, *400 Million Customers*, p. 318.

13. Prasenjit Duara, *The Crisis of Global Modernity: Asian Traditions and a Sustainable Future* (Cambridge: Cambridge University Press, 2015); Paul A. Cohen, *History and Popular Memory: The Power of Story in Moments of Crisis* (New York: Columbia University Press 2014); Wm. Theodore de. Bary, *The Great Civilized Conversation: Education for a World Community* (New York: Columbia University Press, 2013).

14. Karl E. Meyer and Shareen Blair Brysac, *The China Collectors: America's Century-Long Hunt for Asian Art Treasures* (New York: Palgrave Macmillan, 2015).

15. Philippe Berthelot, "Note sur des inscriptions arabes, persanes et chinoises du Chen-Si, du Ho-Nan et du Chan-Toung," *Comptes rendus des séances de l'Academie des Inscriptions et Belles-Lettres* 49, 2 (1905): 186–204; Édouard Chavannes (1865–1918), "Voyage archéologique dans la Mandchourie et dans la Chine septentrionale," *T'oung Pao*, IX, 4 (1908): 513–4.

16. Duara, *The Crisis of Global Modernity*, p. 3.

17. Independently of each other, Christopher Beckwith and Lukas Nickel have recently pushed this time frame back several centuries, perhaps to the fourth or third centuries BCE. Christopher I. Beckwith, *Greek Buddha: Pyrrho's Encounter with Early Buddhism in Central Asia* (Princeton, N.J.: Princeton University Press, 2015), especially the preface and epilogue. Nickel identifies Hellenic influences on Chinese sculpture in artifacts from the Qin Dynasty (221–206 BCE). Lukas Nickel, "The First Emperor and Sculpture in China," *Bulletin of SOAS* 76, no. 3 (2013): 413–447.

On the Chinese intrusions into Central Asia, see Nicola Di Cosmo, "Ancient Inner Asian Nomads: Their Economic Basis and its Significance in Chinese History," *Journal of Asian Studies* 53, no. 4 (November 1994): 1092–1126.

18. Peter Frankopan, "From the Ancient Middle East, Art That Links Past and Present: An Exhibition at the MET Challenges How We Look at History," *Foreign Affairs*, June 7, 2019. https://www.foreignaffairs.com/articles/middle-east/2019-06-07/ancient-middle-east-artlinks-past-and-present (accessed on June 8, 2019).

Appendix

Luoyang as Capital: A Brief Timeline

Xia (2070 BCE–1600 BCE)

It is generally understood that the capital of the Xia dynasty was established in or moved to **Zhenxun**[1] in 2070 BCE. There is firm historical evidence that Luoyang was national capital[2] of the Xia for fifty-two years (1763–1711 BCE).

Shang and Zhou (1600 BCE–256 BCE)

Xibo (Western Bo) was built as the capital of the Shang dynasty and **Chengzhou** established in 1036 as the capital of the Zhou dynasty. **Wangcheng** (also known as **Luoyi**) was built 15 kilometers away to become capital of the Western Zhou (1046–771 BCE) and subsequently the Eastern Zhou (770–256 BCE). The Eastern Zhou capital was relocated back to **Chengzhou** in 510 BCE. Some people believe that Luoyang was the national capital for 954 years (1711–1482 BCE, 770–256 BCE) and subsidiary capital for 249 years (1020–771 BCE) in the Shang and Zhou dynasties under forty-seven different emperors.

Han (202 BCE–220 CE)

During the Eastern Han dynasty, Luoyang was the national capital from 25–190 CE (164 years) under fourteen emperors.

Cao Wei (220–266 CE)

Luoyang was the national capital under five emperors and virtually for the full duration (forty-five years) of the Cao Wei dynasty.

Western Jin (266–316 CE)

Luoyang served as the national capital for four emperors during the fifty years of the Western Jin.

Northern Wei (386–534 CE)

Moving the capital of the Northern Wei to Luoyang in 494 CE crowned the dynasty's effort to unify North China after the fragmentation that took place during the Sixteen States period. It remained the imperial seat for forty years under eight emperors until the dynasty disintegrated in 534 CE.

Northern Zhou (557–581 CE)

After the new divisions that followed the decline of the Northern Wei, the Northern Zhou dynasty forged new unity in North China. Luoyang, which had been under the rule of Chang'an (today's Xi'an) as part of the successor state Western Wei (535–556 CE), was again chosen as the secondary national capital, "eastern capital," (dongdu) during the twenty-five years and under four emperors of the Northern Zhou.

Sui (581–618 CE)

When the Sui dynasty subdued the Northern Zhou and unified north and south China, its national capital was located in Chang'an, now under the new name of Daxing; again Luoyang was given the special status of "eastern capital." Luoyang was reinstated as national capital in 605 CE and functioned as such for thirteen years under the reigns of two emperors.

Tang (618–907 CE)

The Tang dynasty restored Chang'an (Xi'an) as national capital in 618, but Luoyang became the chief capital again between 657 and 907 CE under eight emperors for forty-five years. In 684, Empress Wu Zetian declared Luoyang "holy capital," a unique status the city retained until her regency was terminated by a coup in 705.

Later Liang (907–923 CE)

The short-lived successor dynasty Later Liang established itself in Kaifeng and made Luoyang the "western capital," and after two years turned it into the national capital, a role Luoyang held for four years in 909–913 CE.

Other Minor Dynasties of the Tenth Century

Other weak and transient dynasties that followed (the Later Tang, Later Jin, Later Han, and Later Zhou) variously had Luoyang as their national capital (total of fourteen years) or as the "western capital" (twenty-two years).

Song 960–1279 CE and Jin 1115–1234 CE

The Northern Song dynasty, ruled from Kaifeng, was able to unite political power in North China and upheld the practice of styling Luoyang "western capital" during the incumbency of its nine emperors (for 168 years). As the Song dynasty expanded southward, the Jurchen Jin dynasty began to dominate North China, taking over Kaifeng as capital in 1214 CE. Under the Jin Luoyang became "central capital" (zhongdu), an appellation in use from 1115 to 1234 (for 120 years).

Republic of China 1911–1949 CE

In 1932, Luoyang was for about ten months the seat of China's war-time government, evacuated from Nanjing in response to the threat of Japanese troops already in nearby Shanghai.

Sources: Dangdai Luoyang chengshi jianshe bianwenhui, *Dangdai Luo-yang chengshi jianshe* (Anhui: Nongcun duwu chubanshe, 1990), pp. 9–10. Dynastic information was compiled from national and local histories in English and Chinese, including Endymion Wilkinson, *Chinese History: A New Manual* (Cambridge, Mass.: Harvard University Asia Center, 2012), introduction; Angela Falco Howard, Li Song, Wu Hung, and Yang Hong, *Chinese Sculpture* (New Haven, Conn.: Yale University Press and Foreign Languages Press, 2006), chronology; Wan Guoding, comp., Wan Sinian and Chen Mengjia, supplemented, *Zhongguo lishi jinianbiao* (Beijing: Zhonghua shuju, 2005), 1st ed. 1978, and Luoyang difang shizhi bianzuan weiyuan-hui, comp., *Luoyang shizhi* (Zhengzhou: Zhongzhou guji chubanshe, 2002), 18 vols., vol. 1.

NOTES

1. Place names in bold indicate historical locations identical with today's Luoyang or in its immediate vicinity.

2. The term "national" capital (*guodu*) reflects that it was a true capital of a ruling dynasty in history.

Glossary

Baima Si 白马寺
Baipin 百品
baocun chengshi jiyi 保存城市记忆
Baocun guwu tuiguang banfa 保存古物推广办法
baoluo wanxiang 包罗万象
beiren 北人
Beizhi 悲智
Binji 彬记
Binyang Dong 宾阳洞
Bu Tao 步陶
Bunkazai hogohō 文化財保護法
Cai Yin 蔡愔
Cen Wenben 岑文本
chedi de xiandai hua 彻底的现代化
Chen Yi 陈毅
Cheng Renwei 成仁威
Chu Suiliang 褚遂良
da kuaishi 大快事
datong shehui 大同社会
Daxia 大夏
Daxueyuan 大学院
Dishi shejiyuan 第十设计院
Dongguan 东关
dongyuan xuanchuan 动员宣传
dutexing 独特性
dutong 都统
Ephthalites 嚈哒

Ershipin 二十品
Fan Xuanze 樊玄则
Fang Lüjian 方履籛
Fengjingqu Guanbaochu 风景区管保所
fogu 佛谷
Fojiao Zhonguohua 佛教中国化
Foshafu 佛沙伏
fugu er gengxin 复古而更新
gu qiwuxue 古器物学
guji 古迹
Guobao baocunfa 国宝保存法
guocui 国粹
guoxue 国学
guwu baocun 古物保存
Guwu baocunfa 古物保存法
Guwu baoguan weiyuanhui 古物保管委员会
Guwu chenliesuo 古物陈列所
guwu zhuquan 古物主权
guwu 古物
Guyang dong 古阳洞
Hancheng 韩城
hanhua 汉化
Henan Xian 河南县
Henanfu/Honanfu 河南府
Heyin 河阴
Hua Shana 华沙纳
Huang Xiaosong 黄小松
Huang Yi 黄易
Huangdi lifo tu 皇帝礼佛图
Huanghou lifo tu 皇后礼佛图
jiancha yanshou 检查验收
jiang 匠
Jiangnan 江南
jiaoxian 郊县
Jiaoyu bu 教育部
Jiduo 笈多
Jinglan 镜槛
Jingshi guwan shanghui 京师古玩商会
Jingshi zongshanghui 京师总商会
jinshi 金石
jinshixue 金石学
Jiujianfang 九间房

Jiuqiao shi 九峭石
Ju 苴
ke 科
Khotan 于阗/和田
koki kyūbutsu hozonkata 古器旧物保存方
Li Junzan 李君瓒
Li Shangyin 李商隐
libei 立碑
Lingyan Si 灵岩寺
lishi yiji 历史遗迹
Lisu si 礼俗司
Liu Anguo 刘安国
Liu Xihai 刘喜海
Liu Xu 刘糈
Longmen Guanliju 龙门管理局
Longmen sankan 龙门三龛
Longmen Senlin Guji Baohu Weiyuanhui 龙门森林古迹保护委员会
Longmen Shiku 龙门石窟
Longmen Shiku Yanjiusuo 龙门石窟研究所
Longmen sipin 龙门四品
Longmen ti 龙门体
Longmen Wenwu Baoguansuo 龙门文物保管所
Longmen Wenhua Lüyou Yuanqu Guanli Weiyuanhui 龙门文化旅游园区
    管理委员会
Longmen Yanjiuyuan 龙门研究院
Lu Weiting 陆蔚庭
Luo Yi 洛邑
Luoyang Xian 洛阳县
Ma Lingfu 马凌甫
Ma Longzi 马聋子
Ma Tulong 马图龙
meishu 美术
Minzheng bu 民政部
Miu Quansun 繆荃孙
Mofa 末法
Mudan Huahui 牡丹花会
Neiwu bu 内务部
Nühuang 女皇
pingxiang rentou 平像人头
Pu Ailun 普爱伦
pubianxing 普遍性
Puming 普明

Qian Wangzhuo 钱王倬

qian 钱

qiangxing zhili 强制治理

qiankan 千龛

Qihui 起晖

Qin Jing 秦景

Qinhuai hanbo 秦槐汉柏

Qiusheng 秋胜

quanguo diyipi wenwu baohu danwei 全国第一批文物保护单位

Ruman 如满

Saeki Jōin 佐伯定胤

Sanfan Wufan 三反五反

Shaanyuan 陕垣

shanshui 山水

shenkui 深愧

Shijie yichan zai Zhongguo 世界遗产在中国

Shi Kemen 史克门

shijiehua 世界化

Shiyi 世遗

shizhi guwu 石质古物

Shuiwu chu 税务处

shuori 朔日

Song Yu 宋昱

tiji 题记

Udyāna 乌场国

waijiao 外教

Wakhan 钵和

Wang Hequan 王鹤群

Wang Xiling 王锡龄

Wei Ji 韦机 (韦弘机)

wenhua kuaican 文化快餐

wenhua qiangdao 文化强盗

wenhua yichan 文化遗产

wenren 文人

wenwu 文物

Wenwu baohu guanli zanxing tiaoli 文物保护管理暂行条例

wenwu daoqiefan 文物盗窃犯

Wenxuan 文轩

Wenyi Li 闻义里

Wu Yi 武亿

wushipin 五十品

Xiangjiao 像(象/相)教

xianshi zhi renwu 先时之人物
Xiao Baoyin 萧宝夤
Xijing 西京
xinling 心灵
xionghun 雄浑
xisheng xiaojia gu dajia 牺牲小家顾大家
Xixue dongjian 西学东渐
Xiyu 西域
xi'an 西岸
Xue bu 学部
Yanchen 燕臣
Yanggou Cun 杨沟村
Yao Shiji 姚师积
yaofu 邀福
Yingshan si 营缮司
Yinxu 殷墟
yonggong 用功
Yuan Danqiu 元丹丘
Yue Bin 岳彬
zaoxiang tiji 造像题记
Ze Rong 笮融
Zeng Bingzhang 曾炳章
Zhang Ji 张继
Zhengfa 正法
Zhengfu gongbao 政府公报
Zhongguo Lishi Yanjiuyuan 中国历史研究院
Zhongguo tese de Fojiao wenhua 中国特色的佛教文化
Zhongguo tese 中国特色
Zhongguohua 中国化
Zhonghua Longgong 中华龙宫
Zhonghua Renmin Gongheguo Wenwu Baohufa 中华人民共和国文物保护法
Zhongshu sheren 中书舍人
Zhongyang guwu baoguan weiyuanhui 中央古物保管委员会
Zhu 邾
zhuangyan boda 庄严博大
zixing zhili 自行治理
Zong Huaipu 宗怀璞

Bibliography

Abbott, Kenneth W., and Duncan Snidal. "International 'Standards' and International Governance." *Journal of European Public Policy* 8, no. 3 (2001): 345–70.

Abe, K. "Intermediary Elites in the Treaty Port World: Tong Mow-Chee and His Collaborators in Shanghai, 1873–1897." *Journal of the Royal Asiatic Society* 25, no. 3 (July 2015): 461–80.

Abe, Stanley K. "Inside the Wonder House: Buddhist Art and the West." In *Curators of the Buddha: The Study of Buddhism under Colonialism*, ed. by Jr. Donald S. Lopez, 63–106. Chicago, IL: University of Chicago Press, 1995.

———. *Ordinary Images*. Chicago, IL: University of Chicago Press, 2002.

Adluri, Vishwa P. "Pride and Prejudice: Orientalism and German Indology." *International Journal of Hindu Studies* 15, no. 3 (2011): 253–92.

Agnew, John A. "Slums, Ghettos, and Urban Marginality." *Urban Geography* 31, no. 2 (2010): 144–47.

Ahmadinejad, Tara. "Edward Said's Brilliance Lives On." *Washington Report on Middle East Affairs*, September/October 2005, p. 58.

Al-Sīrāfī, Abū Zayd. *Accounts of China and India*. New York: New York University Press, 2017.

Anderson, Jane, and Haidy Geismar, eds. *The Routledge Company to Cultural Property*. London: Routledge, 2017.

Andreas, Joel, and Shaohua Zhan. "Hukou and Land: Market Reform and Rural Displacement in China." *Journal of Peasant Studies* 43, no. 4 (2016): 798–827.

Appiah, Kwame Anthony. *Cosmopolitanism: Ethics in a World of Strangers*. New York: Penguin, 2006.

Armstrong, A. Hilary, and Henry J. Blumenthal. "Platonism." In *Encyclopædia Britannica*, https://www.britannica.com/topic/Platonism (accessed on December 26, 2017): Encyclopedia Britannica, Inc., 2017.

Arrowsmith, Rupert Richard. *Modernism and the Museum: Asian, African, and Pacific Art and the London Avant-Garde*. Oxford: Oxford University Press, 2010.

———. "The Transcultural Roots of Modernism: Imagist Poetry, Japanese Visual Culture, and the Western Museum System." *Modernism/Modernity* 18, no. 1 (January 2011): 27–42.

Baddeley, John F. *Russia, Mongolia, China*. London: Macmillan, 1919.

Bader, J. "The Political Economy of External Exploitation: A Comparative Investigation of China's Foreign Relations." *Democratization* 22, no. 1 (January 2015): 1–21.

Bai, Juyi (772–846, 白居易), proofed and annotated by Xie Siwei (谢思炜). *Bai Juyi shiji jiaozhu* [白居易诗集校注 An anthology of Bai Juyi's poetry]. Beijing: Zhonghua shuju, 2006, 6 vols.

———. proofed and annotated by Xie Siwei. *Bai Juyi wenji jiaozhu* [白居易文集校注 An anthology of Bai Juyi's essays]. Beijing: Zhonghua shuju, 2015 reprint, 1st ed. in 2011, 4 vols.

———. punctuated and proofed by Gu Xuejie (顾学颉). *Bai Juyi ji* [白居易集 An anthology of Bai Juyi's works]. Beijing: Zhonghua shuju, 1979.

Bai, Qianshen. "Composite Rubbings in Nineteenth Century China: The Case of Wu Dacheng (1835–1902) and His Friends." In *Reinventing the Past: Archaism and Antiquarianism in Chinese Art and Visual Culture*, ed. by Hung Wu, 291–319. Chicago, IL: University of Chicago Press, 2010.

Baker, Alexi Shannon. "Selling the Past: United States v. Frederick Schultz." https:// archive. archaeology.org/online/features/schultz/, April 2002, last updated in June 2003 (accessed on February 5, 2019).

Ban, Zhuo, Shaunak Sastry, and Mohan Jyoti Dutta. "'Shoppers Republic of China': Orientalism in Neoliberal US News Discourse." *Journal of International and Intercultural Communication* 6 (2013): 280–97.

Barnes, Amy Jane. *Museum Representations of Maoist China: From Cultural Revolution to Commie Kitsch*. Farnham: Ashgate, 2014.

Barthel, Diane. *Historic Preservation: Collective Memory and Historical Identity*. New Brunswick, NJ: Rutgers University Press, 1996.

Bator, Paul M. "An Essay on the International Trade in Art." *Stanford Law Review* 34 (1982): 275–348.

Bateson, Gregory. *Mind and Nature*. Cresskill: Hampton Press, 1978.

Bauman, Zygmunt. *Liquid Modernity*. Cambridge: Polity Press, 2015.

BBC Radio4. "Land Power v Sea Power," August 13, 2019, http://www.bbc.co.uk/ programmes/m0007kk3 (accessed on August 15, 2019).

Beard, Charles A., and Mary R. Beard. *The Rise of American Civilization*. New York: The Macmillan Company, 1930.

Beck, Joseph. "Greco-Buddhist Scultpure." *Bulletin of the Metropolitan Museum of Art* 8, no. 6 (June 1913): 133–36.

Beck, Ulrich. *Cosmopolitan Vision*. Cambridge: Polity Press, 2007.

———. *The Risk Society: Towards a New Modernity*. Newbury Park, CA: Sage Publications, 1992.

Beck, Ulrich, and Elisabeth Beck-Gernsheim. *Individualization: Institutionalized Individualism and Its Social and Political Consequences*. Los Angeles, CA: Sage, 2002.

Beckwith, Christopher I. *Greek Buddha: Pyrrho's Encounter with Early Buddhism in Central Asia*. Princeton, NJ: Princeton University Press, 2015.

Beijing Review. "Charting Roadmap for China: Special Report, 17th CPC Congress." *Beijing Review* 50, no. 43 (October 11, 2007).

Benes, Tuska. "Transcending Babel in the Cultural Translation of Friedrich Rückert (1788–1866)." *Modern Intellectual History* 8, no. 1 (2011): 63–64.

Benjamin, Walter, trans. by J. A. Underwood. *The Work of Art in the Age of Mechanical Reproduction.* London: Penguin Books, 2008.

Bennett, Tony. *The Birth of the Museum: History, Theory, Politics.* London: Routledge, 1995.

Berenson, Bernard. "A Sienese Painter of the Franciscan Legend." *Burlington Magazine* 3 (1903): 3–35, 171–84.

Berthelot, Philippe. "Note sur des inscriptions arabes, persanes et chinoises du Chen-Si, du Ho-Nan et du Chan-Toung." *Comptes rendus des séances de l'Academie des Inscriptions et Belles-Lettres* 49, no. 2 (1905): 186–204.

Berlin, Isaiah. *Vico & Herder: Two Studies in the History of Ideas.* New York: The Viking Press, 1976.

Berman, Marshall. *All That Is Solid Melts into Air: The Experience of Modernity.* London: Verso, 2010, 1st ed. 1982 by Simon and Schuster.

Besant, Annie. "Theosophy Is a System of Truths Discoverable and Verifiable by Perfected Men." In *The Theosophical Congress at the Parliament of Religions, World's Fair of 1893, at Chicago, Ill., September 15, 16, 17. Report of Proceedings and Documents*, ed. by Theosophical Society, 24–28. New York: American Section Headquarters, Theosophical Society, 1893.

Bian, Morris. *The Making of the State Enterprise System in Modern China: The Dynamics of Institutional Change.* Cambridge, MA: Harvard University Press, 2005.

Bickers, R. "Moving Stories: Memorialisation and Its Legacies in Treaty Port China." *The Journal of Imperial and Commonwealth History* 42, no. 5 (October 2014): 826–56.

Bigelow, William Sturgis, and John E. Lodge. "Okakura-Kakuzo, 1862–1913." *Museum of Fine Arts Bulletin* 11, no. 67 (December 1913): 72–75.

Billingsley, Phil. *Bandits in Republican China.* Stanford, CA: Stanford University Press, 1988.

———. "Bandits, Bosses, and Bare Sticks: Beneath the Surface of Local Control in Early Republican China." *Modern China* 7, no. 3 (July 1981): 235–87.

Binyon, Laurence. *The Spirit of Man in Asian Art.* Cambridge, MA: Harvard University Press, 1935, Charles Eliot Noten Lectures, 1933/34.

———. *Asiatic Art in the British Museum (Sculpture and Painting).* Paris: Brussels, G. van Oest, 1925.

Blake, Janet. "On Defining the Cultural Heritage." *International and Comparative Law Quarterly* 49 (January 2000): 61–85.

Blavatsky, Helena. *The Secret Doctrine: The Synthesis of Science, Religion, and Philosophy.* London: Theosophy Publishing Company, 1888.

Bloom, Harold. *André Malraux's Man's Fate.* New York: Chelsea House Publishers, 1988.

Blussé, Leonard. "Japanese Historiography and European Sources." In *Reappraisals in Overseas History*, ed. by P. C. Emmer and H. L. Wessling, 193–222. Leiden: Leiden University Press, 1979.

Bonney, Charles C. "The World's Parliament of Religions." *The Monist* 5, no. 3 (1895): 321–44.

Boorman, Howard L., ed. *Biographical Dictionary of Republican China*. New York: Columbia University Press, 1968, 5 vols.

Bourdieu, Pierre, trans. by Gino Raymond and Matthew Adamson. *Language and Symbolic Power*. Cambridge: Polity Press, 1991, original 1982.

Bowles, Samuel, and Herbert Gintis. *A Cooperative Species: Human Reciprocity and Its Evolution*. Princeton, NJ: Princeton University Press, 2011.

Brattain, Michelle. "Race, Racism, and Antiracism: UNESCO and the Politics of Presenting Science to the Postwar Public." *American Historical Review* (December 2007): 1386–1413.

Brenner, Leslie. "Nicholas Roerich: Idealist and Visionary." *Foreign Affairs Journal* (April 1990): 17 and 20, http://afsa.org/foreign-service-journal-april-1990 (accessed on November 23, 2019).

Broc, Numa. "Les voyageurs français et la connaissance de la Chine (1860–1914)." *Revue Historique* 559 (1986): 85–131.

Brook, Timothy, and Gregory Blue, eds. *China and Historical Capitalism: Genealogies of Sinological Knowledge*. Cambridge: Cambridge University Press, 1999.

Brook, Timothy. *Vermeer's Hat: The Seventeenth Century and the Dawn of the Global World*. New York: Bloomsbury Press, 2008.

Brown, Michael F. *Who Owns Native Culture?* Cambridge, MA: Harvard University Press, 2004.

Brown, Shana J. *Pastimes: From Art and Antiquarianism to Modern Chinese Historiography*. Honolulu, Hawaii: University of Hawaii Press, 2011.

Brunnert, H. S., and V. V. Hagelstrom, trans. by A. Beltcheko and E. E. Morgan. *Present Day Political Organization of China*. Shanghai: Kelly and Walsh, Limited, 1912.

Bu, Tao (步陶). "Baocun guwu tan" [保存古物谈 On antiquities preservation]. *Shenbao* [申报], November 26, 1914, no. 15015, p. 7.

Burnett, Katherine P. "Inventing a New 'Old Tradition': Chinese Painting at the Panama-Pacific International Exposition." In *Meishushi yu guannianshi* [美术史与观念史 Art history and the history of ideas], ed. by Fan Jingzhong (范景中), Cao Yiqiang (曹意强), and Liu She (刘赦), 17–57. Nanjing: Nanjing shifan daxue chubanshe, 2010.

Burson, Jeffrey D. "Chinese Novices, Jesuit Missionaries and the Accidental Construction of Sinophobia in Enlightenment France." *French History* 27, no. 1 (2013): 21–44.

———. "Unlikely Tales of Fo and Ignatius: Rethinking the Radical Enlightenment through French Appropriation of Chinese Buddhism." *French Historical Journal* 38, no. 3 (2015): 391–420.

Buruma, Ian, and Avishai Margalit. *Occidentalism: The West in the Eyes of Its Enemies*. New York: Penguin Press, 2004.

Cai, Yaming (蔡亚明). "Cong yulun jiaodu kan jindai wenhuayichan renzhi de zhuanbian" [从舆论角度看近代文化遗产认知的转变 The evolving recognition of cultural heritage: seen from public opinion]. Master's thesis, Shanghai University, 2019.

Calhoun, Craig. *Nations Matter: Culture, History, and the Cosmopolitan Dream.* London: Routledge, 2007.

Cao, Bohan (曹伯韩, 1897–1959), *Guoxue changshi* [国学常识 Basics of national learning]. Beijing: Zhonghua shuju, 2017, 12th printing, based on the 1947 ed. by Shanghai wenguang shudian, 1st ed. under the pen name Cao Pu (曹朴) published by Guowen zazhishe 1943.

Carpenter, Kristen A., Sonia K. Katyal, and Angela R. Riley. "In Defense of Property." *The Yale Law Journal* 118, no. 6 (April 2009): 1022–125.

Carroll, Peter. *Between Heaven and Modernity: Reconstructing Suzhou, 1895–1937,* Cambridge, MA: Harvard University, 2006.

Carus, Paul. *The Gospel of Buddha: Compiled from Ancient Records.* Chicago, IL: The Open Court Publishing Company, 1917, 1st ed., 1894.

Chambers, William. *A Dissertation on Oriental Gardening.* London: W. Griffin, 1772.

Chan, Adrian. *Orientalism in Sinology.* Palo Alto, CA: Academica Press, 2009.

Chan, Anita. *China's Workers under Assault: The Exploitation of Labor in a Globalizing Economy.* London: Routledge, 2015.

Chang, Maolai (1788–1873, 常茂徕). "Luoyang shike lu" [洛阳石刻录A catalog of stone inscriptions from Longmen]. In *Shike shiliao xinbian* [石刻史料新编 A new compilation of historical sources on stone inscriptions], Xin Wenfeng chuban gongsi bianjibu, comp. Taipei: Xin wenfeng, 1986, vol. 1, no. 27.

Chavannes, Édouard (1865–1918). "De L'expression de Voeux Dans L'art Populaire Chinois." *Journal Asiatique* 18 (1901): 193–233.

———. *Dix inscriptions de l'Asie central d'apres les estampages de M. Ch.-E. Bonin.* Paris: Imprimerie Nationale and Librairie C. Klincsieck, 1902.

———. "Le défilé de Long-men dans la province Ho-nan." *Journal Asiatique,* Juillet–Août (1902): 133–59.

———. *Les Inscriptions Chinoises de Bodh-Gayâ.* Paris: Ernest Leroux, 1896.

———. *Mission archéologique dans la Chine septentrionale* [Archeological expedition in northern China]. Paris: Ernest Leroux, 1913–1915, 2 vols.

———. "Traité sur les sacrifices Fong et Chan de Se Ma T'sien." *Journal of the Peking Oriental Society* 3, no. 1 (1890): i–xxxi, 195.

———. "Voyage archéologique dans la Mandchourie et dans la Chine septentrionale." *T'oung Pao* IX, 4 (1908): 503–28.

Ch'en, Kenneth K. S. *The Chinese Transformation of Buddhism.* Princeton, NJ: Princeton University Press, 1973.

Chen, Chongyuan (1928–2010, 陈重远). *Lao gudongshang* [老古董商 Old antique dealers]. Beijing: Beijing chubanshe, 2008.

———. *Liulichang lao zhanggui* [琉璃厂老掌柜 Old traders in Liulichang]. Beijing: Beijing chubanshe, 2015.

Chen, Constance J. S. "From Passion to Discipline: East Asian Art and the Culture of Modernity in the United States, 1876–1945." PhD dissertation, University of California at Los Angeles, 2000.

———. "Merchants of Asianness: Japanese Art Dealers in the United States in the Early Twentieth Century." *Journal of American Studies* 44, no. 1 (February 2010): 31–51.

Chen, Shou (?–297, 陈寿), annotated by Pei Songzhi (372–451, 裴松之). *Sanguo zhi: Wushu* [三国志.吴书 A chronicle of the Three Kingdoms: Wu], vol. 4. Beijing: Zhonghua shuju, 1999, based on 1959 ed.

Chen, Xiaowei (陈小伟). "Longmen liusan wenwu huigui" [龙门流散文物回归 The return of Longmen's stolen artifacts]. *Luoyang wanbao*, October 25, 2005, p. 5.

Chen, Xingcan (陈星灿). *Zhongguo shiqian kaoguxue yanjiu (1895–1949)* [中国史前考古学研究 A study on the history of prehistoric archeology in China (1895–1949)]. Beijing: Zhongguo shehui kexue chubanshe, 2007.

Cheng (诚). "Du Jiaoyu huiyi baocun guwuan ganyan" [读教育会议保存古物案感言 A reaction to the proposal of ancient objects preservation at the education conference]. *Zongsheng huizhi* [宗圣汇志] 1, no. 5 (1913): 10–11.

Ching, Julia, and Willard Gurdon Oxtoby. *Discovering China: European Interpretations in the Enlightenment.* Rochester, NY: University of Rochester Press, 1992.

Christensen, Erleen J. *War and Famine: Missionaries in China's Henan Province in the 1940s.* Montreal: McGill-Queen's University Press, 2005.

Christiansen, Flemming. "Social Division and Peasant Mobility in Mainland China: The Implications of the Hu-K'ou System." *Issues & Studies* 26, no. 4 (April 1990): 23–42.

———. "The Justification and Legalisation of Private Enterprises in China 1983–1988." *China Information* 4, no. 2 (1989): 78–91.

Christy, Arthur. *The Orient in American Transcendentalism: A Study of Emerson, Thoreau, and Alcott.* New York: Columbia University Press, 1932.

Chun, Allen. "An Oriental Orientalism: The Paradox of Tradition and Modernity in Nationalist Taiwan." *History and Anthropology* 9 (1995): 27–56.

Churchman, Michael, ed. *Laurence Sickman: A Tribute.* Kansas City, MO: Nelson-Atkins Museum of Art, 1988.

Clark, Nichols. "Charles Lang Freer: An American Aesthete in the Gilded Era." *The American Art Journal* 11, no. 4 (October 1979): 54–68.

Clunas, Craig. *Art in China.* Oxford: Oxford University Press, 1997.

Cohen, Paul A. *History and Popular Memory: The Power of Story in Moments of Crisis.* New York: Columbia University Press, 2014.

Cohen, Warren. *East Asian Art and American Culture.* New York: Columbia University Press, 1992.

———. "Art Collecting as International Relations: Chinese Art and American Culture." *The Journal of American-East Asian Relations* 1, no. 4 (Winter 1992): 409–34.

Commission on the Bicentennial of the United States Constitution. *The Constitution of the United States with Index and the Declaration of Independence.* Washington, DC: Government Printing Office, 18th ed. 1992.

Convention of 1995 on Stolen or Illegally Exported Cultural Object of the International Institute for the Unification of Private Law (Unidroit), http://portal.unesco.org/en/ev.php-URL_ID=13039&URL_DO=DO_TOPIC&URL_SECTION=201.html (accessed on February 13, 2019).

Cooley, Charles Horton. *Human Nature and the Social Order*. New York: Charles Scribner's Sons, 1902.

Cordier, Henri. *Bibliotheca Sinica: Dictionnaire bibliographique des ouvrages relatifs à l'empire Chinois*. Paris: E. Leroux, 1904.

———. "Édouard Chavannes." *T'oung Pao* XI/18, no. 1/2 (1918): 197–248.

———. "Séance de clôture." *Bulletin historique et philologique du comité des travaux historiques et scientifiques* no. 1–2 (1908): 122–50.

Couling, Samuel. *Encyclopedia Sinica*. London: Humphrey Milford, 1917. Reprinted in Hong Kong: Oxford University Press, 1986.

Crossley, Pamela Kyle. "Thinking about Ethnicity in Early Modern China." *Late Imperial China* 11, no. 2 (June 1990): 1–35.

Crow, Carl. *400 Million Customers: The Experiences—Some Happy, Some Sad of an American in China and What They Taught Him*. Norwalk, CT: EastBridge, 2003.

Cui, Mingde (崔明德), et al. "Lushena weixiao le" [卢舍那微笑了 Buddha Vairocana is smiling]. *Zhongzhou guji* [中州古迹], no. 1 (2001): 4–7.

Cui, Yingke (崔盈科). "Luoyang Longmen zhi zaoxiang" [洛阳龙门之造像 The statues of Luoyang's Longmen]. *Guoli Zhongshan daxue lishixue yanjiusuo zhoukan* [国立中山大学历史学研究所周刊 Weekly review of the Historical Institute of the National Zhongshan University] 5, no. 55 (November 14, 1928): 9–11.

Cuno, J. B. "Ownership and Protection of Heritage: Cultural Property Rights for the 21st Century: U.S. Art Museums and Cultural Property." *Connecticut Journal of International Law* 16, no. 2 (2001): 189–96.

Dalby, Michael. "Nocturnal Labors in the Light of Day." *Journal of Asian Studies* 39, no. 3 (May 1980): 485–93.

Dangdai Luoyang chengshi jianshe bianji weiyuanhui (当代洛阳城市建设编辑委员会), ed. *Dangdai Luoyang chengshi jianshe* [当代洛阳城市建设 Contemporary urban construction of Luoyang]. Anhui: Nongcun duwu chubanshe, 1990.

Dawson, Raymond Stanley. *The Chinese Chameleon: An Analysis of European Conceptions of Chinese Civilization*. London: Oxford University Press, 1967.

Daxueyuan gongbao bianjichu (大学院公报编辑处), ed. *Daxueyuan gongbao* [大学院公报 Council of higher education bulletin], no. 4 (April 1928): 31–32.

Davison, W. Phillips. "Public Opinion." *Britannica Online Encyclopedia*, https://www.britannica.com/print/article/482436 (accessed on August 10, 2019).

de Bary, Wm. Theodore. *The Great Civilized Conversation: Education for a World Community*. New York: Columbia University Press, 2013.

de Bary, Wm. Theodore, and Irene Bloom, eds. *Sources of Chinese Tradition: From Earliest Times to 1600*, 2nd ed. New York: Columbia University Press, 1999.

de Clippele, Marie-Sophie, and Lucie Lambrecht. "Art Law & Balances. Increased Protection of Cultural Heritage Law vs. Private Ownership: Towards Clash or Balance?" *International Journal of Culture Property* 22 (2015): 259–78.

de Pee, Christian. "Wards of Words: Textual Geographies and Urban Space in Song-Dynasty Luoyang, 960–1127." *Journal of the Economic and Social History of the Orient* 52 (2009): 85–116.

de Crespigny, Rafe. *Fire over Luoyang: A History of the Later Han Dynasty 23-220 AD*. Leiden: Brill, 2016.

Delano, Amasa. *A Narrative of Voyages and Travels, in the Northern and Southern Hemispheres, Comprising Three Voyages Round the World; Together with a Voyage of Survey and Discovery, in the Pacific Ocean and Oriental Islands.* Boston, MA: E.G. House, 1817.

Deng, Yong, and Fei-ling Wang, eds. *In the Eyes of the Dragon: China Views the World.* Lanham, MD: Rowman & Littlefield, 1999.

des Froges, Roger V. *Cultural Centrality and Political Change in Chinese History: Northeast Henan in the Fall of the Ming.* Stanford, CA: Stanford University Press, 2003.

di Cosmo, Nicola. "Ancient Inner Asian Nomads: Their Economic Basis and Its Significance in Chinese History." *Journal of Asian Studies* 53, no. 4 (November 1994): 1092–1126.

Diamond, Larry, and Orville Schell, et al., *Chinese Influence & American Interests: Promoting Constructive Vigilance.* Stanford, CA: Hoover Institution Press, 2018.

Dillon, Michael, ed. *China: A Cultural and Historical Dictionary.* Richmond, UK: Curzon Press, 1998.

Dirlik, Arif. "Asia Pacific Studies in an Age of Global Modernity." *Inter-Asia Cultural Studies* 6 (2005): 158–70.

———. "Chinese History and the Question of Orientalism." *History and Theory* 35 (1996): 96–118.

———. "Confucius in the Borderlands: Global Capitalism and the Reinvention of Confucianism." *Boundary 2* 22 (1995): 229–73.

Doucett, Elisabeth. "Finding Aid: Charles Appleton Longfellow (1844–1893) Papers, 1842–1996." Ed. by Longfellow National Historic Site. Cambridge, MA: U.S. National Park Service, U.S. Department of Interior, 2006.

Drake, Fred W. "Protestant Geography in China: E. C. Bridgman's Portrayal of the West." In *Christianity in China: Early Protestant Writings*, ed. by Susan Wilson Barnett and John K. Fairbank, 89–106. Cambridge, MA: Harvard University Press, 1985.

Drew, Isabella M. "Limestone from Rock-Cut Temples at Lung-Men in Honan, China." *MASCA Newsletter* 3, no. 1 (May 1967), Applied Science Center for Archaeology, University Museum of Pennsylvania.

Duan, Pengqi (段鹏琦). *Hanwei Luoyang gucheng* [汉魏洛阳故城 The old city of the Han and Wei]. Beijing: Wenwu chubanshe, 2009.

Duara, Prasenjit. "Asia Redux: Conceptualizing a Region for Our Times." *The Journal of Asian Studies* 69, no. 4 (November 2010): 963–83.

———. *The Crisis of Global Modernity: Asian Traditions and a Sustainable Future.* Cambridge: Cambridge University Press, 2015.

———. "Pan-Asianism and the Discourse of Civilization." *Journal of World History* 12, no. 1 (March 2001): 99–130.

———. "Transnationalism and the Predicament of Sovereignty: China, 1900–1945." *American Historical Review* 102, no. 4 (1997): 1030–1051.

Editorial. *The Guardian*, July 4, 2018, https://www.theguardian.com/commentisfre e/2018/jul/04/the-guardian-view-on-world-heritage-in-the-beginning-was-the-dr eam (accessed on July 12, 2018).

Edkins, Joseph. *China's Place in Philology: An Attempt to Show that the Languages of Europe and Asia Have a Common Origin*. London: Trübner & Co., 1871.

⸻. *The Early Spread of Religious Ideas Especially in the Far East*. London: Religious Tract Society, 1893.

⸻. *Religion in China: Containing a Brief Account of the Three Religions of the Chinese, with Observations on the Prospects of Christian Conversion amongst That People*, 2nd ed. London: James R. Osgood and Company, 1878.

Egan, Ronald. *Word, Image, and Deed in the Life of Su Shi*. Cambridge, MA: Harvard University Press, 1994.

Elbinger, Lewis R. "The Unifying Power of Art." *Foreign Service Journal* (April 1990): 16–17, http://afsa.org/foreign-service-journal-april-1990 (accessed on November 23, 2019).

Ellis, Robert Richmond. "The Middle Kingdom through Spanish Eyes: Depictions of China in the Writings of Juan González de Mendoza and Domingo Fernández Navarrete." *Bulletin of Hispanic Studies* 83 (2006): 469–83.

Empson, William. *The Face of the Buddha*. Oxford: Oxford University Press, 2016.

Endy, Christopher. "Travel and World Power: Americans in Europe, 1890–1917." *Diplomatic History* 22 (Fall 1998): 565–94.

Entman, Robert M. *Projections of Power: Framing News, Public Opinion, and U.S. Foreign Policy*. Chicago, IL: University of Chicago Press, 2004.

Erzioni, Amitai. "Point of Order: Is China More Westphalian Than the West? Changing the Rules." *Foreign Affairs* 90, no. 6 (2011): 172–75.

Fabre-Muller, Bénédicte, Pierre Leboulleux, and Philippe Rothstein. *Léon de Rosny (1837–1914). De L'orient à l'amerique*. Villeneuve d'Ascq: Presses Universitaires du Septentrion, 2014.

Fairclough, Graham, Rodney Harrison, John H. Jameson Jr., and John Schofield, eds. *The Heritage Reader*. New York: Routledge, 2008.

Falkenhausen, Lothar von. "Antiquarianism in East Asia: A Preliminary Overview." In *World Antiquarianism: Comparative Perspectives*, ed. by Alain Schnapp, Lothar von Falkenhausen, Peter N. Miller, and Tim Murray, 35–66. Los Angeles, CA: Getty Research Institute, 2014.

Falser, Michael. "The Graeco-Buddhist Style of Gandhara—a 'Storia Ideologica,' Or: How a Discourse Makes a Global History of Art." *Journal of Art Historiography*, no. 13 (2015): 1–52.

Fan, Ye (398–445, 范晔), annotated by Li Xian (李贤) et al. *Houhan Shu* [后汉书 A chronicle of the Latter Han]. Beijing: Zhonghua shuju, 1999, based on 1965 ed.

Fang, Ruo (方若). *Jiaobei suibi* [校碑随笔 Random notes on steles]. u.p.: Huazhang shuju, 1922, 6 vols.

Fang, Hao (1910–1980, 方豪). *Zhongxi jiaotongshi* [中西交通史 A history of Sino-Western contacs]. Changsha: Yuelu shushe, 1987, 2 vols. 1st ed. in 5 vols. published in Taipei by Zhonghua wenhua chubanshiye weiyuanhui, 1953–1954.

Faure, Bernard. *Double Exposure: Cutting across Buddhist and Western Discourses*. Stanford, CA: Stanford University Press, 2004.

Feng, Youzhen (冯有真). "Shiyun daibiaotuan suizheng ji" [世运代表团随征记(第七信) Embedded reportage from the delegation of the world sports games (7)], *Shenbao*, August 9, 1936, no. 22728.

Fenollosa, Ernest F. "The Coming Fusion of East and West." *Harper's Magazine*, December 1898, pp. 115–22.

———. *Epochs of Chinese and Japanese Art: An Outline History of East Asiatic Design*. London: William Heinemann, 2nd ed. 1921, 2 vols, 1st ed. 1912.

———. "The Collection of Mr. Charles L. Freer." *Pacific Era* 1, no. 2 (1907): 57–66.

Fichter, James. *So Great a Profit: How the East Transformed Anglo-American Capitalism*. Cambridge, MA: Harvard University Press, 2010.

Fiévé, Nicolas, and Paul Waley, eds. *Japanese Capitals in Historical Perspectives: Place, Power and Memory in Kyoto, Edo and Tokyo*. London: RoutledgeCurzon, 2003.

Fine, Gary Alan. "Symbolic Interactionism in the Post-Blumerian Age." In *Frontiers of Social Theory*, ed. by George Ritzer, 117–57. New York: Columbia University Press, 1990.

Fiske, Shanyn. "Orientalism Reconsidered: China and the Chinese in Nineteenth-Century Literature and Victorian Studies." *Literature Compass* 8 (2011): 214–26.

Fiskesjö, Magnus, and Xingcan Chen. *China before China: Johan Gunnar Andersson, Ding Wenjiang, and the Discovery of China's Prehistory*. Stockholm: Museum of Far Eastern Antiquities (Östasiatiska Museet), 2004.

Fogel, Joshua, ed. *The Literature of Travel in the Japanese Discovery of China, 1862–1945*. Stanford, CA: Stanford University Press, 1996.

Forte, Antonino (1940–2006). "On the Origins of the Great Fuxian Monastery 大福先寺 in Luoyang." *Studies in Chinese Religions* 1, no. 1 (2015): 46–69.

———. "Marginalia on the First International Symposium on Longmen Studies." *Studies in Central and East Asian Religions* 7 (1994): 71–82.

Foreign Affairs. February 2019, https://www.foreignaffairs.com/issues/2019/98/2 (accessed on November 23, 2019).

Fortune, Robert. *Three Years' Wanderings in the Northern Provinces of China*. London: John Murray, 1847.

Foster, Kenneth E. *A Handbook of Ancient Chinese Bronzes*. Claremont, CA: The Art Department of Pomona College, revised ed. 1949.

Foucault, Michel. *The Order of Things: An Archaelology of the Human Sciences*. New York: Pantheon Books, 1970, French ed. 1966.

Fourier, Jean Babtiste Joseph. "Préface historique." In *Description de l'Égypte ou recueil des observations et des recherches qui ont été faites en Égypte pendant l'expédition de l'armée française*, i–clv. Tome prémier. Deuxieme ed. Paris: Imprimerie de C. L. F. Panckoucke, 1821.

Frankopan, Peter. "From the Ancient Middle East, Art That Links Past and Present: An Exhibition at the MET Challenges How We Look at History." *Foreign Affairs*, June 7, 2019. https://www.foreignaffairs.com/articles/middle-east/2019-06-07/ancient-middle-east-art-links-past-and-present (accessed on June 8, 2019).

Freer, Charles Lang. Interview. The press cutting published in *Detroit News Tribune*, after February 1911, date suggested by David Hogge.

Charles Lang Freer (CLF) Papers, Freer and Sackler Gallery of Art Archive, Smithsonian Institution in Washington, DC Box 232, Folders 1-3, "American School of Archelogy in China."

―――. Charles Lang Freer's travel journal, October 19-November 14, 1910, transcript and scanned copies provided by David Hogge.

―――. Box 25, Folders 18-22; Box 26, Folders 1-8, Correspondence: Warner, Langdon.

―――. Box 21, Folder 19, Correspondence: Roosevelt, Theodore, 1906–1913.

―――. Freer lecture on Longmen, circa 1911 in Japan, transcript provided by David Hogge.

―――. Box 10, Folders 26-34; Box 11, Folders 1-10, Correspondence: Hecker, Frank, J., Col., 1892–1917.

―――. Freer's letter on a hand scroll to Dwight William Tyron on June 17, 1895 from Amo-no Hashidate (Amanohashidate), Japan, scanned copies provided by David Hogge.

―――. Box 23, Folder 19-27; Box 24, Folder 1-10, Correspondence: Tryon, Dwight William, 1889-1919.

―――. Box 235, Folder 7, Offer of Gifts and Bequests, Freer's letter to Samuel P. Langley, December 27, 1904.

―――. Lecture manuscript on the Buddhist ruins in Ceylon, 1908, date is the author's inference, transcript provided by Daivd Hogge.

―――. Box 22, Folder 1, Correspondence: Siren, Osvald, 1917-1918.

Freer, Charles Lang, and James McNeill Whistler, ed. by Linda Merrill. *With Kindest Regards: The Correspondence of Charles Lang Freer and James Mcneill Whistler, 1890–1903.* Washington, DC: Freer Gallery of Art, Smithsonian Institution Press, 1995.

Fresnais, Jocelyne. *La protection du patrimoine en Réplic Populaire de Chine, 1949–1999.* Paris: Imprimerie Rey Villeurbanne for Comité des travaux historiques et scienctifiques, 2001.

Friedmann, John. "Four Theses in the Study of China's Urbanization." *International Journal of Urban and Regional Research* 30, no. 2 (2006): 440–51.

Fukukita, Yasunosuke, Kakuzō Okakura, and Inazō Nitobe. *Japan's Inner Virility: Selections from Okakura and Nitobe with Introduction, Biographical Sketches and Notes.* Tokyo: Hokuseido Press, 1943.

Galambos, Imre, and Kitsudō Kōichi. "Japanese Exploration of Central Asia: The Ōtani Expeditions and Their British Connections." *Bulletin of School of Oriental and African Studies* 75, no. 1 (2012): 113–34.

Gardner, Isabella Stewart (1840–1924) Papers, 1760–1956, Archives of Isabella Stewart Gardner Museum in Boston, Mass. Okakura Yoshisaburo's Letter to Mrs. Gardner on September 11, 1913.

Gates, Bill. "I worry about U.S.-China relations," *Davos*, January 25, 2019, https://www.youtube.com/watch?v=fGYz5SszZ74 (accessed on June 28, 2019).

"Geguo weihe zhongshi shenbao Shijie Yichan" [各国为何重视申报"世界遗产" Why do all nations value the World Heritage nomination], *Zhongguo wenhua bao* [中国文化报], April 14, 2002, editorial.

Giles, Herbert Allen. *The Civilization of China.* New York: H. Holt, 1911.

Girardot, Norman J. *The Victorian Translation of China: James Legge's Oriental Pilgrimage.* Berkeley, CA: University of California Press, 2002.

Goetzmann, William H. *When the Eagle Screamed: The Romantic Horizon in American Diplomacy 1800–1860*. New York: Wiley, 1966.

Goldman, Andrea S. *Opera and the City: The Politics of Culture in Beijing, 1770–1900*. Stanford, CA: Stanford University Press, 2012.

Gombrich, Ernst Hans Josef. "Malraux's Philosophy of Art in Historical Perspective." In *André Malraux's Man's Fate*, ed. by Harold Bloom, 137–50. New York: Chelsea House Publishers, 1988.

Gong, Ding (公鼎). "Yique Longmen guan shixiang wushier yun" [伊阙龙门观石像五十二韵 Viewing stone icons at Yique Longmen: Fifty-two stanzas]. In *Longyang shizhi*, vol. 15, ed. by Luoyangshi difang shizhi bianzuan weiyuanhui, 1996, p. 404.

Gong, Songlin (龚菘林), and Wang Jian (汪坚), comp. *Luoyang xianzhi* [洛阳县志 Luoyang gazetteer]. u.p.: 1924, reprint of 1745 ed., 24 vols.

Gongbuchabu (1690–1750, 工布查布/衮布紮侦). *Foshuo zaoxiang liangdu jing* [佛说造像量度经 A Buddhist manual for making images]. Beijig: Wenwu chubanshe, reprint 2016, based on 1748 ed.

Goodman, Bryna. "Improvisations on a Semicolonial Theme, or, How to Read a Celebration of Transnational Urban Community." *Journal of Asian Studies* 59, no. 4 (2000): 889–926.

Goodrick-Clarke, Nicholas. *The Western Esoteric Traditions*. Oxford: Oxford University Press, 2008.

Goossaert, Vincent. "The Beginning of the End for Chinese Religion?" *The Journal of Asian Studies* 65, no. 2 (May 2006): 307–36.

Goossaert, Vincent, and David A. Palmer. *The Religious Question in Modern China*. Chicago, IL: The University of Chicago Press, 2011.

Goring, Georgia. "East-West Fusion Is Hope." *The Student Life*, October 6, 1936, p. 1.

Grasskamp, Walter, trans. by Fiona Elliott. *The Book on the Floor and the Imaginary Museum*. Los Angeles, CA: Getty Research Institute, 2016.

Greene, Eric. "The 'Religion of Images'? Buddhist Image Worship in the Early Medieval Chinese Imagination." *Journal of the American Oriental Society* 138, no. 3 (July–September 2018): 455–84.

Gregory, Martyn, ed. *Canton to the West: Historical Pictures by Chinese and Western Artists 1770–1870* (Catalogue 77). London: Martyn Gregory Gallery, 2001.

Greif, Avner. "Cultural Beliefs and the Organization of Society: A Historical and Theoretical Reflection on Collectivist and Individualist Societies." In *The New Institutionalism in Society*, ed. by Mary C. Brinton and Victor Nee, 77–104. Stanford: Stanford University Press, 1998.

Grypma, Sonya. *Healing Henan: Canadian Nurses at the North China Mission, 1888–1947*. Vancouver: Universiy of British Columbia Press, 2008.

Gu, Mingdong. *Sinologism: An Alternative to Orientalism and Postcolonialism*. London: Routledge, 2012.

Gu, Sili (1669–1722, 顾嗣立). "Longmen sishou" [龙门四首 Four poems on Longmen]. In Lu, Chaolin, comp., Xue Ruize and Xu Zhiyin, proofed and annotated, *Luoyang Longmen zhi jiaozhu*, manuscript, 80–81. Jinan: Shandong huabao chubanshe, 2018.

Guan, Baiyi (关百益). *Yique shike tubiao* [伊阙石刻图表 A catalogue of Yique's stone inscriptions]. Kaifeng: Henan bowuguan, 1935.

Goldman, Andrea S. *Opera and the City: The Politics of Culture in Beijing, 1770–1900*. Stanford, CA: Stanford University Press, 2012.

Gong, Dazhong (宫大中). *Longmen shiku yishu* [龙门石窟艺术 The Longmen Grottoes art]. Beijing: Renmin yishu chubanshe, 2002.

Gong, Dazhong, and Gong Wansong (宫万松). "Zhenfen jingshen, jixu xiang 'Shijie Yichan Minglu' jinjun" [振奋精神继续向世界遗产目录进军 With reinvigorated spirits, let's march on toward the World Heritage List], *Heluo chunqiu* [河洛春秋] 1 (2001): 19–23.

Gu, Kefeng. "Luoyang Longmen shiku jinqu baopo chaichu weizhang jianzhu" [洛阳龙门石窟禁区爆破拆除违章建筑 Squatter buildings on the premises of Luoyang's Longmen Grottoes demolished], August 18, 1999, http://news.sina.com .cn/society/1999-8-18/6641.html (accessed on January 13, 2009).

Guo, Moruo (1892–1978, 郭沫若). "Yuqinjin fanggu shiba shou" [豫秦晋访古十八首Eighteen poems on visits to ancient sites in Yuqinjin], *Wenwu* [文物], no. 8 (August 1959): 1–2. DOI:10.13619/j.cnki.cn11-1532/k.1959.08.017.

———. "Guan Longmen shiku chi meidi cuihui daoqie wenwu ershou: Fang Fengxian Si Shiku" [观龙门石窟斥美帝摧毁盗窃文物二首: 访奉先寺石窟 Viewing Longmen caves and blaming American imperialism on ransacking cultural relics: two poems], *Wenwu*, no. 8 (August 1959): 2.

Guo, Nanyan. "Environmental Culture and World Heritage in Pacific Japan: Saving the Ogasawara Islands." *The Asian-Pacific Journal* 7, issue 17, no. 3, Article ID 3130(April 12, 2009). https://apjjf.org/-Nanyan-Guo/3130/article.html (accessed on March 6, 2020).

Guo, Zhan (郭占). "Shijie Yichan zai Zhongguo" [世界遗产在中国 The World Heritage in China], http://www.gscaas.net.cn/bbs/dispbbs.asp?boardid=8&id=223 (accessed on January 3, 2009).

Guo, Zibin (郭子彬), et al., eds. *Luoyang wenxian* [洛陽文獻 Documentary sources on Luoyang]. Luoyang: Luoyang wenxian bianji weiyuanhui, 1969, 2 vols.

Guojia fazhan gaige weiyuanhui (国家发展改革委员会). "Guojia Fazhan Gaige Weiyuanhui guanyu yinfa Zhongyuan chengshiqun guihua de tongzhi" [国家发展改革委员会关于印发中原城市群发展规划的通知 National Development and Reform Commission notice on distributing the development plan for urban agglomeration of the Central Plain], December 29, 2016, http://www.ndrc.gov.cn/ zcfb/zcfbtz/201701/t20170105_834444.html (accessed on August 20, 2018).

———. "Nongye zhuanyi renkou shiminhua anli" [农业转移人口市民化案例 Cases of turning rural migrants living in cities into urban residents], December 2016, http://www.ndrc.gov.cn/fzgggz/fzgh/zcfg/201612/W020161219342511160639. pdf (accessed on April 30, 2018).

Guowuyuan (国务院). "Cujin Zhongbu diqu queqi 'Shisanwu' guihua" [促进中部地区崛起十三五规划 Promote the 13th Five-year Plan for the ascent of the central region], http://www.ndrc.gov.cn/zcfb/zcfbtz/201701/ W020170105517946834722.pdf (accessed on August 20, 2018).

Guth, Christine M. E. "Charles Longfellow and Okakura Kakuzō: Cultural Cross-Dressing in the Colonial Context." *Positions* 8, no. 3 (2000): 605–36.

———. *Longfellow's Tattoos: Tourism, Collecting, and Japan*. Seattle, WA: University of Washington Press, 2004.

Gwinn, Nancy E. "The Library of Congress, the Smithsonian Institution, and the Global Exchange of Government Documents, 1834–1889." *Libraries and the Cultural Record* 45, no. 1 (2010): 107–22.

Ha, Marie-Paule. *Figuring the East: Segalen, Malraux, Duras, and Barthes*. Albany, NY: State University of New York Press, 2000.

Haddad, John R. *America's First Adventure in China: Trade, Treaties, Opium, and Salvation*. Philadelphia, PA: Temple University Press, 2013.

———. "China of the American Imagination: The Influence of Trade on US Portrayals of China, 1820–1850." In *Narratives of Free Trade: The Commercial Cultures of Early US-China Relations*, ed. by Kendall Johnson, ch. 3, 57–82. Hong Kong: Hong Kong University Press, 2011.

Hague Convention. May 14, 1954, http://portal.unesco.org/en/ev.php-URL_ID=13637&URL_DO=DO_TOPIC&URL_SECTION=201.html (accessed on February 13, 2019).

Hägerdal, Hans. "The Orientalism Debate and the Chinese Wall: An Essay on Said and Sinology." *Itinerario* 21 (1997): 19–40.

Hahm, Chaibong. "How the East Was Won: Orientalism and the New Confucian Discourse in East Asia." *Development and Society* 29 (2000): 97–109.

Hall, Jonathan. "The Reception of Victor Segalen in China: Between Literature and Ideology." *China Perspective* 1 (March 1, 2016): 59–63.

Halperin, Mark. *Out of Cloister: Literati Perspectives on Buddhism in Sung China, 960–1279*. Cambridge, MA: Harvard University Asia Center, 2006.

Halpern, A. M., ed. *Policies toward China: Views from Six Continents*. New York McGraw-Hill Book Company, 1965.

Han, Chengwu (韩成武), Zhang Zhimin (张志民). *Dufu shi quanyi* [杜甫诗全译 A complete translation of Du Fu's poetry]. Shijiazhuang: Hebei renmin chubanshe, 1997.

Hancock, Mary Elizabeth. *The Politics of Heritage from Madras to Chennai*. Bloomington, IN: Indiana University Press, 2008.

Harris, Iverson L. "Reminiscences of Lomaland: Madame Tingley and the Theosophical Institute in San Diego." *The Journal of San Diego History* 20, no. 3 (summer 1974), http://sandiegohistory.org/journal/1974/july/reminiscences-lomaland-madame-tingley-theosphical-institute-san-diego/ (accessed on January 8, 2017).

Harrist, Robert E., Jr. *The Landscape of Words: Stone Inscriptions from Early and Medieval China*. Seattle, WA: University of Washington Press 2008.

Hatcher, John. *Laurence Binyon: Poet, Scholar of East and West*. New York: Oxford University Press, 1995.

Hayot, Eric. "Critical Dreams: Orientalism, Modernism, and the Meaning of Pound's China." *Twentieth-Century Literature* 45 (1999): 511–33.

Hayot, Eric, Haun Saussy, and Steven G. Yao. *Sinographies: Writing China*. Minneapolis, MN: University of Minnesota Press, 2008.

He, Jing. "China in Okakura Kakuzō with Special Reference to His First Chinese Trip in 1893." PhD dissertation, the University of California at Los Angeles, 2006.

He, Shengjing, and Desheng Xue. "Identity Building and Communal Resistance against Langrabs in Wukan Village, China." *Current Anthropology* 55, no. Supplement 9 (August 2014): S126–S37.

He, Zhijun (贺志军). "Luoyang Longmen shiku de lishi jienan he wenwu huigui," *Zhongguo wenwu bao* [中国文物报], July 27, 2018, p. 3

Hedges, F. H. "Bandits: A Growing Menace in China." *Current History* 18 (1923): 606–10.

Henan jingji fazhan zhanlue guihua zhidao xiaozu (河南省经济发展战略规划指导小组). *Henan fazhan zhanlüe* [河南发展战略 The development strategy for Henan]. Beijing: Zhongguo tongji chubanshe, 1991.

Henansheng minzhengting (河南省民政厅). *Henansheng zhengqu biaozhun diming tuji* [河南省政区标准地名图集 An atlas of Henan Province]. Xi'an: Xi'an ditu chubanshe, 1997.

Henansheng tongjiju (河南省统计局), comp. *Henan sheng shidi xian shehui jingji gaikuang (1980–1990)* [河南省、市地、县社会经济概况 (1980–1990) A sketch of society and the economy of the province, cities, regions and counties in Henan]. Beijing: Zhongguo tongji chubanshe, 1991.

Heng, Chye Kiang. *Cities of Aristocrats and Bureaucrats: The Development of Medieval Chinese Cityscapes*. Honolulu, Hawaii: University of Hawaii Press, 1999.

Herder, Johann Gottfried. *Abhandlung über den Ursprung der Sprache*. Berlin: Christian Friedrich Voß, 1772.

Hevia, James L. *English Lessons: The Pedagogy of Imperialism in Nineteenth-Century China*. Durham, NC: Duke University Press, 2003.

Hirako, Takurei (平子铎嶺). *Bukkyō geijitsu no kenkyō* [佛教艺术の研究 A study of Buddhist art]. Tokyo: Kinkodō shoseki, 1914.

Hobsbawm, Eric J., ed. *The Invention of Tradition*. Cambridge: Cambridge University Press, 1992.

———. *Nations and Nationalism since 1780: Programme, Myth, Reality*. Cambridge: Cambridge University Press, 1991.

Hockx, Michel. *Questions of Style: Literary Societies and Literary Journals' in Modern China, 1911–1937*. Leiden: Brill, 2003.

Hogge, David. "Freer's Longest Trip to China 1910–1911." *Arts of Asia* 41, no. 5 (September–October 2011): 122–34.

Hollander, Paul. *Political Pilgrims: Travels of Western Intellectuals to the Soviet Union, China, and Cuba 1928–1978*. Oxford: Oxford University Press, 1981.

Hollinger, David. *Protestants Abroad: How Missionaries Tried to Change the World but Changed America*. Princeton, NJ: Princeton University Press, 2017.

Honey, David B. *Incense at the Altar: Pioneering Sinologists and the Development of Classical Chinese Philosophy*. New Haven, CT: American Oriental Society, 2001.

Hopkirk, Peter. *Foreign Devils on the Silk Road: The Search for the Lost Cities and Treasures of Chinese Central Asia*. Amherst, MA: University of Massachusetts Press, 1980.

Howard, Angela Falco, Li Song, Wu Hung, and Yang Hong. *Chinese Sculpture*. New Haven, CT: Yale University Press and Foreign Languages Press, 2006.

Howard, Peter. *Heritage: Management, Interpretation, Identity*. London: Continuum International Publishing, 2003.

Howard, Thomas Albert. "'A Remarkable Gathering': The Conference on Living Religions within the British Empire (1924) and Its Historical Significance." *Journal of the American Academy of Religion* 86, no. 1 (2018): 126–57.

Hsia, Adrian. *Chinesia: The European Construction of China in the Literature of the 17th and 18th Centuries*. Tübingen, Germany: Max Niemeyer Verlag, 1998.

———. *The Vision of China in the English Literature of the Seventeenth and Eighteenth Centuries*. Hong Kong: Chinese University Press, 1998.

Hu, Shih. "The Indianization of China: A Case Study in Cultural Borrowing." In *Independence, Convergence, and Borrowing in Institutions, Thought and Art*, ed. by unknown, 219–47. Cambridge, MA: Harvard University Press, 1937.

Huang, Jiajia (黄加佳). "Guibao yusui: Longmen shiku 'dihou lifo tu,' mengnan ji" [瑰宝玉碎:龙门石窟"帝后礼佛图"蒙难记 Broken treasures: the rape of the offering procession of the empress as donor with her attendants at the Longmen Grottoes], *Beijing ribao*, February 6, 2018, two parts, p. 13 and p. 16.

Huang, Pei. *Reorienting the Manchus: A Study of Sinicization, 1583–1795*. Ithaca, NY: Cornell University, 2011.

Huang, Yi. "Songluo fangbei riji" [嵩洛访碑日记 A diary of the visit to steles in Songluo]. In *Shike shiliao xinbian*, vol. 3, no. 29, Xin wenfeng chuban gongsi bianjibu, comp., based on 1796 ed. Taipei: Xin wenfeng, 1986.

Huffman, James L. *A Yankee in Meiji Japan: The Crusading Jounalist Edward H. House*. Lanham, MD: Rowman & Littlefield, 2003.

Huggan, Graham. "(Not) Reading Orientalism." *Research in African Literatures* 36, no. 3 (Fall 2005): 124–36.

Hummel, Arthur W., ed. *Eminent Chinese of the Ch'ing Period (1644–1912)*. Taipei: Ch'eng Wen Publishing Co., 1975.

Humphreys, Sarah C., and Rudolf G. Wagner, eds. *Modernity's Classics*. Berlin: Springer-Verlag, 2013.

Hung, Ho-Fung. "Orientalist Knowledge and Social Theories: China and the European Conceptions of East-West Differences from 1600 to 1900." *Sociological Theory* 21 (2003): 254–80.

International Dunhuang Project. Website, http://idp.bl.uk.

I-Tsing (635–713, Tripitaka Dharma Master Yijing). *Les religieux éminents qui allèrent chercher la loi dans les pays d'Occident. Mémoire composé à l'époque de la grande dynastie T'ang*. Paris: Ernest Leroux, 1894.

Ishimatsu, Hinako (石松日奈子). "Ryūmon Koyōdō shoki zōzō ni okeru chūgokuka no mondai" [龍門古陽洞初期造像における中国化の問題 The question of the sinicization in the early images of Longmen's Guyan Cave]. *Bukkyō geijutsu* [仏教藝術] 184 (May 1989): 49–69.

Ishwaran, Natarajan. "International Conservation Diplomacy and the World Heritage Convention." *Journal of International Wildlife Law & Policy* 7, no. 1–2 (January 2004): 43–57.

Iwamura, Jane. *Virtual Orientalism: Asian Religions and American Popular Culture.* New York: Oxford University Press, 2010.

Jägerskiöld, Stig. *Mannerheim: Marshall of Finland.* Minneapolis, MN: University of Minnesota Press, 1986.

Jakimów, Małgorzata. "Chinese Citizenship 'After Orientalism': Academic Narratives on Internal Migrants in China." *Citizenship Studies* 16 (2012): 657–71.

James, Patrick. "Externalization of Conflict: Testing a Crisis-Based Model." *Canadian Journal of Political Science* 20, no. 3 (September 1987): 573–98.

Jampoler, Andrew C. A. *Embassy to the Eastern Courts: America's Secret Pivot toward Asia, 1832–37.* Annapolis, MD: Naval Institute Press, 2015.

Jenner, W. J. F. *Memories of Loyang: Yang Hsuan-Chih and the Lost Capital (439–534).* Oxford: Clarendon Press, 1981.

Jennings, Justin. *Globalization and the Ancient World.* Cambridge: Cambridge University Press, 2010.

Ji, Zhe, Gareth Fisher, and André Laliberté, ed. *Buddhism after Mao: Negotiations, Continuities, and Reinventions.* Honolulu, HI: University of Hawaii Press, 2019.

Jiao, Lin (焦琳). "Dihou lifotu yanjiu" [帝后礼佛图研究 A study of the offering procession of the empress as donor with her attendants]. PhD dissertation, Zhongyan meishu xueyuan, 2015.

Jing, Jun. *The Temple of Memories: History, Power, and Morality in a Chinese Village.* Stanford, CA: Stanford University Press, 1996.

Johansson, Perry. *Saluting the Yellow Emperor: A Case of Swedish Sinography.* Boston, MA: Brill, 2012.

Johnson, Kendall A. *The New Middle Kingdom: China and the Early American Romance of Free Trade.* Baltimore, MD: Johns Hopkins University Press, 2017.

Jokilehto, J. "Definition of Cultural Heritage: References to Documents in History." Ed. by ICCROM Working Group "Heritage and Society," 2005.

Juan, E. S. "Edward Said's Use-Value for Asian American Cultural Projects." *Amerasia Journal* 31, no. 1 (2005): 61–63.

Jurgens, Valérie A. M. "The Karlbeck Syndicate 1930–1934: Collecting and Scholarship on Chinese Art in Sweden and Britain." PhD thesis, School of Oriental and African Studies, University of London, 2010.

Kang, Youwei (康有为), organized by Lou Yulie (楼宇烈). *Kang Nanhai zibian nianpu (wai erzhong)* [康南海自编年谱(外二种) The self-compiled chronicle of Kang Nanhai (plus two additions)]. Beijing: Zhonghua shuju, reprint 2017, based on 1992 ed.

———. *Guangyizhou shuangji* [广艺舟双辑 Better paired oars for the boat of art]. Guilin: Guangxi shifan daxue chubanshe, 2016, facsimile of the Jingdong Bieshu version, handwritten and unpunctuated.

———. Zhou Zhenfu (周振甫) and Fang Yuan (方渊), proofed and punctuated. *Datong shu* [大同书 The one-world philosophy]. Beijing: Zhonghua shuju, 2nd ed. 2012, 1st ed. 1956.

———. "Ouzhou shiyiguo youji erzhong" [欧洲十一国游记二种 Two travel accpimts on trips to the eleven European countries]. In *Zouxiang shijie* [走向世界], vol. 10, Zhong Shuhe (钟叔河), comp. Changsha: Yuelu shushe, 2nd reprinting in 2011, based on 2nd ed. in 2008, 10 vols.

———. "Baocun Zhongguo minji guqi shuo" [保存中国名迹古器说 On the preservation of Chinese antiquities]. *Buren* [不忍], no. 3 (June 1913): 12.

Kaogu yanjiusuo ziliaoshi (考古研究所资料室). "Jielu Meidi Yiguan Lueduo Woguo Wenwu De Wuzhi zuicxing" [揭露美帝一贯掠夺我国文物的无耻罪行 Exposing the shameless, habitual criminal behavior to rob our country of the antiquities by American imperialism]. *Kaogu* 4 (1960): 1–10, plus 8 plates.

Kapp, Robert A. "Review Symposium: Edward Said's Orientalism: Introduction." *The Journal of Asian Studies* 39, no. 3 (May 1980): 481–84.

Karetzky, Patricia E. *Early Buddhist Narrative Art: Illustrations of the Life of the Buddha from Central Asia to China, Korea and Japan.* Lanham, Md.: Rowman & Littlefield, 2000.

Katz, Solomon. *The Decline of Rome and the Rise of Medieval Europe.* Ithaca, NY: Cornell University Press, 1955.

Kawakita, Michiaki. trans. and adapted by Charles S. Terry. *Modern Currents in Japanese Art.* New York: Weatherhill, 1974.

Kelman, Herbert C. "Compliance, Identification, and Internalization: Three Processes of Attitude Change." *Journal of Conflict Resolution* 2, no. 1 (1958): 51–60.

Kendall, Timothy. "Marco Polo, Orientalism and the Experience of China: Australian Travel Accounts of Mao's Republic." *Asian Studies Review* 28 (2004): 373–89.

Kieschnick, John. *The Impact of Buddhism on Chinese Material Culture.* Princeton: Princeton University Press, 2003.

Kim, Samuel S, ed. *China and the World: Chinese Foreign Policy Faces the New Millennium.* Boulder, CO: Westview, 1998.

———. *China, the United Nations and World Order.* Princeton, NJ: Princeton University Press, 1979.

———. "The People's Republic of China in the United Nations: A Preliminary Analysis." *World Politics* 26, no. 3 (April 1974): 299–330.

Kingsbury, Benedict. "Sovereignty and Inequality." *European Journal of International Law* 9 (1998): 599–625.

Kling, Blaire B., and M. N. Pearson, eds. *The Age of Partnership: Europeans in Asia before Dominion.* Honolulu, Hawaii: University of Hawaii Press, 1979.

Kopf, David. "Hermeneutics versus History." *The Journal of Asian Studies* 39, no. 3 (May 1980): 495–506.

Kowshik, Dinkar. *Okakura: The Rising Sun of Japanese Renaissance.* New Delhi: National Book Trust, 1988.

Kuo, Ya-Pei. "The Making of the New Culture Movement: A Discursive History." *Twentieth-Century China* 42, no. 1 (January 2017): 52–71.

Lai, Xuezhai. Interviews and conversations with the author, Longmen, Luoyang on January 1–2, 2010, and July 16–20, 2007.

Laidlaw, Christine Wallace, ed. *Charles Appleton Longfellow: Twenty Months in Japan, 1871–1873.* Cambridge, MA: Friends of the Longfellow House, 1998.

Last, Kathryn. "The Resolution of Cultural Property Disputes: Some Issues of Definition." In *Resolution of Cultural Property Disputes*, ed. by The International Bureau of the Permanent Court of Arbitration, 53–84. The Hague: Kluwer Law International, 2004.

Lazreg, Marnia. *Foucault's Orient: The Conundrum of Cultural Difference, from Tunisia to Japan*. New York: Berghahn Books, 2017.

Leahy, Helen Rees. "'For Connoisseurs': The Burlington Magazine 1903–11." In *Art History and Its Institutions: Foundations of a Discipline*, ed. by Elizabeth Mansfield, 231–45. London: Routledge, 2002.

Lecarme, Jacques. "Malraux et Sartre lecteurs de Michelet, ou la vérité d'un mythe." In *La France des écrivains: Éclats d'un mythe* (1945–2005) [online]. Paris: Presses Sorbonne Nouvelle, 2011, http://books.openedition.org/psn/519 (accessed on October 3, 2019).

Leitner, Gottlieb Wilhelm. "Graeco-Buddhistic Sculpture." *The Imperial and Asiatic Quarterly Reviews and Oriental and Colonial Record* 7, no. 13–14 (1894): 186–89.

Leng (冷). "Zhongguo guwu" [中国古物 Chinese antiquities]. *Shibao*, October 21, 1909, p. 3.

Leng, Shaoquan. "Chinese Law." In *Sovereignty within the Law*, ed. by Arthur and C. Wilfred Jenks Larson, et al. Dobbs Ferry, NY: Oceana Publications, 1965.

Levenson, Joseph R. *Confucian China and Its Modern Fate: A Trilogy*. Berkeley, CA: University of California Press, 1965.

Levi, Sylvain, and Édouard Chavannes. "Les seize Arhat proteteurs de la loi," ii, *Journal Asiatique*, September–October (1916): 189–304.

Lewis, Mark Edward. *The Early Chinese Empires: Qin and Han*. Cambridge, MA: Belknap, 2007.

Li, Bai (701–762, 李白). "Qiuye su Longmen Xiangshan Si" [秋夜宿龙门香山寺 Autumn night stay at Longmen's Xiangshan Monastery] 730. In *Luoyang Longmen zhi jiaozhu*, Lu Chaolin, comp., Xue Ruize and Xu Zhiyin, proofed and annotated, manuscript, 69. Jinan: Shandong huabao chubanshe, 2018.

Li, Daoyuan (郦道元, ?–527), annotated and trans. by Chen Qiaoyi (陈桥驿) and supplemented by Wang Dong (王东), *Shuijing zhu* [水经注 The Commentary on the water classic], vol. 15, 119–21. Beijing: Zhonghua shuju, 2017, 1st ed. 2016.

Li, Feng. *Landscape and Power in Early China: The Crisis and Fall of the Western Zhou 1045–771 BC*. Cambridge: University of Cambridge Press, 2006.

Li, Gefei (李格非). *Luoyang Mingyuan Ji* [洛阳名园记 A record on Luoyang's famous gardens]. reprint ed. u.p.: Shulin shuju, no publication date.

Li, Guangzheng. "Reflections on Culture." *Sinorama* 28, no. 11 (November 2003): 2–3.

Li, Jianren (李健人). *Luoyang gujin tan* [洛阳古今谈 On the past and present of Luoyang]. Luoyang: Shixue yanjiushe, 1936.

Li, Tao (1115–1184, 李焘). *Xu Zizhi tongjian changbian* [续资治通鉴长编 A sequence to *Zizhi tongjian*], http://www.guoxuedashi.com/guji/7050l/ (accessed on September 19, 2018).

Li, Wensheng (李文生). "Longmen Shiku dashiji" [龙门石窟大事记 Chronicles of Longmen Grottoes]. In *Zhongguo shiku: Longmen Shiku* [中国石窟:龙门石窟 China's grottoes: Longmen Grottoes], vol. 2, Longmen wenwu baoguansuo and Beijing daxue kaoguxi, comp., 284–95. Tokyo/Beijing: Heibonsha/Wenwu chubanshe, 1992.

———. *Longmen shiku yu Luoyang lishi wenhua* [龙门石窟与洛阳历史文化 The Longmen Grottoes and the history and culture of Luoyang]. Shanghai: Shanghai renmin meishu chubanshe, 1993.

Li, Yuxue (李玉雪). "Yingdui wenwu weiji de lujing xuanze: Yi guoneifa he guojifa dui wenwu de baohu wei fenxi kuangjia" [应对文物危机的路径选择:以国内法和国际法对文物的保护为分析框架 Choices to handle cirisis concerning antiquities: using domestic and international law on the protection of cultural relics as an analytical framework]. *Falü kexue (Xibei Zhengfa Daxue xuebao)* [法律科学(西北政法大学学报)] no. 3 (2009): 106–18.

Liang, Qichao (梁启超). *Yinbingshi heji* [饮冰室合集 Collected essays by Liang Qichao]. Beijing Zhonghua shuju, 1989.

———. Proofed and annotated by Zhu Weizheng (朱维铮). *Qingdai xueshu gailun* [清代学术概论 An outline of the Qing academia]. Beijing: Zhonghua shuju, 5th printing 2015, 1st ed. 2010.

Liang, Sicheng (1901–1972, 梁思成, posthumous), and Lin Zhu (林洙), ed. *Foxiang de lishi* [佛像的历史 The history of the Buddhist images]. Beijing: Zhongguo qingnian chubanshe, 11th reprinting 2018, 1st ed. 2010.

Lin, Zhihong (林志宏). *Minguo nai diguo ye: Zhengzhi wenhua zhuanxing xia de Qing yimin* [民国乃敌国也:政治文化转型下的清遗民 The republic is the enemy state: Qing loyalist in the poltical and cultural transition]. Beijing: Zhonghua shuju, 2013, 1st ed. by Lianjing in Taiwan in 2009.

Liu, Alan. *Mass Politics in the People's Republic: State and Society in Contemporary China*. Boulder, CO: WestviewPress, 1996.

Liu, Jianxin (劉建新). "Longmen shiwen" [龙门十问 Ten questions about Longmen]. *Luoyang ribao* [洛阳日报], April 20, 2001, p. 2.

Liu, Jinglong, Chang Qing, and Wang Zhenguo. *Longmen shiku diaoke cuibian* [龙门石窟雕刻萃编 A select collection of Longmen Grottoes' sculptures]. Beijing: Wenwu chubanshe, 1995.

Liu, Jinzhu (刘金柱). *Tangsong Badajia yu Fojiao.* [唐宋八大家与佛 The Buddha and the eight prominent literary figures of the Tang and Song]. Beijing: Remin chubanshe, 2004.

Liu, Jinglong (刘景龙). "Longmen Shiku de weixiu gongcheng" [龙门石窟的维修工程 The maintenance and repair projects of the Longmen Grottoes]. *Henan wenbo tongxun* [河南文博通讯] 7 (1978): 48–49.

———. "Longmen baohu sishinian" [龙门保护四十年 The protection of Longmen at its forty]. *Zhongyuan wenwu* [中原文物] 4 (1993): 1–4.

———. *Longmen shiku zaoxiang quanji* [龙门石窟造像全集 A complete collection of statues at the Longmen Grottoes]. Beijing: Wenwu chubanshe, 2002, 10 vols.

Liu, Lianxiang (刘连香). "Meiguo daduhui yishu bowuguan cang Longmen Beiwei huangdi lifotu kaobian" [美国大都会艺术博物馆藏龙门北魏"皇帝礼佛图"考辩 An evidential study of Longmen's Northern Wei Emperor Xiaowen and his court]. *Gugong bowuyuan yuankan* [故宫博物院院刊] 165, no. 1 (2013): 120–31.

Liu, Zuozhen. *The Case for Repatriating China's Cultural Objects*. Berlin: Springer, 2016.

Long, Hui (龙晦). "Xiao Wendi yu Longmen shiku de kaizao" [孝文帝与龙门石窟的开凿 Emperor Xiaowen and the carvings of the Longmen caves].

In *Longmen shiku yiqian wubai zhounian guoji xueshu taolunhui lunwenji* [龙门石窟一千五百年国际学术讨论会论文集 Proceedings of the international symposium commemorating the 1500th anniversary of the Longmen Grototes], ed. by Longmen shiku yanjiusuo, 1–8. Beijing: Wenwu chubanshe, 1996.

Longfellow, Alice Mary (1850–1928, AML) Papers, Longfellow National Historic Site archives, Cambridge, Mass. "Morituri Salutamus, or The Old Order Changes" and "Reminiscences of My Father." AML-B20-F13 and AML-B20-F15, transcribed by Amy Harlow in summer 2016.

Longfellow, Charles Appleton (1844–1893, CAL) Papers, Longfellow National Historic Site archives, Cambridge, Mass. "Charles Appleton Longfellow China Journal," March 13 to April 2, 1873, CAL Papers Box 10, Folder 9, transcribed by Regine Thiriez in 2011.

———. CAL Journal, January–June 1874, China and Southeast Asia, transcribed by Frances Ackerly in 2010.

"Longmen daoyouci." [龙门导游词 The tour guide narration of Longmen] July 25, 2008, http://www.doc88.com/p-3092266291369.html (accessed on November 6, 2019).

Longmen shiku yanjiusuo (龙门石窟研究所), Liu Jinglong (刘景龙), and Li Yukun (李玉昆), comp. *Longmen Shiku beike tiji huilu* [龙门石窟碑刻题记汇录 A collection of epigraphic inscriptions at the Longmen Grottos]. Beijing: Zhongguo dabaike quanshu chubanshe, 1998, 2 vols.

Longmen shiku yanjiusuo, ed. *Longmen liusan diaoxiang ji* [龙门流散雕像集 An account of the lost statues of the Longmen Grottoes]. Shanghai: Shanghai renmin meishu shubanshe, 1993.

———. *Longmen shiku yanjiu lunwenxuan* [龙门石窟研究论文选 Selected papers on the Longmen Grottoes]. Shanghai: Shanghai renmin meishu chubanshe, 1993.

———, ed. *Longmen shiku yiqian wubai zhounian guoji xueshu taolunhui lunwenji* [龙门石窟一千五百周年国际学术讨论会论文集 Proceedings of the international academic symposium commemorating the 1500th anniversary of the Longmen Grottoes]. Beijing: Wenwu chubanshe, 1996.

Longmen shiku yanjiuyuan [龙门石窟研究院], ed. *Longmen Baiwen* [龙门百问 One hundred questions about Longmen]. Zhengzhou: Daxiang chubanshe, 2015.

Louie, Kam. "From Orientalists to Bent Bananas: Australasian Research in Chinese Literature in the Last 50 Years." *Journal of the Australasian Universities Language and Literature Association* 100 (2003): 50–60.

Lu, Chaolin (路朝霖). *Luoyang Longmen zhi* [洛阳龙门志 Records on Luoyang's Longmen]. Private ed., 1870/1877, 2 vols. Reprinted in *Zhongguo fosi congshu* [中国佛寺丛书], vol. 8. Yangzhou: Guangling shushe, 1996.

———. comp. and ed. *Luoyang Longmen zhi xuzuan* [洛阳龙门志续纂 A sequel to Longmen's Longmen]. Kaifeng, 1898. Reprinted in *Zhongguo fosi congshu*, vol. 8, 1996.

———. Proofed and annotated by Xue Ruize (薛瑞泽) and Xu Zhiyin (许智银). *Luoyang Longmen Zhi jiaozhu* [《洛阳龙门志》校注 Annotated *Records on Luoyang's Longmen*]. (Jinan: Shandong huabao chubanshe, 2018). Manuscript provided by Xue Ruize.

Lu, Hanchao. "Book Review of Kristin Stapleton's *Civilizing Chengdu: Chinese Urban Reform* and Michael Tsin's *Nation, Governance, and Modernity in China: Canton, 1900–1927.*" *American Historical Review* 106, no. 3 (June 2001): 949–50.

Lu, Jilu (陆继辂), and Wei Xiang (魏襄), comp. *Luoyang xianzhi* [洛阳县志 Luoyang gazetteer]. u.p.: 1813, 60 vols.

Lu, Tracey L.-D. "Heritage Management." In *Oxford Bibliographies in Chinese Studies*, ed. by Tim Wright. New York: Oxford University Press, 2013.

Lu, Wei (路伟). "Beisong shiqi Longmen Shiku yichanyu guankui: Zhonggu yijiang Longmen Shiku yichanyu yanjiu zhiyi" [北宋时期龙门石窟遗产域管窥—中古以降龙门石窟遗产域研究之一 A study of the Longmen heritage zone during the Song period]. *Shikusi yanjiu* [石窟寺研究] 7 (2017): 97–149.

———. "Jijin quzhe zhong kaiyan, xiaotan huihuang yin jinzhao: Longmen shiku shenbao Shijie Yichan jishi" [几尽曲折终开颜,笑谈辉煌吟今朝:龙门石窟申报世界遗产纪实 After all our hard work everybody is smiling, rejoicing over our achievements: a report on the nomination of the Longmen Grottoes for the World Heritage List]. *Heluo chunqiu* 1 (2001): 11–14.

Lufkin, Felicity. *Folk Art and Modern Culture in Republican China*. Lanham, MD: Lexington Books, 2016.

Luoyang guangbo dianshi bao (洛阳广播电视报). *Luoyang mudan huahui wanquan shouce* [洛阳牡丹花会完全手册 A comprehensive handbook on Luoyang's Peony Festival]. *Luoyang guangbo dianshi bao*, no. 14 (April 7, 2006).

"Luoyang Longmen huanjing zhili zhihuibu gonggao" [洛阳龙门环境治理指挥部公告 A public announcement by the Longmen Grottoes environmental enhancement authority]. *Luoyang ribao*, August 5, 1999.

Luoyangshi renmin zhengfu (洛阳市人民政府 The people's government of Luoyang City). "Guanyu jiang Longmen Shiku shenbao wei Shijie Yichan de qingshi" [关于将龙门石窟申报为世界遗产的请示 Seeking advice on nominating the Longmen Grottoes for the World Heritage List], signed by Zhu Guangping, the City of Luoyang archives, file no. 16, February 11, 1999.

———. "Guanyu Longmen baohuqu huanjing zhili de tonggao" [关于龙门保护环境治理的通告 A public announcement on enhancing the environment of Longmen]. *Luoyang ribao*, August 2, 1999.

———. "Guanyu qingqiu jiejue Longmen shiku shenbao shijie yichan huanjing zhili zhong youguan wenti de qingshi" [关于请求解决龙门石窟申报世界遗产环境治理中有关问题的请示 Request for instructions on resolving some issues arising from the environmental cleanup relating to Longmen Grottoes' World Heritage nomination]. City of Luoyang archives, file no. 109, July 8, 1999.

———. "Guanyu tiqing 'Longmen shiku baohu guanli tiaoli (cao'an)' de yi'an" [关于提请《龙门石窟保护管理条例草案》的议案 Motion for approval of the regulations on the protection and management of the Longmen Grottoes, draft], the City of Luoyang archives, file no. 41, April 15, 1999.

———. "Guanyu xietiao chaichu gaizao Luoyang dizhentai jian(gou) zhuwu de han" [关于协调拆除改造洛阳地震台建(构)筑物的函 A letter on the demolition and rebuilding of properties owned by the Luoyang Earthquake Observatory], file no. 141, August 15, 1999.

———. "Guanyu yinfa Longmen shiku baohuqu huanjing zhili shishi fang'an de tongzhi" [关于印发龙门石窟保护区环境治理实施方案的通知 A notice on printing and distributing the implementation plans for the environmental enhancement of the Longmen Grottoes protection area], City of Luoyang archives, file no. 75, July 28, 1999.

———. "Longmen Shiku baohuqu huanjing zhili shishi fang'an" [龙门石窟保护区环境治理实施方案 Implementation plans for the environmental enhancement of the Longmen Grottoes protection zone], the City of Luoyang archives, file no. 75, July 26, 1999.

———. "Longmen shiku shenbao Shijie Yichan neiwai huanjing zhilizhong sheji shengguan danwei he junchan qingkuang diaocha" [龙门石窟申报世界遗产内外环境治理中涉及省管单位和军产情况调查 A survey of properties belonging to work units under the jurisdiction of the province and the army in relation to the internal and external environmental enhancement of the Longmen Grottoes for World Heritage nomination], City of Luoyang archives, file no. 109, July 8, 1999.

———. "Luoyang Longmen huanjing zhili zhihuibu gonggao" [洛阳龙门环境治理指挥部公告 A public announcement from the headquarters of the Longmen Grottoes environmental enhancement project]. *Luoyang ribao*, August 5, 1999.

Luo, Zhenchang (1875–1942, 罗振常). *Huanluo Fanggu Youji* [洹洛访古游记 A travel account on the visit to ancient ruins in Huanluo]. Zhengzhou: Henan renmin chubanshe, 1987. 1st ed. 1936 by Yinyinlu shudian in Shanghai.

Luo, Zhenyu (罗振玉). "Xuetang cang guqiwu mulu xu" [雪堂藏古器物目录序]. In *Luo Zhenyu xueshu lunji* [罗振玉学术论集 A collection of Luo Zhenyu's academic works], vol. 7, ed. by Luo Jizu (罗继祖). Shanghai: Shanghai guji chubanshe, 2013.

———. "*Benchao xueshu yuanliu gailüe*" [本朝学术源流概略 A brief study of the origins of the Qing academia] 1930. In *Luo Zhenyu zishu*. [罗振玉自述 Luo Zhenyu in his own words], ed. by Luo Zhenyu, comp. by Wen Mingguo (文明国), 252–53. Hefei: Anhui wenyi chubanshe, 2014.

———. *Jiliao bian: fulu sanzhong* [集蓼编(附录三种)]. In Luo Zhenyu, *Luo Zhenyu xueshu lunwenji*, vol. 11. Shanghai: Shanghai guji chubanshe, 2013.

———. "Wushiri menghen lu" [五十日梦痕录 A tearful record on the fifty-day trip]. In *Luo Zhenyu xueshu lunwenji*, vol. 11, ed. by Luo Zhenyu. Shanghai: Shanghai guji chubanshe.

———. "Yonglu rizha" (Xu) [俑庐日札] (续). *Guocui xuebao* [国粹学报] 54 (1909): 6.

Luo, Zhenyu, and Wang Guowei (王国维), proofed and annotated by Wang Qingxiang (王庆详) and Xiao Wenli (萧文立). *Luo Zhenyu Wang Guowei wanglai shuxin* [罗振玉王国维往来书信 The correspondence between Luo Zhenyu and Wang Guowei]. Beijing: Dongfang chubanshe, 2000.

Luoshu wang (洛书网). "Luoyang gaiguang" [洛阳概况 A brief introduction to Luoyang], http://www.luoshuw.com/lygl.php (accessed on May 15, 2014).

Luoyang difangshizhi bianzuan weiyuanhui (洛阳地方史志编纂委员会), ed. *Luoyang shizhi* [洛阳市志 A chronicle of municipal Luoyang]. Zhengzhou: Zhongzhou guji chubanshe, 1996–2006, pre-1991, 18 vols; 1991–2000, 6 vols.

Luoyang difanshizhi bianzuan weiyuanhui (洛阳地方史志编纂委员会). *Luoyang dashiji (Gongyuanqian wuwannian-Gongyuan 1990* [洛阳大事记 (公元前五万年-公元1990)]. Chronicles of Luoyang (BCE 50,000–CE 1990) u.p. and u.d.

Mackenzie, Murdoch. *Twenty-Five Years in Honan.* Toronto: Board of Foreign Missions Presbyterian Church in Canada, 1913.

Mackinder, Halford J. "The Geographical Pivot of History." *The Geographical Journal* 23, no. 4 (April 1904): 421–44.

Madsen, Richard, William M. Sullivan, Ann Swidler, and Steven M. Tipton, eds. *Meaning and Modernity: Religion, Polity, and Self.* Berkeley, CA: University of California Press, 2002.

Mahan, A. T. *The Problem of Asia.* Memphis, TN: General Books, 2012 reprint ed., based on 1900 ed.

Mahler, Jane Gaston. "An Assembly of Lung-Men Sculpture." *Archives of Asian Art* 24, no. 1 (1970/1971): 70–75.

Mahoney, Rosemary. *The Early Arrival of Dreams: A Year in China.* New York: Fawcett Columbine, 1990.

Malory, Thomas. *Le Morte Darthur: The Winchester Manuscript.* Oxford: Oxford University Press, 1998.

Malraux, André. *Le musée imaginaire de la sculpture mondiale, vol. 2: Des bas-reliefs aux grottes sacrées.* Paris: La Galerie de la Pleiade, 1954.

———. *Antimemoires.* Paris: Gallimard, 1967.

———. Trans. by Jan Lauts. *Psychologie Der Kunst. Das Imaginäre Museum.* Baden-Baden: Woldemar Klein Verlag, 1949.

———. Trans. by Haakon M Chevalier and Philip Gourevitch. *Man's Fate.* London: Penguin, 2009.

Mannerheim, Carl Gustaf Emil. *Resa Genom Asien: Fältmarskalken Friherre C. G. Mannerheims Dagböcker Förda under Hans Resa Kaspiska Havet—Peking.* Stockholm: Lindfors Bokförlag A. B., 1940.

Mannheim, Karl. *Ideology and Utopia: An Introduction to the Sociology of Knowledge.* San Diego, CA: Harcourt, 1985, 1st ed. 1936.

Mansfield, Elizabeth. "Art History and Modernism." In *Art History and Its Institutions: Foundations of a Discipline*, ed. Elizabeth Mansfield, ch. 1. London: Routledge, 2002.

Mao, Sihui. "Translating the Other: Discursive Contradictions and New Orientalism in Contemporary Advertising in China." *The Translator* 15 (2009): 261–82.

Marchand, Suzanne L. "The Rhetoric of Artifacts and the Decline of Classical Humanism: The Case of Josef Strzygowski." *History and Theory* 33, no. 4 (1994): 106–30.

Marinelli, Maurizio. "The Italian Production of Space in Tianjin: Heterotopia and Emotional Capital." In *Foreigners and Foreign Institutions in Republican China*, ed. by Anne-Marie Brady, and Douglas Brown, 25–51. London: Routledge, 2012.

Marino, Elisabetta, and Tanfer Emin Tunc, eds. *The West in Asia and Asian in the West: Essays on Transnational Interactions.* Jefferson, NC: McFarland & Company, 2015.

Martínez-Robles, David. "The Western Representation of Modern China: Oriental-ism, Culturalism and Historiographical Criticism." *Digithum* 10 (2008): 7–16.

Mayer, Maximilian. "China's Historical Statecraft and the Return of History." *International Affairs* 94, no. 6 (2018): 1217–35.

Mayers, Wiliam Frederick, N.B. Dennys, and Charles King. *The Treaty Ports of China and Japan: A Complete Guide to the Open Ports of Those Countries, Together with Peking, Yedo, Hongkong and Macao.* London: Trübner and Co., 1867.

McCormick, Frederick. "China's Monuments." *Journal of the North China Branch of the Royal Asiatic Society* 43 (1912): 129–88.

———. "Representations made to China by the 'China Monuments' Society (Peking)." November 29, 1913, *Ostasiatische Zeitschrift*, Heft 1 (April/June 1914): 103.

———. Letter of October 4, 1913, *North-China Daily News*, October 7, 1913.

———. *The Flowery Republic.* London: John Murray, 1913.

———. *The Menace of Japan.* Boston: Little, Brown, and Company, 1917.

———. *Treaty of Peace with Germany: Statement of Mr. Frederick McCormick in Regard to Shantung*, August 29, 1919, Committee on Foreign Relations United States Senate, First Session, Sixty-Six Congress, 1919 (Washington, DC: Government Printing Office, 1919).

McKeown, Adam. *Chinese Migrant Networks and Cultural Change: Peru, Chicago, Hawaii, 1900-1936.* Chicago, IL: University of Chicago Press, 2001.

McMahan, David L. *The Making of Buddhist Modernism.* Oxford: Oxford University Press, 2008.

McNair, Amy. *Donors of Longmen: Faith, Politics, and Patronage in Medieval Chinese Buddhist Sculpture.* Honolulu, Hawaii: University of Hawaii, 2007.

———. "Engraved Calligraphy in China: Recension and Reception." *The Art Bulletin* 77, no. 1 (March 1995): 106–14.

———. "Ways of Reading and Writing in Medieval Chinese Relief Shrines: Examples from Guyang Grotto, Longmen." *Zurich Studies in the History of Art* 13/14 (July 2006): 186–205.

Mei, Yaocheng (1002–1060, 梅尧臣). *Wanling xiansheng ji* [宛陵先生集 A collecton of Mr. Wanling], http://skqs.guoxuedashi.com/wen_3230w/74016.html (accessed on September 30, 2018).

Melvin, Sheila. "China Remembers its Lost Treasures." *International Herald Tribune*, October 22, 2010, p. 10.

Meng, Guoqing (孟国庆). "'Tianzi jialiu:' jingshi faxian" ["天子驾六:" 惊世发现 An emperor's six-horse carriage: a stunning archeological discovery]. *Luoyang wanbao* [洛阳晚报], December 22, 2008, online version.

Merrill, Thomas Lawton and Linda. *Freer: A Legacy of Art.* Washington, DC: Freer Gallery of Art, 1993.

Merryman, John Henry. "Two Ways of Thinking about Cultural Property." *The American Journal of International Law* 80, no. 4 (October 1986): 831–53.

———. "Cultural Property, International Trade and Human Rights." *Cardozo Arts & Entertainment Law Journal* 51 (2001): 51–68.

Mertha, Andrew C. *The Politics of Piracy: Intellectual Property in Contemporary China.* Ithaca, NY: Cornell University Press, 2005.

Meyer, Karl E., and Shareen Blair Brysac. *The China Collectors: America's Century-Long Hunt for Asian Art Treasures.* New York: Palgrave Macmillan, 2015.

Mezey, Naomi. "The Paradoxes of Cultural Property." *Columbia Law Review* 107 (2007): 2004–46.

Minear, Richard H. "Orientalism and the Study of Japan." *The Journal of Asian Studies* 39, no. 3 (May 1980): 507–17.

Miyoshi, Masao. *As We Saw Them: The First Japanese Embassy to the United States.* Philadelphia, PA: Paul Dry Books, 2005, 1st ed. 1979.

Mizuno, Seiichi (水野清一), and Nagahiro Toshio (長廣敏雄). *Ryūmon sekkutsu no kenkyū* [龍門石窟の研究 A study of the Buddhist cave-temples at Longmen, Henan]. Tokyo: The Zauho Press, 1941.

Mollier, Christine. *Buddhism and Taoism Face to Face: Scripture, Ritual, and Iconographic Exchange in Medieval China.* Honolulu, Hawaii: Hawaii University Press, 2008.

Moritz, Joshua A. "Darwin's Sacred Cause—the Unity of Humanity." *Theology and Science* 13, no. 1 (2015): 1–3.

Mortimer, Mildred. "Edward Said and Assia Djebar: A Contrapuntal Reading." *Research in African Literatures* 36, no. 3 (Fall 2005): 53–67.

Müller, Max. *Introduction to the Science of Religion: Four Lectures Delivered at the Royal Institute in February and May, 1870.* New ed. Longman, Green, and Co., 1882.

———. *Lectures on the Science of Language Delivered at the Royal Institution of Great Britain in April, May, & June, 1861.* London: Longman, Green, Longman, and Roberts, 1862.

Mungello, David E. *The Great Encounter of China and the West, 1500–1800.* Lanham, MD: Roman & Littlefield Publishers, 2nd ed. 2005, 1st ed. 1999.

Muscolino, Micah S. *The Ecology of War in China: Henan Province, the Yellow River, and Beyond, 1938–1950.* Cambridge: Cambridge University Press, 2014.

Myrdal, Eva. *Mitterns Rike [the Middle Kingdom].* Ed. by Östasiatiska museet. Stockholm: Fälth & Hässler, Värnamo, 2007.

"Neiwu bu tingsi fenke zhangcheng" [内务部厅司分科章程 Regulations on the *tingsike* division of labor in the interior ministry]. (Announced in August 1912). In *Zhonghua minguo faling daquan* [中华民国法令大全 Corpus juris of the Republic of China], ed. by Shangwu yinshuguan bianyisuo, 51–55. Shanghai: Shangwu yinshuguan, 1913.

"Neiwu bu dingding baocun guwu zanxing banfa" [内务部订定保存古物暂行办法 Provisional measures for the preservation of antiquities, the ministry of internal affairs] October 1916. In *Faling daquan* [法令大全三编 A complete collection of statutes], vol. 3, 5th category: Neiwu, 46–47, online database.

Neizheng bu nianjian biancuan weiyuanhui (内政部年鉴编纂委员会编纂), comp. *Neizheng nianjian 3* [内政年鉴(三) Yearbook of interior affairs 3]. Shanghai: Shangwu yinshuguan, 1936.

Netting, Lara Jaishree. *A Perpetual Fire: John C. Ferguson and His Quest for Chinese Art and Culture.* Hong Kong: Hong Kong University Press, 2013.

Ni, Xiying (倪錫英). *Luoyang Youji* [洛阳游记 Travel accounts of Luoyang]. Shanghai: Zhonghua shuju, 1935, reprint ed 2012 in Beijing by Zhongguo qingnian chubanshe.

Nian, Ming (念铭). "Quan dajia baocun guwu" [劝大家保存本国古物 Urge everyone to preserve our country's ancient relics]. *Yanjiang huibian: Lousu gailiang* [演讲汇编陋俗改良], no. 52 (1917): 53–65.

Nickel, Lukas. "The First Emperor and Sculpture in China." *Bulletin of SOAS* 76, no. 3 (2013): 413–47.

"Nongye zhuanyi renkou shiminhua anli." [农业转移人口市民化案例 Cases of granting permanent residence to rural people living in cities), December 2016, http://www.ndrc.gov.cn/fzgggz/fzgh/zcfg/201612/W020161219342511160639.pdf (accessed on April 30, 2018).

Notehelfer, F. G. "On Idealism and Realism in the Thought of Okakura Tensin." *The Journal of Japanese Studies* 16, no. 2 (Summer 1990): 309–55.

Novalis, [Friedrich von Hardenberg]. *Heinrich von Ofterdingen. Ein nachgelassener Roman von Novalis.* Berlin: Buchhandlung der Realschule, 1802.

Nowak, Martin A., with Roger Highfield. *Supercooperators: Altruism, Evolution, and Why We Need Each Other to Succeed.* New York: Free Press, 2011.

O'Keefe, Patrick J. *Commentary on the UNESCO 1970 Convention on the Means of Prohibiting and Preventing the Illicit Import, Export and Transfer of Ownership of Cultural Property.* Leicester: Institute of Art and Law, 2007.

Oakes, Tim, and Louisa Schein. *Translocal China: Linkages, Identities, and the Reimaging of Space.* London: Routledge, 2006.

Okakura, Kakuzō/Tenshin (岡倉覚三). *The Awakening of Japan.* New York: The Century Co., 1905.

———. "Ōshū Shisatsu Nisshi." In *Okakura Tenshin Zenshū*, vol. 5, 281–448. Tokyo: Rikugeisha, 1939/Heibonsha, 1979–1981.

———. "Shina Ryokō Nisshi." In *Okakura Tenshin Zenshū*, vol. 5, 120–26, 492.

———. *Tenshin zenshū* [天心全集 A complete collection of works by Tenshin]. Tokyo: Nihon Bijutsuin, 1922, 2 vols.

———. "Kangakai ni oite" [鑑画会に於て A lecture to the painting appreciation soceity]. In *Okakura Tenshin Zenshū*, vol. 3, 173–78.

———. *Okakura Tenshin Zenshū* [岡倉天心/覚三全集 A complete collection of works by Okakura Tenshin/Kakuzō]. Tokyo: Rikugeisha, 1939/Heibonsha, 1979–1981, 5 vols.

———. *The Book of Tea.* New York: Dover Publications, 1964, 1st ed. 1906.

———. *The Ideals of the East: The Spirit of Japanese Art.* New York: Cosimo, 2007, 1st ed. 1904.

Olcott, Henry Steel. *The Buddhist Catechism.* London: Theosophical Publishing Company, 44th ed. 1915, 1st ed. 1881.

———. *Le bouddhisme selon le canon de l'église du sud, sous forme de catéchisme.* Paris: Publications Théosophiques, 1905.

Ouyang, Xiu (欧阳修). "Song Chenjing xiucai xu." [送陈经秀才序 Farewell to Chen Jin] In *Zhongguo youji sanwen daxi: Henan juan* [中国游记散文大系: 河南卷 A collection of Chinese travels essays: Henan], 36-38. Taiyuan: Shuhai chubanshe, 2011 reprint, 1st ed. 2004.

———. Annotated by Li Zhiliang (李之亮). *Ouyang Xiu ji biannian jianzhu* [欧阳修集编年笺注 An annotated chronicle of Ouyang Xiu's works]. Chengdu: Bashu chubanshe, 2007, 8 vols.

———. *Jigu lu* [集古录Records of collecting antiquities]. In Ji Yun (纪昀), et al., comp. *Qinding siku quanshu* [清代四库全书 A complete library of books in the four brances of literature], http://www.guoxuedashi.com/zj/jiucuo.php?id=264167k (accessed on October 27, 2018).

Owen, Stephen. *The Late Tang: Chinese Poetry of the Mid-Ninth Century (827-860)*. Cambridge, MA: Harvard University, 2007.

Palat, Ravi Arvind. "Beyond Orientalism: Decolonizing Asian Studies." *Development and Society* 29 (2000): 105–35.

Pascoe, Stephen, Virginie Rey, and Paul James, eds. *Making Modernity: From the Mashriq to the Maghreb*. Melbourne: Arena Publications, 2015.

Pelliot, Paul. "Le terme de 象教siang-kiao comme designation du bouddhisme." *T'oung Pao* 25 (1928): 92–94.

Pemberton, Jo-Anne. *Global Metaphors: Modernity and the Quest for One World*. Sydney: Pluto, 2001.

Pence, Mike. "Remarks by Vice President Pence on the Administration's Policy toward China," issued on October 4, 2018, https://www.whitehouse.gov/briefings-statements/remarks-vice-pre (accessed on October 5, 2019).

Peng, Dingqiu (1645–1719, 彭定求), et al., comp. *Quantang shi* [全唐诗 A complete collecton of Tang poetry]. Zhengzhou: Zhongzhou guji chubanshe, 2018, 8 vols.

Peng, Gang (彭纲, imperial degree holder of 1475). "Ti Longmen shixiang" [题龙门石像 On Longmen's stone icons]. In *Songyue wenxian congkan* [嵩岳文献丛刊], vol. 3, reprint of *Shuosong* [说嵩 On Song], Jing Rizhen (景日昣,1658–?), Zhengzhou shi tushuguan wenxian bianji weiyuanhui [郑州市图书馆文献编辑委员会], comp., vol. 31, *Fengshi* 4 [风什]. Zhengzhou: Zhongzhou guji chubanshe, 2003.

Peng, Lei (彭蕾). *Wenwu fanhuan fazhi kao* [文物返还法制考 A study of laws on the return of ancient relices]. Nanjing: Yilin chubanshe, 2012.

———. "Wenwu fazhi jianshe zhong ying zhuyi de jige wenti" [文物法制建设中应注意的几个问题 Some issues that should be attended to in the construction of antiquity laws]. *Zhongguo wenwu kexue yanjiu* [中国文物科学研究], December 15, 2015, pp. 28–32.

Phillips, Kim M. *Before Orientalism: Asian Peoples and Cultures in European Travel Writing, 1245–1510*. Philadelphia, PA: University of Pennsylvania Press, 2013.

Pnevmonidou, Elena. "Veiled Narratives: Novalis' Heinrich von Ofterdingen as a Staging of Oriental Discourse." *The German Quarterly* 84, no. 1 (2011): 21–40.

Posner, Eric A. "The International Protection of Cultural Property: Some Skeptical Observations." *Chicago Journal of International Law* 8, no. 1 (summer 2007): 213–31, https://chicagounbound.uchicago.edu/cjil/vol8/iss1/12 (accessed on February 5, 2019).

Pound, Ezra. *Cathay*. London: Elkin Mathews, 1915.

Priest, Alan. *Chinese Sculpture in the Metropolitan Museum of Art*. New York: The Metropolitan Museum of Art, 1944.

Pumpelly, Raphael. *Across America and Asia: Notes of a Five Year Journey around the World and of Residence of Arizona, Japan, and China*. New York: Leypoldt & Holt, 1870, 2 vols.

Pung, Kwang Yu. "Confucianism." In *The World's Parliament of Religions: An Illustrated and Popular Story of the World's First Parlimanet of Religions, Held in Chicago in Connection with the Columbia Exhibition of 1893*, ed. by J. H. Barrows, 374–439. n.p.: The Parliament Publishing Company, 1893.

Pyne, Kathleen. "Portrait of a Collector as an Agnostic: Charles Long Freer and Connoisseurship." *The Art Bulletin* 78, no. 1 (1996): 75–97.

Qi, Yongchang (齐永长), ed. *Jingdian Luoyang* [经典洛阳 Classical Luoyang]. Hong Kong: Zhongguo wenhua chubanshe, 2007.

Qian, Zhaoming. *Orientalism and Modernism: The Legacy of China in Pound and Williams*. Durham, NC: Duke University Press, 1995.

Qu, Changrong (曲昌荣). "Luoyang Longmen Xishan jingxian 29 tao shenmi bieshu!" [洛阳龙门西山惊现29套神秘别墅 The 29 mysterious villas on the West Hill of Longmen in Luoyang]. *Renmin ribao*, December 10, 2008.

Racel, Masako N. "Okakura Kakuzō's Art History, Cross-cultural Encounters, Hegelian Dialectics, and Darwinian Evolution." *Asian Review of World Histories* 2, no. 1 (2014): 17–45.

Reid, Gilbert. *A Christian's Appreciation of Other Faiths: A Study of the Best in the World's Greatest Religions*. Chicago, IL: The Open Court Publishing Company, 1921.

Ren, Jiyu (任继愈), ed., *Zhongguo fojiao shi* [中国佛教史 A history of Chinese Buddhism]. Beijing: Zhongguo shehui kexue chubanshe, 1988, 3 vols, 2018 reprint.

Rich, Paul. "European Identity and the Myth of Islam: A Reassessment." *Review of International Studies* 25, no. 3 (1999): 435–51.

Rieff, David. *In Praise of Forgetting: Historical Memory and Its Ironies*. New Haven, CT: Yale University Press, 2016.

Rogaski, Ruth. *Hygienic Modernity: Meanings of Health and Disease in Treaty-Port China*. Berkeley, CA: University of California Press, 2004.

Romos, Maria, and David Duganne, Harris Interactive, Society for American Archaeology, "Exploring public perceptions and attitudes about archaeology," February 2000, https://documents.saa.org/con-tainer/docs/defaultsource/docpublicoutreach/harris_poll1999.pdf?sfvrsn=8fefd9a4_4 (accessed on February 4, 2019).

Rong, Yuan (容媛). "Yusheng Luoyang Longmen Huixian wenwu duo beidao" [豫省洛阳辉县文物多被盗 Ancient objects stolen in Luoyang and Huixian of Henan Province]. In *Yanjing xuebao* [燕京学报], no. 21 (June 1937): 292–94.

Roosevelt, Theodore. "The Pacific Era." *The Pacific Era* 1, no. 1 (October 1907): 1–4.

Rosny, Léon de. *Le bouddhisme éclectique. Exposé de quelques-uns de principes de l'école*. Paris: E. Leroux, 1894.

———. *Les origines bouddhiques du christianisme*. u.p.: Vve Krüsi, 1894.

Rothschild, N. Harry. *Emperor Wu Zhao and Her Pantheon of Devis, Divinities, and Dynastic Mothers*. New York: Columbia University Press, 2015.

———. *Wu Zhao: China's Only Woman Emperor*. New York: Longman, 2008.

Roy, Ananya. "Slumdog Cities: Rethinking Subaltern Urbanism." *International Journal of Urban and Regional Research* 35, no. 2 (2011): 223–38.

Rubiés, Joan-Pau. "Oriental Despotism and European Orientalism: Botero to Montesquieu." *Journal of Early Modern History* 9 (2005): 1–2.

Ryckmans, Pierre. "Orientalism and Sinology." *Asian Studies Review* 7 (1984): 18–20.

Saarinen, Aline. *The Proud Possessors: The Lives, Times, and Tastes of some Adventurous American Art Collectors*. New York: Random House, 1958.

Sadula (萨都剌). "Longmen ji" [龙门记 An account of Longmen]. In *Zhongguo youji sanwen daxi*, Zhang Chengde, et al., comp., 41–42. Taiyuan: Shuhai chubanshe, 2011.

Said, Edward W. *Culture and Imperialism*. New York: Knopf, 1993.

———. *Orientalism*. New York: Vintage Books, 1994, 1st ed. 1978.

Salmony, Alfred. *Die Chinesische Steinplastik*, vol. 1. Berlin: Verlag für Kunstwissenschaft, 1922.

Sandler, Joseph. *Projection, Identification, Projective Identification*. London: Karnac Books, 1988.

Schmidt-Glintzer, Helwig. *Sinologie und das Interesse an China*. Mainz, Germany: Akademie der Wissenschaften und der Literatur, 2007.

Schoppa, R. Keith. *Twentieth Century China: A History in Documents*. Oxford: Oxford University Press, 2004.

Schwab, Louise. "Le parlement des religions à Chicago." *Bulletin de la Société d'Ethnographie* 36/78 (1894): 165–72.

Scobell, Andrew, et al. *At Dawn of Belt and Road: China in the Developing World*. Santa Monica, CA: RAND, 2018.

Scott, David. "Rohmer's 'Orient'–Pulp Orientalism?" *Archiv orientální* 80 (2012): 1–27.

Scott, Katie. "Playing Games with Otherness: Watteau's Chinese Cabinet at the Château de la Muette." *Journal of the Warburg and Courtauld Institutes* 66 (2003): 189–248.

Segalen, Victor. *Chine. La grande statuaire. Les origines de la statuaire en Chine*. Paris: Collections Bouquins, Editions Robert Laffont, 2nd ed. 1995, 1st ed. 1972.

———. Trans. and ed. by Yaël Rachel Schlick, with a foreword by Harry Harootunian. *Essay on Exoticism: An Aesthetic of Diversity*. Durham, NC: Duke University Press, 2002.

———. *René Leys*. Paris: Georges Crès et Cie, 1971, 1st ed. 1922.

Sekino, Tadashi (1868–1935, 關野貞), and Tokiwa Daijō (1870–1945, 常盤大定). *Shina Bukkyō shiseki* [支那佛教史蹟 Historical sites of Chinese Buddhism]. Tokyo: Bukkyō shiseki kenkyūkai, 1925–28, 5 vols.

———. *Chūgoku bunka shiseki* [中國文化史蹟 Monuments of Chinese culture]. Kyoto: Hōzōkan, 1975–76, 13 vols.

Sell, Susan K. "Intellectual Property Protection and Antitrust in the Developing World: Crisis, Coercion, and Choice." *International Organization* 49, no. 2 (Spring 1995): 315–49.

Sen, Tansen. *Buddhism, Diplomacy, and Trade: The Realignment of India-China Relations, 600–1400*. Lanham, MD: Rowman & Littlefield, 2nd ed. 2016, 1st ed. 2003.

Shao, Yong (邵雍). "You Longmen" [游龙门 Touring Longmen]. In *Luoyang shizhi*, vol. 15, p. 400, ed. by Luoyang difang shizhi bianzuan weiyuanhui, 1996. Zhengzhou: Zhongzhou guji chubanshe, 1996.

Sharf, Robert H. "The Scripture on the Production of Buddha Images." In *Religions of China in Practice*, ed. by Jr. Donald S. Lopez, 261–67. Princeton, NJ: Princeton University Press, 1996.

———. "On the Allure of Buddhist Relics." *Representations* 66 (1999): 75–99.

———. *Coming to Terms with Chinese Buddhism: A Reading of the Treasure Store Treatise*. Honolulu, Hawaii: University of Hawaii Press, 2002.

Shemo, Connie A. "Imperialism, Mission, and Global Power Relations in East Asian Religions in the United States." In *Oxford Research Encyclopedia of Religion*, August 2017, DOI: 10.1093/acrefore/9780199340378.013.403.

Shi, Baoyin (史宝银). "Guomingdang ronyu zhuxi Lian Zhan: Henan shi zhonghua ernü xinling de guxiang" [河南是中华儿女心灵的故乡 Henan is the home to the soul of Chinese sons and daughters], April 17, 2007, http://tw.people.com.cn/GB/14810/5617855.html# (acess- ed on October 8, 2019).

Shi, Cheng (施诚), comp. *Henan fuzhi* [河南府志 Gazetteer of Henanfu], 24 vols., u.p.: 1867, https://ctext.org/wiki.pl?if=gb&res=122627&remap=gb (accesed on March 6, 2020).

Shi, Hongtao (石洪涛). "Dichen yisheng xiang, 'julong' bian wali: Zhonghua longgong baopo ji" [低沉一声响, "巨龙"变瓦砾:中华龙宫爆破记 One low sound blew the 'mighty dragon' to pieces]. *Luoyang ribao*, August 17, 1999.

———. "Longmen shiku huanjing zhili zhanyi daxiang" [龙门石窟环境治理战役打响 The launching of the environmental cleanup campaign at the Longmen Grottoes]. *Luoyang ribao*, August 4, 1999, http://travel. sohu.com/82/37/travel_article15013782.shtml (accessed on January 25, 2009).

Shi, Jun (石峻), Lou Yulie (楼宇烈), Fang Litian (方立天), Xu Kangsheng (许抗生), and Le Shouming (乐寿明), comp. *Zhongguo Fojiao sixiang ziliao xuanbian* [中国佛教思想资料选编 Selected sources on Chinese Buddhist thought]. Beijing: Zhonghua shuju, 2014, 10 vols.

Shieh, Leslie. "Becoming Urban: Rural-Urban Integration in Nanjing, Jiangsu Province." *Pacific Affairs* 84, no. 3 (September 2011): 475–94.

Shih, David. "The Color of Fu-Manchu: Orientalist Method in the Novels of Sax Rohmer." *Journal of Popular Culture* 42 (2009): 304–17.

Shih, Shu-mei. *The Lure of the Modern: Writing Modernism in Semicolonial China, 1917–1937*. Berkeley, CA: University of California Press, 2001.

Shin, K. Ian. "The Chinese Art 'Arms Race': Comsmopolitanism and Nationalism in Chinese Art Collecting and Scholarship between the United States and Europe, 1900–1920." *The Journal of American-East Asian Relations* 23 (2016): 229–56.

Shin, Kin-Yee Ian. "Making 'Chinese Art': Knowledge and Authority in the Transpacific Progressive Era." PhD dissertation, Columbia University, 2016.

Scholze, Marko. "Arrested Heritage: The Politics of Inscription into the UNESCO World Heritage List: The Case of Agadez in Niger." *Journal of Material Culture* 13, no. 2 (2008): 215–31.

Siciliano, Giuseppina. "Rural-Urban Migration and Domestic Land Grabbing in China." *Population, Space and Place* 20 (2014): 333–51.

Sifa gongbao [司法公报 Judicial bulletin], online database, 1930, no. 75.

Sima, Guang (司马光), comp. *Zizhi tongjian* [资治通鉴 The mirror for the wise ruler]. Beijing: Zhonghua shuju, 2017 15th reprint, based on 2007 ed.

Sima, Qian (ca. 145 BCE-? 司马迁), annotated by Pei Yin (between 420–479 CE, 裴駰). *Shiji* [史记 The Grand scriber's record]. Beijing: Zhonghua shuju, 1999, 3 vols., 1st ed. in 1959.

Sirén, Osvald (1879–1966). Sirénarkiv (Osvald Sirén Archive), Östasiatiska Museets (Museum of Far Eastern Antiquities, Stockholm, Sweden), 1907–1957. "Brev Och Document."

———. Lopnr. File no. 1–28, A: 1 (Box 1), Brev Och Document (Document) 1907–1919, Sirénarkiv, Östasiatiska Museets, 1907–1919. A: 2, Box 2, Files no. 29–221, 1920–1929. Document Group 17, 1907–1957.

———. Letter from Iverson L. Harris (quoting Sirén) to Osvald Sirén. Sirénarkiv, December 5, 1957.

———. Letters from Orvar Karlbeck to Sirén, July 17 and October 11, 1921, Sirénarkiv, A2: 1921–29.

———. Letter of November 30, 1921 from Feng Yuxiang to Sirén, Sirénarkiv, A2: 1921–29.

———. "Michaelangelos Medici-grafvårdar." *Ord och Bild* 16 (1907): 417–35.

———. "Mrs. Katharine Tingley och Point-Loma-Institutionen." *Hufvudstadsbladet*, no. 230, 6, August 29, 1923.

———. "Primitiv och modern konst." *Ord och Bild*, no. 47 (1915): 35–47.

———. "Professor Sirén's Address." In Freer Gallery of Art, *First Presentation of the Charles Lang Freer Medal*. Washington, DC: Freer Gallery of Art, Smithsonian Institution, 1956.

———. "Studies of Chinese and European Painting." *The Theosophical Path* 14–15, nos. 2–6 and 1 (February–July 1918): 163–77, 229–48, 336–43, 431–52, 530–50, 56–65.

———. *China and Gardens of Europe*. New York: Ronald Press, 1950.

———. *Chinese Sculpture from the Fifth to the Fourteenth Century*. London: Ernest Benn, 1925, 4 vols.

———. *Den gyllene paviljongen: Minnen och studier från Japan*. Stockholm: P.A. Norstedt and Söner, 1919.

———. *History of Early Chinese Art*. London: E. Benn, 1929, 4 vols.

———. *Imperial Palaces of Peking*. Brussels: G. van Oest, 1926.

———. *Italienska handteckningar från 1400–och 1500–talen i Nationalmuseum: Catalogue raisonné*. Stockholm: Bröderna Lagerströms Förlag, 1917.

———. *Rytm och form*. Stockholm: Bröderna Lagerström, 1917.

———. *Walls and Gates of Peking: Researches and Impressions*. London: John Lane Ltd., 1924.

———. Xi, Renlong (喜仁龙 Osvald Sirén), trans. Xu Yongquan (许永全). *Beijing de chengqiang he chengmen* [北京的城墙和城门 Walls and gates of Beijing]. Beijing: Yanshan chubanshe, 1985.

———. Xi, Renlong, trans. Deng Ke (邓可). *Beijing de chengqiang he chengmen.* Chengdu: Sichu renmin chubanshe, 2017.

———. Xi, Renlong, trans. Song Xibing (宋惕冰) and Xu Yongquan (许永全). *Beijing de chengqiang he chengmen.* Beijing: Beijing lianhe chubanshe, 2017.

Smith, Harold F. *American Travelers Abroad: A Bibliography of Accounts Published before 1900.* Carbondale, IL: Southern Illinois University, 1969.

Smith, Richard J. *China's Cultural Heritage: The Qing Dynasty, 1644–1912.* Boulder, CO: Westview Press, 2nd ed. 1994, 1st ed. in 1983, 3rd and expanded ed. in 2015 by Rowman & Littlefield.

Société d'ethnographie de Paris. *Comptes rendus des séances de la Société d'Ethnographie Américaine et Orientale.* Paris: Challamel Aîné, 1860.

Soper, Alexander Coburn. *Literary Evidence for Early Buddhist Art in China.* Ascona: Artibus Asiae Publishers, 1959.

———. "Review of *Chinese Sculpture from the Fifth to the Fourteenth Century.*" *Artibus Asiae* 32 (1970): 336–38.

Spence, Jonathan D. *The Gate of Heavenly Peace: The Chinese and Their Revolution.* New York: Penguin Books, reprint 1987, 1981 1st ed.

Stapleton, Kristin. *Fact in Fiction: 1920s China and Ba Jin's Family.* Stanford, CA: Stanford University Press, 2016.

Steuber, Jason, and Guolong Lai, eds. *Collectors, Collections, and Collecting the Arts of China: Histories and Challenges.* Gainesville, FL: University Press of Florida, 2014.

Stowe, William W. *Going Abroad: European Travel in Nineteenth-Century American Culture.* Princeton, NJ: Princeton University Press, 1994.

Strehlke, Carl Brandon. "Bernard Berenson and Asian Art." In *Bernard Berenson: Formation and Heritage*, ed. by Joseph Connors and Louis A. Waldman, 223–34. Florence: Villa I Tatti, 2014.

Su, Bai (宿白). *Zhongguo Fojiao Shikusi Yiji: San Zhi Ba Shiji Zhongguo Fojiao Kaoguxue* [中国佛教石窟遗迹:3至8世纪中国佛教考古学 Chinese Buddhist grottoes sites: Chinese Buddhist archeology from the third to the eighth centuries]. Beijing: Wenwu chubanshe, 2010.

Su, Guo (1072–1123, 苏过). "Wuti" [无题 No title]. In *Luoyang shizhi*, Luoyang difangshizhi bianzuan weiyuanhui, comp., vol. 15, p.402. Zhengzhou: Zhongzhou guji chubanshe, 1996.

Sun, Changwu (孙昌武). "Bai Juyi de Fojiao xinyang yu shenghuo taidu" [白居易的佛教信仰与生活态度 Bai Juyi's Buddhist belief and attitude towards life]. In *Tangdai wenxue yu Fojiao* [唐代文学与佛教 Tang literature and Buddhism], ed. by Sun Changwu, 102–25. Xi'an: Shaanxi renmin chubanshe, 1985.

Sun, Di (孙迪). *Zhongguo liushi haiwai Fojiao zaoxiang zonghe tumu* [中国流失海外佛教造像总合图目 A comprehensive list of Buddhist statues lost overseas]. Beijing: Waiwen chubanshe, 2005.

Sun, Guanwen (孙贯文). "Longmen zaoxiang tiji jianjie" [龙门造像题记简介 A brief introduction to Longmen's epigraphic inscriptions]. In *Longmen shiku yanjiu lunwenxuan*, ed. by Longmen shiku yanjiusuo, 109–42, Shanghai: Shanghai ren-min meishu chubanshe, 1993.

Sun, Qinliang (孙钦良). "Beiwei de Longmen he da Tang de Longmen" [北魏的龙门和大唐的龙门 Northern Wei's Longmen and Tang's Longmen]. In *Jingdian Luoyang*, ed. by Qi Yongchang (齐永长), 89–93. Hong Kong: Zhongguo wenhua chubanshe, 2007.

———. "Luoyang de Longmen he shijie de Longmen" [洛阳的龙门和世界的龙门 Luoyang's Longmen and the world's Longmen]. In *Jingdian Luoyang*, ed. by Qi Yongchang, 94–99. Hong Kong: Zhongguo wenhua chubanshe, 2007.

Sutter, Robert. "Pushback: America's New China Strategy." *The Diplomat*, November 2, 2018, https://thediplomat.com/2018/11/pushback-americas-new-china-strategy (accessed on November 8, 2018).

Svensson, Marina. "In the Ancestors' Shadow: Cultural Heritage Contestations in Chinese Villages." Working paper no 17, 2006, Centre for East and Southeast Asian Studies, Lund University.Svensson, Marina, and Christina Maags. "Mapping the Chinese Heritage Regime." In *Chinese Heritage in the Making: Experience, Negotiations and Contestations*, ed. by Christina Maags, and Marina Svensson, 1-38. Amsterdam: Amsterdam University Press, 2018.

Taam, Cheuk-woon. "The Discovery of the Tun-Huang Library and Its Effect on Chinese Studies." *The Library Quarterly: Information, Community Policy* 12, no. 3 (July 1942): 686–705.

Tachiki, Satoko Fujita. "Okakura Kakuzo (1862–1913) and Boston Brahmins." PhD dissertation, the University of Michigan, 1986.

Tan, Qixiang (谭其骧), ed. *Jianming Zhongguo lishi dituji* [简明中国历史地图集 The abridged historical atlas of China]. Beijing: Zhongguo ditu chubanshe, 2nd ed. 1996, 1st ed. 1991.

Taylor, Patrick. "Nation Dance: Religion, Identity and Cultural Difference in the Caribbean." In *Sanfancon: Orientalism, Confucianism and the Construction of Chineseness in Cuba, 1847–1997*, ed. by Frank F. Scherer, 153–70. Bloomington: Indiana University Press, 2001.

Thai, Philip. *China's War on Smuggling: Law, Economic Life, and the Making of the Modern State, 1842–1965*. New York: Columbia University Press, 2018.

Theosophical Society. *The Theosophical Congress at the Parliament of Religions, World's Fair of 1893, at Chicago, Ill., September 15, 16, 17. Report of Proceedings and Documents*. New York: American Section Headquarters, Theosophical Society, 1893.

Thomson, John. *Illustrations of China and Its People: A Series of Two Hundred Photographs with Letterpress Descriptive of the Places and People Represented*. New Delhi: India Isha Books, 2013. 4 vols, 1st ed. 1874 by Sampson Low, Marston, Low, and Searle in London.

Thornberry, Robert S. "A Spanish Civil War Polemic: Trotsky versus Malraux." *Twentieth-Century Literature* 24, no. 3, Andre Malraux Issue (Autumn 1978): 324–34.

Thorp, Robert L. "Review of East Asian Art and American Culture: A Study in International Relations." *The Journal of the American Oriental Society* 114, no. 2 (April–June 1994): 329–31.

Thouard, Denis, and Tao Wang. "Making New Classics: The Archaeology of Luo Zhenyu and Victor Segalen." In *Modernity's Classics*, ed. by Sarah C. Humphreys and Rudolf G. Wagner, 231–60. Berlin: Springer Verlag, 2013.

Titchen, Sarah M. "On the Construction of Outstanding Universal Value. UNESCO's World Heritage Convention (Convention concerning the protection of the world cultural and natural heritage, 1972) and the Identification and Assessment of Cultural Places for Inclusion in the World Heritage List," PhD dissertation, Australian National University, 1995.

Todd, Olivier, trans. by Joseph West. *Malraux. A Life.* New York: Alfred A. Knopf, 2005.

Tokiwa, Daijō (常盤大定), and Sekino Tadashi (關野貞). *Shina bunka shiseki: kaisetsu* [支那文化史蹟 The historical sites of Chinese culture]. Tokyo: Hōzōkan, 1939–1941, 12 vols.

Tong, Qing Sheng. "Inventing China: The Use of Orientalist Views on the Chinese Language." *Interventions* 2 (2000): 6–20.

"Tongchi chabao baocun guju" [通饬查报保存古迹 Decree on the investigation and preservation of ancient relics]. *Ta Kung Pao* [大公报], December 17, 1910, online database.

Toqto'a (1314–1356, 脱脱), et al. *Songshi* [宋史 The history of the Qing]. Beijing: Zhonghua shuju, 1999.

Törmä, Minna. *Enchanted by Lohans: Osvald Sirén's Journey into Chinese Art.* Hong Kong: Hong Kong University Press, 2013.

———. "Osvald Sirén's Encounter with the Arts of China and Japan." In *Questioning Oriental Aesthetics and Thinking: Conflicting Visions of "Asia" under the Colonial Empires*, ed. by Shigemi Inaga, 83–90. Kyoto: International Research Center for Japanese Studies, 2010.

Townsend, James R. *Political Participation in Communist China.* Berkeley, CA: University of California Press, 1967.

Tsai, Weiping. *Reading Shenbao: Nationalism, Consumerism, and Individuality in China, 1919–1937.* New York: Palgrave, 2010.

Tseng, Lillian Lan-Ying. "Retrieving the Past, Inventing the Memorable: Huang Yi's Visit to the Song-Luo Monuments." In *Monuments and Memory, Made and Unmade*, ed. by Roberts S. Nelson and Margaret Olin, 37–58. Chicago, IL: University of Chicago Press, 2003.

Tsou, Mingteh. "Christian Missionary as Confucian Intellectual: Gilbert Reid (1857–1927) and the Reform Movement in the Late Qing." In *Christianity in China: From the Eighteenth Century to the Present*, ed. by Daniel H. Bays, 73–90. Stanford, CA: Stanford University Press, 1996.

Tsukamoto, Yasushi (塚本靖). *Shinkoku kōgeihin ishō chōsa hōkokusho* [清國工藝品意匠調査報告書 A survey report on the decorative arts in Qing China]. Tokyo: Nōshōmushō Shōkōkyoku, 1908.

———. *Nohon no Bukkyō kenchiku gaisetsu* [日本の佛教建築概說 An outline of Japanese Buddhist architecture]. Tokyo: Yūzankaku, 1936.

Tweed, Thomas A. *The American Encounter with Buddhism, 1844–1912: Victorian Culture & the Limits of Dissent.* With a new preface, Chapel Hill, NC: University of North Carolina Press, 2000, 1st ed. 1992.

UNESCO. "Convention Concerning the Protection of the World Cultural and Natural Heritage, 1972, http://whc.unesco.org/en/conventiontext/ (accessed November 24, 2019).

UNESCO Archives. "Report of the 24th Session," WHC-2000/CON F.204/21, also available online at http://whc.unesco.org/archive/repcom00.htm (accessed on August 11, 2007).

———. World Heritage Centre, CLT/WHC/NOM 542. The State Administration of Cultural Heritage of the People's Republic of China, World Heritage Convention, Nomination of Cultural Properties for Inscription on the World Heritage List: China, Longmen Grottoes, 2001.

———. World Heritage Centre, CLT/WHC/NOM542, China folder, Longmen Grottoes, no. 1003. Two letters dated June 30, 1999, to Mr. Mounir Bouchenaki, Director, UNESCO World Heritage Center, from Yu Fuzeng, Secretary-General, the National Commission of the People's Republic of China for UNESCO.

UNESCO Intergovernmental Committee for the Protection of World Cultural and Natural Heritage Sites. "Operational Guidelines for the Implementation of the World Heritage Convention," WHC-99/2, March 1999, http://whc.unesco.org/archive/opguide99.pdf (accessed on January 1, 2009).

UNESCO World Heritage Centre. "Operational Guidelines for the Implementation of the World Heritage Convention," WHC-99/2, March 1999.

UNESCO World Heritage Convention. "World Heritage List Statitics." August 2019 statistics, https://whc.unesco.org/en/list/stat#s2 (accessed on August 13, 2019).

UNESCO World Heritage Convention, the United Nations Foundation, and National Geographic, "World Heritage, 2008-09." (source provided by Jing Feng).

United Nations, International Law Commission. *Yearbook of the International Law Commission*. New York: The United Nations, 1949-.

Unknown author. "A Compliment for McCormick." *Service Bulletin of the Associated Press* 18 (June 15, 1908): 13.

———. "American School of Archelogy in China." *Journal of the American Asiatic Association* 13, no. 1 (1913): 6–7.

———. "Celing" [策令 Policy ordinaces]. *Shenbao* [申报], June 16, 1914, p. 2.

———. "China's Precious Relics." An interview with Langdon Warner, *Central-China Post,* March 28, 1914.

———. "Gugong de guwu" [故宫的古物 Antiquities in the Imperial Palace]. *Huanian* [华年] 1, no. 21 (1932): 405.

———. "Henan baohu yuxi gudai lingmu" [河南保护豫西古代陵墓 Henan guarding the ancient tombs in western Yu]. *Shenbao*, August 8, 1914, no. 14905, p. 7.

———. "Kang Youwei huanjing li Shan" [康有为还经离陕 Kang Youwei returning the scriptures and departing Shaan]. *Shenbao*, January 18, 1924, no. 18283.

———. "Kaogujia jiqi tuzhi" [考古家急起图之 Archaeologists eager to do something]. *Shenbao*, January 28, 1913, no. 14354, p. 7.

———. "Lunshuo: Baocun guwu" [论说: 保存古物 A commentary: preserving ancient objects]. *Shizheng tongbao* [市政通报], 1914, no. 74, pp. 1–3.

———. "Shoushi Longmen shifo cansheng ji" [收拾龙门石佛残胜纪 A report on protecting Longmen's remains of stone buddhas]. *Shenbao*, March 23, 1916, no.

15483, p. 6. Reprinted in *Dongfang zazhi* [东方杂志 The Eastern Miscellany] 13, no. 7 (July 10, 1916): 13–14.

———. "The Prevention of Vandalism in China." *Art and Progress* 1, no. 1 (November 1909), Notes: 42–43.

———. "Treasures of Archeology in China." *Journal of the American Asiatic Association* 13, no. 1 (1913): 5–6.

———. "Waijiaozhang zhuyi baocun guwu" [外交长注意保存古物 Head of Foreign Affairs pays attention to preserve antiquities]. *Shenbao*, January 21, 1913, p. 3.

———. "Yibao guji" [议保古迹 On protecting ancient sites]. *Shenbao*, January 29, 1913, p. 6.

———. "Yuren baocun tiaojinjiaobei zhi zhuojian" [豫人保存挑筋教碑之拙见 A humble opinion on the protection of Judaist sculptures in Henan Province]. *Shenbao*, December 31, 1912, p. 6.

———. "Guanyu zhongguo guwu beidao zhi tanpian ji jisi" [关于中国古物被盗之谈片及纪事 On the stealing of Chinese antiquities] and "Lun Zhongguo gubei zhi beidao." [论中国古碑之被盗 On the stealing of Chinese ancient steles]. In *Dongfang zazhi* [东方杂志 Eastern Miscellany] 10, no. 12 (1914): 34–36.

———. "Henan Luoyang Shijie wenhua yichan Longmen shiku pang maochu bieshuqun" [河南洛阳世界文化遗产龙门石窟旁冒出别墅群 A group of cottages suddenly appeared next to the World Heritage Site Longmen Grottoes in Henan's Luoyang], http://www.ha.xinhua.org/add/hnnews/2008-12/10/content_15140498.htm, posted December 10, 2008 (accessed on December 26, 2008).

———. "In the Magazines." *Art and Progress* 3, no. 1 (November 1911): 405.

———. "Longmen shenbao shijie wenhua yichan shimo" [龙门申报世界文化遗产始末 The nomination of the Longmen Grottoes for the world cultural heritage list: a full story]. http://travel.sohu.com/82/37/travel_article15013782.shtml (accessed on January 25, 2009).

———. "Makemi jun baocun Zhongguo guwu banfa zhi hanjian" [马克密君保存中国古物办法之函件 Mr. McCromick's letter concerning the methods to preserve Chinese antiquities]. *Dongfang zazhi* 11, no. 6 (1914): 15–18.

———. "Notes." *Museum of Fine Arts Bulletin* (1916): 8.

———. "Shui zhan le Bai Juyi de di?" [谁占了白居易的地 Who is occupying Bai Juyi's site?] http://yl.peoplexz.com/2273/2289/20081223105300.htm, posted December 23, 2008 (accessed on January 13, 2009).

———. "Xi'anfu baohu Beilin" [西安府保护碑林 Xi'an Prefecture protecting the Stele Forest]. *Shen bao*, no. 14122, p. 6, June 16, 1912.

———. "Xijia Houpianqu guoyou tudi cheqian pinggu" [西夹后片区国有土地拆迁评估 Impact assessment of demolition and relocation on state-owned land in the area behind Xijia]. December 26, 2013, http://www.lmsk.gov.cn/news/show-570.aspx (last accessed April 24, 2018, no longer available).

———. "Yusheng guwu beidao shenduo, Yuan Tongli chakan hou baogao" [豫省古物被盗甚多, 袁同礼查勘后报告 Many of antiquities in Henan Province stolen; a report of Yuan Tongli upon inspection], *Shenbao*, January 14, 1937.

———. "Zuohao shenyi gongzuo, tisheng gudu xingxiang" [做好申遗工作, 提升古都形象 Let us prepare for the World Heritage application and improve the appearance of our ancient city]. undated (2008, my inference), manuscript provided by Lu Wei.

Valone, David A. "Language, Race, and History: The Origin of the Whitney-Müller Debate and the Transformation of the Human Sciences." *Journal of the History of the Behavioral Sciences* 32, no. 2 (1996): 119–34.

van den Bosch, Lourens P. "Language as the Barrier between Brute and Man. Friedrich Max Müller and the Darwinian Debate on Language." *Saeculum Jahrbuch für Universalgeschichte* 51, no. 1 (2000): 57–89.

Vincent, Steven. "The Stake in the Schultz Trial." *Orientations* 33, no. 2 (February 2002), Commentary.

———. "Schultz Convicted." *Orientations* 33, no. 4 (April 2002), Commentary.

von Richthofen, Ferdinand Freiherr. *China. Ergebnisse eigener Reisen und darauf gegründeter Studien*, vol. 2. Berlin: Verlag von Dietrich Reimer, 1882.

Vukovich, Daniel. *China and Orientalism: Western Knowledge Production and the PRC*. London: Routledge, 2013.

Wacquant, Loïc. "Urban Desolation and Symbolic Denigration in the Hyperghetto." *Social Psychology Quarterly* 73, no. 3 (2010): 215–19.

Wallerstein, Immanuel. *Geopolitics and Geoculture: Essays on the Changing World-System*. New York: Columbia University Press, 1991.

Walmsley, Lewis C. *Bishop in Honan: Mission and Museum in the Life of William C. White*. Toronto: University of Toronto Press, 1974.

Waln, Robert, Jr. *China: Comprehending a View of the Origin, Antiquity History, Religion, Morals, Government, Laws, Population, Literature, Drama, Festivals, Games, Women, Beggars, Manners, Customs, &C of That Empire*. Philadelphia, PA: J. Maxwell, 1823.

Wan, Guoding (万国鼎), comp., Wan Sinian (万斯年) and Chen Mengjia (陈梦家), supplemented. *Zhongguo lishi jinianbiao* [中国历史纪年表 An chronological chart of Chinese history]. Beijing: Zhonghua shuju, 2005, 1st ed. 1978.

Wang, Daisy Yiyou. "Charles Lang Freer and the Collecting of Chinese Buddhist Art in Early-Twentieht-Century America." *Journal of the History of Collections* (July 25, 2015): 1–16, online version.

Wang, Dong. "China and the World, 1900–1949." In *Oxford Bibliographies in Chinese Studies*, ed by Tim Wright. New York Oxford University Press, 2013.

———. "The United States, Asia, and the Pacific, 1815–1919." In *The Society for Historians of American Foreign Relations (SHAFR) Guide: An Annotated Bibliography of American Foreign Relations since 1600*, ed. by Alan McPherson. Leiden: Brill, 2017, ch. 9.

———. "Internationalizing Heritage: UNESCO and China's Longmen Grottoes." *China Information* 24, no. 2 (July 2010): 123–47.

———. "Redeeming 'a Century of National Ignomiy': Nationalism and Party Rivalry over the Unequal Treaties, 1928–1947." *Twentieth-Century China* 30 (2005): 72–100.

———. "Restructuring Governance in Contemporary Urban China: Perspectives on State and Society." *Journal of Contemporary China* 20, no. 72 (November 2011): 723–33.

———. "The 'Letter Should Not Beg': Chinese Diaspora Philanthropy in Higher Education." In *Chinese Diaspora Charity and the Cantonese Pacific, 1850–1949,* ed. by John Fitzgerald, and Hon-ming Yip, 99–120. Hong Kong: University of Hong Kong Press, 2019.

———. "The Discourse of Unequal Treaties in Modern China." *Pacific Affairs* 76 (2003): 399–425.

———. *China's Unequal Treaties: Narrating National History.* Lanham, MD: Lexington Books, 2005.

———. *Managing God's Higher Learning: U.S.-China Cultural Encounter and Canton Christian College (Lingnan University), 1888–1952.* Lanham, MD: Lexington Books, 2007.

———. *The United States and China: A History from the Eighteenth Century to the Present.* Lanham, MD: Rowman & Littlefield, 2013.

Wang, Hui. *Translating Chinese Classics in a Colonial Context: James Legge and His Two Versions of the Zhongyong.* Bern: Peter Lang, 2008.

Wang, Jing, ed. *Locating China: Space, Place, and Popular Culture.* London: Routledge, 2005.

Wang, Mingming. *The West as the Other. A Genealogy of Chinese Occidentalism.* Hong Kong: The Chinese University Press, 2014.

Wang, Ning. "Orientalism versus Occidentalism?" *New Literary History* 28 (1997): 57–67.

Wang, Q. Edward. "Beyond East and West: Antquarianism, Evidential Learning, and Global Trends in Historical Study." *The Journal of World History* 19, no. 4 (December 2008): 489–519.

Wang, Qingxiang (王庆祥). "Luo Zhenyu de zhengzhi shengya he xueshu chengjiu" [罗振玉的政治生涯和学术成就 Luo Zhenyu's political career and academic achievements]. *Shehui kexue zhanxian* 5 (2002): 152–61.

Wang, Shixiang (王世襄). "Ji Meidi sougua woguo wenwu de qida zhongxin" [记美帝搜刮我国文物的七大中心 On the seven centers pillaging our county's antiquities by American imperialism]. *Wenwu cankao ziliao* 7 (1955): 45–55, plus 34 plates.

Wang, Ti (王惕). *Fojiao zaoxiang fa* [佛教造像法 Rules for making Buddhist images]. Tianjin: Tianjin renmin chubanshe, 1999.

Wang, Yanwei (王彦威), and Wang Liang (王亮). eds. *Qingji waijiao shiliao* [清季外交史料 diplomatic sources for the late Qing], 10 vols. Changsha: Hunan shifan daxue chubanshe, 2015, 1st ed. 1935.

Wang, Yiyou. "The Loouvre from China: A Critical Study of C. T. Loo and the Framing of Chinese Art in the United States, 1915–1950." PhD dissertation, Ohio University, 2007.

Wang, Zhenguo (王振国). *Longmen Shiku yu Luoyang Fojiao wenhua* [龙门石窟与洛阳佛教文化 The Longmen Grottoes and Luoyang's Buddhist culture]. Zhengzhou: Zhongzhou guji chubanshe, 2006.

———. "Longmen Shiku pohuai canji diaocha" [龙门石窟破坏残迹调查 A survey of the destruction at the Longmen Grottoes]. In *Longmen liusan diaoxiang ji,* Shanghai renmin chubanshe, and Longmen shiku yanjiusuo, comp., 107–26, Shanghai: Shanghai renmin chubanshe, 1993.

Wang, Zhiqiang (王志强). Interview with the author at the Administration of the Longmen Cultural Tourism Zone at Longmen on January 1, 2010.

Warner, Langdon. Langdon Warner (LW) Papers, Harvard Houghton Library, 1900–1959. Langdon Warner's letter to Charles Lang Freer on November 27, 1913, p. 8. MS Am 3138, Box 8, Folder 26 "American School of Archaeology Expedition, Freer, 1913–1914."

———. LW Papers, Box 10, Warner's diary.

———. LW Papers, Box 2 Folder 30, Okakura, Kakuzo, circa 1906–1912: Warner's diary, Harvard Houghton Library. Letter of May 1, 1912 from Okakura Kakuzō from Peking to Warner.

———. Langdon Warner (LW) Personal Archive, Harvard University Archives, 1881–1955. Warner's letter of September 10, 1931 in response to Bahr's letter of August 25, Box 1, Folder: Langdon Warner Correspondence.

———. LW Personal Archive, Harvard University Archives 1881–1955. Warner's letter of April 11, 1947 to Liang Ssu-ch'eng, Box 5, Folder 15, "L"-2, 1937–1949.

———. ed. by Theodore Bowie. *Langdon Warner through His Letters*. Bloomington, IN: Indiana University Press, 1966.

Watson, Burton. "Buddhism in the Poetry of Po Chü-i." *Eastern Buddhist* 21, no. 1 (Spring 1988): 1–22.

Watson, William (1917–2007). Obituary of Osvald Sirén, 1966. "Professor Osvald Sirén." *The Burlington Magazine* 108, no. 762 (September 1966): 484–85.

Weber, Max. *Die Wirtschaftsethik der Weltreligionen: Konfuzianismus und Taoismus*. Tübingen: J. C. B Mohr, 1991.

Wei, Boxiao (魏搏霄). "Longmen" [龙门 Longmen]. In *Luoyang shizhi*, Luoyang difangshizhi bianzuan weiyuanhui, comp., vol. 15, p. 403. Zhengzhou: Zhongzhou guji chubanshe, 1996.

Wei, Shou (505–572, 魏收). *Weishu* [魏书 The history of the Wei]. Beijing: Zhonghua shuju, 1999.

Wen, Ruzhang (温如璋). "Jiuri tong Lü Wenchuan su Longmen dongzhong" [九日同吕文川宿龙门洞中 Staying overnight with Lü Wenchuan in Longmen's cave on the nineth day]. In Zhengzhou shi, *Songyue wenxian congkan*, vols. 3, *Shuosong*, vol. 31, *Fengshi* 4, p. 778. Zhengzhou: Zhongzhou guji chubanshe, 2003.

Wen, Yucheng (温玉成). "Luoyang Longmen Xiangshan Si yizhi diaochao shijue" [洛阳龙门香山寺遗址调查试掘 The preliminary findings from the excavation of Luoyang Longmen's Xiangshan Monastery]. *Kaogu*, no. 1 (1986): 40–43.

———. "Zheren weixiao, qiangu miaodi" [哲人微笑, 千古妙谛 Wise men smiling, miraculous truth from antiquity]. In *Longmen liusan diaoxiang ji*. ed. by Longmen shiku yanjiusuo, preface, 1-3. Shanghai: Shanghai reminchubanshe, 1993.

———. "Longmen Tangku painian" [龙门唐窟排年 The chronology of Longmen's Tang caves]. In *Zhongguo shiku: Longmen shiku*, vol. 2, Longmen Wenwu Baoguansuo and Beijing Daxue Kaoguxi, comp., 172–216. Tokyo/Beijing: Heibonsha/ Wenwu chubanshe, 1992.

———. "Dangnian manfu lingyunzhi, erjin wuren bu baitou" [当年满腹凌云志,而今无人不白头 Past ambitions, and now nobody can escape from having white hair]. *Shijie zongjiao yanjiu* 3 (2001): 6–7.

Weng, Fanggang (1733–1818, 翁方纲). "Ti Songluo fangbei tu" [题嵩洛访碑图 On *Songluo fangbei tu*]. In *Shike shiliao xinbian*, vol. 3, issue 29, ed. by Xin Wenfeng, 591–93. Taipei: Xin wenfeng, 1986.

Whitney, William Dwight. *Max Müller and the Science of Language: A Criticism.* New York: D. Appleton and Company, 1892.

Whittaker, C. R. *Frontiers of the Roman Empire: A Social and Economic Study.* Baltimore, MD: Johns Hopkins University Press, rev. ed. 1997, 1st ed. 1994.

Wilhelm, Richard. *Die Seele Chinas*. Berlin: Reimar Hobbing, 1925.

Wilkinson, Endymion. *Chinese History: A New Manual.* Cambridge, MA: Harvard University Asia Center, 2012.

Wintle, Michael. "Image into Identity: Constructing and Assigning Identity in a Culture of Modernity." In *On Being Chinese*, ed. by Adrian Chan, 159–74. Amsterdam: Rodopi, 2006.

Wolin, Richard. *The Wind from the East: French Intellectuals, the Cultural Revolution and the Legacy of the 1960s.* Princeton, NJ: Princeton University Press, 2nd ed. 2018, 1st ed. 2010.

Wong, Aida Yuen. *The Other Kang Youwei: Calligrapher, Art Activist, and Aesthetic Reformer in Modern China.* Leiden: Brill, 2016.

Wong, Dorothy C. *Chinese Steles: Pre-Buddhist and Buddhist Use of a Symbolic Form.* Honolulu, Hawaii: University of Hawaii Press, 2004.

Wong, Laura Elizabeth. "Relocating East and West: UNESCO's Major Project on the Mutual Appreciation of Eastern and Western Cultural Values." *The Journal of World History* 19, no. 3 (2008): 349–74.

Wou, Odoric Y. K. "Development, Underdevelopment and Degeneration: The Introduction of Rail Transport into Honan." *Asia Profile* (Hong Kong) 12, no. 3 (June 1984): 215–30.

———. *Mobilizing the Masses: Building Revolution in Henan.* Stanford, CA: Stanford University Press, 1994.

Wright, Arthur F. Review of *Ryūmon sekkutsu no kenkyū* by Mizuno Seiichi, Nagahiro Toshio, et al. *Harvard Journal of Asiatic Studies* 7, no. 3 (February 1943): 261–66.

Wu, Fengshi. "Environmental Activism and Civil Society Development in China," talk at the China Lunchtime Seminar, the Fairbank Center for Chinese Studies, Harvard University, May 12, 2009.

Wu, Hung, ed. *Reinventing the Past: Archaism and Antiquarianism in Chinese Art and Visual Culture.* Chicago, IL: University of Chicago Press, 2010.

Wu, Qingyang (武清旸). "Song Zhenzong de Daojiao Xinyang yu qi chongdao zhence" [宋真宗的道教信仰与其崇道政策 Emperor Zhenzong's Daoist belief and his pro-religious policy]. *Laozi xuekan* 1 (2016): 109–16.

Wu, Shaomin (吴少珉). *Huihuang de Luoyang* [辉煌的洛阳 Splendid Luoyang]. Kaifeng: Henan daxue chubanshe, rev. ed. 2003, 1st ed. 1995.

Wu, Shellen. "The Search for Coal in the Age of Empires: Ferdinand Von Richthofen's Odyssey in China, 1860–1920." *American Historical Review* 119, no. 2 (April 2014): 339–63.

Wu, Shellen Xiao. *Empires of Coal: Fueling China's Entry into the Modern World Order, 1860–1920.* Stanford, CA: Stanford University Press, 2015.

Wu, Xiaoding (吴晓丁). *Liushi haiwai Zhongguo Fojiao zaoxiang* [流失海外中国佛教造像 The lost Chinese Buddhist statues overseas]. Tianjin: Tianjin renmin meishu chubanshe, 2001.

Wyatt, Don J. *The Recluse of Loyang: Shao Yung and the Moral Evolution of Early Sung Thought.* Honolulu, HI: University of Hawaii Press, 1996.

Xinhua wang (新华网). "Luoyang Longmen shiku Xishan bieshuqun chaichu wanbi, jiuming guanyuan bei zewen" [洛阳龙门石窟西山别墅群拆除完毕, 九名官员被责问 The villa complex on the West Hill at Longmen, Luoyang, demolished, and 9 officials punished], http://www.ha.xinhuanet.com/add/2008-12/18/content_15211088.htm, posted on December 18, 2008 (accessed on December 26, 2008).

Xi, Jinping. *The Governance of China.* Beijing: Foreign Language Press, 2014.

———. "Xi Jinping zai Lianheguo Jiaokewen Zuzhi zongbu de yanjiang" [习近平在联合国教科文组织总部的演讲 Xi Jinping's speech at the headquares of the UNESCO], March 28, 2014, http://www.xinhuanet.com/world/2014-03/28/c_119982831_2.htm (accessed on November 17, 2019).

———. "Jianding wenhua zixin, jianshe shehui zhuyi wenhua qianguo" [坚定文化自信, 建设社会主义文化强国 Strengthening cultural confidence, building a strong state of socialist culture], https://article.xuexi.cn/articles/index.html?art_id=10234064154315503061&study_style_id=video_default&pid=&ptype=1&source=share&share_to=wx_feed&from=groupmessage&isappinstalled=0 (accessed on June 25, 2019).

Xia, Xiaohong (夏晓虹), comp. *Zhuiyi Kang Youwei* [追忆康有为 Remembering Kang Youwei]. Beijing: Sanlian shudian, 2009.

Xin, Deyong (辛德勇). *Suitang liangjing congkao* [隋唐两京丛考 A study of the two capitals of the Suitang]. Xi'an: Sanqin chubanshe, 2006.

Xiong, Bingming (1922–200, 熊秉明). *Zhongguo shufa lilun tixi* [中国书法理论体系 The theoretical system of Chinese calligraphy]. Beijing: Renmin meishu chubanshe, 2017, 1st ed. 1985 by the Hong Kong Commercial Press.

Xiong, Victor Cunrui. *Capital Cities and Urban Form in Premodern China: Luoyang, 1038 BCE to 938 CE.* London: Routledge, 2017.

———. "Sui Yangdi and the Building of Sui-Tang Luoyang." *The Journal of Asian Studies* 52, no. 1 (February 1993): 66–89.

"Xisheng xiaojia gu dajia, jiji xingdong zhua luoshi: Longmen shiku huaijing zhili jinzhan shunli" [牺牲小家顾大家, 积极行动抓落实 Sacrificing the small family for the big family, taking action to fulfill our goals: good progress on improving Longmen's environs]. *Luoyang ribao*, 7 August 1999, editorial.

"Xiuzhen Neizheng bu gesi fenke guize" [修正内政部各司分科规则 Rules guiding the revised division of labor in the Ministry of Internal Affairs]. In *Neizhengfa huibian* [内政法汇编 A collection of laws of internal affairs], 225-36, Neizheng bu zongwusi dierke (内政部总务司第二科), comp. Beijing: Jinghua yinshuguan, 1931.

Xu, Jinxing. Interview with the author, July 19, 2007, Luoyang.

Xu, Senyu (徐森玉), ed., *Zhongguo Jiawu yihou liuru Riben zhi wenwu mulu* [中国甲午以后流入日本之文物目录 A catalog of Chinese antiquities flowing into Japan after 1894]. Shanghai: Zhongxi shuju, 2012.

Xu, Song (1781–1848, 徐松), comp. *Henan zhi* [河南志 A record on Henan]. Beijing: Zhonghua shuju, 2012, based on circa 1060 ed.

———. Proofed and supplemented by Zhang Mu (张穆). *Tang liangjing chengfang kao* [唐两京城坊考 An evidential study of the two capitals of the Tang]. Beijing: Zhonghua shuju, 2013, 1st ed. 1985.

———. Annoated and expanded by Li Jianchao (李健超). *Zengding Tang liangjingcheng fangkao* [增订唐两京城坊考 An expanded evidential study of the two capitals of the Tang]. Xi'an: Sanqin chubanshe, 2006.

Xu, Xiaoqun. *Cosmopolitanism, Nationalism, and Individualism in Modern China: The Chenbao Fukan and the New Culture Era, 1918–1928*. Lanham, MD: Lexington Books, 2014.

———. "Law, Custom, and Social Norms: Civil Adjudications in Qing and Republican China." *Law and History Review* 36, no. 1 (2017): 77–104.

———. "The Rule of Law without Due Process: Punishing Robbers and Bandits in Early-Twentieth-Century China." *Modern China* 33 (2007): 230–57.

Xu, Kangsheng (许抗生). *Fojiao de Zhongguohua* [佛教的中国化 The sinicization of Buddhism]. Beijing: Zongjiao wenhua chubanshe, 2008.

Yan, Grace, and Carla Almeida Santos. "'China Forever': Tourism Discourse and Self-Orientalism." *Annals of Tourism Research* 36 (2009): 295–315.

Yan, Yunxiang. "The Chinese Path to Individualization." *The British Journal of Sociology* 61, no. 3 (2010): 489–511.

———. *The Individualization of Chinese Society*. Oxford: Berg, 2010.

Yang, Chia-Ling, and Roderick Whitfield, eds. *Lost Generation: Luo Zhenyu, Qing Loyalists and the Formation of Modern Chinese Culture*. London: Saffron Books, 2012.

Yang, Mayfair Mei-Hui. "Spatial Struggles: Postcolonial Complex, State Disenchantment, and Popular Reappropriation of Space in Rural Southeast China." *The Journal of Asian Studies* 63, no. 3 (August 2004): 719–56.

Yang, Xuanzhi (?-? 杨衒之), annotated and trans. Xiang Rong (向荣). *Luoyang qielan ji.* [洛阳伽蓝记 The Buddhist monasteries of Luoyang]. Beijing: Zhonghua shuju, 2012.

Yang, Zuolong (杨作龙), and Mao Yangguang (毛阳光), eds. *Luoyang kaogu jicheng: Qinhan Weijin Nanbeichao juan* [洛阳考古集成:秦汉魏晋南北朝卷 Archeological findings in Luoyang: Qinhan Weijin and Northern and Southern dynasties]. Beijing: Beijing tushuguan chubanshe, 2007, 2 vols.

Yang, Zuolong (杨作龙), ed., *Luoyang guanli shiyue* [洛阳古代官吏事约 Records on Luoyang's ancient officials]. Beijing: Zhaohua chubanshe, 2007.

Yang, Zuolong (杨作龙), Zhao Shuisen (赵水森), et al., comp., *Luoyang xin chutu muzhi shilu* [洛阳新出土墓志释录 Notes on the newly excavated tomb steles]. Beijing: Beijing tushuguan chubanshe, 2004.

Yasaitis, Kelly Elizabeth. "National Ownership Laws as Cultural Property Protection Policy: The Emerging Trend in United States v. Schultz." *International Journal of Culture Property* 12 (2005): 95–113.

Ye, Gongping (叶公平). "Er'shi shijie zaoqi Beijing de yishupin jiancang yanjiu" [二十世纪早期北京的艺术品鉴藏研究 Research on antiquarianism in early twentieth century Beijing]. PhD dissertation, Nanjing shifan daxue, 2014.

Yeung, King-To, and John Levi Martin. "The Looking Glass Self: An Empirical Test and Elaboration." *Social Forces* 81, no. 3 (March 2003): 843–79.

Yi, Ming (佚名). *Kangyi meidi lüeduo woguo wenwu* [抗议美帝掠夺我国文物 Protesting against American imperialist robbery of our country's antiquities]. Beijing: Wenwu chubanshe, 1960.

Yu, Dan (于丹). *Gu Yanwu Jinshi Wenzi Ji yanjiu* [顾炎武《金石文字记》研究 A study of Gu Yanwu's *Jinshi Wenzi Ji*]. Masters' thesis, Huadong shifan daxue, 2009.

Yu, Pauline. "Travels of a Culture: Chinese Poetry and the European Imagination." *Proceedings of the American Philosophical Society* 151 (2007): 218–29.

Yuan, Haowen (元好问). "Longmen zashi ershou" [龙门杂诗二首 Two peoms on Longmen]. In *Luoyang shizhi*, Luoyang difangshizhi bianzuan weiyuanhui, comp., vol. 15, p. 403. Zhengzhou: Zhongzhou guji chubanshe, 1996.

Yuan, T'ung-li. *China in Western Literature: A Continuation of Cordier's Bibliotheca Sinica*. New Haven, CT: Yale University Press, 1958.

Yuan, Xitao (袁希涛). "Luoyang Yique shiku foxiang ji" [洛阳伊阙石窟佛像记 An account of the Buddhist icons at Luoyang's Yique]. *Dongfang zazhi* 17, no. 23 (December 19, 1920): 88.

Yue, Isaac. "Missionaries (Mis-)Representing China: Orientalism, Religion, and the Conceptualization of Victorian Cultural Identity." *Victorian Literature and Culture* 37 (2009): 1–10.

Zan, Luca, Bing Yu, Jianli Yu, and Haiming Yan. *Heritage Sites in Contemporary China: Cultural Policies and Management Practices*. London: Routledge, 2018.

Zan, Luca, and Sara Bonini Baraldi. "Managing Cultural Heritage in China: A View from the Outisde." *China Quarterly* 210 (June 2012): 456–81.

Zan, Luca, Sara Bonini Baraldi, et al., eds. *Managing Cultural Heritage: An International Research Perspective*. Farnham: Ashgate, 2015.

Zeleza, Paul Tiyambe. "The Politics and Poetics of Exile: Edward Said in Africa." *Research in African Literatures* 36, no. 3 (Fall 2005): 1–22.

Zeng yi ahan jing (Skt. Ekottarāgama-sūtra). In *Taishō shinshū daizōkyō* [大正新脩大藏經 Revised version of the canon, compiled during the Taishō era], ed. by Takakusu Junjirō (1866–1945, 高楠順次郎) and Watanabe Kaikyoku (1872–1933 渡辺海旭) et al. Tokyo: Taishō Issaikyō Kankōkai, 1924–1935, 100 vols.

Zhang, Fan Jeremy. "Asian Art for U.S. College Museums: Two Pioneering Collectors, Charles Freer and Dwight Tryon." In *The West in Asia and Asia in the West: Essays on Transnational Interactions*, ed. by Elisabetta Marino, and Tanfer Emin Tunc, 192–202. Jefferson, NC: McFarland & Company, 2015.

Zhang, Guangda. "À propos d'Edouard Chavannes, le premier sinologue complet," https://www.youtube.com/watch?v=YCd6grzkYMU, published on *Cap33 WebTV* on August 30, 2014 (accessed on July 3, 2018).

Zhang, Jian (张健). *Guobao jienan beiwanglu* [国宝劫难备忘录 A memorandum on the plundering of national treasures]. Beijing: Zhongguo lüyou chubanshe, 2000.

Zhang, Jianhua (张建华). "Beixue de fayang: Kang Youwei 'Guangyizhou shuangji' jiqi shuxue sixiang yanjiu" [碑学的发扬:康有为《广艺舟双楫》及其书学思想研究 Advances in the study of steles: Kang Youwei's *Better paired oars for the boat of art* and his academic thoughts]. PhD dissertation, Zhongguo meishu yanjiu yuan, 2012.

Zhang, Kaisheng (张锴生). "Luoyang Longmen Fengxiansi daxiangkan kaizao nian-dai qianshuo" [洛阳龙门奉先寺大像龛开凿年代浅说 A preliminary study of the start year to carve the large Buddha in Luoyang Longmen's Fengxian Monastery]. In *Longmen shiku yiqian wubai zhounian guoji xueshu taolunhui lunwenji*, ed. by Longmen shiku yanjiusuo, 151–56. Beijing: Wenwu chubanshe, 1996.

Zhang, Kuan. "The Dilemma of Postcolonial Criticism in Contemporary China." *ARIEL: A Review of International English Literature* 40 (2009): 143–59.

Zhang, Lei (1054–1114, 张耒). "Sankan" [三龛 The three niches]. In *Luoyang shizhi*, Luoyang difangshizhi bianzuan weiyuanhui, comp., vol. 15, p. 402. Zhengzhou: Zhongzhou guji chubanshe, 1996.

Zhang, Li. *Strangers in the City: Reconfigurations of Space, Power, and Social Net-workds within China's Floating Population*. Stanford, CA: Stanford University Press, 2001.

Zhang, Longxi. "The Myth of the Other: China in the Eyes of the West." *Critical Inquiry* (1988): 108–31.

Zhang, Naizhu (张乃翥). *Longmen Shiku yu Xiyu wenming* [龙门石窟与西域文明 The Longmen Grottoes and the civilization of the Western Regions]. Zhengzhou: Zhongzhou guji, 2006.

———. "Wenhua renleixue shiyu xia Yiluohe yan'an de Tangdai huren buluo: yi Longmen Shiku xinfanxian de Jingjiao yiku wei yuanqi" [文化人类学视域下伊洛河沿岸的唐代胡人部落：以龙门石窟新发现的景教瘗窟为缘起 The cen-tral Asian community on the banks of the Yi and Luo Rivers from the perspective of cultural anthropology: The case of the newly discovered Nestorian burial niches at the Longmen Grottoes]. *Shikusi yanjiu*, part 1, no. 5 (December 2014):154–74; part 2, no. 6 (January 2016): 255–99.

Zhang, Tingyu (张廷玉), et al., *Mingshi* [明史 The history of the Ming]. Beijing: Zhonghua shuju, 1974.

Zhang, Xiangyun (张祥云). *Beisong Xijing Henanfu Yanjiu* [北宋西京河南府研究 Research on Henanfu, the Western capital of the Northern Song]. Zhengzhou: Henan daxue chubanshe, 2012.

Zhang, Xin. *Social Transformation in Modern China: The State and Local Elites in Henan, 1900–1937*. Cambridge: Cambridge University Press, 2000.

Zhang, Xinglang (1881–1951, 张星烺). *Zhongxi jiaotong shiliao huibian* [中西交通史料汇编 A collection of sources on Sino-Western contacts]. Beijing: Zhonghua shuju, 2003, 4 vols., 1st ed. 1930, in 6 vols.

Zhang, Yawu (张亚武). "Nongmo zhongcai 'Longmen song'" [浓墨重彩龙门颂 Ode to Longmen]. *Luoyang ribao*, 4 April 2008, special issue, T31.

Zhang, Yongjin. *China in International Society since 1949: Alienation and Beyond*. New York: St. Martin's Press, 1998.

Zhang, Zicheng (张自成), ed. *Bainian Zhongguo wenwu liushi beiwanglu* [百年中国文物流失备忘录 A memorandum on the loss of Chinese antiquities in the past one hundred years]. Beijing: Zhongguo lüyou chubanshe, 2001.

Zhang, Ziyu (张子羽). "You Longmen fang Qianxi qingshe" [游龙门访潜溪清舍 A visit to Qianxi Inn at Longmen]. In *Luoyang shizhi*, Luoyang difangshizhi bian-zuan weiyuanhui, comp., vol. 15, p. 403. Zhengzhou: Zhongzhou guji chubanshe, 1996.

Zhao, Erxun (赵尔巽), et al. *Qingshi Gao* [清史稿 The draft history of the Qing]. Beijing: Zhonghua shuju, 2013, 1928 1st ed., 536 vols.

Zhao, Mingcheng (赵明诚), corrected by Jin Wenming (金文明). *Jinshilu jiaozheng* [金石录校正 Errata to *Jinshi lu*]. Guilin: Guangxi shifan daxue chubanshe, 2005.

Zhao, Shanshan (赵姗姗). "Wenhua yichan de falü baohu: Zhongri bijiao yu bentu xuanze" [文化遗产的法律保护: 中日比较与本土选择 The legal protection of cultural heritage: a Chinese-Japanese comparison and local options]. *Guowai shehui kexue*, no. 6 (2018): 25–33.

Zhao, Zhenhua (赵振华). "Longmen Shiku daozao shi [龙门石窟盗凿史 The plunder of the Longmen Grottoes: a history]." In *2004 nian Longmen Shiku guoji xueshu yantaohui wenji* [2004 年龙门石窟国际学术研讨会文集 Proceedings of 2004 international symposium on the Longmen Grottoes], ed. by Li Zhengang, 269–78. Zhengzhou: Henan remin chubanshe, 2006.

———. "Longmen shiku de daozao" [龙门石窟的盗凿 The plunder of the Longmen Caves]. *Jingdian Zhongguo shufa* 227, no. 3 (2012): 96–105.

Zheng, An (郑安). "Yique guanlan ting ji." [伊阙观澜亭记 An account of Yique's Guanlan Pavilion] 1461. In *Zhongguo youji sanwen daxi*, ed. by Zhang Chengde, 49–52. Taiyuan: Shuhai chubanshe, 2011 reprint, 1st ed. 2004.

Zhipan (13th century, 志磐). *Fozu tongji* [佛祖统纪 Records of the Buddha and the patriarchs]. Jinan: Qilu shushe, 1997 reprint.

"Zhicai daomai wenwu de jianshang"[制裁倒卖文物的奸商 Punish antiquities traffickers]. *Renmin ribao*, December 16, 1952, online.

Zhong, Shuhe (钟叔河), comp. *Zouxiang shijie congshu* [走向世界丛书 From the East to the West: Chinese Travelers before 1911, sic], 10 vols. Changsha: Yuelu shushe, 2008.

Zhongguo di'er lishi dang'anguan (中国第二历史档案馆), comp. *Zhonghua mingua dang'an ziliao huibian* [中华民国史档案资料汇编 Collected archival sources on the history of the Republic of China]. Nanjing: Jiangsu guji chubanshe, 1991, diwuji (vol. 5], part 1, waijiao.

———. Diwuji (vol. 5), wenhua 2. "Guwu chuguo huzhao guize" [古物出国护照规则 Regulations on overseas travel passport for antiquities], March 16, 1935, pp. 630–31.

———. Diwuji, wenhua 2. "Guwu baocun fa," [古物保存法 The Antiquities Preservation Act] and "Guwu baocunfa shishi xize." [古物保存法实施细则 Detailed Regulations on Implementing Antiquities Protection], pp. 609–11, 622–25.

———. Disanji (vol. 3], wenhua. "Neiwubu wei tuoshan baohu Longmen guji yu Henan shengzhang gongshu wanglai wen." [内务部为妥善保护龙门古迹与河南省长公署往来文 Correspondence from the Ministry of Internal Affairs to the Governor's Office of Henan Province concerning the proper protection of the Longmen ancient site] Correspondence no. 1: "Neiwubu zhi Henan minzhengzhang xunling" [内务部致河南民政长训令 Order from the Ministry of Internal Affairs to the director of the Henan branch office of internal affairs], February 26, 1914, pp. 190–91.

———. Correspondence no. 2: "Neiwubu zhi Henan shengzhang zi" [内务部致河南省长咨 The Ministry of Internal Affairs to Governor of Henan Province], October 2, 1916, p. 191.

———. Correspondence no. 3: "Henan shengzhang Tian Wenlie zhi Neiwubu" [河南省长田文烈致内务部 Governor of Henan to Ministry of Internal Affairs], October 18, 1916, and two enclosures, "Baoshou Longmenshan shifo guitiao" [保守龙门山石佛规条 Rules for guarding stone buddhas of the Longmen Hill] and "Longmenshan dengchu zaoxiang shumubiao," [龙门山等处造象[像]数目表 Table of the images on the Longmen Hill], pp. 191–96.

———. Correspondence 4: "Neiwubu wei qieshi baocun qiandai wenwu guji zhi gesheng minzhengzhang xunling" [内务部为切实保存前代文物古迹致各省民政长训令 An order to all heads of provincial branch offices from the Ministry of the Interior to effectively protect cultural relics and historical sites], p. 197.

———. Correspondence 9: "Neiwubu guanyu Yungang, Longmeng zaoxiang daliang wailiushi zhi Shanxi, Henan shengzhang zi" [内务部关于云岗、龙门造像大量外流致山西、河南省长咨 Correspondence to the head of Shanxi and Henan Provinces from the Ministry of the Interior regarding the loss of a large quantity of Yungang's and Longmen's statues overseas], pp. 203–05.

———. "Da Zongtong fabu xianzhi guwu chukou ling" [大总统发布限制古物出口令 Presidential decree on limiting antiquities exports], June 14, 1914, p. 185.

———. "Baocun guwu zanxing banfa" [保存古物暂行办法 Provisional Measures for the Preservation of Antiquities], pp. 198–99.

———. "Neiwubu wei diaocha guwu liebiao baobu zhe ge shengzhang/dutong zi" [内务部为调查古物列表报部致各省长/都统咨 Letter from the Ministry of Internal Affairs to all governors/military governors concerning the inventory of antiquities], pp. 199–200.

———. "Shuiwuchu zhi Neiwubu gonghan" [税务处致内务部公函 Letter from the Chinese Customs to the Ministry of Internal Affairs], December 14, 1925, p. 186.

———. "Zhou Zhaoxiang zhi neiwu zongzhang cheng" [周肇祥致内务总长呈 Letter from Zhou Zhaoxiang to the Minister of Internal Affairs], pp. 204–05.

"Zhonghua Renmin Gongheguo wenwu baohufa" [中华人民共和国文物保护法 The Law of the PRC on the Protection of Cultural Heritage], Guojia wenwuju, http://www.sach.gov.cn/art/2017/11/28/art1034121351.html (accessed on February 8, 2019).

Zhongyan Dianshitai (中央电视台 Chinese Central Television). "Longmen daoying" [龙门盗影 Thefts at Longmen]. In "Zhongyuan dafaxian," [中原大发现 The great discovery on the North China Plan], 5th episode of the documentary series, 2007, http://www.cctv.com/program/tsfx/topic/geography/C20322/20071228/104498_1.shtml (accessed on October 22, 2016).

Zhou, Ti (周倜). *Guwan shichang jinxi kao* [古玩市场今昔考 An examination of the past and present antiques markets]. Hong Kong: Xianggang tianma chuban youxian gongsi, 3rd expanded ed. 2007, 1st ed. by Zhongguo wenlian chubanshe in 2001.

Zhou, Xing (周星) and Liao Mingjun (廖明君). "Fei wuzhi wenhua yichan baohu de Riben jingyan." [非物质文化遗产保护的日本经验 Lessons from Japan for the protection of intangible cultural heritage]. *Minzu yishu* 1 (2007): 26–35.

Zhu, Jian, Michael D. Glascock, Changsui Wang, Xiaojun Zhao, and Wei Lu. "A Study of Limestone from the Longmen Grottoes." *Journal of Archaeological Science* 39 (2012): 2568–73.

Zhu, Qianzhi (朱谦之). *Zhongguo zhexue duiyu Ouzhou de yingxiang* [中国哲学对于欧洲的影响 The influence of Chinese philosophy on Europe]. Fuzhou: Fujian renmin chubanshe, 2nd ed. 1983, based on 1940 ed. published in Shanghai by Shangwu shuju.

Zhu, Qiling (朱启钤). "Neiwubu ling (wei baocun guwu)" [内务部令(为保存古物) Ordinance of the Ministry of the Interior (for the preservation of antiquities]; "Guwu chenliesuo zhangcheng" [古物陈列所章程 By-laws for the Institute of Antiquity Exhibition] and "Baocun guwu xiejin hui zhangcheng." [保存古物协进会章程 By-laws for the Association for the Preservation and Promotion of Antiquities] all issued in December 1913, *Tongsu jiaoyu zazhi*, no. 5 (1914): 2–8.

Zhu, Yu (朱昱). "Ti Shikusi" [题石窟寺 Inscribing Shiku Si]. Also titled as "Ti Shiku Si Xiao Wendi suozhi." In *Luoyang xianzhi*, Gong Songlin (龚崧林), and Wang Jian (汪堅), comp., vol. 22, 9b. u.p.: 1924, reprint of 1745 ed.

Zürcher, Erik. *The Buddhist Conquest of China: The Spread and Adaptation of Buddhism in Early Medieval China*, with a foreword by Stephen F. Teiser. Leiden: Brill, 2007, 3rd ed., 1st ed. in 1959.

Index

About the Author

Dr. Dong Wang is distinguished university professor of history, director of the Wellington Koo Institute for Modern China in World History at Shanghai University, and has been a research associate at the Fairbank Center of Harvard University since 2002. A director of the 2014–2015 U.S. National Endowment for the Humanities program, Dr. Wang currently serves on seven international editorial boards including the U.S.-based Association for Asian Studies, *American Foreign Relations Since 1600: A Guide to the Literature*, *Twentieth-Century China*, and *the Journal of American-East Asian Relations*. With bases in the Boston, Massachusetts, Shanghai, and German Lower Rhine areas, she is also a council member of the Royal Asiatic Society China.

Books in English that Dr. Wang authored are: *Longmen's Stone Buddhas and Cultural Heritage: When Antiquity Met Modernity in China* (2020), *The United States and China: A History from the Eighteenth Century to the Present* (2013, 2nd ed. 2020), *Managing God's Higher Learning: U.S.-China Cultural Encounter and Canton Christian College (Lingnan University), 1888-1952* (2007), and *China's Unequal Treaties: Narrating National History* (2005). Among other edited works, she edited "The United States, Asia, and the Pacific, 1815-1919," which was published in *The Society for Historians of American Foreign Relations (SHAFR) Guide: An Annotated Bibliography of American Foreign Relations since 1600* (2017).

Asia/Pacific/Perspectives

Series Editor: Mark Selden

Printed in Poland
by Amazon Fulfillment
Poland Sp. z o.o., Wrocław

91287200R00177